Hermeneutical Community

Hermeneutical Community

Pursuing Local Theology in Historical
and Cross-Cultural Perspective

C. S. BAREFOOT

WIPF & STOCK · Eugene, Oregon

HERMENEUTICAL COMMUNITY
Pursuing Local Theology in Historical and Cross-Cultural Perspective

Copyright © 2024 C. S. Barefoot. All rights reserved. Except for brief quotations in critical publications or reviews, no part of this book may be reproduced in any manner without prior written permission from the publisher. Write: Permissions, Wipf and Stock Publishers, 199 W. 8th Ave., Suite 3, Eugene, OR 97401.

Wipf & Stock
An Imprint of Wipf and Stock Publishers
199 W. 8th Ave., Suite 3
Eugene, OR 97401

www.wipfandstock.com

PAPERBACK ISBN: 979-8-3852-2154-7
HARDCOVER ISBN: 979-8-3852-2155-4
EBOOK ISBN: 979-8-3852-2156-1

12/23/24

Unless otherwise stated, Scripture quotations are from the ESV® Bible (The Holy Bible, English Standard Version®), © 2001 by Crossway, a publishing ministry of Good News Publishers. Used by permission. All rights reserved.

"The White Man's Burden," by Rudyard Kipling quoted under public domain and with permission from the National Trust, UK.

The section entitled "Royal Priesthood of All Believers (1 Pet 2:9)" was previously published in C. S. Barefoot, "Local Ownership of the Theological Task," *Great Commission Baptist Journal of Missions* 2.2 (2023) 1–16. It is republished here with permission from the International Mission Board.

For Kristin,
a joy and blessing to me
and all who know her.

Contents

Acknowledgments | ix

List of Abbreviations | xi

1 **Lack of Clarity for Missionary Outsiders** | 1
  Aim | 8
  Agenda | 11
  Acknowledgments | 13
  Abstract | 18

2 **Colonial Pattern of Theological Imposition** | 19
  Overview of Colonial Period | 23
  Examples of Theological Imposition | 29
  Commonalities of Practice and Presupposition | 80

3 **Post-Colonial Rejection of Theological Imposition** | 85
  Voices from the Majority World | 95
  Arguments against Theological Imposition | 111
  Commonalities of Contention | 138
  Evaluation of Theological Imposition | 140

4 **Hermeneutical Community for Local Theological Development** | 152
  Conceptions of Hermeneutical Community | 152
  Biblical Foundations for Hermeneutical Community | 202
  Relevance of Hermeneutical Community | 226
  Function of Hermeneutical Community | 231

CONTENTS

5 **Outsider Role in Local Theological Development** | 235
   Warrant for the Outsider | 236
   Metaphors for the Outsider | 242
   Role of the Outsider | 246
   Examples for the Outsider | 274

6 **A Way Forward for Missionary Outsiders** | 293
   Summary | 294
   Implications | 296
   Further Research | 300
   Conclusion | 301

Appendix: *Indigenous Statement of Faith on Soteriology* | 305

Bibliography | 307

Acknowledgments

THROUGHOUT THE PROCESS OF this research and writing, I have been in debt to the grace and help of the Lord Jesus Christ: "Here I raise my Ebenezer; hither by thy help I've come." For his faithfulness in this endeavor, I cannot give enough thanks. Yet more importantly, I rejoice that he has written my name in heaven (Luke 10:20).

I am also tremendously grateful for Dr. Chuck Lawless, whose resolute insistence on clear and exact writing and thinking has benefited me greatly. My research would not have fared well without his guidance from beginning to end. I also owe gratitude to Dr. George Robinson, whose teaching and passion helped stoke in me a heart for the nations and God's mission among them. His encouragement to me over the years has helped me press on in the task of mission and missiological research. Additionally, I am thankful for Dr. William Dyrness, who humbly and generously offered me his insight into the field of Majority World theologizing. This work owes much to his guidance, which helped clarify my thinking regarding hermeneutical community as an approach to local theological development.

I am grateful for my organization's field leadership, who graciously allowed me to pursue this research and writing. I am also thankful for the co-laborers with whom I have ministered in South Asia over the years. These brothers and their families have been a source of great encouragement to me. Further, I am thankful for the many national brothers and sisters alongside whom I have lived and labored. They have taught me much about remaining steadfast in faith, in prayer, and in trials, all for the glory of "him who called [us] out of darkness into his marvelous light" (1 Pet 2:9).

For Debra, Randy, Jerry, Brenda, Rick, and Lou—I am very appreciative. They have regularly taken interest in my research and encouraged

ACKNOWLEDGMENTS

me in the task. For my siblings and their spouses—Spencer, Liz, LeAnna, Kevin, Tyler, Anna, Jay, Richard, and Emily—I give much thanks.

For my two wonderful children—Joshua and Sarah—I am abundantly thankful. Their lives are a source of great joy for me, and to be their father is an honor far greater than having my research published.

Finally, for my wife Kristin, who is lovely in every way, I am beyond grateful. Without her constant help, encouragement, and respect, I would not have reached this milestone. I am very thankful for the many sacrifices she has made for me over the course of this research. Her grace and kindness are unmatched, and her love and friendship are worth far more to me than she knows.

List of Abbreviations

All Africa Conference of Churches	AACC
Baker Exegetical Commentary on the New Testament	BECNT
Baptist Faith and Message 2000	BF&M
Church Missionary Society	CMS
Church of South India	CSI
Doctrina Christiana y Catecismo para Instrucción de los Indios	DCC
Ecumenical Association of Third World Theologians	EATWOT
Greek-English Lexicon of the New Testament	BDAG
International Critical Commentary	ICC
IVP New Testament Commentary	IVPNTC
London Missionary Society	LMS
New American Commentary	NAC
New International Commentary on the New Testament	NICNT
Pillar New Testament Commentary	PNTC
Sacra Pagina	SP
South India United Church	SIUC
Theological Education Fund	TEF
Theological Interpretation of Scripture	TIS
Third Lima Council	TLC
Tyndale New Testament Commentaries	TNTC
World Council of Churches	WCC
Word Biblical Commentary	WBC

LIST OF ABBREVIATIONS

Zondervan Exegetical Commentary on the New Testament   ZECNT

1

Lack of Clarity for Missionary Outsiders

SOUND LOCAL THEOLOGY PLAYS a vital role in the development of healthy local churches.[1] Local theology refers to implicit and explicit biblical-theological convictions that develop within and in relation to a local context. Further, the task of local theologizing entails believers seeking to understand the truth of Scripture and to bring that truth to bear upon the questions and challenges that a given context raises. When those questions and challenges remain unaddressed, the local church remains susceptible to theological syncretism and split-level Christianity[2]—in which believers adhere to Christianity on a formal level yet continue seeking out pagan belief systems to address their deeper concerns. As Dean Flemming points out, "In modern times, missionaries and mission organizations have sometimes imposed an imported brand of theology and Christian behavior on younger churches in a well-meaning effort to prevent heresy or syncretism. But short-circuiting the development of a contextualized theology has often had the opposite effect. When the Christian message appears to be irrelevant to peoples' lives and worldview questions, they will likely turn elsewhere for answers, especially to

---

1. "Health" here refers to the state in which a local church is seeking to uphold and embody sound doctrine, according to the Scriptures.

2. On "split-level Christianity," see Jaime Bulatao, "Split-Level Christianity," *Philipp. Sociol. Rev.* 13.2 (1965) 119–21; Paul G. Hiebert et al., "Responding to Split-Level Christianity and Folk Religion," *Int. J. Front. Missions* 16.4 (1999) 173–82; Paul G. Hiebert et al., *Understanding Folk Religion: A Christian Response to Popular Beliefs and Practices* (Grand Rapids: Baker, 1999), 10–21.

traditional religious beliefs and practices."[3] Thus, a perennial need is for local theology that can help transform believers' worldviews and buttress the church in the face of local challenges.[4]

However, instead of fostering such local theological development, Western missionaries have often imported and imposed foreign theology on local churches. Andrew F. Walls explains, "Over most of the nineteenth and even the twentieth centuries, centuries that have entirely changed the face of the Christian world, most missionaries saw theology as a given, something already formed and ready for transfer to China or India or Africa."[5] One finds historical examples of this precedent across the world.[6] As a result, many of the contextual issues with which local Christians have to grapple remained unaddressed.[7] Indeed, as Wilbert R. Shenk notes, the reality and impact of foreign theological imposition "is widely recognized and there is ample documentation of the unsatisfactory results that have been produced in the life of the mission-established church."[8]

This precedent of foreign theological imposition stemmed, in part, from a failure to recognize that all theology is local, or contextual, in nature. As Anri Morimoto claims, "Theology has always been contextualised, whether theologians of each generation were aware of the fact or not. As long as it is a human endeavor carried out in the language and conceptuality of a given time and place, all theology is contextualised from the very beginning of its history."[9] In other words, all theology bears marks of the locale in which it has developed.[10] Yet the Western theological tradition

---

3. Dean E. Flemming, *Contextualization in the New Testament: Patterns for Theology and Mission* (Downers Grove, IL: IVP Academic, 2005), 303.

4. Tite Tiénou, "The Church and Its Theology," *Evang. Rev. Theol.* 7.2 (1983) 246; Tokunboh Adeyemo, "Contemporary Issues in Africa and the Future of Evangelicals," *Evang. Rev. Theol.* 2.1 (1978) 7.

5. Andrew F. Walls, *The Cross-Cultural Process in Christian History: Studies in the Transmission and Appropriation of Faith* (Maryknoll, NY: Orbis, 2002), 242–43.

6. Chapter 2 provides case studies of this precedent in Latin America, Africa, and Asia.

7. For example, Bong Rin Ro, "Theological Trends in Asia," *Themelios* 13.2 (1988) 57, highlights several pertinent challenges in Asia—including, among others, idolatry, ancestor worship, caste realities, poverty, and major world religions—that Western theologies have, historically, not sufficiently addressed.

8. Wilbert R. Shenk, "Theology and the Missionary Task," *Missiology* 1.3 (1973) 300–301.

9. Anri Morimoto, "Contextualised and Cumulative: Tradition, Orthodoxy and Identity from the Perspective of Asian Theology," *Stud. World Christ.* 15.1 (2009) 66.

10. Shenk, "Theology and the Missionary Task," 296–97, elaborates, "Christian

has not always accounted for this reality.[11] That is not to say that theology has no relevance beyond its immediate context; it is to say, however, that all theology derives from a given context and that each context warrants localized theology that addresses pertinent cultural issues.[12]

Additionally, the practice of theological imposition derived from an assumption that the Western tradition had already addressed every major theological issue. Even as the Iberian powers set out to explore and colonize the world at the dawn of the sixteenth century, "Christian theology," according to Walls, "could be described as virtually complete; it appeared that every important question had been canvassed and settled."[13] For colonial era missionaries then, the transfer of Western theology to the Majority World appeared sensical. Few considered the possibility that their own culture and context conditioned—at least to a certain extent—their theological perceptions. Instead, most operated with an assumption that their theology was sufficient and normative across cultures.[14] The Western

---

theology bears the impress of the historical periods and cultural contexts in which it has developed. . . . In the first place, theology has developed within Hellenic thought categories and formulations. This has encouraged development of theology as a set of abstractions organized into doctrinal systems. . . . Second, particularly the recent history of theology is the record of the rise and decline of various schools or systems of thought typically organized around a certain motif or controlling principles. . . . Modern theology, in the third place, has been tempted by the urge to be 'relevant' with the result, in the words of Peter Berger, that there have appeared a 'sequence of "mood theologies."'"

11. As Richard B. Cunningham, "Theologizing in a Global Context: Changing Contours," *Rev. Expo.* 94.3 (1997) 351, explains, "In earlier eras, classical theologians thought that theology is an objective science which could interpret scripture and tradition into a formal dogmatic system that transcends cultures and is universally applicable in all times and places. Their presumed catholicity of theology was and is an illusion. All systems are deeply embedded in specific cultural situations."

12. The historic creeds (e.g., Apostles' Creed, Nicene Creed), for example, have rightly served the global church, even though they developed in a particular historical context. However, while those statements of faith provide helpful contributions to theological development on various local levels, they do not exhaust the truth of Scripture and what Scripture has to say regarding local cultural issues.

13. Walls, *Cross-Cultural Process*, 37–38.

14. David J. Bosch, *Transforming Mission: Paradigm Shifts in Theology of Mission* (Maryknoll, NY: Orbis, 1991), 448; Harvie M. Conn, *Eternal Word and Changing Worlds: Theology, Anthropology, and Mission in Trialogue* (Grand Rapids: Zondervan, 1984), 116. Bruce J. Nicholls, "From Colosse to India: Some Reflections on the Life of the Church in Cultural Contexts," in *Integral Mission: The Way Forward: Essays in Honour of Dr. Saphir Athyal*, ed. C. V. Mathew (Tiruvalla, India: Christava Sahitya Samithi, 2006), 394, declares, "Some Christians have been slow to reflect critically on their own cultural heritage and personal experience of Christ. An earlier generation of missionaries assumed that their western understanding of the gospel was the biblical one. They merely transplanted the gospel from one pot to another."

theological tradition has since been slow to recognize limitations within its own theology.[15]

Recent demographic shifts have challenged this assumption concerning the supposed normativity of Western theology, however. As the twentieth century waned, a massive shift in Christianity's global "center of gravity" was afoot.[16] That is, Christianity had grown to the extent that the Majority World Christian population began to overtake that of the Western world. With that shift came the emergence of new theological perspectives that challenged Western theological sentiments. According to Timothy C. Tennent,

> We can no longer afford to ignore the theological implications inherent in the demographic reality that Christianity is currently experiencing a precipitous decline in the West and that the vast majority of Christians now live outside the West.... This reality will inevitably shape and form the development of theology since new questions are being posed to the text within the larger context of poverty, powerlessness, pluralism, and the inevitable challenges that occur when vernacular languages begin to wrestle with theological issues.[17]

Philip Jenkins presses further: "We can reasonably ask whether the emerging Christian traditions of the Two-Thirds World have recaptured themes and trends in Christianity that the older churches have forgotten, and if so, what we can learn from their insights."[18]

---

15. Charles E. Van Engen, "The Glocal Church: Locality and Catholicity in a Globalizing World," in *Globalizing Theology: Belief and Practice in an Era of World Christianity*, ed. Craig Ott and Harold A. Netland (Grand Rapids: Baker Academic, 2006), 173, traces this issue all the way back to the fourth century AD. He maintains, "Since Constantine, the Christian church has tended to do its theology from a predominantly monocentric and monocultural perspective, formulating a set of theological dogmas that were assumed to be universally true for everyone, everywhere, always.... This perspective also permeated Protestant missions for over 150 years during the time of colonial missions."

16. Scholars documenting this demographic shift include Philip Jenkins, *The Next Christendom: The Coming of Global Christianity*, 3rd ed. (New York: Oxford University Press, 2011); Walls, *Cross-Cultural Process*. Timothy C. Tennent, *Theology in the Context of World Christianity: How the Global Church Is Influencing the Way We Think About and Discuss Theology* (Grand Rapids: Zondervan, 2007), 8, explains, "The statistical center of gravity refers to that point on the globe with an equal number of Christians living north, south, east, and west of that point."

17. Tennent, *Theology in the Context*, 17.

18. Philip Jenkins, *The New Faces of Christianity: Believing the Bible in the Global South* (New York: Oxford University Press, 2006), 178.

LACK OF CLARITY FOR MISSIONARY OUTSIDERS

Western theological and missionary stakeholders have thus begun to realize the inadequacy of offering old theological formulae as blanket answers to those in the Majority World who wrestle with new theological questions. Robert J. Schreiter notes that as the post-colonial era dawned, "*New questions* were being asked, questions for which there were no ready traditional answers. Indeed, so many new questions were emerging that the credibility of existing forms of theology was weakened."[19] Yet despite this incongruity between local issues and those which occupied traditional Western theology, such theology continued to proliferate among Majority World churches. Schreiter explains,

> *Old answers* were being urged upon cultures and regions with new questions. People outside the North Atlantic communities felt that the older churches were not taking their questions seriously, or were trying to foist their own agenda upon them. They detected a continuing and consistent colonialism and paternalism on the part of the North Atlantic churches, which seemed to be insisting that, if they wished to be considered full-fledged Christian communities, they would have to come to think and respond like the older churches.[20]

Walls also highlights the inadequacy of such a response: "Africa is already revealing the limitations of theology as generally taught in the West. . . . [Western] models of theology cannot cope with some of the most urgent pastoral needs. They have no answers for some of the most desolating aspects of life—because they have no questions."[21]

A growing conviction has thus emerged among Western theologians and missiologists that local theological development is vital to the

---

19. Robert J. Schreiter, *Constructing Local Theologies* (Maryknoll, NY: Orbis, 1985), 2, emphasis original.

20. Schreiter, *Constructing Local Theologies*, 3, emphasis original.

21. Andrew F. Walls, "Globalization and the Study of Christian History," in *Globalizing Theology: Belief and Practice in an Era of World Christianity*, ed. Craig Ott and Harold A. Netland (Grand Rapids: Baker Academic, 2006), 75–76; Craig Ott, "Conclusion: Globalizing Theology," in *Globalizing Theology: Belief and Practice in an Era of World Christianity*, ed. Craig Ott and Harold A. Netland (Grand Rapids: Baker Academic, 2006), 315, adds, "Theological formulations in the Western tradition are no less true in Africa or Asia than they are in Europe or America. However, they are not necessarily equally relevant, understandable, or adequate in all contexts. Nor are such formulations exhaustive. Here is where theological insights from non-Western perspectives hold so much promise. They open the door not necessarily for *alternative* but rather for *fuller* theological understanding" (emphasis original).

maturation of churches across the world.[22] Christians in every generation and culture must articulate their faith in relation to local issues; they cannot afford, according to Richard Lints, to "remain parasitic on the faith of generations past."[23] Theologies of former generations and other contexts do not always address the cultural and contextual challenges that confront churches today. In order to remain faithful in the face of such challenges, churches everywhere need to seek Scripture for guidance and articulate its truth as it applies to confronting issues. Failure to do so imperils the local church. D. A. Carson thus contends, "If by African, Scottish, Indian and Burmese theologies we are referring to attempts by nationals to work directly from Scripture in order to construct a biblically controlled theology each for its own language, culture and generation, the enterprise cannot be too highly lauded and encouraged."[24]

Majority World church leaders have expressed similar sentiments, and a host of voices among them have—understandably—reacted strongly against the colonial pattern of theological imposition. Richard B. Cunningham explains, "The younger churches no longer take for granted the normative and undisputed nature of Western theology, church structures, and practices, and now assert their autonomy—in practice and

---

22. That is not to say, however, that patterns of colonial theological imposition no longer exist. Werner Mischke, *The Global Gospel: Achieving Missional Impact in Our Multicultural World* (Scottsdale, AZ: Mission ONE, 2015), 208–9, rightly questions whether Western missionaries and mission agencies have moved on from colonial patterns of theological control. He asserts, "Could it be that the days of colonialism in mission methods may be largely behind us—while colonialism in theology is still an issue? The Western Christian academy still dominates, and Western theological approaches are usually considered universally valid by Western mission practitioners and cross-cultural workers. Ponder the many Western organizations that offer theological training for all pastors anywhere—all with an unconscious Western theological bias. For the massive short-term mission movement, this is certainly the case. It's difficult to come to terms with the fact that the 'Western air' we breathe actually influences the way we *think-and-do theology*" (emphasis original). Tennent, *Theology in the Context*, 11, adds, "Despite the dramatic growth of the Majority World church, the center of theological education and Christian scholarship remains in the Western world. In fact, despite the growth of Majority World Christianity and the corresponding decline in the vitality of Western Christianity, there remains the view that Western theological writings and reflection somehow represent the normative, universal Christian reflection whereas non-Western theology is more localized, ad hoc, and contextual."

23. Richard Lints, *The Fabric of Theology: A Prolegomenon to Evangelical Theology* (Grand Rapids: Eerdmans, 1993), 86.

24. D. A. Carson, "Reflections on Contextualization: A Critical Appraisal of Daniel von Allmen's 'Birth of Theology,'" *East Afr. J. Evang. Theol.* 3.1 (1984) 52.

theology."[25] As previously noted, some have lamented Western theology's silence on major issues facing churches in other contexts. John Mbiti typifies this reaction in claiming that traditional Western theology "is largely ignorant of, and often embarrassingly impotent in the face of, human questions in the churches of Africa, Latin America, parts of Asia, and the South Pacific."[26]

Others have decried the hermeneutical and epistemological hegemony that the Western theological tradition tends to exert over others.[27] Tite Tiénou highlights the perception that the West serves as the arbiter of knowledge.[28] Even within the field of theology, "the assumption is that the West represents the center of scholarship and the rest (usually Africa, Asia and Latin America) fits in the margins."[29] The development of contextual theologies in the Majority World over the past half-century has served as a means of contesting such hegemonic control over the theological enterprise. R. S. Sugirtharajah explains, "Third World theologies, especially the liberation variety, arose as a way of critiquing the universalistic, Eurocentric, individualistic, patriarchal and anti-environmental tendencies of . . . Western theologies."[30]

This post-colonial rejection of foreign theological imposition places the outsider's role in local theological development in a precarious spot. If, as some in the post-colonial era have argued, the outsider's role is not to control the theology of local churches, then what is his or her role? Some have moved in the direction of the opposite extreme—the withdrawal of

---

25. Cunningham, "Theologizing in a Global Context," 357.

26. John S. Mbiti, "Theological Impotence and the Universality of the Church," in *Third World Theologies*, ed. Gerald H. Anderson and Thomas F. Stransky, Mission Trends 3 (New York: Paulist, 1976), 8.

27. For example, see Pui-lan Kwok, "Discovering the Bible in the Non-Biblical World," in *Voices from the Margin: Interpreting the Bible in the Third World*, ed. R. S. Sugirtharajah (Maryknoll, NY: Orbis, 1995), 289–305; Elsa Tamez, "Women's Rereading of the Bible," in *Voices from the Margin: Interpreting the Bible in the Third World*, ed. R. S. Sugirtharajah (Maryknoll, NY: Orbis, 1995), 48–57; Oscar García-Johnson, "Transoccidentalism and the Making of Global Theology," in *Theology Without Borders: An Introduction to Global Conversations*, by William A. Dyrness and Oscar García-Johnson (Grand Rapids: Baker Academic, 2015), 1–22; Walter Mignolo, "Epistemic Disobedience and the Decolonial Option: A Manifesto," *Transmodernity* 1.2 (2011) 44–66.

28. Tite Tiénou, "Indigenous Theologizing: From the Margins to the Center," *J. NAIITS* 6 (2008) 118–21.

29. Tiénou, "Indigenous Theologizing," 119.

30. R. S. Sugirtharajah, *Postcolonial Reconfigurations: An Alternative Way of Reading the Bible and Doing Theology* (St. Louis, MO: Chalice, 2003), 123.

outsiders.[31] Other post-colonial voices refrain from such a broad pendulum swing and recognize value in the incorporation and consideration of multiple voices in the task of theologizing.[32] Even these proposals, though, tend to leave ambiguous the specific role that outsiders might play in local theological development.[33] Thus, neither colonialism, with its practice of theological imposition, nor postcolonial discourse, seeking to counteract the overextension of Western theology, has elucidated a constructive role for outsiders in local theological development.

To clarify the outsider's role, this book presents an approach that delineates a constructive way forward beyond the impasse between theological imposition and theological withdrawal. The role advocated here is constructive because it features the outsider as one who speaks into the development of local theology, yet encourages and promotes the voices of local believers in that process. Such a role circumvents the pitfalls of colonial missionary practice, heeds legitimate post-colonial critiques, and at the same time avoids the potential post-colonial extreme of total outsider withdrawal from local theological development. What animates this approach is the idea of *hermeneutical community*—the notion that multiple constituents together can and should contribute to the task of biblical interpretation and theology.

AIM

The concept of hermeneutical community is not new. Various theologians—as far back as the early church—have called for the believing community to remain the primary location and context for the interpretation

---

31. For example, see Emerito Nacpil, "Mission but not Missionaries," *Int. Rev. Mission* 60.239 (1971) 356–62; Choan-Seng Song, "From Israel to Asia: A Theological Leap," in *Third World Theologies*, ed. Gerald H. Anderson and Thomas F. Stransky, Mission Trends 3 (New York: Paulist, 1976), 211–22.

32. For example, see Pui-lan Kwok, "Teaching Theology from a Global Perspective," in *Teaching Global Theologies: Power and Praxis*, ed. Pui-lan Kwok et al. (Waco, TX: Baylor University Press, 2015), 14; Kwok, "Discovering the Bible," 302–3; R. S. Sugirtharajah, "Inter-Faith Hermeneutics: An Example and Some Implications," in *Voices from the Margin: Interpreting the Bible in the Third World*, ed. R. S. Sugirtharajah (Maryknoll, NY: Orbis, 1995), 314.

33. For example, both Pui-Lan Kwok and R. S. Sugirtharajah, in the citations of the preceding footnote, recognize the general value of incorporating multiple voices from different backgrounds into the work of theologizing. However, they do not spell out the specifics of what an outsider's role might be.

of Scripture.[34] Recent scholarship has highlighted and studied communal hermeneutics from different vantage points.[35] This work does so from a missiological perspective and seeks to discern the relevance of hermeneutical community for cross-cultural missionaries laboring to establish healthy churches.

Building on prior developments of this concept, the thesis of this work is that a hermeneutical community approach to local theological development delineates a constructive role for outsiders that avoids the colonial extreme of theological imposition and the post-colonial extreme of theological withdrawal. "Hermeneutical community" refers to the practice of interpreting the Scriptures in conversation with others and within the community of the church as a means of guarding and enriching theological reflection and expression. As this book seeks to show, this approach to biblical interpretation and theology has developed in several different fields of discourse and provides a helpful framework for understanding the outsider's place in local theological development. Such a framework recasts the outsider's role to include five key components:

---

34. Robert W. Jenson, "Hermeneutics and the Life of the Church," in *Reclaiming the Bible for the Church*, ed. Carl E. Braaten and Robert W. Jenson (Eugene, OR: Wipf & Stock, 2016), 95–98, for example, points to second-century bishop Irenaeus of Lyon as someone who argued in favor of such ecclesial interpretation. Chapter 4 of this book highlights various scholars and theologians who follow suit. Jenson himself similarly contends that the primary context for scriptural interpretation ought to be the church, as opposed to the academy.

35. In addition to the literature explored in chapter 4 of this book, see for example Cecilio Arrastía, "La Iglesia como Comunidad Hermenéutica," *Apuntes* 1.1 (1981) 7–13; John Howard Yoder, "The Hermeneutics of Peoplehood: A Protestant Perspective on Practical Moral Reasoning," *J. Relig. Ethics* 10.1 (1982) 40–67; Michael G. Cartwright, "The Practice and Performance of Scripture: Grounding Christian Ethics in a Communal Hermeneutic," *Annu. Soc. Christ. Ethics* 8 (1988) 31–53; Adolf Ens, "Theology of the Hermeneutical Community in Anabaptist-Mennonite Thought," in *The Church as Theological Community: Essays in Honour of David Schroeder*, ed. Harry Huebner (Winnipeg: CMBC Publications, 1990), 69–80; Simone Sinn, "Hermeneutics and Ecclesiology," in *The Routledge Companion to the Christian Church*, ed. Gerard Mannion and Lewis S. Mudge (New York: Routledge, 2008), 576–93; Tim Conder and Daniel Rhodes, *Free for All: Rediscovering the Bible in Community* (Grand Rapids: Baker, 2009); Mary McCaughey, *The Church as Hermeneutical Community and the Place of Embodied Faith in Joseph Ratzinger and Lewis S. Mudge*, Religions and Discourse 58 (Oxford: Peter Lang, 2015); Andrew P. Rogers, *Congregational Hermeneutics: How Do We Read?* (New York: Routledge, 2016); Jeppe Bach Nikolajsen, "The Formative Power of Scripture: The Church as a Hermeneutical Community," *Eur. J. Theol.* 27.2 (2018) 130–38; Doug Heidebrecht, "Community Hermeneutics in Practice: Following the Interpretive Path Together," *Direction* 49.2 (2020) 123–40. Such scholars broach the topic of communal hermeneutics from various historical, theological, empirical, ethical, philosophical, homiletical, and practical perspectives.

teaching Scripture, modeling sound hermeneutics, cultivating theological agency, challenging blind spots, and broadening perspectives.

This argument is significant for at least three reasons. First, it helps to chart a path beyond both theological imposition and theological withdrawal by outsiders. In a hermeneutical community approach to local theological development, the outsider remains involved in the process but does not dominate it. Rather, the outsider serves to facilitate and promote what DeVries calls "ecclesial contextualization," a stage at which the local church takes ownership of the task of biblical interpretation and theological expression.[36] This book seeks to show how a hermeneutical community approach provides a way to do just that while avoiding the two extremes of imposition and withdrawal.

Second, this thesis provides clarity on how outsiders should function in local theological development—a clarity which has been lacking in the wake of post-colonial critiques.[37] If the foreigner should neither control local theology nor withdraw from its development, then what exactly is his or her role? Appealing to the notion of hermeneutical community, this book outlines several fundamental components of the outsider's role. One aspect, for example, is the work of cultivating theological agency among local believers. That is, the outsider should not stop at merely teaching theology, but rather should press on toward teaching the *doing* of theology. In this way, outsiders can help local believers become active agents of their own theological convictions rather than mere passive recipients.

Third, this proposal offers a way to achieve the theological vision which evangelicals outlined in the "Willowbank Report," a joint statement from Lausanne's Consultation on Gospel and Culture in 1978.[38] The consultation at Willowbank, Bermuda, was an important step forward for evangelicals in exploring the implications of culture for theology and mission. John Stott notes, "Only, I suspect, as a result of the

---

36. Brian A. DeVries, "The Contexts of Contextualization: Different Methods for Different Ministry Situations," *Evang. Missions Q.* 55.4 (2019) 12.

37. For example, although he promotes "communitarian exegesis," Sugirtharajah, *Postcolonial Reconfigurations*, 160, yet advocates "keeping a constant vigilance over the predatory nature of Western values and treating circumspectly the immaculate qualities of the vernacular." Thus, there remain deep suspicions of Western outsiders and their role in the local theological enterprise.

38. Lausanne Theology and Education Group, "The Willowbank Report," in *Down to Earth: Studies in Christianity and Culture*, ed. Robert T. Coote and John R. W. Stott (Grand Rapids: Eerdmans, 1980), 308–42.

Lausanne Congress on World Evangelization in 1974 has the evangelical constituency as a whole come to acknowledge the central importance of culture for the effective communication of the Gospel."[39] The Willowbank consultation served as an important follow up to the 1974 Lausanne gathering and provided an outlet for evangelicals from across the world to further consider the relationship between culture and the gospel.[40] In their final report, participants at Willowbank charted an initial way forward for evangelicals seeking to better understand that relationship.[41]

Concerning local theological development, the Willowbank Report declares, "Thus we should seek with equal care to avoid theological imperialism or theological provincialism. A church's theology should be developed by the community of faith out of the Scripture in interaction with other theologies of the past and present, and with the local culture and its needs."[42] This book puts forward a way for outsiders to labor in local theological development while achieving each component of this evangelical vision from Willowbank: (1) treatment of contextual issues, (2) engagement with historical theology and theology from other locales, (3) study of the biblical text, (4) involvement of the community of believers, (5) avoidance theological imposition from without, and (6) avoidance of theological provincialism within the local community.

In sum, by appealing to the practice of hermeneutical community, this work aims to both demonstrate *that* outsiders should remain involved in local theological development—which is not a given from a post-colonial perspective—and draw implications for *how* they should be involved. In doing so, it seeks to provide a sound theological and missiological foundation for the outsider's work in local theological development.

---

39. John R. W. Stott, "Foreword," in *Down to Earth: Studies in Christianity and Culture*, ed. Robert T. Coote and John R. W. Stott (Grand Rapids: Eerdmans, 1980), vii.

40. John Gration, "Willowbank to Zaire: The Doing of Theology," *Missiology* 12.3 (1984) 297.

41. Participants included Saphir Athyal, Kwame Bediako, Peter P. J. Beyerhaus, Harvie M. Conn, Orlando E. Costas, Charles Kraft, Jacob Loewen, I. Howard Marshall, Bruce J. Nicholls, James I. Packer, C. René Padilla, Pedro Savage, John Stott, Charles R. Taber, Tite Tiénou, and Alan R. Tippett, among others. A little less than half of the participants were from the Majority World. See Lausanne Theology and Education Group, "Willowbank Report," 340–42.

42. Lausanne Theology and Education Group, "Willowbank Report," 334.

AGENDA

In order to substantiate its thesis, this work will first provide, in chapter 2, a historical analysis of colonial theological imposition through the use of case studies. Regarding the purpose of case study methodology, Deborah Court explains, "We study a particular case in order to gain detailed understanding of that case, and hope from this understanding to shed light on the wider phenomenon of which that case is an example."[43] Phil Hodkinson and Heather Hodkinson similarly assert that a strength of a case study approach is that "it facilitates the construction of detailed, in depth understanding of what is to be studied."[44] Seeking such an understanding of the wider phenomenon of colonial theological imposition, this chapter therefore employs a case study approach.[45]

It will explore the work of sixteenth-century Jesuits in Peru, the Church Missionary Society in Uganda around the turn of the twentieth century, and the early twentieth-century Protestant union movement in South India. The chapter will provide an analysis of these cases, first, because they serve as microcosms of ways outsiders exerted control over the theological enterprise during the colonial era, and second, because they demonstrate the reality of theological imposition across different continents and time periods. In its analysis, this book will examine how outsiders imposed theology in each case and then synthesize the findings to discern commonalities in practice and presupposition.

After seeking to establish the historical precedent of theological imposition, this book will, in chapter 3, survey and assess various postcolonial reactions to outside theological control. It will examine such responses from both ecumenical and evangelical perspectives. Further,

---

43. Deborah Court, "Ethnography and Case Study: A Comparative Analysis," *Acad. Exch. Q.* (2003), https://www.thefreelibrary.com/Ethnography+and+case+study%3a+a+comparative+analysis.-a0111848865.

44. Phil Hodkinson and Heather Hodkinson, "The Strengths and Limitations of Case Study Research" (paper presented at the Learning and Skills Development Agency conference, "Making an Impact on Policy and Practice," Cambridge, December 5–7, 2001), 3.

45. Regarding historical case studies in particular, Stephen Petrina, "Methods of Analysis: Historical Case Study," 2020, 1, https://blogs.ubc.ca/researchmethods/files/2020/11/Historical-Case.pdf, a professor at the University of British Columbia, explains, "A historical case is a particular someone or something in the past that can be conceptually aggregated and temporally limited. . . . Typically chosen and assembled with a purpose, a historical case is an example or exemplification used to demonstrate, exemplify, and illustrate or alternatively contradict and undermine a claim or thesis. Indeed, a case provides evidence."

it will synthesize and evaluate reactions, noting both a warrant for their rejection of Western theological imposition and ways in which they leave the outsider's role in local theological development ambiguous.

This book will then, in chapter 4, critically assess the concept of hermeneutical community. It will provide a descriptive analysis of the concept's historical development in different realms of hermeneutical thought—including Anabaptist, philosophical, theological, postliberal, Pentecostal, and ecumenical hermeneutical discourse—and offer an evangelical understanding of hermeneutical community. The chapter will also present an evaluation of the concept's biblical-theological moorings in order to assess the legitimacy of employing a hermeneutical community approach as a means of framing the outsider's role in local theological development. The book will then synthesize the historical and biblical-theological data in order to establish the contemporary relevance of hermeneutical community for the local theological enterprise, particularly in light of colonial shortcomings and post-colonial critiques.

In chapter 5, this book will then apply this hermeneutical community framework to the outsider's role in local theological development. In doing so, it will seek to demonstrate how a hermeneutical community approach provides legitimate rationale for outsider involvement in local theological development. Further, it will demonstrate how such an approach helps shape a constructive role for the outsider in that process—something lacking in both colonial practice and post-colonial reactions. Lastly, the book will consider implications of this research and propose areas for further study.

ACKNOWLEDGMENTS

Before commencing, I need to acknowledge and set forth various delimitations, assumptions, and definitions which shape and constrain this missiological exploration of hermeneutical community. To begin with, this study is delimited in three significant ways. First, in order to demonstrate the reality and nature of colonial theological imposition, this work focuses strictly on three different case studies, one each in Latin America, Africa, and Asia.[46] In particular, it will assess how theological

---

46. As chapter 2 will point out, both the modern enterprise of colonialism and the Modern Missionary Movement transpired among these three continents. Therefore, these regions present opportunities to explore the precedent of colonial control over local theological conviction.

imposition featured in the work of sixteenth-century Jesuits in Peru, the Church Missionary Society's ministry in Uganda in the late nineteenth and early twentieth centuries, and in early twentieth-century church unification schemes that developed in South India at the hands of various Protestant mission leaders. These cases are presented as representative of the broader, general missionary approach throughout most of the colonial period. Walls—an eminent historian of Christianity—underscores the warrant for this generalization, asserting that this pattern of theological imposition remained commonplace in the colonial missionary enterprise.[47]

As a second delimitation, this study's exploration of post-colonial reactions to Western theological imposition focuses strictly on literature of the Ecumenical Association of Third World Theologians (EATWOT) and three different evangelical associations—the Latin American Theological Fraternity, the Association of Evangelicals of Africa, and the Asia Theological Association. By delimiting this study to the aforementioned organizations and their bodies of literature, author and reader alike are able to engage important discourses (e.g., liberation theology, postcolonial theological studies) as well as significant theological voices of the Majority World (e.g., Gustavo Gutiérrez, Enrique Dussel, John Mbiti, Aloysius Pieris, René Padilla, Byang Kato, Tite Tiénou, Bong Rin Ro, etc.). Moreover, because these organizations incorporate diverse ecclesial and theological orientations, this delimitation allows this work to engage a wide variety of reactions within a more narrow body of literature.

Third, this work delimits the context for applying the following proposal regarding the outsider's role in local theological development. Specifically, this book focuses on the outsider's role among local churches moving from the "missional contextualization" phase to the "ecclesial contextualization" phase.[48] According to DeVries, the missional contextualization phase features the outsider as the dominant agent of theological conviction and communication. At this stage, outsiders assume responsibility for theological formation among local believers. However, in the ecclesial contextualization phase, local Christians become the agents of theology—that is, rather than remaining recipients of theology, they become self-theologizing. This book outlines a role for the outsider

---

47. Walls, *Cross-Cultural Process*, 37–38, 242–43.
48. DeVries, "Contexts of Contextualization," 11–12.

to help local churches who are not yet self-theologizing to become agents of their own theological conviction and expression.

In addition to the aforementioned delimitations, this work proceeds with two major assumptions. First, I assume an evangelical view of Scripture[49] and remain committed to the biblical text as the supreme authority and norm for all theology. By extension, I reject the notion that context serves as an equally authoritative basis for theology, deny that liberative praxis or the analysis of historical events serve as conduits of divine revelation, and reject theological methods that subsume the authority of Scripture under the perceived authority of the interpreting community. Second, I assume the priority of establishing healthy local churches within the Christian missionary task. This assumption provides the backdrop for my argument in favor of sound theological development in and among local churches. This priority of church planting derives from Jesus' promise to build his church (Matt 16:18) and the precedent of church planting in the New Testament (e.g., Acts 9:31; 14:23; 16:5; 20:28; 1 Cor 3:6–17; Rev 2–3).

This work also frequently employs several significant terms in making its case, the definitions of which are below. These definitions will shape and constrain the use of these terms throughout the book.

Hermeneutical community. This term refers to a group of Christians—either as a smaller set of believers or the broader, global church—who interpret and apply the Scriptures together in order to pool insight and guard against errant interpretations. A hermeneutical community approach to theological development incorporates multiple voices and different perspectives.

Outsider. This term here mainly refers to someone who grew up in the North Atlantic world but ministers in a context outside of the countries therein. Generally, it refers to one who has not grown up from within a given local context.

Local theology. The notion of "local" has become more complex in today's globally interconnected world.[50] While acknowledging such com-

---

49. That is, I affirm the view of Scripture set forth by the International Council on Biblical Inerrancy, "Chicago Statement on Biblical Inerrancy," *J. Evang. Theol. Soc.* 21.4 (1978) 289–96.

50. As Robert J. Schreiter, *The New Catholicity: Theology between the Global and the Local* (Maryknoll: Orbis, 1997), ix, notes, "Theology stands today between the global and the local. The global is not the same as the old universal or perennial theologies. Despite the homogenizing aims of globalization, local situations remain robust in their resistance. And there is no 'local' any more that is not touched by powerful outside

plexity, this book employs the term as a simple descriptor of theology arising out of a specific context. "Local theology" here refers to implicit and explicit biblical-theological convictions that develop within and in relation to a local context. It is roughly synonymous with terms like "contextual theology" and "indigenous theology."

Majority World. This term here refers to the area outside the North Atlantic context of Western Europe and North America, an area that assumed the moniker "Third World" over the last half of the twentieth century. In adopting this term, this book follows other recent missiological literature.[51]

West. While recognizing that the West is by no means monolithic, this book will employ this term (and its cognates) to refer to the broad context of Europe and North America—that is, the "North Atlantic."

Western theology. Recognizing likewise that Western theology is far from monolithic, this term here will refer to the implicit and explicit biblical-theological convictions which have developed in the contexts of Europe and North America. In this sense, Western theology is itself local theology, having developed within and in relation to contexts of the West.

Theologizing. This term refers both to the formal articulating of theological beliefs—in forms like confessions or songs—and to the work applying biblical truth to contextual issues.

Theological agency. This term refers to the state in which a person or group of people is able to articulate theology and develop theological conviction. That is, they are "agents" of their own beliefs rather than mere "recipients" who receive and embrace the theological convictions of others.

Theological imposition. This term refers to the common practice among colonial-era missionaries of binding native churches to Western understandings and formulations of theology, and treating those as normative for the life and faith of local believers. It refers to the way in

---

forces. In fact, the local itself increasingly cannot be defined simply in territorial terms." For an overview of this complexity, see John Cheong, "Polycentrism in Majority World Theologizing: An Engagement with Power and Essentialism," in *Majority World Theologies: Theologizing from Africa, Asia, Latin America, and the Ends of the Earth*, ed. Allen L. Yeh and Tite Tiénou, Evangelical Missiological Society Series 26 (Pasadena, CA: William Carey Library, 2018), 24–26.

51. Allen L. Yeh and Tite Tiénou, eds., *Majority World Theologies: Theologizing from Africa, Asia, Latin America, and the Ends of the Earth*, Evangelical Missiological Society Series 26 (Pasadena, CA: William Carey Library, 2018); Gene L. Green et al., eds., *Majority World Theology: Christian Doctrine in Global Context* (Downers Grove, IL: IVP Academic, 2020).

which missionaries controlled the theology that governed life in native churches.

Colonial. This term here refers generally to the era in which Western nations expanded and exerted their power over regions throughout the world for economic and political gain (ca. AD 1500–1950). In this book, the term will also refer more specifically to the controlling or domineering ways in which Western missionaries exerted authority over native churches during that era.

Post-colonial. This term here refers mostly to the period following the end of formal colonialism in the mid-twentieth century. In recent decades the term has assumed different meanings. According to Henning Wrogemann, "The term postcolonial initially came to be used as an historic term designating the time after the colonial era, but its definition was then broadened to refer to the continuation of colonial dependencies ('neocolonial') in the economic and cultural spheres following the independence of former colonial territories. In this sense, postcolonial was used as a systematic term designating a discourse formation."[52] The discourse to which Wrogemann refers is usually categorized as "postcolonial studies," with *postcolonial* as one word without a hyphen. Because this book employs the term not in reference to that emerging discourse but rather in reference to the time after the end of formal colonialism, it will do so by using the hyphenated construction (i.e., *post-colonial*) for clarity. It will also feature this term as a descriptor of scholars and practitioners who have leveled critiques against Western theological imposition in the wake of the colonial era.

Younger churches. For many years this term referred to the churches that mission agencies planted in the Majority World over the course of the Modern Missionary Movement. They were "younger" relative to the established churches of Europe and North America. This book will instead employ the descriptor "Majority World" in reference to such churches. Yet because the term "younger" shows up often in the literature explored in this research, this work will employ it on occasion, usually as a continuation of the wording in references cited.

Evangelical. It is important to define the adjective "evangelical," particularly considering its contemporary socio-political connotations in North America. While recognizing the difficulty of attaching a fixed definition to so wide a concept, this book will employ the term to designate

---

52. Henning Wrogemann, *Intercultural Hermeneutics*, vol. 1 of *Intercultural Theology*, trans. Karl E. Böhmer (Downers Grove, IL: IVP Academic, 2016), 348.

those people and dispositions that approximate David Bebbington's well-known quadrilateral of convictions: Biblicism, crucicentrism, conversionism, and activism.[53]

Finally, this work admittedly does not give attention to every contributing voice, particularly in its exploration of how the notion of hermeneutical community has developed within the broad realms of philosophical, theological, and postliberal hermeneutics.[54] The absence of certain voices stems from an endeavor to survey a vast landscape of literature associated with those discourses and present a concise overview of them in relation to hermeneutical community and its development as a concept. The overviews offered here serve simply to trace those broad lines of development.

ABSTRACT

Historically, Western missionaries have not gone far enough in the work of local theological development. They have settled for imparting existing theologies from the North Atlantic world rather than cultivate among local believers and church leaders an ability to read, interpret, apply, and express scriptural truth on their own and in their own context. Post-colonial voices—particularly those from the Majority World—have roundly criticized this precedent.

In the wake of this post-colonial development, the outsider's role in local theological development has remained unclear. This book seeks to offer clarity. It argues that a hermeneutical community approach to local theological development delineates a constructive role for outsiders that avoids the colonial extreme of theological imposition and the post-colonial extreme of theological withdrawal.

---

53. Bebbington first highlighted this quadrilateral in his *Evangelicalism in Modern Britain: A History from the 1730s to the 1980s* (London: Routledge, 1989). For an assessment of Bebbington's quadrilateral, see Brian Harris, "Beyond Bebbington: The Quest for Evangelical Identity in a Postmodern Era," *Churchman* 122.3 (2008) 201–19.

54. Those under-represented in this survey include prominent voices like Karl Barth, H. Richard Niebuhr, John Webster, Stanley Fish, David Kelsey, Francis Watson, Stephen Fowl, R. W. L. Moberly, Craig Bartholomew, Brevard Childs, Ronald Thiemann, Kathryn Tanner, Bruce Marshall, James K. A. Smith, John Howard Yoder, Stanley Hauerwas, James William McClendon, and Lewis Mudge, to name just a few. More remains to be said regarding how each of these theologians, and others, have shaped the idea of communal/ecclesial hermeneutics.

2

Colonial Pattern of Theological Imposition

"Take up the white man's burden," Rudyard Kipling urged in his famous 1899 poem.¹ The poem was not just an endorsement of the United States' military pursuit of control over the Philippines, it was an ode to broader Western imperialism. Kipling begins,

> Take up the White Man's burden—
> Send forth the best ye breed—
> Go bind your sons to exile
> To serve your captives' need;
> To wait in heavy harness,
> On fluttered folk and wild—
> Your new-caught, sullen peoples,
> Half-devil and half-child.²

Here Kipling conceives of Western peoples (i.e., the "White Man") in a superlative way. Conversely, he pictures many outside the West as somehow less than fully human—in need of someone to take them captive for their own good (i.e., that the "White Man" might "serve" them). He continues,

> Take up the White Man's burden—
> The savage wars of peace—

---

1. Rudyard Kipling, "The White Man's Burden," in *The Five Nations* (London: Methuen and Co., 1903), 79–81.
2. Kipling, "White Man's Burden," 79.

> Fill full the mouth of Famine
> And bid the sickness cease;³

Kipling understands the task of Western colonialism as a laudable one; it was one of humanitarian aid and liberation. However, he recognized that it was an endeavor which people of the Majority World would not necessarily receive well:

> And when your goal is nearest
> The end for others sought,
> Watch Sloth and heathen Folly
> Bring all your hope to nought.. . .
>
> Take up the White Man's burden—
> And reap his old reward:
> The blame of those ye better,
> The hate of those ye guard—
> The cry of hosts ye humour
> (Ah, slowly!) toward the light :—
> "Why brought ye us from bondage,
> Our loved Egyptian night?"⁴

Despite the potential that locals would disparage such colonization, Kipling urges those in the West to press on. To shrink from the burden of the task—no matter how thankless or difficult it may be—was, for Kipling, unacceptable. The West must nobly bear such an obligation for the sake of the backward, primitive peoples of the world.

Kipling's poem embodies much of the rationale behind Western colonialism. Throughout most of the period spanning from the 1400s through the early 1900s, Western nations held to a set of convictions that animated their foreign policies.⁵ Those convictions centered on the ideas of Natural Law and Natural Rights.⁶ Many believed that European na-

---

3. Kipling, "White Man's Burden," 80.

4. Kipling, "White Man's Burden," 80–81.

5. Robert Delavignette, *Christianity and Colonialism*, trans. J. R. Foster (New York: Hawthorn, 1964), 37–46, highlights some of the differences between early colonial expansion and its later manifestations. Yet, David Boucher, "Invoking a World of Ideas: Theory and Interpretation in the Justification of Colonialism," *Theoria* 63.2 (2016) 19, contends that the same set of ideological convictions remained fairly common throughout the colonial period, even as late as 1930. He highlights how these convictions even undergirded "European Trusteeship in Africa in the latter part of the nineteenth century" (18).

6. Boucher, "Invoking a World of Ideas," 11–13.

tions rightly recognized and lived according to God's natural ordering of the universe.[7] That is, they were civilized people who did not maintain the kind of barbaric practices prevalent outside the West and in earlier periods of history. Western nations therefore maintained certain rights (e.g., the right to land) for which certain barbaric peoples did not qualify, precisely because they failed to abide by God's Natural Law.

A built-in hierarchy of humanity thus existed within the prevailing Western worldview, one which warranted—in foreign policy—the subjugation of peoples on the lower rungs of humankind.[8] At the top were the people of the West; far below them were the indigenous peoples of the Majority World. These peoples were backward and primitive, and they required, at most, others to conquer and subjugate them due to their Natural Law violations, or, at least, they needed the guiding and controlling hand of a superior people—one who could civilize them out of barbaric ways.[9] Thus many Western nations surmised, as did Kipling, that it was their duty to colonize and control the non-Western world, and that doing so was ultimately for the good of the peoples therein.[10]

This rationale of control and imposition also surfaced in a movement corollary to Western colonialism—the Christian missionary enterprise. Many within Christian missions embraced the idea that the West—its culture and its people—remained superior to the peoples and cultures in other parts of the world.[11] This notion led, in part, to pat-

---

7. Boucher, "Invoking a World of Ideas," 16, explains this conception of Natural Law: "It is the duty imposed by God upon humanity of self-preservation which requires making the earth productive and bountiful. The more efficiently this is done the better. To optimise productivity of the soil and fulfil one's duty to God requires the development of techniques of cultivation, and just as importantly the establishment of civil society, or sovereignty, to ensure good governance and security in order to protect oneself from harm and to cultivate in safety. To judge indigenous peoples against the universal obligation to cultivate or exploit the land to its optimum meant that they fell short of their moral duty in a number of respects."

8. Boucher, "Invoking a World of Ideas," 11–13.

9. For an overview of how colonizers projected identities onto peoples outside the West, and how those projections undergirded and shaped Western efforts to colonize and control them, see Henning Wrogemann, *Intercultural Hermeneutics*, vol. 1 of *Intercultural Theology*, trans. Karl E. Böhmer (Downers Grove, IL: IVP Academic, 2016), 151–53.

10. Boucher, "Invoking a World of Ideas," 11–13, 19–20.

11. This idea surfaced clearly in the work of James S. Dennis, *Christian Missions and Social Progress: A Sociological Study of Foreign Missions*, 3 vols. (New York: Fleming H. Revell, 1897–1906), whose three-volume work extolling social amelioration through Christian mission also roundly denounced non-Western cultures (see, for example,

terns of dominance and control within Christian missions, as missionaries consolidated and retained near total control over local churches, believers, and ministries.[12] It was such patterns of foreign dominance that missionary statesmen Rufus Anderson and Henry Venn famously decried.[13] For Venn and Anderson, Christian missions had inculcated in local churches far too much dependency on the West. Rather than being self-governing, self-supporting, and self-propagating, many native churches remained dependent on Western missionary societies and their heavy-handed control over ecclesiastical affairs. Yet, it was not only over church polity, finance, and ministry that missionaries exerted control.

1:75–76, 380). William R. Hutchison, *Errand to the World: American Protestant Thought and Foreign Missions* (Chicago: University of Chicago Press, 1993), 110–11, notes that Dennis's views and analysis received wide praise and approval upon its publication. In both Dennis's work and reviews of it, "the unspoken assumption, in what passed for intercultural inquiry, continued to be that Western civilization is entitled to phrase the questions as well as provide most of the answers. The unspoken, and mostly unconscious, watchword was still 'define and conquer'" (111). David J. Bosch, *Transforming Mission: Paradigm Shifts in Theology of Mission* (Maryknoll, NY: Orbis, 1991), 293, summarizes, "Mission writers and speakers, then, had little doubt about the depravity of life in non-Western societies. Some of them, particularly around the transition from the nineteenth century to the twentieth, excelled in portraying the depravity of pagan life from which 'Christian civilization' could rescue people." Moreover, Bosch notes that around the turn of the twentieth century, the Western missionary enterprise "proceeded not only from the assumption of the superiority of Western culture over all other cultures, but also from the conviction that God, in his providence, had chosen the Western nations, because of their unique qualities, to be the standard-bearers of his cause even to the uttermost ends of the world. This conviction, commonly referred to as the notion of 'manifest destiny,' was only barely identifiable during the early decades of the nineteenth century but gradually deepened and reached its most pronounced expression during the period 1880–1920" (298).

12. Bosch, *Transforming Mission*, 294–96. Bosch asserts that in the eyes of Western missionaries, local churches overseas "were churches, yes, but of a lesser order than those in the West, and they needed benevolent control and guidance, like children not yet come of age" (295).

13. Both Anderson and Venn sought to move missions away from patterns of dominance and in the direction of planting self-supporting, self-governing, and self-propagating churches. See Rufus Anderson, *Foreign Missions: Their Relations and Claims* (New York: Charles Scribner, 1869), 44–61, 109–19; Henry Venn, "The Native Pastorate and Organization of Native Churches. First Paper, Issued 1851. Minute upon the Employment and Ordination of Native Teachers," in *Memoir of Henry Venn, B.D.: Prependary of St. Paul's, and Honorary Secretary of the Church Missionary Society*, by William Knight (London, 1882), 412–14; Henry Venn, "The Native Pastorate and Organization of Native Churches. Second Paper, Issued July, 1861," in *Memoir of Henry Venn, B.D.: Prependary of St. Paul's, and Honorary Secretary of the Church Missionary Society*, by William Knight (London, 1882), 414–20.

This chapter explores, in particular, how the colonial pattern of control in the missionary enterprise of the West extended to the realm of theology. In doing so, this chapter will first provide an overview of the colonial era and its relationship to Western missions. Second, it will examine three case studies which highlight how missionaries imposed Western theology onto local, native churches and believers. Finally, this chapter will identify commonalities among the case studies to give shape to the broader pattern of theological imposition in the colonial period.

OVERVIEW OF COLONIAL PERIOD

The term "colonialism" has assumed different definitions. Edward Said—the late literary scholar and founder of postcolonial studies—offers a basic, somewhat neutral definition. According to him, colonialism is "the implanting of settlements on distant territory."[14] Historian Wolfgang Reinhard, professor emeritus at Freiburg University, offers a more detailed and more value-laden definition. He employs the term "colonialism" to mean "one people's control over another people through the economic, political and ideological exploitation of a development gap between the two."[15] Reinhard thus sees control and exploitation as part of the nature of colonialism; it entails the "alien rule" of one people over another.[16]

Closely related to the term colonialism is that of "imperialism." Both Said and Reinhard understand imperialism as a process that has often led to colonialism. According to Said, imperialism "means the practice, the theory, and the attitudes of a dominating metropolitan center ruling a distant territory. 'Colonialism' . . . is almost always a consequence of imperialism."[17] Similarly, Reinhard defines the term "imperialism" as "the measures undertaken in order to establish colonialism."[18]

With regard to the Western colonial era, the two terms are often conflated. That is, colonialism has come to replace imperialism, the former a more pejorative moniker for the latter, which held an altruistic connotation among the colonizing nations throughout much of the

---

14. Edward W. Said, *Culture and Imperialism* (New York: Knopf, 1993), 9.
15. Wolfgang Reinhard, *A Short History of Colonialism* (New York: Manchester University Press, 2011), 1.
16. Reinhard, *Short History of Colonialism*, 1.
17. Said, *Culture and Imperialism*, 9.
18. Reinhard, *Short History of Colonialism*, 1.

colonial period.[19] Missions historian Stephen Neill asserts, "The term 'colonialism' appears to be a recent arrival in the languages of the western world, taking the place of the older and more familiar 'imperialism.' It is used almost exclusively as a term of reproach, implying that the only aim of colonial rule has been the exploitation and impoverishment of weaker and defenceless [sic] peoples, and that its only results have been the destruction of what was good in ancient civilizations and the multiplications of measureless evils."[20] Neill highlights here the negative connotation of Western colonialism, yet—writing two decades after its collapse—believed that not enough time had lapsed to make an objective evaluation.[21] Moreover, he—as well as others—calls attention to the reality that Western nations have not been the only ones to engage in such colonialism/imperialism.[22]

Yet however one understands and evaluates Western colonialism, it remains a historical fact—from the late fifteenth century to the mid-twentieth century, various Western nations extended their claim and control over vast regions beyond their borders.[23] This colonial period began in the 1400s with the Age of Discovery, as the Iberian powers of Spain and Portugal launched their maritime explorations behind men like Christopher Columbus, Vasco de Gama, and Ferdinand Magellan.[24] Their hope was to find an alternative path to Asia as a means of circumventing the Turkish empire's monopoly on key global trade routes through the Middle East.[25] Western colonialism ultimately culminated in a period known as "High Imperialism," which spanned roughly the latter part of the nineteenth century and the first half of the twentieth.[26]

---

19. Hans Kohn, "Reflections on Colonialism," in *The Idea of Colonialism*, ed. Robert Strausz-Hupé and Harry W. Hazard (New York: Frederick A. Praeger, 1958), 2; Kipling's aforementioned poem underscores this positive connotation that imperialism had in popular Western imagination. See also Said, *Culture and Imperialism*, 9–14.

20. Stephen Neill, *Colonialism and Christian Missions* (New York: McGraw-Hill, 1966), 11.

21. Neill, *Colonialism and Christian Missions*, 11.

22. Neill, *Colonialism and Christian Missions*, 11; see also Marc Ferro, *Colonization: A Global History*, trans. K. D. Prithipaul (Quebec: World Heritage, 1997), 1; Reinhard, *Short History of Colonialism*, 5, 7.

23. Mary Gilmartin, "Colonialism/Imperialism," in *Key Concepts in Political Geography*, ed. Carolyn Gallaher et al. (London: Sage, 2009), 115–16.

24. For an overview of Spain and Portugal's initial foray into maritime exploration, see Reinhard, *Short History of Colonialism*, 8–19.

25. Neill, *Colonialism and Christian Missions*, 35–39.

26. For a brief overview of High Imperialism, see Reinhard, *Short History of*

COLONIAL PATTERN OF THEOLOGICAL IMPOSITION

During this time, the Western colonial enterprise reached its zenith, as world powers jostled for control over global markets and raw materials in an effort to strengthen domestic economies and outgain competing nations.[27]

Over the course of these centuries, European nations claimed and established control over immense tracts of territory.[28] At the fore of this endeavor were Spain and Portugal, who effectively conquered and controlled the whole of Central and South America.[29] Under the rule of either England or France came countries like Canada, Australia, New Zealand, and India, as well as massive portions of Africa and the Middle East.[30] The expansion of such nations over time was so extensive that by 1914, European nations claimed some sort of control over about 85 percent of the earth.[31] Said adds that by the turn of the twentieth century, "Scarcely a corner of life was untouched by the facts of empire; the economies were hungry for overseas markets, raw materials, cheap labor, and hugely profitable land, and defense and foreign-policy establishments were more and more committed to the maintenance of vast tracts of distant territory and large numbers of subjugated peoples."[32] Western colonialism was thus immense in geographical scope.

A number of motivations undergirded this broad colonial endeavor. Reinhard identifies three types.[33] First, socio-economic factors led colonial powers to expand their control into foreign territories. That is, "the acquisition of profits and thus of enhanced social status" impelled various rulers to invest in the development of foreign markets. Second, political motivations existed. Colonial powers, particularly in the period of High Imperialism, leveraged colonial holdings to gain advantages against one another. Third, ideological, religious, and cultural motivations factored

---

Colonialism, 178–80.

27. Reinhard, *Short History of Colonialism*, 178–80.

28. Delavignette, *Christianity and Colonialism*, 15–17, provides a statistical overview of the geographic scope of Western colonial expansion. He notes that by the year 1900, Western colonial powers controlled about a third of the world's population.

29. Neill, *Colonialism and Christian Missions*, 38–39.

30. Said, *Culture and Imperialism*, 5–6. Said highlights other nations, including the United States, Russia, Japan, and Turkey, who were also involved in imperialism in the nineteenth century.

31. Said, *Culture and Imperialism*, 8.

32. Said, *Culture and Imperialism*, 8.

33. Reinhard, *Short History of Colonialism*, 6.

Hermeneutical Community

into colonial expansion. Per Reinhard, "At stake was often a desire to bring true faith to the heathens, true culture to the barbarians."[34]

Of particular importance here is the motivating desire to Christianize people outside the West. That such a desire helped sustain the colonial enterprise is not surprising, considering that Western colonialism developed out of a European context in which the church and society remained bound up with one another.[35] As historian Marc Ferro explains, "Conversion to Christianity became identified with the duty to civilize, for civilization could not be other than Christian."[36] Neill adds,

> The ideas of conquest and of conversion lay side by side in the consciousness of the Christians of the western world. Trade, and the hopes of fame and wealth, were without doubt the dominant motives. But there is no reason to doubt the sincerity of those who supposed that the addition of so many lands to the Christian world was an enterprise which could count on the divine blessing, and that nothing could be more beneficial to the inhabitants of those dark lands than their admission to the Christian Church.[37]

For many then, the expansion of European dominion was also the expansion of the church's dominion—an expansion of Christendom.

This intricate tie between Christianity and colonialism serves, in some ways, as an indictment of the missionary enterprise of that era—since the aims and means of political expansion did not necessarily align with Christian virtue. Jesuit scholar Ana Carolina Hosne, for one, calls attention to the ills of the confluence of colonial statecraft and missions:

> The Columbus voyage—or rather the date 1492—sparked the Catholic monarchs' claim to sovereignty, riches and mission in America. The claim set off a rush towards European imperial rivalry and indigenous disaster, and towards the building of power and prosperity on foundations of racial dominance and violence. . . . One of the natural outcomes of the conquest was "Occidentalization," meaning the setting up of European institutions, beliefs and practices in the "New World," which went

---

34. Reinhard, *Short History of Colonialism*, 6.

35. Neill, *Colonialism and Christian Missions*, 39, explains, "In the Middle Ages all history was Church history. The Church was effectively present in every aspect of the lives of men, even of those who most emphatically denied by their lives what they professed with their lips."

36. Ferro, *Colonization*, 11.

37. Neill, *Colonialism and Christian Missions*, 39.

alongside both the exploitation of its resources and energy and the transformation of its natives.[38]

In certain places and certain times, Christianity advanced on the heels of such colonial power. On occasion, Christianity even moved forward under the threat of violence from "Christian" kings in Europe.[39] Although not every mission of the colonial era was an accomplice to the violent and domineering ways of the colonizing nations from which they came, one can hardly deny that Christianity and colonialism often remained intricately tied to one another, often for ill.[40]

However, the history of Christian missions defies a reductionistic equation of the processes of colonialism and Christianization. That is, although the Christian missionary enterprise weaved itself into the political expansion of European powers, it was not necessarily *thoroughly* colonial.[41] Neither was colonialism *thoroughly* Christian. Many colonial agents, in fact, opposed the presence and work of missionaries, believing them to be an impediment to the work of the state.[42] Moreover, mis-

---

38. Ana Carolina Hosne, *The Jesuit Missions to China and Peru, 1570–1610: Expectations and Appraisals of Expansionism* (New York: Routledge, 2013), 71.

39. For example, see Lee M. Penyak and Walter J. Petry, eds., "The Requerimiento," in *Religion in Latin America: A Documentary History* (Maryknoll, NY: Orbis, 2006), 25–27, a document drafted in 1513 which the king of Spain ordered to be read to natives at the outset of Spanish conquest. The document threatens severe violence for those who do not acknowledge the supremacy of the church, the pope, and the Spanish crown as well as properly receive the Catholic missionaries in their presence.

40. Neill, *Colonialism and Christian Missions*, 11–12, notes that among many people, "It is now widely taken for granted that, whatever may have been the beneficent intentions of the missionaries, they were in fact the tools of governments, and that missions can be classed as one of the instruments of western infiltration and control." Neill argues against this reductionistic conclusion.

41. After surveying six different missionary case studies from the latter half of the nineteenth century, John H. Darch, *Missionary Imperialists? Missionaries, Government and the Growth of the British Empire in the Tropics, 1860–1885*, Studies in Christian History and Thought (Colorado Springs: Paternoster, 2009), 244, concludes, "It cannot be denied that their presence and sometimes their actions aided that spread of western influence, authority and power that we refer to as 'imperialism.' Nevertheless, where their actions aided the development of the empire it was as a secondary consequence, what may appropriately be described as incidental imperialism." That is, in such cases they fostered "an 'imperialism of result' rather than an 'imperialism of intent.' Missionaries were primarily messengers of the Christian gospel and its attendant values" (246). Regarding British Protestant missions from the period 1880–1914, Porter, "Introduction," 4, similarly claims, "Most missionaries were not conscious imperialists in either a political or denominational sense."

42. Lamin Sanneh, *Encountering the West: Christianity and the Global Cultural Process: The African Dimension* (Maryknoll, NY: Orbis, 1993), 206, asserts, "Many senior

sionaries at times counteracted the aims of colonial powers, whether by advocating for native rights over and against colonial injustices (e.g., Bartolomé de Las Casas)[43] or through the promotion of vernacular languages and local cultures (e.g., William Carey).[44]

The relationship between colonialism and Christianity is thus complex, which undermines the possibility of descriptive generalizations. Neill rightly maintains,

> The slapdash assertion that the penetration of the world by the political power and the culture of the West has nowhere produced anything but destruction, and that Christian missions without distinction have been involved in the guilt of that destruction, will not stand up to the light of sober historical investigation. On the other hand, idealizing representations, whether of colonial expansion as the bearing of the white man's burden, or of missionary progress in which the good missionary always appears as the friend of the simple Asian or African, are gravely distorted by mythological importations.[45]

Nevertheless, Western colonialism certainly played a significant role in shaping Christian missions during the colonial period, particularly in

---

colonial officials were anti-clerical and combated the Church with administrative measures, at times spiced with personal prejudice." Sanneh is referring here to missionary labors in Africa, yet the same anti-clericalism among colonial agents manifested itself in other regions too. Neill, *Colonialism and Christian Missions*, 14, adds, "The record shows that in innumerable cases the entrance of missionaries into non-Christian countries was opposed by governments, public opinion, traders, and local authorities alike."

43. Fernando Cervantes, "'The Defender of the Indians': Bartolomé de Las Casas in Context," *The Way* 38.3 (1998) 271–81.

44. Lamin Sanneh, *Translating the Message: The Missionary Impact on Culture*, American Society of Missiology Series 13 (Maryknoll, NY: Orbis, 1989), 101–5, demonstrates how Carey's translation of various works into vernacular languages subtly undermined colonial aims. With reference to Carey's translation work, he contends, "Christian mission, by furnishing a systematic account of the indigenous heritage, tacitly encouraged pride and confidence in the people, and in time this must prevail against the unstated logic of colonial overlordship" (102). Regarding missionaries at odds with colonial powers, see also Darch, *Missionary Imperialists?*, 237–46; Hutchison, *Errand to the World*, 9–10, adds, "From the sixteenth-century Spanish priest Bartolomé de Las Casas, railing against a society that had institutionalized Indian slavery; through Roger Williams, proclaiming the superior virtue of the native Americans; to the premillennialists and social radicals of the late nineteenth and early twentieth centuries; one could always hear a few voices within the churches and the missionary enterprise raising sharp questions about the purported overall superiority of Western or American civilization."

45. Neill, *Colonialism and Christian Missions*, 412.

how Western missionaries exerted control over native Christians and churches. Despite missionaries' genuine care for the well-being of locals, their outlook toward them was often one of a superior looking down on subordinates.[46] Moreover, missionaries often maintained positions of control over native churches.[47] And while there were prophetic voices calling them away from such domineering patterns (e.g., Rufus Anderson, Henry Venn), missionaries were slow in divesting themselves of positions of control.[48]

Further, such colonial control over the lives of native churches and believers extended quite naturally to the realm of theology. That is, missionaries in the colonial era often controlled local theological conviction by imposing Western understandings and formulations of theology on local, native churches.[49] As Bosch notes, "By the time the large-scale Western colonial expansion began, Western Christians were unconscious of the fact that their theology was culturally conditioned; they simply assumed that it was supracultural and universally valid."[50] Theological imposition thus appeared sensical to missionaries of this colonial era.

EXAMPLES OF THEOLOGICAL IMPOSITION

To explore this dynamic of Western theological imposition, this chapter will examine and assess three case studies which serve as examples of foreign control over local theological reflection and expression. Geographically, these case studies span three different continents (i.e., South America, Africa, and Asia), while temporally, they span from the earliest stage of the colonial period to the latest. First, this chapter will examine the missionary labors of early Jesuits in Peru toward the end of the sixteenth century. Second, it will examine the work of the Church Missionary Society in Uganda in the late nineteenth and early twentieth centuries. Finally, it will examine the Protestant union movement in South India during the first half of the twentieth century. This chapter seeks to demonstrate that each case evidences foreign theological imposition, though in different and varying ways.

---

46. Neill, *Colonialism and Christian Missions*, 413.
47. Neill, *Colonialism and Christian Missions*, 417.
48. Neill, *Colonialism and Christian Missions*, 417.
49. The following sections seek to substantiate this claim.
50. Bosch, *Transforming Mission*, 448.

Latin America: Early Jesuits in Peru

The first example of theological imposition comes from the ministry of early Jesuits in Peru during the latter half of the sixteenth century. The land of Peru at that time covered a much wider region than the modern nation-state. According to Jesuit scholar Claudio Burgaleta, "It encompassed all of South America with the exception of Brazil and the Caribbean coast of the continent east of Colombia."[51] The Spanish assumed control over this region after conquering the Incas in 1532.[52] The decades following featured social upheaval and unrest, as Spanish conquistadors subjugated the native population and exploited them and their land for economic gain through the *encomienda* system, a system which allowed conquistadors to exact labor and taxes from the indigenous population.[53]

Entering this context in 1568 was the Society of Jesus (i.e., the Jesuits)—a Catholic missionary organization.[54] This Society finds its origin in Ignatius of Loyola, who played a major role in founding it in the early sixteenth century.[55] Ignatius and his young Catholic compatriots desired to establish a new religious order in which members offered themselves as ministers to be sent—whether within Europe or overseas—at the discretion of the church.[56] The society thus placed a missional obligation on all of its members. Hosne explains, "The society established that, apart from the three vows of religious life—obedience, poverty and chastity, the Jesuits must make a fourth vow to the Pope, *circa misiones*, to allow themselves to be sent wherever they were needed.

---

51. Claudio M. Burgaleta, *José de Acosta, S.J. (1540–1600): His Life and Thought* (Chicago: Loyola University Press, 1999), 33.

52. Gregory J. Shepherd, *José de Acosta's "De Procuranda Indorum Salute": A Call for Evangelical Reforms in Colonial Peru* (New York: Peter Lang, 2014), 13.

53. Hosne, *Jesuit Missions*, 62–63; Shepherd, *José de Acosta's "De Procuranda,"* 13.

54. Hosne, *Jesuit Missions*, 4.

55. For a survey of the origin of the Society of Jesus, and the role that Ignatius played in it, see John W. O'Malley, *The First Jesuits* (Cambridge, MA: Harvard University Press, 1993), 23–50.

56. John W. O'Malley, *The Jesuits: A History from Ignatius to the Present* (New York: Rowman & Littlefield, 2014), 4, maintains that the founders "seemed to envisage the Society as an updated version of the so-called mendicant orders such as the Dominicans and Franciscans founded in the thirteenth century. They described themselves as engaging primarily in the same ministries of preaching and hearing confessions. They, like the Dominicans and Franciscans, saw these ministries as almost by definition itinerant and without geographical limits, which thus implicitly entailed overseas missions. They in fact conceived the Society as essentially a missionary order."

In effect, the Jesuit's fourth vow ... is a vow about 'missions.'"[57] The Jesuits eventually became the most prominent Catholic society of its kind in decades following.[58]

The king of Spain—Philip II—directly summoned the Society to work within the Spanish viceroyalty of Peru, and the Jesuits, entering into Spain's broader colonial enterprise, would go on to exhibit a kind of colonial control over the local church and its theology.[59] This reality became evident in the person of José de Acosta, in the resolutions of the Third Lima Council, and in the Jesuit parish ministry at Juli.

Jesuit Arrival in Peru—The Beginnings

The context of Peru was in transition at the time Jesuit missionaries arrived. According to Hosne, it was a "harsh Counter-Reformation context," in which King Philip II was attempting to consolidate control over the viceroyalty. The king, she adds, "decided to carry out an entire political, economic and religious reorganization in the Indies, which resulted in the arrival in Peru of Viceroy Toledo (1515–82), the Society of Jesus and the Inquisition."[60] Upon his appointment in 1569, the new viceroy—Francisco de Toledo—became an important figure in that reorganization process. As an agent of the Spanish Crown, Toledo sought to wrest control from *encomenderos*—often conquistadors who had long ruled over various areas of Peru through the *encomienda* system. According to Hosne, his aim was "to build a strong and powerful colonial state."[61]

One of Viceroy Toledo's major reforms was the introduction of a system of *reducciones*—large towns in which Toledo resettled the native population.[62] While the forced migration of indigenous peoples was not new to Peru, the new viceroy expanded that operation to benefit the burgeoning colonial state. Hosne explains, "With this forced relocation into the *reducciones*, Toledo could more easily impose effective labour, tax, and religious controls on the already overexploited Andean population. The *corregidores de indios*, or provincial magistrates, controlled the

---

57. Hosne, *Jesuit Missions*, 2.
58. O'Malley, *Jesuits*, 3–4.
59. The following sections will provide support for this claim.
60. Hosne, *Jesuit Missions*, 4.
61. Hosne, *Jesuit Missions*, 64.
62. Shepherd, *José de Acosta's "De Procuranda,"* 13.

Hermeneutical Community

Andean communities and were put in charge of tithe collection and the administration of justice."[63] This system allowed, for example, Toledo to utilize indigenous labor to tap the lucrative Peruvian mining economy.[64]

Toledo also sought to reassert the *patronato real* (i.e., royal patronage) system—a scheme by which the Spanish monarchy maintained significant control over the Catholic Church in foreign lands.[65] This system grew out of the medieval ideal for a synthesis between church and state and the ends which they sought.[66] Latin American history scholar Nicholas Cushner succinctly describes this scheme:

> As the Iberian powers moved into the Atlantic in search of new land and peoples, papal intervention through decrees and statements gave a framework of legitimacy to Portuguese and Spanish conquests. In 1508 a separate, more radical version of Royal Patronage was applied to America. The pope granted the Spanish Crown jurisdiction in essence over the Catholic Church in America. The enterprise of building churches and establishing clerics and the infrastructure of the church in the vast domains of America required large sums of money. Church construction and transportation of missionaries and their maintenance in America was a financial burden that Rome could not easily afford. So a bargain was struck between the King of Spain and the pope.[67]

That bargain involved the Spanish Crown bearing the burden for all costs related to the establishment and extension of the Catholic Church in the New World, in exchange for a significant measure of control over the church. Cushner asserts, "The king thus became the legal patron of the church in America, enjoying a sweeping control even greater than that enjoyed in Spain. The crown controlled the clergy, the clergy controlled the faithful, and so Catholicism was indissolubly linked with Royal Authority."[68] Toledo thus reclaimed the colonial state's power over the Catholic Church in Peru.

---

63. Hosne, *Jesuit Missions*, 64.
64. Hosne, *Jesuit Missions*, 64.
65. Hosne, *Jesuit Missions*, 64–65.
66. Nicholas P. Cushner, *Why Have You Come Here? The Jesuits and the First Evangelization of Native America* (New York: Oxford University Press, 2006), 28.
67. Cushner, *Why Have You Come Here?*, 28–29.
68. Cushner, *Why Have You Come Here?*, 29.

COLONIAL PATTERN OF THEOLOGICAL IMPOSITION

Not only did Toledo maintain control over the appointment and distribution of clergy, he also determined the methods by which they would minister.[69] The method he preferred was ministry by parishes, which tied into his system of *reducciones*. Hosne explains, "Together with the *reducciones*, the parish system was fundamental to the implementation of the Tridentine decrees in Peru; Toledo created hundreds of new parishes, making it easier to control the religious instruction of the Indians."[70] The parishes comprised strictly of Indians he called *doctrinas*, and it was Toledo's desire for the Jesuits to take up residence in these *doctrinas* as parish priests.[71]

After their arrival in 1568, the Jesuits had to grapple with these newly instituted reforms. Initially, they focused on catechetical work in Lima, while also traveling itinerantly outside the city to evangelize rural towns.[72] Before long, however, these early Jesuits faced a dilemma precipitated by Toledo's desire for them to assume full-time clerical duties in outlying rural *doctrinas*. If they were to accept such stationary roles, they would be sacrificing the mobility which Jesuit missionaries valued so highly.[73] Furthermore, they would be breaking their commitment to abstain from receiving remuneration for their services, which was typical for such parish priests.[74] However, if they refused the viceroy's orders, they might jeopardize the whole Jesuit operation in Peru—dependent as it was on royal patronage.[75] In other words, they could either sacrifice part of their identity and principles or risk drawing the ire of the one who held sway over the Catholic Church in Peru.[76]

---

69. Hosne, *Jesuit Missions*, 64–65.
70. Hosne, *Jesuit Missions*, 65.
71. Hosne, *Jesuit Missions*, 18, 65.
72. Cushner, *Why Have You Come Here?*, 80.
73. O'Malley, *First Jesuits*, 74.
74. O'Malley, *First Jesuits*, 74, explains, "The Jesuits forswore the parish for a variety of reasons. They believed it belonged more properly to the diocesan clergy than to members of an order. The benefice, or 'living,' attached to it conflicted with their version of the vow of poverty. Its fixity, generally as a lifetime appointment, restricted the mobility that was so intrinsic to their theory about their calling. It implied, finally, a ministry to those who already had pastors, a ministry to those who already had somebody to care for them."
75. Hosne, *Jesuit Missions*, 18.
76. Burgaleta, *José de Acosta*, 34, notes, "The society entered Peru at the dawn of a new age for the patronato real. This expansionist and centralized vision of the patronato would ensure that part of the Society's early years in Peru would be characterized by the tensions of an organization that had to protect its unique way of proceeding against the

Hermeneutical Community

Eventually, the Jesuits were able to navigate the uneasy terrain which Toledo's socio-political and ecclesiological emphases created. While they ended up accepting several *doctrinas* around Peru, the Jesuits nevertheless settled into a familiar routine of ministry in the city of Lima, which included college teaching, general pastoral care, catechetical work, and humanitarian aid among both the native Peruvian and displaced African populations in the city.[77]

One of the key figures leading the Society through the tension with Toledo and his reforms was José de Acosta, a Jesuit missionary-theologian who, in Hosne's words, took a more "conciliatory approach regarding the *doctrinas*."[78] Acosta averred, "In the midst of all the difficulties... and until we can see something more sure and certain, the position of the Compañía is, that it will not take over the parishes in a hurry, but neither will it reject the possibility completely."[79] Acosta eventually led the Society to embrace ministry within the *doctrina* system as a means of evangelizing the natives.[80] Gregory Shepherd, a scholar in the field of Latin American literature and culture, maintains, "The Jesuits began to coordinate their efforts to reform the missions with the sweeping changes being instituted by Toledo. Toledo's use of the famous 'reducciones' was of special interest to the Jesuits because the gathering and unification of scattered native groups would eventually facilitate the evangelization process."[81]

Theological Imposition in Person—José de Acosta

Acosta not only led these early Jesuit missionaries to embrace certain missionary methods, but he also played a significant role in establishing

---

crown's policies of centralized control of all religious affairs in the Americas."

77. Burgaleta, *José de Acosta*, 35.

78. Hosne, *Jesuit Missions*, 18.

79. José de Acosta, *De Procuranda Indorum Salute—Jose De Acosta S.J. 1540–1600: An English Introduction and Translation*, trans. G. Stewart McIntosh (2020), Kindle, loc. 8319.

80. Hosne, *Jesuit Missions*, 67, contends, "Through Acosta, the Society adjusted to—and finally accepted—the conditions imposed by the colonial authorities, specifically regarding the doctrinas, which, in fact, the Society eventually incorporated as an evangelization method.... In short, Acosta's intervention as the main theologian of the mission was both conciliatory and instrumental, as there was no possible way that Toledo would let the Society impose its preferences when it came to the principal Christianization methods in Peru." See also Shepherd, *José de Acosta's "De Procuranda,"* 38.

81. Shepherd, *José de Acosta's "De Procuranda,"* 36.

COLONIAL PATTERN OF THEOLOGICAL IMPOSITION

a precedent for theological imposition within the work of the Society in Peru. After the completion of his theological studies at a preeminent Jesuit university outside of Madrid, and while ministering in smaller Spanish towns, he began voicing his desire to minister in the New World.[82] Jesuit authorities eventually granted his request, and Acosta set sail for Peru in 1571.[83] More than just a missionary practitioner during his subsequent fourteen-year stay in the Americas, he went on to become one of the most influential theologians of the early modern period, spanning from the late fifteenth century to the late eighteenth century.[84] Two of his most famous books are *De Procuranda Indorum Salute*[85] (i.e., *On Procuring the Salvation of Indians*) and *Natural and Moral History of the Indies*.[86]

Acosta's predilection for theological imposition was both subtle and obvious. It was subtle because it resided, in part, at the level of epistemology. That is, Acosta assumed a position in which his claim on knowledge—as well as that of the European tradition he represented—remained wholly authoritative. Upon his arrival in Peru, Acosta started recognizing the incongruity between his Old World conceptualities and the physical realities he faced in the New World.[87] In the midst of this epistemological dilemma, he reconceptualized the New World and its geographic realities—particularly in his *Natural and Moral History of the Indies*—so as to remain commensurate with the European theological tradition with which he was so familiar.[88] Yet in doing so, he rendered the natives silent, unable to speak for themselves in their own land.

Acosta's reconceptualization of the New World in light of the Old was an epistemological move that helped ensure the ongoing normativity

82. For an overview of Acosta's early life, see Burgaleta, *José de Acosta*, 12–31.

83. Burgaleta, *José de Acosta*, 12–31.

84. Willie James Jennings, *The Christian Imagination: Theology and the Origins of Race* (New Haven, CT: Yale University Press, 2010), 68, claims, "Not simply a Catholic theologian in the New World, [Acosta] was one of the most important, if not the most important, bearer of the theological tradition of Christianity to set foot in the New World in his time and arguably for at least one hundred years after his arrival. Indeed Acosta was the embodiment of theological tradition. He was a traditioned Christian intellectual of the highest order who precisely, powerfully, and unrelentingly performed that tradition in the New World."

85. Acosta, *De Procuranda*.

86. José de Acosta, *Natural and Moral History of the Indies*, ed. Jane E. Mangan, trans. Frances M. López-Morillas, Chronicles of the New World Order (Durham, NC: Duke University Press, 2002).

87. Jennings, *Christian Imagination*, 85.

88. Jennings, *Christian Imagination*, 84–87.

of his theology in the Americas. According to Willie James Jennings, a professor and theologian at Yale University, that move reflected a thoroughly colonial mindset. He explains, "Although [Acosta] entered the New World, his central epistemological gesture was bringing the New World inside of his theological vision, rendering it intelligible inside Christian Theology. Acosta's would be a totalizing epistemological gesture that was a harbinger of the kind of Western conceptual hegemony that has come upon the world since the sixteenth century."[89]

What Acosta did was extract geography—which, through the discovery of new lands, was then challenging conventional European ideas about that nature of the world—from theology and philosophy.[90] Rather than allowing New World realities to challenge Old World textual authorities (whether theological or philosophical), Acosta took it upon himself to conceptualize the New World in a way that left Old World authorities intact.[91] On one hand, this move helped Acosta maintain the inner coherence of European theology and philosophy.[92] On the other hand, it ensured that Christian knowledge in South America—not having to account for the local context—would remain beholden to Europe.

Thus, Acosta's imperialistic epistemology led him to an imperialistic theological pedagogy, in which local subjects remained bound to his theological convictions. In Acosta's eyes, natives were essentially children, and the more advanced Europeans must teach them accordingly.[93] Jennings contends, "Acosta's quest to teach and thereby create orthodoxy even in those he designates the most ignorant flesh . . . produced a reductive theological vision in which the world's people become perpetual students, even where and when faith is formed."[94] For Acosta, natives (whom he evaluated through a "racial optic") brought little to nothing to the table when it came to theological reflection.[95] Jennings explains, "Acosta believes that natives can be trained in the faith, but only with much struggle, much effort, and with their world shaped in disciplinary realities."[96]

89. Jennings, *Christian Imagination*, 87.
90. Jennings, *Christian Imagination*, 84–85.
91. Jennings, *Christian Imagination*, 85–88.
92. Jennings, *Christian Imagination*, 88.
93. Acosta, *De Procuranda*, loc. 3899.
94. Jennings, *Christian Imagination*, 112.
95. Jennings, *Christian Imagination*, 104–6.
96. Jennings, *Christian Imagination*, 108–9.

COLONIAL PATTERN OF THEOLOGICAL IMPOSITION

Acosta's theological imposition did not remain at the subtle level of epistemology, however; it became more pronounced in the missionary methods he advocated and employed, particularly evident in *De Procuranda*. In the book, Acosta revealed what he believed to be the nature of the Society's missionary task within the viceroyalty. He was displeased with the missiological approach of previous Dominican missionaries, and thus sought to clarify both the rationale for the Catholic mission to Peru and its proper methods.

Acosta's methodological starting point for the mission rested on an ethnic hierarchy which classified different kinds of Amerindians. Shepherd explains, "In order to develop a more fertile climate for missionary work in Peru, Acosta investigates or reads the nature of Amerindians measuring their cognitive capacity and empowering their position as prospective Christians."[97] The hierarchy Acosta developed sought to categorize different types of "barbarians." According to him, barbarians were "peoples who are not only all deprived of the light of the Gospel but are also unaware of civilization."[98] In other words, they were those who resided outside of European Christendom.

Acosta offered three categories in his hierarchy of barbarian peoples. The first category, he maintained, "are those who do not depart greatly from true reason and the common way-of-life. They have a stable form of government, legal system, fortified cities, magistrates who are obeyed and well established, prosperous commerce and what is most important, the use and knowledge of letters, for where there are books and engraved monuments there the people are more human and civilized."[99] He tentatively placed the Chinese and Japanese in this category. He acknowledged respectable institutions in those societies, yet contended that they nevertheless fail to reason properly and remain in need of salvation.[100]

Acosta's second category occupies a lower rung on the hierarchy than his first. Included in this category, he maintained, are "Barbarians who did not achieve the use of writing nor the knowledge of philosophy or civil rights, but nevertheless have their nationhood and government defined by leaders, and where they have fixed settlements and custodians of law and order, armed forces and captains, and finally some form of

---

97. Shepherd, *José de Acosta's "De Procuranda,"* 15.
98. Acosta, *De Procuranda*, loc. 893.
99. Acosta, *De Procuranda*, loc. 908.
100. Acosta, *De Procuranda*, loc. 908.

Hermeneutical Community

solemn religious worship."[101] In this category Acosta placed those who were part of Mexican and Peruvian empires in the Americas.

Acosta took a particularly negative view of those who reside in his last and lowest category of humanity. He asserted, "Among them are the savages similar to wild animals, who hardly have human feelings—without law, without agreements, without government, without nationhood, who move from place to place, or if they live in one place they are more like wild animals' caves or animal cages. Such are those that our people call Caribes, always hungry for blood, cruel to foreigners, who devour human flesh, walk naked or barely cover their private parts."[102] He believed that there are many such groups in the New World. Regarding this hierarchy, Shepherd summarizes, "Acosta's three categories of non-European cultures attempt to define the cognitive abilities of the different Amerindian groups based on cultural evidence deemed valid by the European mind."[103] Moreover, for Acosta, the proper method of evangelization of a given population depended on where that people group fell within these three hierarchical categories.[104]

In Acosta's eyes, the indigenous populations of the New World fell into the second and third rungs of this hierarchy, and thus the way to Christianize them was through imposition and control. Regarding missionary methods among the second category of barbarians, Acosta argued, "If they are not controlled by a higher authority, they will find it difficult to receive the light of the Gospel and to take on customs that are worthy of humanity. And if they do receive the Gospel without that sort of control, then one doubts if they will continue in it."[105] For the third and lowest category of people, he maintained,

> All these are hardly men, or are only half men, so it is best to teach them to become men and instruct them like children. . . . [A]nd if they go against their own best interests and their salvation, and become exasperated with the doctors and teachers, then we shall have to constrain them by controlled and proper means of force, obliging them to leave the jungle and reside in urban centers, and even carry it out, up to a certain point,

---

101. Acosta, *De Procuranda*, loc. 922.
102. Acosta, *De Procuranda*, loc. 936–51.
103. Shepherd, *José de Acosta's "De Procuranda,"* 57.
104. Shepherd, *José de Acosta's "De Procuranda,"* 54.
105. Acosta, *De Procuranda*, loc. 936.

against their wills in order to constrain (Luke 14:23) them to enter the Kingdom of Heaven.[106]

Thus, for Acosta, the way of Christianizing the Americas was through coercion and, if necessary, force.

The imperial nature of such political and ecclesial subjugation of natives extended quite naturally to the arena of theology. That is, as part of the overall process of Christianization, Acosta envisioned his own Roman Catholic tradition serving as the ecclesiological and theological norm throughout the world. He contended that the Amerindians must learn that

> [the church] is the congregation of people who profess Christ and His doctrine. It is not merely for Spaniards or Barbarians, not something limited to a particular nation, or certain type of people, or a specific geographical location, but something that covers all parts of the earth and all periods of time.... We are sons and members of the Church, but all together we are the Mother Church herself. Its head is the Pontiff of Rome, the successor of Peter, the vicar of Christ, who exercises, on earth, all His power, and whom all Christians must obey, even kings and princes. That is what is meant by believing in the Universal Catholic Church.[107]

For Acosta, the doctrine of Christ was the doctrine of the Roman Catholic Church. There was thus no room for deviation; all must adhere to theology issuing forth from Rome.

Acosta's approach thus rendered natives dependent on Europe for their Christian knowledge. Shepherd highlights this dependency:

> [Acosta's] hierarchy of social and political achievement was measured against European epistemological standards. The behavior of non-Europeans is translated into terms recognizable by European systems of representation and inserted into the Western archive of knowledge. While this insertion organizes the Amerindian demeanor into distinct levels of "Europeaness," it also prepares Native Americans for a teleological conversion to a pre-Christian state within Western consciousness. Once they undergo this conversion, Christian teaching attempts to

---

106. Acosta, *De Procuranda*, loc. 964.
107. Acosta, *De Procuranda*, loc. 7670.

assist as Amerindians progress up the hierarchical ladder of civility.[108]

Knowledge here both emanates from Europe and seeks to make subjects more European. Moreover, this Christian knowledge merged into colonial systems of power and racial subjugation. As Jennings contends, "The native peoples of the world received a Christianity exaggerated in evaluative habit and poised to merge brutality with intellectual formation. It would create a deeply troubled theological subjectivity."[109]

In sum, Acosta demonstrated—both epistemologically and methodologically—a predilection for theological imposition. For Jennings, "Acosta marks the theological beginning of imperialist modernity."[110] He envisioned the wholesale implementation in Peru of the European Catholic theological tradition. Further, in order to bring that about, he maintained that Jesuit missionaries in Peru must teach and train locals as if they were children—children learning from those who had already mastered true doctrine.

Theological Imposition en Route—The Third Lima Council

The Third Lima Council of 1582–83 further codified this pattern of theological imposition Acosta had set. This council followed two others, one in 1551–52 and another in 1567–68, which set the stage for the third. Both of these earlier Catholic councils sought to establish and impose a standard of doctrine on the emerging church in Peru. The First Lima Council, according to Hosne, was "conceived and created, among other purposes, to unify doctrine and erase contradictions and divergences," which had become a problem with different orders and clergymen ministering in that context.[111] The Second Lima Council aimed to bring to bear on the Peruvian church the decrees issued at the Council of Trent (1545–1563), a European program that aimed to reform the Catholic Church in the wake of the broader Reformation.[112] Both councils, how-

---

108. Shepherd, *José de Acosta's "De Procuranda,"* 57.
109. Jennings, *Christian Imagination*, 114.
110. Jennings, *Christian Imagination*, 71.
111. Hosne, *Jesuit Missions*, 109.
112. Hosne, *Jesuit Missions*, 111–12; Robert Edwin McNally, "The Council of Trent, the Spiritual Exercises and the Catholic Reform," *Church Hist.* 34.1 (1965) 36, states regarding the Council of Trent, "Paul III's bull of convocation (May 22, 1542) aptly marked out the purpose of the Council which he was summoning: 'to ponder, discuss,

ever, failed to establish an authoritative standard of doctrine for the viceroyalty.[113]

It would be the Third Lima Council (TLC) over a decade later which finally codified Acosta's vision for the imposition of European theology on the developing Peruvian church.[114] The council hosted almost every Catholic bishop from the areas in South America that Spain controlled.[115] According to Hosne, "The TLC of 1582–83 made an old dream come true: that of imposing an authoritative catechism embodying a unified doctrine in Peru, as well as in the suffragan dioceses. Indeed, this general catechism, in a Spanish version translated into Quechua and Aymara, was for use in all the provinces."[116] At this council, church leaders accomplished what they had not done previously—namely, work out the decrees of the Council of Trent within the Peruvian context.[117] The TLC thus served as a landmark conference in Catholic history and, as Burgaleta notes, became known as the "Trent of the Americas."[118]

Out of this conference came an influential doctrinal text—*Doctrina Christiana y Catecismo para Instrucción de los Indios* (henceforth DCC).[119] Acosta, the leading theologian of the conference, played a significant role in its composition.[120] The text features a brief catechism, a longer catechism, an exhortation concerning the rite of confession among natives, instruction for priests regarding the rituals and superstitions of the

---

execute and bring speedily and happily to the desired result whatever things pertain to the purity and truth of the Christian religion, to the restoration of what is good and the correction of bad morals, to the peace, unity and harmony of Christians among themselves, of the princes as well as of the people. . . .' The conciliar program is clear: reformation of the Christian religion, restoration of Christian morality and reunion of all Christian people."

113. Hosne, *Jesuit Missions*, 107.

114. Although this council was a broader Catholic gathering, the Jesuits nevertheless played an important role in it, most evident in the appointment of Acosta as the council's official theologian. Acosta later served as the primary author of the council's doctrinal text. See Burgaleta, *José de Acosta*, 50–52; for a detailed overview of the Third Lima Council and its catechetical text, see Alan Durston, *Pastoral Quechua: The History of Christian Translation in Colonial Peru, 1550–1650* (Notre Dame, IN: University of Notre Dame Press, 2007), 86–104.

115. Burgaleta, *José de Acosta*, 51.

116. Hosne, *Jesuit Missions*, 117.

117. For an overview of the TLC and its full set of decrees, see Rubén Vargas Ugarte, ed., *Concilios Limenses (1551–1772)* (Lima: Tipografia Peruana, 1951), 1:259–375.

118. Burgaleta, *José de Acosta*, 51.

119. *Doctrina Christiana y Catecismo para Instrucción de los Indios* (Lima, 1584).

120. Hosne, *Jesuit Missions*, 120–22.

Hermeneutical Community

local population and a set of scripted sermons that further expound the doctrine contained in the catechisms. Additionally, the council ordered its translation into two of the main indigenous languages of Peru—Quechua and Aymara—to aid its implementation throughout the region. As Monica Barnes—editor of the journal *Andean Past*—notes, "The Lima Catechism of 1584 and its accompanying materials were composed to make orthodox Catholic belief, as accepted by the Council of Trent, accessible to Andeans."[121]

The council aimed for DCC to be the standard which would regulate all theology within the Catholic Church in Peru. In Hosne's words, DCC was "to establish Tridentine orthodoxy as a final direction" for church doctrine.[122] The TLC itself issued the following decree concerning the theology which would govern the church:

> In order that the masses of Indians who remain uninstructed in the Christian religion may be more properly and more safely trained in the doctrine of the redeeming (salvific) faith, and in order that they may find everywhere the same form of a single doctrine, it has pleased the Holy Synod, following in the footsteps of the general Council of Trent, to publish a proper catechism for this entire Province; a catechism which all the Indians should be taught according to their capacity, and which at least the children should memorize and repeat on Sundays and on the feast days of the Church in public meetings. Or at least they should recite some part of it, as may seem appropriate, for the benefit of the others. The Holy Synod orders, therefore, to all the parish priests of the Indians, by virtue of Holy Obedience and under pain of excommunication, that they use this catechism which has been published by its [the Synod's] authority, to the exclusion of all others, and that they take care to instruct the people entrusted to them according to it.[123]

DCC thus centralized theological conviction in Peru. Again, no room existed for deviation; what the European authorities declared theologically was to remain the controlling norm.

---

121. Monica Barnes, "Catechisms and Confessionarios: Distorting Mirrors of Andean Societies," in *Andean Cosmologies Through Time: Persistence and Emergence*, ed. Robert V. H. Dover et al. (Bloomington: Indiana University Press, 1992), 80.

122. Hosne, *Jesuit Missions*, 5.

123. Vargas Ugarte, *Concilios Limenses*, 1:266. Robert Babcock, distinguished professor of classics at the University of North Carolina Chapel Hill, provided this English translation of the decree from Latin. This decree also appears in the early pages of *Doctrina Christiana y Catecismo para Instrucción de los Indios*.

Thus, the TLC and its influential catechetical text—DCC—played a significant part in further establishing the pattern of theological imposition in Peru. Hosne points out that over a decade earlier, the Second Lima Council "had stopped short of introducing a positive theology to frame doctrine and impose it as authoritative and exclusive."[124] That is, the council did not establish a constructive theological text to regulate Latin American Catholicism. Yet DCC became just that—a doctrinal confession that would serve as the theological standard for the Catholic Church in Peru. Hosne maintains, however, that DCC did not ignore the Peruvian context, and that its framers did not intend it to be a set of "abstract doctrines, meaning by 'abstract' an 'exported' orthodoxy from Europe expected to be imposed while ignoring the question of 'where.'"[125] Yet even if DCC accounted for the local context, it was still a product of European minds at a European-controlled council, which registered no input from indigenous Catholic voices. Further, it addressed Latin American contextual realities from a cultural distance and without the involvement of native Christians who best understood those realities.[126] The TLC and DCC thus further reveal the kind of foreign theological imposition at work within the early Jesuit mission to Peru.[127]

Theological Imposition Exemplified—The Juli Reduccion

One area in which Jesuit missionaries demonstrated the kind of theological imposition which Acosta and the TLC advocated was the *reduccion* at Juli. Burgaleta contends, "It was among those who directly ministered to the native peoples at Juli that Acosta's ideas had their greatest impact."[128] Juli was a town of around fifteen thousand that rested at the edge of Lake

---

124. Hosne, *Jesuit Missions*, 125.

125. Hosne, *Jesuit Missions*, 141.

126. Burgaleta, *José de Acosta*, 51, notes that the TLC was a gathering of Catholic bishops in Latin America. Bishops were, at that time, all from Europe. John Frederick Schwaller, *The History of the Catholic Church in Latin America: From Conquest to Revolution and Beyond* (New York: New York University Press, 2011), 64, states, "Ordination was not an option for native men until nearly a century after the conquest. The local bishops simply did not believe that the natives were well enough versed in Christianity to become priests."

127. Burgaleta, *José de Acosta*, 51, notes, "The catechism [the TLC] designed for the indigenous population became the standard catechetical tool throughout the continent well into the nineteenth century."

128. Burgaleta, *José de Acosta*, 45.

Hermeneutical Community

Titicaca in the Andes Mountains.[129] It also served as one of Toledo's *doctrinas*, or native parishes. Of all the *doctrinas* which the early Jesuits accepted, the one at Juli became Acosta's most cherished.[130]

The Society accepted the *doctrina* at Juli in 1576, following the departure of Dominican clergy from the region. The Dominicans had previously ministered there for over two decades, having assumed ministerial responsibility for this native parish back in the mid-1500s. However, for various reasons they backed out of that commitment in 1572.[131] Not long afterward, Viceroy Toledo made it clear that he wanted the Jesuits to take over responsibility for the Juli *doctrina*.[132] Acosta saw great potential for ministry in the region, but had to convince his compatriots, many of whom were leery of settling down permanently in a location like Juli.[133] Ultimately, the local Society acquiesced.[134]

The Jesuits went on to establish a robust, multifaceted ministry in and around the town of Juli. Cushner posits, "The mission at Julí of the Andes functioned as Jesuit residence, language school, parish, and experimental mission station. The European missionaries applied a vertical approach to their activity. Social work, religious indoctrination, contact with Indians, as well as the Indians' political and economic lives were influenced wholly or in part by the missionary."[135] Thus, on many levels, the Society exerted significant control over the natives of Juli and their religious life.

One of the principal ministries of the Jesuits at Juli—one that also highlights theological imposition in their work—was the indoctrination of local parishioners. According to Burgaleta, "Most of these native peoples had been baptized but not fully catechized, and so catechesis became an immediate and perennial concern of the Jesuits who labored at Juli."[136] Playing a significant role in that work was DCC. Cushner notes, "The gauge by which the Jesuit missionaries in Julí measured whether the Indians were progressing toward the formation of a true Christian

---

129. Cushner, *Why Have You Come Here?*, 80–81.
130. Burgaleta, *José de Acosta*, 45–46.
131. Burgaleta, *José de Acosta*, 45.
132. Cushner, *Why Have You Come Here?*, 81–82.
133. Alexandre Coello de la Rosa, "La Doctrina de Juli a Debate (1575–1585)," *Rev. Estud. Extremeño* 63.2 (2007) 952–54.
134. de la Rosa, "La Doctrina de Juli," 952–54.
135. Cushner, *Why Have You Come Here?*, 87.
136. Burgaleta, *José de Acosta*, 46.

community was their knowledge, understanding, and application of the *Doctrina Christiana*."[137] Local Jesuits expected the natives to memorize doctrinal truths therein as a means of demonstrating the legitimacy of their commitment to the Catholic faith.[138]

The work of indoctrinating the local population according to European theological conviction became pervasive in Juli. Burgaleta describes the routine:

> Each morning the Indian children, both boys and girls, under sixteen years of age went to one of the local parish churches, and under the supervision of an Indian catechist they repeated the short form of the catechism and various prayers. This also occurred at the Angelus each day. On Sundays the children were joined by their elders. Also on Sundays there were open-air sermons for the whole town followed by a sung solemn high mass accompanied by exquisite musical compositions. After mass, alms were distributed to the needy accompanied by another period of catechetical instruction. After a few hours of free time the whole village would once again gather at two o'clock for a massive procession and public recitation of the catechism.[139]

As in other places in Peru, the Jesuits required the people of Juli to memorize the shorter catechism of DCC.[140] With this insistence on doctrinal memorization through various means, Jesuits endeavored to bind the whole population to European Catholic theology by way of the TLC and its catechetical corpus.[141]

Consequently, Juli came to exemplify what Acosta and the TLC envisioned—the establishment of a native church which would fully adhere to—at least theoretically—the theological tradition emanating from the Catholic Church in Europe. For some, it appeared to be a utopia of

---

137. Cushner, *Why Have You Come Here?*, 87.

138. Cushner, *Why Have You Come Here?*, 92.

139. Burgaleta, *José de Acosta*, 48; Durston, *Pastoral Quechua*, 81–82, highlights this broad pattern among the Jesuits in Peru of forcing natives to internalize catechetical doctrine through various means: "Jesuit missionaries focused on producing highly choreographed catechetical performances in which the population of a pueblo walked in processions through the plaza and streets while reciting the cartilla and catechism."

140. Barnes, "Catechisms and Confessionarios," 67, 78, notes the emphasis that Catholic clerics in Peru placed on having natives memorize the catechism of DCC.

141. For an overview of the general pattern of catechesis in Peru, see Fernando de Armas Medina, *Cristianizacion del Peru (1532–1600)* (Sevilla: Escuela de Estudios Hispano-Americanos de Sevilla, 1953), 269–305.

sorts.[142] Others however, noting the manifold way in which the Society wielded near total control over the lives of natives, suggested that the Juli *doctrina* was more akin to a theocracy.[143] Either way, it is hard for these early Jesuits to avoid the charge of paternalism, both on a general level and a theological one. As historian Alan Durston points out, "Jesuits in Peru imposed a narrower and more dogmatic Catholicism which allowed little leeway for the development of specifically Andean forms of Christianity."[144]

Africa: Church Missionary Society in Uganda

A second example of theological imposition comes from the work of the Church Missionary Society (CMS) in the region of Uganda during the late nineteenth and early twentieth centuries. This region remained somewhat unknown to Europe prior to the mid-1800s, but went on to acquire significant notoriety, at least in the eyes of the English. Johannes du Plessis explains, "Uganda, or more correctly Buganda, the land and kingdom of the Baganda people, was a discovery of the mid-nineteenth century. Up to that time no one had guessed that a compact, well-organised and highly civilized kingdom of [Africans] existed at the sources of the Nile."[145] Winston Churchill later called Uganda the "pearl" of Africa in light of its beauty, and he believed it to hold great promise for colonial development.[146]

---

142. de la Rosa, "Doctrina de Juli," 959–60, highlights, for example, Acosta's glowing reports of the mission work in Juli. Additionally, Ricardo Gonzalez, "El Juli Jesuítico: ¿Modelo Misional o Proyección Historiográfica?," *IHS Antig. Jesuit. En Iberoam.* 2.1 (2014) 87–88, cites Rubén Vargas Ugarte, Norman Meiklejohn, and Ramón Gutiérrez as contemporary scholars who have seen in the Juli *reduccion* a superlative model of Jesuit missions.

143. See Cushner, *Why Have You Come Here?*, 99. In fact, Cushner titles his inquiry into the Jesuit mission to Juli "Julí: Utopia or Theocracy." Additionally, Gonzalez, "Juli Jesuítico," 85–100, highlights dissenting voices of those who were quite critical of Jesuit missionary labors at Juli; de la Rosa, "Doctrina de Juli," 960–61, also notes critical views of the Juli mission.

144. Durston, *Pastoral Quechua*, 83.

145. Johannes du Plessis, *The Evangelisation of Pagan Africa: A History of Christian Missions to the Pagan Tribes of Central Africa* (Cape Town: J.C. Juta, 1929), 265.

146. Winston S. Churchill, *My African Journey* (Toronto: William Briggs, 1909), 197, 211.

COLONIAL PATTERN OF THEOLOGICAL IMPOSITION

The first missionary society to engage Buganda was the renowned CMS in 1877.[147] According to Kevin Ward, this Anglican society "was a response from within the established Church of England to the widespread rediscovery of the obligation laid on Christians to engage in mission, which had been one of the important consequences of the eighteenth-century evangelical awakening in Britain."[148] From there, the CMS became one of the most influential missionary societies of the Modern Missionary Movement. Ward explains, "The existence of the CMS helped revivify the older Anglican mission societies and was crucial in the global spread of an Anglican communion. By 1899 the CMS had become one of the largest Protestant missions in terms of resources, personnel, and influence."[149]

One of the distinguishing missiological features of the CMS was its emphasis on planting self-supporting, self-extending (or self-propagating), and self-governing native churches. That is, native churches should develop the ability to financially support themselves, propagate themselves evangelistically, and govern themselves apart from foreign aid. The venerable CMS secretary Henry Venn developed this three-self formula with an eye toward preventing ongoing missionary dominance within native churches. He contended, "If the elementary principles of self-support and self-government and self-extension be thus sown with the seed of the Gospel, we may hope to see the healthy growth and expansion of the Native Church."[150] These ideals of Venn for planting indigenous churches remained influential in the work of the society over the latter half of the nineteenth century.[151]

The CMS missionaries to Buganda, however, never fully lived up to these ideals for indigeneity.[152] Although their mission was successful in

---

147. Eugene Stock, *The History of the Church Missionary Society: Its Environment, Its Men and Its Work*, 4 vols. (London: Church Missionary Society, 1899–1916), 3:101. French Catholic missionaries arrived later in 1879 (105).

148. Kevin Ward, "Introduction," in *The Church Mission Society and World Christianity, 1799–1999*, ed. Kevin Ward and Brian Stanley (Grand Rapids: Eerdmans, 2000), 1.

149. Ward, "Introduction," 2.

150. Venn, "Native Pastorate and Organization of Native Churches. Second Paper," 420.

151. C. Peter Williams, "The Church Missionary Society and the Indigenous Church in the Second Half of the Nineteenth Century: The Defense and Destruction of the Venn Ideals," in *Converting Colonialism: Visions and Realities in Mission History, 1706–1914*, ed. Dana L. Robert (Grand Rapids: Eerdmans, 2008), 93–106.

152. The proceeding sections seek to substantiate the claims made here.

establishing a native church that was self-supporting and self-extending, they were far less successful in establishing a truly self-governing church. Rather, they persisted in maintaining a form of colonial control over the Bugandan church. Moreover, their professed desire for local church indigeneity remained confined to Venn's three selves, which focused strictly on the ecclesiological issues of finance, evangelism, and polity; it did not extend to the realm of theology within the Bugandan church, which remained bound to the confessional theology of its mother church—the Church of England. Thus, as the proceeding sections seek to demonstrate, the CMS mission to Buganda represents a case of colonial theological imposition.

Beginning of the Uganda Mission

In 1875, Henry Morton Stanley—a British-American journalist and explorer—arrived in Buganda and became a forerunner to the CMS mission.[153] Although evangelism was not the object of his expedition into central Africa, Stanley nevertheless "spoke and acted as a Protestant lay missionary," according to Bengt Sundkler and Christopher Steed.[154] He arrived at a time when the Baganda were becoming increasingly dissatisfied with their traditional religion and their king, Mutesa, was becoming suspicious of the increasing Muslim influence in the region.[155] For Mutesa, Stanley and the Bible represented an alternative.[156] For Stanley,

---

153. Although Stanley's exploration in Central Africa became a decisive factor in CMS engagement of Uganda, James A. Casada, "James A. Grant and the Introduction of Christianity in Uganda," *J. Church State* 25.3 (1983) 507–22, demonstrates that John Speke and James A. Grant, earlier explorers in the region, also served as important forerunners to the spread of Christianity in Uganda. Twelve years prior to Morton's appeal, Speke declared, "Of all places in Africa by far the most inviting to missionary enterprise are the kingdoms of Karague, Uganda and Unyoro," all of which were governed by a single ruler. See du Plessis, *Evangelisation of Pagan Africa*, 265.

154. Bengt Sundkler and Christopher Steed, *A History of the Church in Africa* (New York: Cambridge University Press, 2000), 567.

155. Brian Stanley, "East African Revival: African Initiative within a European Tradition," *Churchman* 92.1 (1978) 6; Adrian Hastings, "From Mission to Church in Buganda," *Z. Für Mission. Relig.* 53.3 (1969) 210; Kevin Ward, "A History of Christianity in Uganda," in *From Mission to Church: A Handbook of Christianity in East Africa*, ed. Zablon Nthamburi (Nairobi: Uzima, 1991), 82–83.

156. Although Mutesa would go on to look favorably upon Christianity in its own right, a primary motive of his initial engagement with Stanley and his later reception of the first CMS missionaries was the desire for guns and ammunition. See Stock, *History of the Church Missionary Society*, 3:101.

the king and his people represented a ripe field for missionary service.[157] Having garnered favor with Mutesa, he spent several months teaching the king and his chiefs the message of the Bible. Stanley then sent a letter to England in late 1875, published in the *Daily Telegraph*, imploring the church to send missionaries to the region.[158]

Soon after Stanley's public appeal for missionaries, the CMS decided to organize a mission to the region of Uganda.[159] The society promptly made the decision after someone donated £5,000 to the organization in response to Stanley's letter.[160] The first two CMS missionaries—C. T. Wilson and Shergold Smith—eventually reached Mutesa's capital in June of 1877.[161] However, in light of Smith's unfortunate death a few months later and Wilson's subsequent traveling, Anglican ministry in Uganda only truly began in late 1878 with the arrival of Alexander Mackay, a bright young missionary from Scotland.[162] Several other Anglican missionaries eventually joined Wilson and Mackay in 1879, and over the proceeding years, this group began laying the foundations for an Anglican church in Buganda.[163]

The CMS intended from the outset to establish a local church in Buganda that would operate independently from the mission.[164] This goal

---

157. Sundkler and Steed, *History of the Church*, 567.

158. Stanley, quoted in du Plessis, *Evangelisation of Pagan Africa*, 266, claimed, "I assure you that in one year you will have more converts to Christianity than all other missions united can muster."

159. For a detailed account of the sending of the first CMS missionaries to Uganda, see A. T. Matson, "The Instructions Issued in 1876 and 1878 to the Pioneer CMS Parties to Karagwe and Uganda: Part I," *J. Relig. Afr.* 12.3 (1981) 192–237; A. T. Matson, "The Instructions Issued in 1876 and 1878 to the Pioneer CMS Parties to Karagwe and Uganda: Part II," *J. Relig. Afr.* 13.1 (1982) 25–46.

160. Matson, "Pioneer CMS Parties: Part I," 192; for a detailed overview of the response of the CMS to Stanley's letter and subsequent financial donation, see Stock, *History of the Church Missionary Society*, 3:94–99.

161. Hastings, "From Mission to Church," 208; John V. Taylor, *The Growth of the Church in Buganda* (London: SCM, 1958), 36–37, documents Wilson and Smith's arrival and reception at Mutesa's court.

162. Hastings, "From Mission to Church," 208; for an overview of the circumstances of Smith's death, see Matson, "Pioneer CMS Parties: Part II," 27; Taylor, *Growth of the Church*, 38, explains that Smith and another missionary became unwittingly involved in a dispute between a local chief and an Arab trader. See also du Plessis, *Evangelisation of Pagan Africa*, 267.

163. Taylor, *Growth of the Church*, 39–59.

164. Holger Bernt Hansen, "Church and State in Early Colonial Uganda," *Afr. Aff.* 85.338 (1986) 58, explains, "In the tradition of the CMS, the overriding objective of the Uganda mission was to build an independent African church and make itself

Hermeneutical Community

derived in no small measure from the influence of Venn's missiology. Venn viewed the mission as a temporary scaffolding, as it were, around what was to become the permanent building—i.e., the church.[165] He therefore advocated for the dissolution, or "euthanasia," of the mission once the missionaries had sufficiently established the native church:

> Regarding the ultimate object of a mission, viewed under its ecclesiastical aspect, to be the settlement of a native Church, under native pastors, upon a self-supporting system, it should be borne in mind that the progress of a mission mainly depends upon the training up and the location of native pastors; and that, as it has been happily expressed, "the euthanasia of a mission" takes place when a missionary, surrounded by well-trained native congregations, under native pastors, is able to resign all pastoral work into their hands, and gradually relax his superintendence over the pastors themselves, till it insensibly ceases; and so the mission passes into a settled Christian community. Then the missionary and all missionary agency should be transferred to "the regions beyond."[166]

Thus, the missionaries were not to oversee the church in perpetuity; they were to entrust that responsibility to the native church itself. This ideal became a central objective of the first wave of CMS missionaries in Buganda.

There appeared promising early indicators that their vision for an independent church in Buganda might indeed become a reality. That is, two of Venn's three selves—which served as key marks of a native church ready for independence—became manifest early on in the work. For one, the Bugandan church was remarkably self-propagating.[167] Many of the early converts that joined the emerging Christian community did so in light of contact with native believers.[168] John V. Taylor notes, "It had been

---

superfluous. To achieve that goal the mission followed three major principles which served as a yardstick in measuring the maturity of the church. These three criteria were known as the three-selves formula: self-government, self-support and self-extension."

165. C. Peter Williams, "'Not Transplanting': Henry Venn's Strategic Vision," in *The Church Mission Society and World Christianity, 1799–1999*, ed. Kevin Ward and Brian Stanley (Grand Rapids: Eerdmans, 2000), 156.

166. Venn, "Native Pastorate and Organization of Native Churches. First Paper," 413–14.

167. Stock, *History of the Church Missionary Society*, 4:95; Hastings, "From Mission to Church," 215–16.

168. Taylor, *Growth of the Church*, 45, explains, "In the experience of the Baganda converts their contact with the missionaries counted far less than the missionaries

COLONIAL PATTERN OF THEOLOGICAL IMPOSITION

the constant refrain of the heads of the Christian groups in the early days that their pupils and followers must be witnesses of the Gospel."[169] Then in the early 1890s, a local revival broke out that led to further native evangelistic initiative, which was particularly evident in the activities of the local church council—a group of native Christian men who helped lead the church. According to Taylor,

> The revival . . . only fanned a flame that was already burning, and renewed in ordinary Christians the impulse to offer themselves as evangelists. On the following Easter Sunday thirteen young men were sent out to the islands of the lake by the church council, which undertook to support them. Every month "missionary meetings" were organized by the council at which some evangelists reported on their work and called for fresh recruits. Within one year of the beginning of the revival, 260 new evangelists were at work, occupying 85 stations, of which twenty were beyond the borders of Buganda. The number of catechumens in the Anglican Church had risen from 170 to 1,500.[170]

This emerging Bugandan church thus demonstrated a significant willingness and ability to extend itself through evangelism.

Not only was the native church self-propagating at an early stage, it was also self-supporting in certain ways. Particularly worthy of note is the fact that the local church council financially supported the evangelists it sent out during the aforementioned season of revival.[171] Furthermore, Taylor records that when the local Anglican cathedral burned down in 1910, "and £20,000 was needed for a new one, each Anglican chief undertook to contribute a third of his income for three years, and some continued to do so when that time was over."[172] Thus in regard to self-

---

supposed; their contact with other African 'readers', and their attachment to the Christian community-groups that were beginning to appear, had a more decisive influence."

169. Taylor, *Growth of the Church*, 63. This lay evangelistic initiative impressed Bishop Alfred Tucker when he first arrived in Buganda in 1890. Tucker claimed, "No sooner was a reading sheet mastered than at once the learner became a teacher. It was the same with the Gospels; every fact noted, every truth mastered, was at once repeated to groups of eager enquirers. It was a most touching sight to see little groups scattered about here and there in the church, each of which had in its centre a native teacher who was himself at other times in the day an eager learner" (63).

170. Taylor, *Growth of the Church*, 64.

171. Taylor, *Growth of the Church*, 64; Hastings, "From Mission to Church," 215.

172. Taylor, *Growth of the Church*, 83.

support and self-propagation, this young Bugandan church appeared well on its way to independence.

However, mitigating the establishment of a truly independent church in Buganda was one significant factor—ongoing missionary control over church governance. The CMS mission to Buganda, despite its affirmation of Venn's missiological ideals, never fully embraced the prospect of handing over governing authority to local church leaders.[173] As the number of missionaries grew over time, and as those missionaries centralized ecclesiastical structure and authority in themselves, the local church became more and more dependent.[174] Taylor maintains, "One cannot escape from the suspicion that the institution which emerged was not the authentic answer to the needs of the time made by a responsible church, but a pattern of preconceptions built up by architects from Europe."[175] The missionaries' consolidation of control over the church's governance not only led to foreign dependency in church polity, but also resulted in theological dependency, as the "architects from Europe" bound the emerging Bugandan church to its own theological blueprints.

Colonial Sensibilities Within the Mission

The trend toward greater colonial control of the emerging Anglican church in Buganda became more pronounced with the increase of European missionaries from 1890 onward. In fact, Adrian Hastings claims, "December 1890 marks a new beginning as regards the European presence in Buganda."[176] By that time the initial wave of CMS missionaries had departed, and a new wave was entering the fray.[177] This second group of missionaries proved to be more controlling of the native church than the first. For example, one of them—George Baskerville—wrote of a confrontation he had with the local church council, saying, "Our meeting

---

173. The proceeding section seeks to substantiate this claim.

174. Hastings, "From Mission to Church," 214, explains, "[The] years after 1890 were ones of constant missionary expansion and of a vast increase in the number of Christians.... There is no doubt of the continued fervour and energy of the new converts. Nevertheless, the more the missionaries increased, the less room there seemed to be for African initiative." See also Taylor, *Growth of the Church*, 71–82.

175. Taylor, *Growth of the Church*, 78.

176. Hastings, "From Mission to Church," 209.

177. For an overview of the first wave of missionaries and their work, see Arthur Shepherd, *Tucker of Uganda: Artist and Apostle, 1849–1914* (London: Student Christian Movement, 1929), 34–44.

with the elders on Saturday did a lot of good, and I think they will not be so independent in future."[178] Taylor concludes, "The old type of African church-leadership could not for long be maintained in partnership with this new missionary assertiveness."[179]

Two of the foremost leaders of this second, more colonial, wave of CMS missionaries were Bishop Alfred Tucker and Archdeacon R. H. Walker. Tucker arrived in Buganda in late 1890 as the newly consecrated bishop of the Anglican diocese of Eastern Equatorial Africa.[180] He then served as the bishop of that region until 1911. Walker's time in Buganda largely coincided with Tucker's. Several years after Walker's arrival in 1888, Tucker appointed him to serve as archdeacon.[181] He later became the secretary of the CMS mission and went on to become one of the most established and influential members of the group.[182] Both of these men embodied the trend toward greater control over the native church.

Colonial sensibilities of the mission and its leaders surfaced in a long-standing debate regarding whether or not the Bugandan church should have its own independent constitution. Oddly, both Tucker and Walker betrayed such sensibilities, despite the fact that the two remained on opposite sides of this constitutional debate. In the late 1890s, Tucker began advocating for the establishment of a local church constitution which would effectively dissolve the mission and incorporate all the missionaries into the church under native leadership.[183] On one hand, he believed that such an arrangement—in which missionaries and locals would govern the church together—would allow native believers to slowly grow in their capacity for church leadership. On the other hand, he recognized that the full incorporation of CMS missionaries into the native church would still afford them a means of supervising the natives (in this case from within rather than from without).[184] The major-

178. Quoted in Taylor, *Growth of the Church*, 71.

179. Taylor, *Growth of the Church*, 71.

180. Shepherd, *Tucker of Uganda*, 32; du Plessis, *Evangelisation of Pagan Africa*, 275.

181. du Plessis, *Evangelisation of Pagan Africa*, 275–76.

182. Holger Bernt Hansen, "European Ideas, Colonial Attitudes and African Realities: The Introduction of a Church Constitution in Uganda 1898–1909," *Int. J. Afr. Hist. Stud.* 13.2 (1980) 246.

183. Alfred R. Tucker, *Eighteen Years in Uganda and East Africa*, 2 vols. (London: Edward Arnold, 1908), 2:146–50.

184. Tucker, *Eighteen Years in Uganda*, 2:148–49. Tucker also reasoned that, owing to its size and continuing growth, the Bugandan church needed a more formal

ity of the missionaries, including Walker, opposed this move, believing that such a church constitution was premature for the still developing Bugandan church, which was not ready to come out from under direct foreign oversight.[185] In the ensuing—and sometimes convoluted—debate within the mission, one can discern both a functional retreat from the ideal of self-governance and a clear propensity toward colonial control.

Walker's penchant for missionary control is, perhaps, not surprising considering his opposition to Tucker's constitutional proposal to place the CMS missionaries under native church leadership. Early on, Walker's opposition to the proposal derived, in large part, from a desire to promote ecclesial indigeneity.[186] Walker rooted himself in the Venn tradition, a missiological tradition that promoted self-governing churches and provisional missionary leadership.[187] Holger Bernt Hansen, an African studies scholar and professor emeritus at the University of Copenhagen, explains that, as with Venn, "It was for [Walker] of the greatest importance to emphasize to the Africans the temporary character of the mission and its final withdrawal to other regions."[188] Additionally, Walker believed that the amalgamation of the church and the mission would impede the Bugandan church from becoming an independent church. According to Hansen, Walker's fear was that "Africans would always leave all responsibility to the missionaries if the latter became full members of the church and not just temporary advisors."[189] Considering Walker's desire to develop and empower native church leadership and, ultimately,

---

organizational structure, which is what he sought to provide in his constitution (146); Hansen, "Church and State," 59, also points out that part of Tucker's rationale for a formal constitution was to provide a foundation upon which the church could interact with the colonial government. It would allow the church to "receive recognition from the state and thus be entitled to own property."

185. Hansen, "European Ideas," 246–47; see also Tudor Griffiths, "Bishop A. R. Tucker of Uganda and the Implementation of an Evangelical Tradition of Mission" (PhD diss., University of Leeds, 1998), 223–24. Griffiths here highlights some of the claims of Walker and others who opposed Tucker's constitutional proposal. Additionally, Griffiths maintains that those in opposition to Tucker failed to realize that Tucker was not arguing for total native control over the church. Rather, he saw the incorporation of missionaries into the local church as the appropriate next step toward establishing a truly self-governing church (235).

186. Hansen, "European Ideas," 248.

187. Concerning the provisional nature of missionary leadership over native churches, see Venn, "Native Pastorate and Organization of Native Churches. First Paper," 413–14.

188. Hansen, "European Ideas," 248.

189. Hansen, "European Ideas," 248.

relinquish control over the local church, he did not initially appear to embody colonial sensibilities. However, over the course of his time in Buganda, Walker and those who sided with him became increasingly insistent on maintaining authority over the native church.

Walker's proclivity for missionary control emerged, first, in his qualitative assessment of Bugandan Christian leaders. Hansen notes that his view of the natives was not always negative: "Walker expressed great confidence in the African leadership of the church and their competence to give Christianity and the church a truly African expression."[190] Over the last decade of the nineteenth century, however, Walker and other CMS missionaries began sensing a decline in religious fervor within the Bugandan church. As a result, they embraced an increasingly negative view of the capabilities of Bugandan believers to govern their own church.[191] By the early 1900s, a considerable "hardening of attitudes" toward the natives had set in.[192] After attending a 1904 conference in Buganda for CMS missionaries, a member of the CMS Home Committee reported, "A good deal was said on . . . [the native believers'] unfitness on the whole for bearing responsibility; they were 'still mere children,' as one leading missionary remarked."[193] One missionary even said at the conference, "In neither the moral, spiritual, or intellectual sense were the Baganda able to take their place alongside Europeans in the government of their Church. Their standard was not equal to the Europeans; therefore their vote should not be equal. It was unjust to give weaker men any equal vote with stronger and abler."[194] For Walker and those on his side of the debate, this kind of negative assessment became a foundational motivation for retaining control of the Bugandan church.[195] As Hansen claims, "By projecting equality between Europeans and Africans into a remote future, the missionaries had a powerful argument for European guidance and trusteeship at that time and for years to come."[196]

---

190. Hansen, "European Ideas," 263n96.

191. Hansen, "European Ideas," 263–64, 271–73.

192. Hansen, "European Ideas," 264.

193. Victor Buxton, quoted in Taylor, *Growth of the Church*, 61. At that same conference, one CMS missionary reportedly asserted, "The spirit of the Baganda (has) entirely changed and their qualities [have] gone down" (82).

194. Quoted in Hansen, "European Ideas," 262.

195. Hansen, "European Ideas," 261, 264.

196. Hansen, "European Ideas," 255.

Walker's desire for missionary control surfaced more clearly in his later retreat from the Venn ideal of planting self-governing churches. He remained in opposition to Bishop Tucker's constitutional proposal over the years, but his reasoning shifted from the original convictions he shared with Venn. Hansen notes that during a third round of discussion regarding a potential church constitution, "Walker repeated the argument from 1901 that Africans lacked competence in the light of the Europeans' qualifications and that they had too low an educational standard."[197] Yet, "This time he did not base his arguments upon theories of missionary work, as he had in 1898–1899. All talk of withdrawal of the mission and independence of the church have [sic] disappeared."[198] In other words, Walker maintained his original argument against Tucker and in favor of missionary control not by appealing to the Venn tradition, but by retreating from it. In fact, Peter Williams contends that this opposition to the bishop's proposal stood in direct opposition to Venn's missiological ideals.[199] Thus, both Walker's qualitative assessment of Africans and his retreat from the Venn tradition betrayed a colonial approach to local church governance.

Although Walker's colonial sensibilities were perhaps clearer and stronger, Bishop Tucker's were more surprising. They are surprising because Tucker consistently lamented the refusal of Walker and others to incorporate themselves into the native church and under native church leadership.[200] For Tucker, the time had come to dissolve the mission and entrust leadership of the Bugandan church to the local believers.[201] In light of this reality, scholars have identified Tucker as embodying the Venn heritage—a tradition that seeks to counteract colonial tendencies in the missionary enterprise.[202] According to Hastings, Tucker represented that

197. Hansen, "European Ideas," 261.
198. Hansen, "European Ideas," 261.
199. Williams, "Defense and Destruction," 106–11.
200. Tucker, *Eighteen Years in Uganda*, 1:241, reasoned, "In training native Christians in the art of self-government it is a tremendous mistake to hold aloof from their organization, and this for the simple reason that if the work of the European Missionaries is carried on outside the limits of the native Church, there must be an outside organization. In that case the native Christians will not be slow to realize that the outside organization is the one which really settles whatever questions may be under discussion in the Church and that their own organization is more or less a sham."
201. Tucker, *Eighteen Years in Uganda*, 2:148–49.
202. Williams, "Defense and Destruction," 110–11; see also Brian Stanley, "Afterword," in *The Church Mission Society and World Christianity, 1799–1999*, ed. Kevin Ward and Brian Stanley (Grand Rapids: Eerdmans, 2000), 350.

move away from colonial control. He asserts, "The missionaries [in Buganda] remained only too clearly in ultimate control. There was certainly no real parity of dignity between priests white and black. Bishop Tucker had earnestly striven for this, and his plans for a church constitution, first proposed as early as 1897, were extremely far-sighted and in the line of Henry Venn and the C.M.S. tradition at its very best."[203] Thus, in some ways it appears as if Tucker—who fought for the establishment of native leadership and the dissolution of the Buganda mission—did not maintain the colonial mentality of his compatriots.[204]

Yet for all of Tucker's insistence on developing native church leadership, he never appeared ready to relinquish the supervisory role that CMS missionaries had maintained. African history scholar Joan Plubell Mattia contends, "It is clear from Tucker's letters that he believed the African church needed supervision as it evolved into maturity and that Tucker's admiration of the innate abilities of the East Africans did not include an across-the-board reliance on their organizational ability."[205] For example, in one letter, Tucker actually justified his proposal to incorporate CMS missionaries into the Bugandan church by claiming that the move would circumscribe total native control over the church. In reference to Walker's alternative, Tucker asserted, "The second alternative, that of having two separate organizations—one for the European Missionaries and one for the Native Church, is to my mind an absolute impossible one.... It would not be safe to give at present to a purely native governing body the power of enacting laws for the church."[206] To be fair, Tucker believed that the leadership of CMS missionaries within the Bugandan church would be temporary and would one day fade away as native leaders grew in their capacity for self-governance.[207] However, for Tucker, that day remained in the indeterminate future, and until then the

---

203. Hastings, "From Mission to Church," 216.

204. Tucker, quoted in Griffiths, "Bishop A. R. Tucker," 217, recognized "the deep-rooted tendency which there is in the Anglo-Saxon character to anglicise everything with which it comes into contact." Further, he advocated for native methods in church polity, claiming, "We should take this matter in hand at the very earliest stages of our work and never rest satisfied until we see springing up into life the vigorous shoots of a healthy system of self-government" (217).

205. Joan Plubell Mattia, "Walking the Rift: Alfred Robert Tucker in East Africa Idealism and Imperialism 1890–1911" (PhD diss., University of Birmingham, 2007), 233.

206. Quoted in Mattia, "Walking the Rift," 236.

207. Tucker, *Eighteen Years in Uganda*, 1:241–42, 2:148–49; Griffiths, "Bishop A. R. Tucker," 224–25, 235–36.

missionaries must necessarily continue in their oversight of the church—only from within it rather than from the outside.

Thus, in Tucker's proposal, the euthanasia of the mission—rather than being a means of divesting control and moving on to unreached regions, as Venn had urged—effectively consolidated the missionaries' control over the Bugandan church.[208] As Mattia asserts, "Even when Tucker's approach was placed into operation with a heartfelt appreciation for African abilities, two attitudes were frequently and simultaneously present; first, that the Africans were the back-up personnel to be used when there were not enough Europeans, and secondly that the Africans needed tutoring before they would be ready to take responsibilities alone at which time it was the duty of the western missionaries to allow them their part."[209] Thus, in spite of the affinity he seemed to share with Venn and his own stated conviction regarding the impermanence of the mission, Tucker never appeared ready to surrender the mission's authority over to the Baganda.

There is thus an irony in the reasoning of both Walker and Tucker—that is, both men assented to the value of native leadership and the ideal of self-governance, yet at the same time promoted ecclesial arrangements that undermined native agency. Walker, in Venn-like fashion, argued for the strict separation of the mission from the local church. Tucker, also in Venn-like fashion, argued for the dissolution of the mission. Yet Walker claimed that the time for dissolution had not yet arrived and that to incorporate the missionaries into the local church would lead to ongoing foreign dominance.[210] Tucker, meanwhile, believed the time for dissolution had indeed arrived and that maintaining two distinct entities—mission and local church—would undermine native leadership.[211] Thus both men postured themselves as proponents of native leadership. However, as

---

208. For further evidence of Tucker's colonial sensibilities, see Mattia, "Walking the Rift," 232–40. She notes, "For all of Tucker's advocacy of African approaches to church government and leadership he still maintained an easily distinguishable separateness" (237).

209. Mattia, "Walking the Rift," 239.

210. Griffiths, "Bishop A. R. Tucker," 224, explains, "Walker identified the key issue as whether or not the European missionaries were to be regarded as an integral part of the Ugandan Church or 'friends and advisers' solely. He argued that the former would destroy the temporary nature of the residence of Europeans and that furthermore the Europeans would dominate the Church Council if they sat as members."

211. Griffiths, "Bishop A. R. Tucker," 208–47, provides a helpful overview of Tucker's argument for a church constitution that would effectively dissolve the mission and incorporate the CMS missionaries into the local church.

the foregoing pages have demonstrated, neither was ready to relinquish foreign control over church polity. In sum, both of these important mission leaders demonstrated—whether overtly or covertly—a penchant for preserving some level of missionary control over the Bugandan church.

Theological Imposition Within the Mission

The colonial sensibilities of these two key leaders came to a head in their final resolution to the long-standing constitutional debate within the mission. After several rounds of discussions over the better part of a decade, the two sides—which Walker and Tucker led, respectively—came to an agreement in 1907 and adopted a constitution for the Bugandan church.[212] Tucker thus finally succeeded in his enduring quest to establish for the church a formal constitution—one which recognized, in principle, equality between locals and expatriate missionaries.[213] However, in the process, he conceded his insistence on the full incorporation of CMS missionaries into the Bugandan church, which was a clear win for Walker and those on his side of the debate.[214]

The resolution effectively cemented the missionaries' control over the native church.[215] Although they "accepted in principle that the missionaries should join the church and work under the constitution," Hansen explains that the agreement ultimately allowed CMS missionaries to continue operating as "an independent organization outside the authority of the church."[216] This arrangement afforded the missionaries an ongoing means of directing and controlling the native church, even in the face of a constitution which declared equality between the Baganda and expatriate missionaries.[217] According to Hansen, "The missionaries were thus

212. Hansen, "European Ideas," 275.

213. Hansen, "European Ideas," 276.

214. Hansen, "European Ideas," 275–77.

215. Griffiths, "Bishop A. R. Tucker," 236, notes, "Missionaries would exercise a double veto in the Synod in the person of the Bishop and because a majority of the clergy were European."

216. Hansen, "European Ideas," 275; this independent organization was the Missionary Committee, which was composed strictly of Europeans and continued to wield a significant amount of control over the Bugandan church. See Griffiths, "Bishop A. R. Tucker," 245–46. Years later, Walker understood the CMS mission as still being in existence, distinct from the Bugandan church. See R. H. Walker, "The Native Church of Uganda," *Church Mission. Rev.* 64.2 (1913) 434.

217. Griffiths, "Bishop A. R. Tucker," 244, adds, "The fact of an integrated Church

placed in a special position by deriving their authority from two sources. In some respects they were external to the church, while in others they were full members and filled positions of authority and control, thereby blurring the distinction between mission and church and causing doubt about the autonomy of the church."[218] The CMS missionaries thus neither dissolved the mission nor kept it distinct from the local church, and in the muddle that resulted, they continued to wield control over the Bugandan church in the years that followed.[219] According to Hastings, "A situation in which the top levels of the ministry were confined to expatriate clergy came to be accepted as a quasi-permanent one."[220]

This reified missionary control over the Bugandan church's polity extended quite naturally to its theology, for the constitution which the missionaries adopted explicitly bound the church to Anglican doctrine. Their constitution stated, "The Church of Uganda doth hold and maintain the doctrine and Sacraments of Christ as the Lord hath commanded in His Holy Word, and as the Church of England hath received and explained the same in the Book of Common Prayer, in the form of manner of making, ordaining and consecrating of Bishops, Priests and

---

made possible complete local domination by European missionaries, excluding Africans altogether from the Church Council. That this was not entirely a theoretical problem is shown by the fact that the inaugural Bukedi Church Council consisted solely of Europeans."

218. Hansen, "European Ideas," 277.

219. Thus, while both Tucker and Walker claimed adherence to the Venn tradition, they abandoned it in practice. According to Hansen, "European Ideas," 278, their new arrangement "allowed for continued missionary influence and control without any built-in mechanisms for an African replacement of Europeans, which had been the essential element in Tucker's original scheme." John V. Taylor, *Processes of Growth in an African Church*, International Missionary Council Research Pamphlets 6 (London: SCM, 1958), 14, adds, "Missionaries were committed to a policy of handing over responsibility into African hands, but the Church structure enabled them to do so always by withdrawing upwards into a higher level in the administrative hierarchy, instead of withdrawing sideways so as to make room for African colleagues working beside them as fellow-members of the same category."

220. Hastings, "From Mission to Church," 223; J. J. Willis, who succeeded Tucker as bishop, would later claim, quoted in Hansen, "European Ideas," 277, "The position of the European within a Native Church must necessarily be that of a leader. This is the sole justification of his presence." Additionally, he declared that the Missionary Committee "has a dominant voice in the conduct of the native Church affairs, inasmuch as it directly advises as to the locations of the European leaders" (277). Griffiths, "Bishop A. R. Tucker," 247, concludes, "The Constitution of 1909 assuredly provided a structure in which the African Church could exercise genuine responsibility, but required considerable trust on the part of the missionary body to ensure that this was the case. Sadly, there was failure at precisely this point."

Deacons, and in the 39 articles of religion."[221] The Thirty-Nine Articles of 1571 formed the Anglican confession of faith, which, according to Mark D. Thompson, was "meant to stake out the theological position of the reformed Church of England, especially on issues which were currently in dispute either in England or on the continent [of Europe]."[222] In writing this confession into the Bugandan church's constitution, the CMS mission thus imported a foreign theology and imposed it on the local congregation.

Such theological imposition becomes more apparent when one recognizes the absence of Bugandan believers in the development of their own church's constitution. The CMS missionaries granted the native Christian leaders little to no input in the discussions—and thus little to no input regarding the theology which would govern and direct their church.[223] Tucker himself even acknowledged the absence of African voices in the discussion.[224] According to Hansen, "The missionaries did not register any African interest or pressure in the whole constitutional matter."[225] Moreover, "leaving aside the fact that the African leaders were not brought into the procedure, it was a discussion entirely based upon European presuppositions originating in longstanding theories of missionary work."[226] Tudor Griffiths adds that, despite some of Tucker's Venn-like sentiments, his "consultations about the shape of the constitution for the new diocese took place entirely in a European milieu."[227] Thus, the missionaries spoke on behalf of the Baganda, while the Baganda remained silent.

Yet not only did CMS missionaries exclude local Christian leaders from important constitutional and theological discussions, they also forbade them from altering the theological standard which the missionaries had established for the church. As their constitution stated, the Church of Uganda "disclaims for itself the right of altering any of the aforesaid

---

221. Quoted in Walker, "Native Church of Uganda," 437.

222. Mark D. Thompson, "The Origin of the Thirty-Nine Articles," *Churchman* 125.1 (2011) 40.

223. Tucker, *Eighteen Years in Uganda*, 2:150; see also Hansen, "European Ideas," 268.

224. Tucker, *Eighteen Years in Uganda*, 2:150.

225. Hansen, "European Ideas," 268–69.

226. Hansen, "European Ideas," 270.

227. Griffiths, "Bishop A. R. Tucker," 217.

standards of faith and doctrine."[228] Moreover, it concluded, "it shall not be within the powers of the Provincial Synod (assembly) or of any Diocesan Synod to alter, revoke, add to, or diminish any of the same."[229] It is understandable that missionaries of a given denomination would seek to plant churches in accord with the doctrinal standards of that denomination; nevertheless, the fact that CMS missionaries prohibited the Bugandan church from shaping its own theology in any way betrays a theological colonialism that was commonplace in the Modern Missionary Movement.[230]

Underscoring such theological imposition was the belief that Bugandan Christians had neither the ability to theologize nor the need to do so. In a revealing statement, Walker asserted, "The Baganda are not abstract thinkers, and to formulate afresh for themselves their own articles of belief would be a task as much beyond them as it would be unnecessary."[231] Thus according to Walker, the native believers—having neither ability to reason theologically nor the need for a theology of their own—understandably looked to the Church of England in matters of doctrine. He claimed, "It was inevitable that the Baganda should turn to some one of the older Churches for guidance in this matter, and, like the Thessalonians, become 'imitators of the Churches of God' which were before them."[232]

For Walker and his compatriots then, their consolidation of control over the Bugandan church's theology seemed reasonable. One must be careful, therefore, not to read ill motives into their actions, especially considering that these CMS missionaries in Buganda were, according to Taylor, "as remarkable a group of missionaries as can be found in the annals of any mission field."[233] He adds, "It ill becomes a missionary of these latter days to find fault with predecessors of such calibre, or to condemn what was, essentially, a form of love," albeit a "protective and possessive"

---

228. Quoted in Wilson Muyinda Mande, "An Ethics for Leadership Power and the Anglican Church in Buganda" (PhD diss., University of Aberdeen, 1996), 75.

229. Quoted in Mande, "Ethics for Leadership Power," 75–76. Mande thus notes, "The powers of the Church Constitution which were exercisable concerned mainly leadership, and not regulations of liturgies and doctrine" (76).

230. Andrew F. Walls, *The Cross-Cultural Process in Christian History: Studies in the Transmission and Appropriation of Faith* (Maryknoll, NY: Orbis, 2002), 242–43.

231. Walker, "Native Church of Uganda," 437.

232. Walker, "Native Church of Uganda," 437.

233. Taylor, *Growth of the Church*, 82.

love.²³⁴ These CMS missionaries honorably served the Baganda and in many ways advanced the cause of Christ.²³⁵ Furthermore, they were, in some ways, quite effective in their goal of establishing an indigenous church—one that was at least self-supporting and self-extending to varying degrees.

However, despite their reasoning and their laudable endeavor to promote ecclesial indigeneity, the CMS missionaries fell short of establishing a truly indigenous church—one which was also indigenous in its theological reflection.²³⁶ Rather, they bound the Bugandan church to the theology of the Church of England. This reality eventually factored into various church schisms of the first half of the twentieth century. According to G. C. Oosthuizen, "The lack of real theological conversation with the Buganda Society led to different separatist movements, some of which are flourishing in Uganda."²³⁷ That lack of theological conversation in the Bugandan church thus persisted long after Tucker and Walker helped establish the precedent. Even as of 1958, Oosthuizen concluded, "The [Bugandan] Church has a great need of discovering the Scripture and what it has to say about the church's present situation and that of the Buganda society; it has to become a confessional church in the true sense of the word."²³⁸

Asia: Protestant Union Movement in South India

The last example of theological imposition comes from the Protestant union movement in South India in the first half of the twentieth century.

234. Taylor, *Growth of the Church*, 82–83.

235. Shepherd, *Tucker of Uganda*, 13–16, lauds Bishop Tucker, for example, as a man of great missionary acumen and faithfulness.

236. As Dean S. Gilliland, "Contextual Theology as Incarnational Mission," in *The Word Among Us: Contextualizing Theology for Mission Today*, ed. Dean S. Gilliland (Dallas: Word, 1989), 13–15, maintains, it is possible for a local church to appear indigenous based on certain external metrics, yet fail to be indigenous on a deeper level. For true indigeneity, native churches must be able to reflect theologically on the issues that pervade their contexts. See also Paul G. Hiebert, *Anthropological Insights for Missionaries* (Grand Rapids: Baker, 1985), 193–224, who advocates for a "fourth self" (self-theologizing) in addition to Venn's formula.

237. G. C. Oosthuizen, *Theological Discussions and Confessional Developments in the Churches of Asia and Africa* (Franeker, Netherlands: T. Wever, 1958), 273. For an overview of such separatist movements, see Ward, "History of Christianity in Uganda," 102; Hastings, "From Mission to Church," 223; Taylor, *Growth of the Church*, 15–17.

238. Oosthuizen, *Theological Discussions*, 274.

Hermeneutical Community

Protestantism by then had maintained a presence in India for almost two centuries. The first Protestant missionaries to India were Bartholomew Ziegenbalg and Heinrich Plütschau, who arrived at Tranquebar (a coastal city of modern day Tamil Nadu) in 1706.[239] The king of Denmark at that time—Frederick IV—considered it his responsibility, as a Christian prince claiming dominion over portions of the Indian subcontinent, to promote the conversion of natives within his dominion. Meeting no response to his demand for missionaries in Denmark, he turned to the University of Halle in Germany, where he found Ziegenbalg and Plütschau ready for the task.[240] After settling in at Tranquebar, the two ministered through education, Bible translation and evangelism, and even built up a native Lutheran church over time.[241]

Later, over the course of the nineteenth century, Protestant missionaries spread out across the Indian subcontinent. Baptists, Anglicans, Lutherans, Congregationalists, Methodists, and Presbyterians all established missions in various parts of India.[242] In South India alone by the turn of the twentieth century, no fewer than forty-five missionary organizations were at work.[243] Sundkler highlights this diversity of the Protestant missionary presence across India, noting that the CMS and the Society for the Propagation of the Gospel in Foreign Parts (SPG), both predominantly Anglican, had nearly one hundred and fifty thousand Indian members within their churches. The London Missionary Society (LMS) claimed around fifty thousand in membership, the Wesleyans twelve thousand, and the American Baptist Mission over fifty thousand. Additionally, Lutheran mission organizations had around thirty-eight thousand native church members, while the inter-denominational Basel Mission claimed fourteen thousand.[244]

---

239. Stephen Neill, *A History of Christianity in India 1707–1858* (New York: Cambridge University Press, 1985), 28.

240. Neill, *History of Christianity in India*, 29–30.

241. Stephen Neill, *A History of Christian Missions*, 2nd ed. (New York: Penguin, 1990), 195–97. For an overview of the missionary labors of Ziegenbalg and Plütschau, see also Robert Eric Frykenberg, *Christianity in India: From Beginnings to the Present* (New York: Oxford University Press, 2010), 146–51; Neill, *History of Christianity in India*, 28–40.

242. Neill, *History of Christianity in India*, 331–33.

243. Bengt Sundkler, *Church of South India: The Movement Towards Union, 1900–1947* (London: Lutterworth, 1954), 27.

244. Sundkler, *Church of South India*, 27–28.

COLONIAL PATTERN OF THEOLOGICAL IMPOSITION

This proliferation of Protestant missions—and the planting of denominational churches that resulted—gave Christianity in India a factional appearance, which in turn gave rise to a movement for establishing a more united church. Missionaries began to conclude that in a context where Christianity composed a small minority of the population, their denominational differences were not as significant as they had appeared in the West.[245] For example, one Congregationalist missionary to South India noted, "I have lived in a station where the Christian Church was represented by a feeble handful, despised by the great mass of surrounding Hindus in a sacred city of Saivism, and that feeble handful broken into three portions, Lutheran, Anglican and South Indian United Church, over the communion question. You can scarcely imagine how insane seem our ecclesiastical divisions in those circumstances."[246]

Indians also came to this conviction, believing that a divided Christianity was an impediment to the church's missionary task. At a 1919 ministers conference at Tranquebar, an Indian constituency of Anglicans, Presbyterians, and Congregationalists concluded, "We face together the titanic task of the winning of India for Christ. . . . Yet, confronted by such an overwhelming responsibility, we find ourselves rendered weak and relatively impotent by our unhappy divisions—divisions for which we were not responsible, and which have been, as it were, imposed upon us from without; divisions which we did not create, and which we do not desire to perpetuate."[247] Thus there was, among both missionaries and national ministers, a growing desire to establish a united church bereft of Western denominationalism.[248]

---

245. Sundkler, *Church of South India*, 24.

246. G. E. Phillips, quoted in Sundkler, *Church of South India*, 28.

247. G. K. A. Bell, ed., "Statement Drawn Up by Thirty-Three Ministers of the Anglican and South India United Churches at Tranquebar, May 1 and 2, 1919," in *Documents on Christian Unity: A Selection from the First and Second Series 1920-30* (New York: Oxford University Press, 1955), 122-23.

248. G. V. Job, "The Christian Movement in India," in *Rethinking Christianity in India*, ed. G. V. Job et al. (Madras, India: A. N. Sudarisanam, 1939), 24, stated that there is "indignant impatience at the wedges which keep Indian Christianity divided." Michael Hollis, *The Significance of South India* (Richmond, VA: John Knox, 1966), 32, an early bishop of the Church of South India, would later add, "In a country torn by racialism the Church must bear relevant witness by transcending race; in a country divided into competing communities it is vital that it demonstrates the truth of its claim that in Christ all walls of partition are broken down. If not, why should those outside believe in the new creation in Christ?"

Hermeneutical Community

Yet the impetus for church union in India went beyond concerns about the outward appearance of the church; for many, the sectarian presence of Christianity in the midst of a non-Christian society was an affront to the witness of Scripture and Jesus' prayer for unity in John 17.[249] The Tranquebar Manifesto quoted above thus also stated, "We believe that the union is the will of God, even as our Lord prayed that we might be one, that the world might believe. We believe that union is the teaching of Scripture."[250] Stephen Neill, esteemed historian and also an Anglican priest involved in the later stages of union negotiations in South India, added, "The only reasons for seeking unity are that God is one and that Christ is one, and that He prayed that His Church might be one. Here all else is irrelevant; only on this basis can irreconcilable traditions be reconciled, and a true organic unity grow out of the *disiecta membra* of the separated Christian bodies."[251] With these convictions in place, the notion of uniting various Protestant denominations in South India became appealing to various factions.

While the ensuing movement toward church union in South India was, for some, a laudable endeavor,[252] it nevertheless featured a form of foreign control over the theology of the emerging, united church. As the proceeding sections seek to demonstrate, the negotiating actors throughout much of the union movement were mostly foreign to Indian soil. That is, it was largely foreign missionaries and other Western denominational representatives who were negotiating the union and determining the theological convictions which would govern the united church.

---

249. David G. Moses, "The Spiritual Significance of Church Union in South India," *Christ. Crisis* 7.21 (1947) 3, maintained, "The union of the churches in South India means, in the first place, the fulfillment, however partial, of the great high-priestly prayer of our Lord and Master." See also Bell, "Statement Drawn Up," 122; Stephen Neill, "Co-Operation and Unity," *Int. Rev. Mission* 44.176 (1955) 446.

250. Bell, "Statement Drawn Up," 122.

251. Neill, "Co-Operation and Unity," 446.

252. Moses, "Spiritual Significance of Church Union," 2, declared regarding the union, "A miracle it certainly is. It is not an achievement of man; it is not the triumph of Christian statesmanship. It is the work of the Holy Spirit and those who have striven for it, Indian and non-Indian, will enthusiastically testify." According to F. M. Potter, "Churches Unite in South India," *Christ. Century* 64.43 (1947) 1264, in a sermon from the service inaugurating the Church of South India, J. S. M. Hooper proclaimed, "The reconciliation between our divergent elements which has this day been effected by the grace of God enables us with fresh conviction and force to proclaim the gospel of reconciliation to all the clashing elements in this nation's life. It should provide an example of God's working which we pray may lead many to ask for its secret."

Movement Toward Union from 1900 to 1947

Although various discussions regarding union took place in the late 1800s, it was not until the year 1902 that empirical union began in earnest with the union of several Presbyterian groups in South India.[253] Presbyterian missionaries in India began discussing the topic of union in 1863 but were not able to achieve it in the decades that followed.[254] However, around the turn of the century, the impetus for organic union in Presbyterian circles began growing in the aftermath of the formation of the United Free Church of Scotland and the union of two missionary societies in China that each held to Presbyterian polity.[255] These events reignited union discussions among Presbyterians in South Asia, and ultimately led to the formation in 1902 of the South India United Church (SIUC) from the union of three separate missionary bodies that were Presbyterian in their church polity.[256]

The broader union movement gathered further steam in 1908 as Congregationalists of the LMS and American Board united with the Presbyterians of the SIUC. Such a union between Congregationalists and Presbyterians was unprecedented. Yet, according to Clifford Manshardt, "It was felt strongly by leaders in both churches that the time was ripe for the abandonment of sectarian ruts, and to give the Indian church the encouragement of larger numbers and a broader horizon of fellowship."[257] In the union, both parties recognized and sought to maintain key aspects of Congregational and Presbyterian polity.[258] Then just over a decade later, the Basel Mission in Malabar (along the southwestern coast of the subcontinent) formally joined the SIUC.[259]

---

253. The term "Presbyterian" here refers not to an official Presbyterian denomination, but to various denominations and missionary organizations that held to Presbyterian church polity.

254. Clifford Manshardt, "Movements Toward Church Union in South India," *J. Relig.* 6.6 (1926) 617.

255. Sundkler, *Church of South India*, 36.

256. Manshardt, "Movements Toward Church Union," 618; Sundkler, *Church of South India*, 37–39.

257. Manshardt, "Movements Toward Church Union," 619.

258. For an overview of this union between the SIUC and Congregationalists, see Sundkler, *Church of South India*, 39–49.

259. Manshardt, "Movements Toward Church Union," 620; Sundkler, *Church of South India*, 81.

Hermeneutical Community

Another significant event leading to an even wider union of Protestant denominations in South India was the Tranquebar conference of 1919, in which thirty-three representatives—thirty-one of whom were Indian—began considering a union between Anglicans and the SIUC.[260] Anglicans at the conference were keen to preserve, in any potential union, their notion of a historic episcopate, while the SIUC constituency insisted on maintaining the spiritual equality of members (i.e., the priesthood of believers and an emphasis on lay participation in church life) within the potential united church.

The outcome of their deliberations came in the form of a manifesto, which they intended to serve as a basis for potential union in the years that followed. The manifesto states, "Upon this common ground of the Historic Episcopate and of the spiritual equality of all members of the two churches, we propose union on the following basis: (1) The Holy Scriptures of the Old and New Testaments, as containing all things necessary to salvation. (2) The Apostles' Creed and the Nicene Creed. (3) The two Sacraments ordained by Christ Himself—Baptism and the Lord's Supper."[261] This group of Indian ministers understood that they were merely laying the groundwork for potential union. They claimed, "While not committing our respective bodies, we, unofficially and individually, with the blessing of God, agree to work toward union on such a basis."[262] This Tranquebar Manifesto went on to become a catalytic force in the movement toward union in South India. Sundkler posits, "The Tranquebar Manifesto had its strength, not as a detailed programme on Faith and Order—that was worked out later for South India by others—but as a challenge, a moving appeal to union which stirred the hearts of men."[263]

During the decade following Tranquebar's plea, Anglicans, Methodists, and the SIUC began negotiating terms of a potential union.[264] The Anglicans and SIUC set up after the Tranquebar conference a Joint Committee on Union, which held a number of meetings in the 1920s in an

---

260. For a detailed overview of the Tranquebar Conference of 1919, see Sundkler, *Church of South India*, 91–130.

261. Bell, "Statement Drawn Up," 124.

262. Bell, "Statement Drawn Up," 124–25.

263. Sundkler, *Church of South India*, 104.

264. See Manshardt, "Movements Toward Church Union"; Clifford Manshardt, "The Movement Toward Church Union in South India," *J. Relig.* 9.1 (1929) 109–15; Clifford Manshardt, "Church Union in South India," *J. Relig.* 9.4 (1929) 607–13.

effort to establish a united church between them.²⁶⁵ Wesleyan Methodists began taking part in these joint meetings from 1925 onward.²⁶⁶ The most contentious points of debate were the issues of intercommunion between constituent churches and ministerial authority vis-à-vis ordination and the right to administer sacraments.²⁶⁷

After a decade of discussion, the negotiating parties formally issued the first draft of their Scheme of Union in 1929. Building on the 1919 Tranquebar basis of union and subsequent deliberations between the uniting churches, the scheme clarified the theological and ministerial convictions which would govern and shape the potential united church. It addressed what would be the doctrine, ministry, membership, governance, and worship of the church, along with how it would relate to other churches.²⁶⁸ Sundkler captures the significance of this publication:

> The three churches in South India were not officially committed to any part of it. They had been able to give general approval to the basic principles involved. So far the home churches had been able to content themselves with nodding approval to the bold endeavors of the younger church. The publication of the first edition of the scheme in 1929 changed the situation fundamentally. The ideas and ideals were now brought down to earth. They were translated into paragraphs and words which might have consequences not only for South India but, by example and precedence, for other parts of the world where church union was considered.²⁶⁹

This scheme underwent a number of revisions over the course of the 1930s.²⁷⁰

The decade following the first publication of the scheme was replete with inter- and intra-church disputes on a wide variety of theological issues related to the potential union. Anglican bishops at the 1930 Lambeth

---

265. Manshardt, "Movements Toward Church Union," 621.

266. D. M. Devasahayam, "The South India Church Union Movement," in *Rethinking Christianity in India*, ed. G. V. Job et al. (Madras, India: A. N. Sudarisanam, 1939), 233.

267. Manshardt, "Movements Toward Church Union," 621–24. For a detailed account of the negotiations between the constituent churches over the course of the 1920s, see Sundkler, *Church of South India*, 108–68.

268. Sundkler, *Church of South India*, 168–72.

269. Sundkler, *Church of South India*, 172.

270. Sundkler, *Church of South India*, 216–17, diagrams the various iterations of the scheme from 1929 onward.

Conference granted tentative approval of the first edition of the scheme, while also voicing reservations. According to D. M. Devasahayam, the bishops perceived the scheme to be "within the traditional framework of faith and order. But the proposed united church of South India would not be in full communion with the Church of England or even the North Indian branch of that Church, for the time being, until irregularities from the Anglican standpoint were all removed."[271]

Among both Methodists and the SIUC, opposition to the scheme and the Anglican stance at Lambeth 1930 was strong and varied. Various factions of the SIUC voiced concern over the authority granted to bishops in the scheme. Some contended that such an episcopalian authority structure would deemphasize lay initiative, while some believed it would undermine the role of presbyters.[272] The Methodists also expressed misgivings regarding the place of bishops in the scheme and how such "sacerdotalism" might undercut lay spiritual fervor.[273] Later in the decade, other issues like the doctrinal basis of the church and the priesthood of believers came to the fore.[274]

A central point of contention among Methodists and the SIUC following the 1929 Scheme of Union and the 1930 Lambeth Conference was the issue of intercommunion. That is, non-Anglican constituents decried the unwillingness of Anglicans to partake in the Lord's Supper together with members of the SIUC and Methodist churches, which carried an implicit denial of the legitimacy of SIUC and Methodist church order. A. Streckeisen of the Basel Mission spoke on behalf of both the SIUC and the Methodists when he stated, "The refusal of the Anglican Church to have intercommunion is a real offence to me. What then is the Scheme but an absorption into that church? If we can't recognize each other even so much, is there much use in trying for union, while the necessary presuppositions are missing?"[275] Although the Joint Committee went on to promote a degree of intercommunion between the uniting parties, the SIUC remained unsatisfied, which appeared to put the whole union movement in peril.[276]

---

271. Devasahayam, "South India Church Union Movement," 233.
272. Sundkler, *Church of South India*, 221–25.
273. Sundkler, *Church of South India*, 227.
274. Oosthuizen, *Theological Discussions*, 83–92; Sundkler, *Church of South India*, 283–95.
275. Quoted in Sundkler, *Church of South India*, 229.
276. Sundkler, *Church of South India*, 228–44. There arose in the SIUC

COLONIAL PATTERN OF THEOLOGICAL IMPOSITION

In 1937, the General Assembly of the SIUC thus issued a significant resolution, which in its eyes provided the only legitimate way forward in the quest for church union in South India. The assembly stated,

> Resolved that as a confirmation of the mutual recognition of the Ministers of the Word and Sacraments in the three negotiating Churches, so clearly expressed in the Basis of Union and in the governing principles of the Church, the General Assembly urges the Joint Committee to take steps to secure the adoption of the practice of inter-communion and inter-celebration between the negotiating churches before union. The Assembly believes that if this is done, one of the chief obstacles to Union would be removed.[277]

From their perspective, if Anglican church leaders were unwilling to take part in SIUC worship gatherings—as well as those of the Methodists—before uniting, then they were not likely to acknowledge the validity of their ministries after uniting. Devasahayam, an Indian member of the SIUC, averred, "The demand of the S.I.U.C. for intercommunion and intercelebration before Union is amply justified as the only guarantee that will secure the recognition of the equality of the ministries and members of the united churches even after union."[278]

The Joint Committee ultimately came to a conclusion in 1941 that satisfied, for the most part, the negotiating parties.[279] While not heeding the SIUC's aforementioned demand for full intercommunion prior to union, they nevertheless recognized the need to widen the practice of intercommunion before inaugurating the union. Additionally, they determined that full intercommunion among the churches should begin taking place as soon as each of the uniting churches had formally voted in favor of uniting. This resolution satisfied the majority of SIUC and Methodist leaders. From that point, the decision regarding the potential union rested in the hands of the three churches as they considered the latest Scheme of Union.

---

dissatisfaction with the reedited Scheme of Union in 1935 and its stance on the validity of the ministries of the constituent churches. This dissatisfaction led, in part, to a crisis in the overall union negotiations (266–72).

277. Quoted in Devasahayam, "South India Church Union Movement," 234–35.
278. Devasahayam, "South India Church Union Movement," 237.
279. Sundkler, *Church of South India*, 295–96.

After decades of debate and negotiation, each of the three churches approved of the scheme and decided to formalize the union.[280] The Methodists, voting in 1943, were the first to decide in favor of consummating the union.[281] The Anglicans followed suit in 1945,[282] while the SIUC—after further deliberation—formally voted to unite in 1946.[283] The official inauguration of the union took place on September 27, 1947, in Madras. The three constituent churches became one Church of South India (CSI).[284]

Foreign Theological Dominance Within the Movement

An irony of the union movement in South India is that although it sought to establish a truly local, Indian church, the movement's negotiating actors—those who decided the theological convictions which would govern the united church—were mostly foreign missionaries tied to foreign theological traditions. Indian theologian P. Chenchiah observed,

> The missionary was a member of the home-church sent to do its work. The early converts were overseas members of the denomination. They were ruled by home boards, financed from the church funds. The converts got their religion straight from the headquarters. It was in this soil that the seeds of union first sprouted. The originators easily perceived that in these circumstances, any scheme of church union can be carried on only by the home churches. The missionaries themselves could not move without the sanction of their masters.[285]

---

280. Sundkler, *Church of South India*, 322–38.

281. G. K. A. Bell, ed., "The South India Provincial Synod of the Methodist Church. Resolution of Acceptance. January and July 1943," in *Documents on Christian Unity: Third Series 1930-48* (New York: Oxford University Press, 1948), 224.

282. G. K. A. Bell, ed., "The General Council of the Church of India, Burma, and Ceylon. Resolution of Acceptance. January 1945," in *Documents on Christian Unity: Third Series 1930-48* (New York: Oxford University Press, 1948), 228.

283. G. K. A. Bell, ed., "The General Assembly of the South India United Church. Resolutions of Acceptance. September 1946," in *Documents on Christian Unity: Third Series 1930-48* (New York: Oxford University Press, 1948), 228–29.

284. For a detailed overview of the inauguration service, see Potter, "Churches Unite in South India"; Carol Graham, "The Inauguration of the Church of South India," *Int. Rev. Mission* 37.1 (1948) 49–53.

285. P. Chenchiah, "Church Union: A Study of Underlying Ideas," in *Rethinking Christianity in India*, ed. G. V. Job et al. (Madras, India: A. N. Sudarisanam, 1939), 211; Sundkler, *Church of South India*, 187, highlights an example of this close connection

Thus, foreign agents played a dominant role in the movement toward union.

This reality was true from the beginning, when various Presbyterian groups in India were considering union. A significant catalyst for Presbyterian union in South India was the South Indian Missionary Conference of 1900. Of the one hundred and fifty attendees of this conference, there were only twenty-four Indians; the rest were foreign missionaries.[286] In the aftermath of this conference, the missionaries determined that organic union between the different missions and churches was the only proper way forward.[287] Additionally, they also decided that Westminster theology would govern the new, united church. According to Sundkler, "The Confession of Faith [of the united church] was based on the 'Statement of Doctrine and Questions for the Ordaining of Office-bearers in the Native Churches of India,' a shortened and modified form of the Westminster Confession."[288]

This pattern of foreign theological dominance continued as the SIUC considered uniting with Congregationalists. It was the missionaries and their respective boards who authorized the union and established its confessional basis.[289] Per Manshardt, although the intention was to build up the Indian church, "The movement was inaugurated by missionaries and largely negotiated by them."[290] They were the ones asking and seeking answers to theological questions related to union.[291] Indians, on the other hand, played a minimal role in the process.[292] Ironically, some of

---

between missionaries in India and denominational leaders back in Europe, noting that Methodist missionaries "kept the Home Board in London effectively informed about every move and change in South India."

286. Sundkler, *Church of South India*, 33.

287. Manshardt, "Movements Toward Church Union," 618.

288. Sundkler, *Church of South India*, 37; Oosthuizen, *Theological Discussions*, 72, notes that the churches of the uniting Presbyterian missions adhered to transplanted Western confessions of faith even prior to their union.

289. Sundkler, *Church of South India*, 42.

290. Manshardt, "Movements Toward Church Union," 620.

291. Oosthuizen, *Theological Discussions*, 75.

292. Sundkler, *Church of South India*, 43. However, the SIUC would later give a larger platform to Indian leaders as broader union discussions took place. Sundkler notes, "Perhaps the most positive contribution of the S.I.U.C. to organic church union was the scope it gave to the initiative of Indian leaders. Two of the greatest among these had passed away in 1930: K. T. Paul and V. Santiago. Their contemporaries, such as Meshach Peter and B. Samuel and C. J. Jones, had responsible positions and used these in furthering the cause of union; C. J. Lucas made an important contribution to

the Indians reacted strongly against this union, because they had learned to embrace their denominational confessions as the sole standard bearers of theology. J. H. Wyckoff, then a Presbyterian missionary in India, reported that the Indian opponents "had been wedded so long to the Canons of Dort and the Westminster Confession, that they heartily believed that the organization which held those symbols of orthodoxy was the only true Reformed Church."[293]

Foreign actors also dominated the negotiations that led to an even wider union in the formation of the CSI. Although Indian leaders were largely responsible for catalyzing this broader union and establishing its basis at the 1919 Tranquebar conference, Western missionaries dominated the theological negotiating from that point onward. While Indian Christian leaders took part in the Joint Committee on Church Union, it appears that foreigners assumed its main offices and also composed important sub-committees like the business committee and drafting committee.[294] Further, Sundkler notes that it was E. J. Palmer—an Anglican missionary—who served as the "main architect" of the CSI union.[295]

Yet foreign theological influence within the union movement went beyond Western missionaries on the ground; scholars in Europe also exerted significant pressure on the union negotiations.[296] Many Joint

---

the debate at Edinburgh in 1937. There was also a younger generation of well-educated leaders in particularly strategic positions" (193–94).

293. Quoted in Sundkler, *Church of South India*, 47; Oosthuizen, *Theological Discussions*, 75, adds, "Indians were of the strongest opponents of the formation of the S.I.U.C. They considered that these canons of Dort, the confession of Westminster and of the Heidelberg Catechism became part and parcel of their churches as they had them so long. This attitude may be ascribed to the fact that, with ecclesiastical authority, these doctrines were inculcated as the only true orthodoxy, as exhibiting the purity of the faith, and as the unquestionable standards of faith." Job, "Christian Movement in India," 22, recognized that even apart from active foreign agency, the long-inculcated prestige of Western Christendom among native Christians is hard to overcome.

294. For example, in both the thirteenth and seventeenth meetings of the Joint Committee, about equal number of Indian constituents and non-Indian constituents took part. However, for each gathering, non-Indian participants assumed the offices of chairman and secretary. Further, between the two meetings, V. S. Azariah was the only Indian to serve on either the business committee or drafting committee. See "Report of the Thirteenth Session of the Joint Committee on Church Union" (Madras, 1935; Yale Divinity School archives); "Report of the Seventeenth Session of the Joint Committee on Church Union in South India" (Madras, 1941; Yale Divinity School archives).

295. Sundkler, *Church of South India*, 115.

296. Sundkler, *Church of South India*, 144, maintains, "Tranquebar had been an Indian ministers' conference. They had decided that they wished to join forces. But South India was not alone. Behind the different churches were different traditions

Committee members looked regularly to "theological and ecclesiastical experts" in the West for input and guidance as the union movement progressed.[297] Among those consulted were J. Vernon Bartlett of Oxford, A. C. Headlam of Gloucester, William Temple of Manchester and York, O. C. Quick of Durham and Oxford, B. J. Kidd of Oxford, H. L. Goudge of Oxford, Alexander Martin of Edinburgh, J. Scott Lidgett of London, Newton Flew of Cambridge, and Karl Hartenstein and K. G. Goetz of Basel.[298] In fact, the Joint Committee members spent their first ten meetings together grappling with the theological input of their respective missionary society home boards and the theological scholars associated with them.[299]

Occasionally Western theologians contributed to theological discussions within the union movement in more official ways, beyond personal correspondence with missionaries on the ground. Sundkler notes, for example, "The intercommunion problem in 1932 led to the publication of the so-called Oxford Theologians' Note, signed by H. L. Goudge, B. J. Kidd, K. E. Kirk, W. B. O'Brien, F. W. Puller, Darwell Stone and N. P. Williams."[300] On one occasion, a prominent missionary in India, J. J. Banninga, even sent a questionnaire to around two hundred theologians in America and Great Britain, seeking input on the issue of lay celebration of the Lord's Supper. He was of the opinion that the movement's "[theological] battle should be fought in Europe" rather than in India.[301]

With so many Western voices dominating theological deliberations, the Protestant union movement in South India was, from the start, theologically dependent on the West. The Madras *Christo Samaj* group, or the "Rethinking Group"—a well-known collection of progressive, nationalistic Indian Christian thinkers—was at the forefront of calling attention to this Western character of the movement.[302] V. Chakkarai, one of its most prominent members, maintained,

---

and loyalties, and when the theological technicians stepped in to discuss matters of validity and 'economy,' something of the first enthusiasm, that 'rushing mighty wind' which Palmer had heard in the Indian quest for unity, subsided. The appeal to the home churches and constituencies became an important matter, and that appeal meant necessarily a stiffening of the relations between the parties concerned." See also 207–13.

297. Sundkler, *Church of South India*, 145.
298. Sundkler, *Church of South India*, 212.
299. John J. Banninga, "Union in South India," *Christ. Century* 64.15 (1947) 459.
300. Sundkler, *Church of South India*, 213.
301. Quoted in Sundkler, *Church of South India*, 213.
302. The group became known as the "Rethinking Group" in light of their

> The South Indian scheme had no Indian origin. It was based on the Lambeth Quadrilateral.... [T]he presence of Anglican bishops and Western missionaries on the Joint Committee has deflected the Indian mind into channels that are not its own. ... The mission field is not a fit scene where to fight out the battle of Western ecclesiasticism. They ought to be transferred to Rome, Canterbury or Geneva which is their native habitat. Strange that they should try to impose a Western solution of Western controversies on the Eastern mind![303]

Devasahayam also objected, claiming, "The Indian Church should not be treated as pliable material for conducting experiments for the solution of the denominational problems of Western Christendom."[304] According to Sundkler, the *Christo Samaj* group believed that the establishment of a single ecclesiastical structure was "a grievous mistake caused by the preponderance of Western missionary influence, which reduced the Indians to mere pawns in the game of missionary diplomacy."[305]

J. C. Chatterjee—who served as the president of the All Indian Christian Conference in 1928—went so far as to contend that it was the Western missionary societies who were actually doing the uniting, not necessarily local, Indian churches. He asserted,

> To my mind all our talk about church unity is premature, for by whatever names we may like to distinguish our churches, practically none of them has achieved an independent church life. Till then we can only talk of the union of missionary societies and not of the Indian Church. I must frankly state my belief that church unity as well as the establishment of a truly national church can only be achieved by spontaneous enthusiasm resulting from indigenous movements from within the Indian Christian community and not by elaborate conferences

---

endeavors to indigenize Christianity in India according to its prevailing Hindu context. Their most famous publication is G. V. Job et al., eds., *Rethinking Christianity in India* (Madras, India: A. N. Sudarisanam, 1939).

303. V. Chakkarai, "The South India Rapprochement," in *Rethinking Christianity in India*, ed. G. V. Job et al. (Madras, India: A. N. Sudarisanam, 1939), 281–82.

304. Devasahayam, "South India Church Union Movement," 263. Elsewhere he added, "The ecclesiastical systems evolved in the West are foreign to the Indian soil. ... Farther removed from the Indian spirit is the elaborate institutional conception of Christianity connected with the historic episcopate or the Papacy. Young Christian India does not need the trammels of heavy ecclesiastical machinery, but the simplicity of the Gospel in Faith and Order" (253).

305. Sundkler, *Church of South India*, 143–44.

and constitution-making on Western lines, functioning under Western guidance.[306]

Such Western tutelage became abhorrent to many of the progressive Indian Christian thinkers.[307]

Additionally, the *Christo Samaj* group asserted that most Indian Christians were largely unaware of and unconcerned with the theological debates dominating the union movement. In its weekly newspaper, *The Christian Patriot*, the group claimed, "We take it that 99.99 per cent of the Christian people have not any inkling of an idea" regarding the union movement and its theological currents.[308] Moreover, the theological difference between the Protestant denominations apparently meant little to the ordinary Indian Christian; most did not hold dogmatically to denominational loyalties. This stance contributed to the push for union—insofar as the impetus for union came from Indians.[309]

Yet not all shared the convictions of this *Christo Samaj* group. In particular, many missionaries and not a few prominent Indians rejected the notion that the union movement was a disservice to Indian Christianity. Sundkler notes that many Western missionaries "were convinced that in drawing together they were serving the national interests of India."[310] There were also prominent Indian church leaders, like V. S. Azariah, V. Santiago, and A. J. Appasamy who likewise believed in the merits of the union movement as it proceeded from Tranquebar 1919.[311] Moreover, other mission and church leaders distanced themselves from the more liberal, progressive theological convictions of *Christo Samaj*.[312]

306. Quoted in Devasahayam, "South India Church Union Movement," 237–38. It is unclear if Chatterjee himself was a member of *Christo Samaj*, but Devasahayam quoted him approvingly.

307. Job, "Christian Movement in India," 20, argued that an Indian church "cannot be brought into being by transplanting on the Indian soil Western churches. It cannot be built upon outworn creeds, borrowed theology, alien ceremonials, sacerdotalism and priestcraft."

308. Quoted in Sundkler, *Church of South India*, 143.

309. Devasahayam, "South India Church Union Movement," 230; Chenchiah, "Church Union," 223, posited, "The normal Indian Christian has a healthy mind in this matter and treats denominations as accidental misfortunes, not as spiritual assets."

310. Sundkler, *Church of South India*, 144.

311. For Appasamy's stance on church union in contradistinction to the *Christo Samaj* group, see Sundkler, *Church of South India*, 205–6.

312. Oosthuizen, *Theological Discussions*, 86–87, notes, for example, that A. Streckeisen led a charge in the SIUC to establish a stronger, more precise biblical-theological basis for union in order to guard against the syncretistic theological convictions of men

However, the group rightly recognized Western theological dependence within the movement. After a thorough study of the union negotiations, Sundkler acknowledges, "There was a sense in which the West, or rather the theology of the West, was fighting a battle on South India's behalf."[313] Michael Hollis, who occupied the highest leadership position in the CSI during its first three years of existence, later recognized such foreign theological dependence. He admitted, "Our error was, and in a great measure still is, that we of the West have tried to give the answers to the churches of other lands, to those who are as truly God's people as we are and who have as really received the Holy Spirit as we have."[314]

It bears mentioning that the movement's foreign negotiators stopped short of developing a fully formed theology to govern the church. The three not-yet-united churches believed that such a theology must necessarily come after union.[315] Hollis maintained, "Union cannot be brought about either by the rigid imposition of the ancient creeds and confessions or by drawing up a detailed new statement of belief. As with worship, so with matters of belief, the right answers can only be found after uniting."[316] The CSI thus wrote into its constitution the expectation that it would, in time, develop its own confession of faith: "The Church of South India desires, therefore, conserving all that is of spiritual value in its Indian heritage, to express under Indian conditions, and in Indian forms the Spirit, the thought, and the life of the Church Universal."[317]

---

like Chakkarai and Chenchiah. For a critical overview of the theological convictions of several members of the Rethinking Group, see 37–50.

313. Sundkler, *Church of South India*, 213.

314. Michael Hollis, *Paternalism and the Church: A Study of South Indian Church History* (New York: Oxford University Press, 1962), 6. It is not entirely clear if Hollis here was making a general statement about a common pattern within the Western missionary enterprise or a specific statement regarding the missionary approach in South India. However, other statements of his in the book (14–15, 35–36) indicate that Hollis believed that this general pattern was also evident in South India.

315. Marcus Ward, *The Pilgrim Church: An Account of the First Five Years in the Life of the Church of South India* (London: Epworth, 1953), 198–99; Hollis, *Significance of South India*, 65, asserted, "It is necessary to recognize the impossibility of reaching full agreement while the negotiating Churches are still in their separation. The essential aim of any viable plan must be to make it possible for life in unity to begin, leaving many decisions to be taken by the united Church."

316. Hollis, *Significance of South India*, 22–23.

317. Church of South India, *The Constitution of the Church of South India with Amendments up to 31st December 1951* (Madras: The Christian Literature Society for India, 1952), 3.

Nevertheless, foreign theological dominance was still at work in the union movement, as Western missionary leaders did most of the grappling over theological issues like intercommunion, ordination, church polity, and the priesthood of believers.[318] The CSI's Basis of Union and Constitution later codified the committee's joint resolutions on such issues, therefore cementing the influence of Westerners on the theological convictions of this Indian church.[319]

Thus, although Western agents stopped short of articulating a fully orbed confession of faith, they nevertheless exerted a significant amount of control over the theological convictions that lay at the heart of the united church. As a result, Western theology continued to dominate the church's life even after union.[320] In the words of an editorial in the *South India Churchman*, the CSI "is not only foreign in its personnel; it is foreign in its ethos; it is foreign in its administrative machinery; it is foreign in its theology; and, above all, it is foreign in its material resources."[321] In the face of such foreign theological dominance, CSI Bishop Sabapathy Kulandran thus urged,

> If it is really to fulfill its calling, the Indian Church must realise its Indian setting, must begin to grapple with Indian problems, see the world through its own eyes, and must think out its theology with its own mind. That the Indian Church should be Christian in its outlook and its presuppositions is fundamental but, unless its judgements and actions are its own, coming out of its own soul, and not from a Cambridge- or Oxford-educated

---

318. Hollis, *Significance of South India*, 36–37, asserts that the negotiating parties were mostly agreed on issues of "faith," or theology; it was the issue of church "order" that occasioned debate within the movement. However, issues of church order are no less theological than those of doctrine, for undergirding convictions about intercommunion, ordination, church polity, and the priesthood of believers are fundamental biblical and theological convictions.

319. Church of South India, *Constitution*, contained fourteen chapters on theological topics like church membership, ordination, church governance, and the ministry of the laity. The church also addressed such topics in their Basis of Union (68–89).

320. Moses, "Spiritual Significance of Church Union," 4, contended, "The church in India has yet to bring her peculiar honors to her King, our Lord Jesus Christ. So far she has been too much of an uninspiring replica of the Western denominational churches." F. Burton Nelson, "The Church of South India: A Report," *Covenant Q.* 22.3 (1964) 35, added that "the majority of the [CSI] bishops are from overseas. Some Indian leaders consequently feel, and rightly so, that the Church of South India is far too foreign in its theology, in its administrative machinery, and in its material resources."

321. Quoted in Ward, *Pilgrim Church*, 163.

missionary of the West, the Indian Church would only be a possibility and not a reality in the Church Universal.[322]

Although some have recognized growth in the area of indigenous theological development within the CSI,[323] the pattern of foreign theological dominance remained the norm throughout the union negotiations and the early life of the united church.

COMMONALITIES OF PRACTICE AND PRESUPPOSITION

The strongest similarities among these three case studies exist between the first two—the early Jesuits in Peru and the CMS in Uganda. Missionaries in both cases betrayed a presupposed belief in a form of cultural evolution—i.e., that European civilization and its people reside at the top of an ordered hierarchy, while the inferior peoples of the Majority World remain on lower rungs of humanity.[324] This conviction was clearly at work among the early Jesuits in Peru, and particularly in the thought of José de Acosta. Quoting him, Sabine MacCormack explains, "Human knowledge and institutions, Acosta thus thought, had reached their most perfect state in Europe, and compared to the Americas, Europe was 'the better and more noble part of the world.'"[325] Conversely, Peru was, accord-

---

322. Quoted in Ward, *Pilgrim Church*, 169.

323. For example, see Nelson, "Church of South India," 38–39; Ward, *Pilgrim Church*, 156.

324. Wrogemann, *Intercultural Hermeneutics*, 121–22, contends, "The evolutionary understanding of culture had a widespread theological impact within the movement of cultural Protestantism, which proceeded on the basis of a religiocultural evolution of humanity, assuming that Western Protestantism comprised the consummation of this evolutionary development. As was observed in the approach of Ernst Troeltsch, here too the spiritual underpinnings of the scientific, technical-industrial, and ethically superior Western civilization were located in the fundamental convictions of Protestant Christianity. The individuality of particular cultures was plotted as a point in the greater continuum of the course of human history. At the same time, a value was assigned to each culture. Only *that culture seen as having reached the highest stage of development*—i.e., a constituent culture—could serve as the criterion of culture in the sense of a progressive civilization" (emphasis original). He points to Georg Friedrich Wilhelm Hegel, Auguste Comte, James George Frazer, and Lewis Henry Morgan as exponents of cultural evolution (121).

325. Sabine MacCormack, *Religion in the Andes: Vision and Imagination in Early Colonial Peru* (Princeton, NJ: Princeton University Press, 1993), 264.

ing to a metaphor Acosta employed, "an ugly daughter whose appearance was redeemed only by her dowry, that is, Peru's mineral wealth."[326]

R. H. Walker of the CMS mission to Uganda betrayed, though less explicitly, a similar sense of local inferiority. In arguing against the need to develop local theology, Walker asserted, "The Baganda are not abstract thinkers, and to formulate afresh for themselves their own articles of belief would be a task beyond them as it would be unnecessary."[327] By claiming that the task of theology is beyond the Baganda, he aligned himself and the mission with the notion of cultural evolution, which perceives natives as "primitive" or "pre-logical," and thus inferior in their capabilities.[328]

Additionally, in both the Jesuit and CMS cases, missionary outsiders explicitly bound local churches and believers to Western confessions of theology. For the Jesuits, the standard of doctrine was *Doctrina Christiana y Catecismo para Instrucción de los Indios*[329] (DCC), which was a reappropriation of Tridentine Catholic theology emanating from Europe. For the CMS, the standard which missionaries imposed was the Church of England's Thirty-Nine Articles, a confession of faith developed in light of and in reference to contextual and theological issues of late sixteenth-century Europe.[330] Further, missionaries of both societies aimed to prevent deviation from these established Western standards.

The third case study—the Protestant union movement in South India—differs from the first two in certain ways. For one, appeals to cultural evolution do not appear to have factored into the union movement. That is, major Western negotiators within the movement do not seem to have viewed South Indians as inferior to themselves. Additionally, although missionaries at the outset of the movement did bind early united churches to established Western theological confessions, the broader union movement stopped short of doing so. Though informed

---

326. MacCormack, *Religion in the Andes*, 264. MacCormack highlights how these convictions contributed to the Jesuit emphasis on first civilizing natives as a prerequisite for evangelization (268, 276).

327. Walker, "Native Church of Uganda," 437.

328. Paul G. Hiebert, "Beyond Anti-Colonialism to Globalism," *Missiology Int. Rev.* 19.3 (1991) 266, explains, "Evolution accounted for cultural variations by arranging them along a scale from 'primitive,' and 'pre-logical' to 'civilized' with the West at the top. . . . These theories of evolution justified the initial response of Westerners to other peoples and cultures. They 'proved' Western superiority, and gave scientific support for colonial rule, and for efforts to 'civilize' other peoples."

329. *Doctrina Christiana y Catecismo para Instrucción de los Indios*.

330. Thompson, "Origin of the Thirty-Nine Articles," 40.

Hermeneutical Community

by Western theology, the Basis of Union, the various schemes of union, and the CSI's first, formal constitution were all new theological documents which negotiating actors developed over the course of the movement, not preexisting standards from without.

However, among all three case studies, there exist two significant commonalities. First, in each case, outside agents betrayed an assumption of Western theological universality and normativity. The early Jesuits in Peru—following the stance of the Third Lima Council (TLC)—presupposed as much, and therefore established DCC as the definitive standard of faith among their Peruvian churches. Western missionaries within the Protestant union movement in South India also betrayed this assumption in the way they constantly looked to Western scholars for theological input and guidance. As Sundkler notes regarding the negotiating parties, "South India was not alone. Behind the different churches were different traditions and loyalties," and often "the theological technicians [of the West] stepped in to discuss matters of validity and 'economy.'"[331] It thus appears that a key presupposition undergirding these theological discussions was the belief that final theological authority resides in the West.

Walker of the CMS mission to Uganda revealed this assumption in his endorsement of the fact that the Ugandan church, though native, was yet Anglican in doctrine. He asserted, "While giving the fullest possible scope to national aspiration, and without it the church stands doomed to failure, it would be the height of unwisdom to suppose that any local Church, certainly not a Church less than forty years old, and least of all a Church in Central Africa, could stand alone independent of Christendom."[332] The assumption here is that theology emanating out of Christian Europe—in this case the Church of England—serves as the standard bearer of orthodoxy, to which every other church must orient itself. In other words, Majority World churches are theologically dependent on "Christendom," and it would be "unwise" for those churches to evade such dependency. It is not hard then to imagine how these missionary outsiders, with this assumption in tow, would operate by way of theological imposition.

Second, in each case, outsiders remained in positions of control over local theology. The TLC, which set the theological standard for the ministry of early Jesuits in Peru, was a gathering of European Catholic clerics; they do not appear to have registered any local input regarding the

---

331. Sundkler, *Church of South India*, 144.
332. Walker, "Native Church of Uganda," 437.

theology which would govern the Catholic Church in Peru.³³³ In Uganda, the CMS mission—rather than the local church—retained the final word in matters of theology. Even in Bishop Tucker's proposal to bring the missionaries under the leadership of the local Ugandan church, there remained a Western bishop who held veto power over any new theological development.³³⁴ Within the Protestant union movement in South India, missionary outsiders—not to mention their scholar colleagues in the West—dominated theological negotiations. In fact, there were only two secretaries of the Joint Committee (which oversaw the negotiations leading to the formation of the CSI), and both were Western missionaries.³³⁵ Additionally, those who filled leadership positions in the early life of the CSI came mostly from outside of India.³³⁶ Such was the case with the CSI's moderator position (its highest level of leadership), a post which a Western missionary filled for the church's first six years of existence.³³⁷ Thus in each case, theological control remained largely in the hands of outsiders.

CONCLUSION

These case studies typify a broader pattern in the colonial period, in which Western outsiders perceived (whether explicitly or implicitly) their role in local theological development as one of imposition.³³⁸ They assumed near total control over local theological reflection and expression and permitted little to no space for locals to rethink or develop theology on their own, according to their own categorical frame of reference, or with

---

333. Burgaleta, *José de Acosta*, 51, notes that the TLC was a gathering of Catholic bishops in Latin America. Bishops were, at that time, all from Europe; Schwaller, *History of the Catholic Church*, 64, states, "Ordination was not an option for native men until nearly a century after the conquest. The local bishops simply did not believe that the natives were well enough versed in Christianity to become priests."

334. Griffiths, "Bishop A. R. Tucker," 236, notes in reference to Tucker's proposal, "Missionaries would exercise a double veto in the Synod in the person of the Bishop and because a majority of the clergy were European."

335. The two were J. J. Banninga and J. S. M. Hooper. Sundkler, *Church of South India*, 188, notes that Hooper took over as secretary in 1934 after Banninga stepped aside.

336. Hollis, *Paternalism and the Church*, 159.

337. K. M. George, *Church of South India: Life in Union (1947–1997)* (Delhi: ISPCK, 1999), 275. Michael Hollis of England filled this position from 1948 to 1954.

338. Walls, *Cross-Cultural Process*, 37–38, 242–43; Bosch, *Transforming Mission*, 427; Charles E. Van Engen, "The Glocal Church: Locality and Catholicity in a Globalizing World," in *Globalizing Theology: Belief and Practice in an Era of World Christianity*, ed. Craig Ott and Harold A. Netland (Grand Rapids: Baker Academic, 2006), 173.

their own contextual questions and issues in mind. Rather, outsiders often expected locals to embrace Western theology wholesale. As historical theologian Justo González explains, "When mission theoreticians in past decades spoke of the 'three selfs' as a goal for younger churches, they included self-support, self-government, and self-propagation. They did not envision self-interpretation or self-theologizing. They expected theology to continue being what it was, for the meaning of the gospel was fully understood by the sending churches, and all that the younger ones had to do was continue proclaiming the same message."[339] Such an approach was the theological outworking of what Wilbert R. Shenk calls the "replication model" of missions, in which "the missionary seeks to replicate or reproduce a church in another culture patterned after that of the church from which the missionary originated."[340]

This practice of theological imposition ultimately left Majority World churches without a theology of their own.[341] Thus even as late as 1976, John Mbiti observed that "the Church has become kerygmatically universal, but is still theologically provincial, in spite of the great giants of theology."[342] That is, although Christianity had spread throughout the world, theological reflection remained mostly Western in orientation. This reality ultimately undermined ecclesial indigeneity in the Majority World, for such indigeneity stems not just from external metrics like self-support, self-governance, and self-propagation, but even more deeply from the ability of locals to reflect theologically on the issues that confront them in context.[343] This lack of local theological reflection stemmed, in no small measure, from the imposing role that Western missionaries played in local theological development throughout the colonial period.

---

339. Justo L. González, *Mañana: Christian Theology from a Hispanic Perspective* (Nashville: Abingdon, 1990), 49.

340. Wilbert R. Shenk, *Changing Frontiers of Mission* (Maryknoll, NY: Orbis, 1999), 51.

341. C. René Padilla, "The Contextualization of the Gospel," in *Readings in Dynamic Indigeneity*, ed. Charles H. Kraft and Tom N. Wisley (Pasadena, CA: William Carey Library, 1979), 298.

342. John S. Mbiti, "Theological Impotence and the Universality of the Church," in *Third World Theologies*, ed. Gerald H. Anderson and Thomas F. Stransky, Mission Trends 3 (New York: Paulist, 1976), 8.

343. Gilliland, "Contextual Theology as Incarnational Mission," 13–15.

3

Post-Colonial Rejection of Theological Imposition

WESTERN MISSION SCHOLARS AND practitioners eventually began to recognize the pattern of theological imposition coming from the West. Throughout much of the Modern Missionary Movement, foreign control over local theology appeared sensical to Western outsiders. However, that very movement created—ironically—the necessary conditions for Western Christians to rethink their theological presuppositions, especially concerning the supposed completeness and normativity of their theology[1] and the way they so often imposed that theology on younger churches across the globe.[2] Andrew Walls notes that as the gospel spread throughout much of the world during the modern era, that movement then "challenge[d] . . . many of the assumptions that had originally undergirded the movement, assumptions about the nature of sin, assumptions about the values of Western society, and, eventually, about the adequacy of Western theology. Part of the story of the missionary movement as a learning experience is the creation of an instrument for Western self-criticism."[3] As foreign missionaries engaged a myriad

---

1. Chapters 1 and 2 highlighted that reality that Westerners often assumed that their Western theology was complete (i.e., that it had completely addressed every major issue) and that it was universally normative (i.e., that it served as the standard to which churches across the world should adhere).

2. Chapter 2 presented the precedent of theological imposition by missionary outsiders.

3. Andrew F. Walls, *The Cross-Cultural Process in Christian History: Studies in the Transmission and Appropriation of Faith* (Maryknoll, NY: Orbis, 2002), 258.

of different contextual and theological issues throughout the world, they and the churches they represented began to recognize not just the incompleteness of Western theology, but also the weaknesses of binding Majority World churches to that theology.

Over the course of the twentieth century, a growing number of scholars began voicing concerns with this pattern of imposition. Such concern was evident at the 1910 World Missionary Conference in Edinburgh.[4] Others expressing this sentiment included Charles Cuthbert Hall,[5] Roland Allen,[6] Arthur Judson Brown,[7] Kenneth Scott Latourette,[8] G. C. Oosthuizen,[9] J. H. Bavinck,[10] John V. Taylor,[11] and Michael Hollis.[12] Each highlighted shortcomings of this pattern which was commonplace in the Modern Missionary Movement. Wilbert R. Shenk typified their concerns, claiming, "The church which is the product of this historic movement suffers seriously from spiritual and intellectual rootlessness.... [I]t is, in a significant measure, a result of a particular approach to theology which has kept the young church a dependent of Western Christian thought and the missionary unassimilated into a new milieu."[13]

---

4. *The Church in the Mission Field: Report of Commission II* (Edinburgh: Oliphant, Anderson and Ferrier, 1910), 189–91.

5. Charles Cuthbert Hall, *The Universal Elements of the Christian Religion: An Attempt to Interpret Contemporary Religious Conditions* (New York: Fleming H. Revell, 1905), 42–46, 51–53, 154–56.

6. Roland Allen, *Missionary Methods: St. Paul's or Ours* (London: Robert Scott, 1912), 187–99.

7. Arthur J. Brown, *Rising Churches in Non-Christian Lands* (New York: Missionary Education Movement of the United States and Canada, 1915), 188–90.

8. Kenneth Scott Latourette, *Missions Tomorrow* (New York: Harper and Brothers, 1936), 211–12.

9. G. C. Oosthuizen, *Theological Discussions and Confessional Developments in the Churches of Asia and Africa* (Franeker, Netherlands: T. Wever, 1958); this book was later published as G. C. Oosthuizen, *Theological Battleground in Asia and Africa: The Issues Facing the Churches and the Efforts to Overcome Western Divisions* (New York: Humanities, 1972).

10. J. H. Bavinck, *An Introduction to the Science of Missions*, trans. David Hugh Freeman (Grand Rapids: Baker, 1960), 203–4.

11. John V. Taylor, *The Primal Vision: Christian Presence amid African Religion* (Philadelphia: Fortress, 1963), 21–24.

12. Michael Hollis, *The Significance of South India* (Richmond, VA: John Knox, 1966), 23, 40–41, 51; Michael Hollis, *Paternalism and the Church: A Study of South Indian Church History* (New York: Oxford University Press, 1962), 15, 35–36.

13. Wilbert R. Shenk, "Theology and the Missionary Task," *Missiology* 1.3 (1973) 295–96.

Recognition of Western theological imposition became more pronounced from the latter part of the twentieth century onward, particularly after the World Council of Churches' (WCC) push for "contextualization"[14] and the Lausanne movement's Willowbank Report.[15] In the early 1970s, the Theological Education Fund (TEF) of the WCC began promoting contextualization as a means of reform in Majority World theological education. The term itself emerged in the TEF committee's deliberations as part of its Third Mandate period,[16] in which it sought to foster theological education that was more responsive to local contexts.[17] According to then TEF director Shoki Coe, "Contextualization is the interpretation of the imperative call of the Third Mandate—'that the gospel be expressed and ministry undertaken *in response to*' . . . the urgent issues in the historic realities, particularly those of the Third World."[18]

The ecumenical promotion of contextualization emphasized that traditional, Western theologies do not adequately address the dynamic issues of contemporary contexts.[19] Already within the TEF was an in-

---

14. For an overview, from an evangelical perspective, of the historical development of the term "contextualization" see Harvie M. Conn, "Contextualization: Where Do We Begin?," in *Evangelicals and Liberation*, ed. Carl E. Armerding (Grand Rapids: Baker, 1977), 90–97; Bruce C. E. Fleming, *Contextualization of Theology: An Evangelical Assessment* (Pasadena, CA: William Carey Library, 1980), 1–44.

15. Lausanne Theology and Education Group, "The Willowbank Report," in *Down to Earth: Studies in Christianity and Culture*, ed. Robert T. Coote and John R. W. Stott (Grand Rapids: Eerdmans, 1980), 308–42.

16. Shoki Coe, "In Search of Renewal in Theological Education," *Theol. Educ.* 9.4 (1973) 233–43, explains that over the years following its inception, the TEF organized three distinct, sequential initiatives—called mandates—for its work in the field of theological education across the world. The First Mandate focused advancing the quality of theological education in the Majority World by granting financial and material resources to theological institutions. The Second Mandate then focused on rethinking the nature and purpose of theological education with an eye toward equipping students and teachers to better understand the gospel in relation to their contexts and the role of the church in participating in the mission of God around them. The Third Mandate focused on reforming theological education through granting funds to institutions which focus on contextualizing the gospel in response to the dynamic realities of contemporary contexts. Regarding the Third Mandate, see Theological Education Fund, "A Working Policy for the Implementation of the Third Mandate of the Theological Education Fund," in *Contextualization of Theology: An Evangelical Assessment*, by Bruce C. E. Fleming (Pasadena, CA: William Carey Library, 1980), 83–87.

17. Coe, "In Search of Renewal," 237, 239–43.

18. Coe, "In Search of Renewal," 243, emphasis original.

19. According to the Theological Education Fund, "Working Policy for the Implementation," 86, contextualization "means all that is implied in the familiar term 'indigenization' and yet seeks to press beyond. Contextualization has to do with how we

creasing concern that Western theological standards were impeding the development of indigenous theological education, and thus hindering Majority World Christians from responding meaningfully to local exigencies.[20] With the introduction of the term "contextualization" in 1972, the TEF addressed the issue more directly. In its working policy statement for the Third Mandate period, it asserted, "Throughout much of the Third World . . . the basic crisis in theological education can often be traced to the continued dominance of inherited and traditional patterns."[21] Moreover according to the TEF, this educational crisis had precipitated local theological problems: "Theologically, both the approach and content of theological reflection tend to move within the framework of Western questions and cultural presuppositions, failing to vigorously address the Gospel of Jesus Christ to the particular situation. Western formulations are sometimes wrongly understood as identical with the universal in Christian theology."[22] For ecumenicals of the TEF and WCC, contextualization was the hopeful answer to such Western theological dominance.

Some of the issues which the TEF raised in its call for contextualization later occupied evangelicals at the 1974 Lausanne Congress on World Evangelization, and ultimately led to the convening of a smaller consultation at Willowbank, Bermuda, in order for evangelical leaders to further explore the complex relationship between the gospel and culture.[23] According to John Gration, Lausanne 1974 "introduced many evangelicals to the concept of contextualization. The Willowbank Consultation on the Gospel and Culture (1978) provided a giant step forward in examining its multi-faceted dimensions."[24] The outcome of this consultation—the Willowbank Report—was a document that tentatively addressed, from an evangelical perspective, how culture interacts with topics like biblical

---

assess the peculiarity of third world contexts. Indigenization tends to be used in the sense of responding to the Gospel in terms of traditional culture. Contextualization, while not ignoring this, takes into account the process of secularity, technology, and the struggle for human justice, which characterize the historical moment of nations in the Third World."

20. Coe, "In Search of Renewal," 235–36.

21. Theological Education Fund, "Working Policy for the Implementation," 84.

22. Theological Education Fund, "Working Policy for the Implementation," 84.

23. For an overview of early evangelical reactions to the TEF's promotion of contextualization, see Conn, "Contextualization"; Harvie M. Conn, *Eternal Word and Changing Worlds: Theology, Anthropology, and Mission in Trialogue* (Grand Rapids: Zondervan, 1984), 177–84; Fleming, *Contextualization of Theology*.

24. John Gration, "Willowbank to Zaire: The Doing of Theology," *Missiology* 12.3 (1984) 297.

revelation, gospel content, evangelism, conversion, ecclesiology, and Christian ethics.[25]

Lausanne's Willowbank Report acknowledged the legacy of Western missionary control over theology and sought to direct evangelicals away from such theological imposition. It stated that some missions had indoctrinated Majority World Christian leaders "in western ways of thought and procedure. These westernized local leaders have then preserved a very western-looking church, and the foreign orientation has persisted, only lightly cloaked by the appearance of indigeneity."[26] In light of this precedent, the report declared, "cross-cultural witnesses must not attempt to impose a ready-made theological tradition on the church in which they serve, either by personal teaching or by literature or by controlling seminary and Bible college curricula."[27] Rather, such witnesses should "seek with equal care to avoid theological imperialism or theological provincialism. A church's theology should be developed by the community of faith out of the Scripture in interaction with other theologies of the past and present, and with the local culture and its needs."[28]

Since Willowbank and the TEF's Third Mandate, the recognition of such "theological imperialism" has continued to grow among Western missiological and theological scholars.[29] Paul G. Hiebert issued in 1985 perhaps the most significant call among evangelicals to move beyond Western theological imposition by proposing his seminal concept of "self-theologizing."[30] In addition to the notion that younger churches ought to be self-governing, self-supporting, and self-propagating, Hiebert argued that they must also be able to do theology on their own. Thus he consciously connected self-theologizing to Henry Venn and Rufus Anderson's classic three-self formula. He observed, "After much discussion about the three 'selves,' there has emerged a general consensus that young churches must be allowed to mature and take responsibility for the work

---

25. Lausanne Theology and Education Group, "Willowbank Report."
26. Lausanne Theology and Education Group, "Willowbank Report," 329.
27. Lausanne Theology and Education Group, "Willowbank Report," 333.
28. Lausanne Theology and Education Group, "Willowbank Report."

29. For example, J. Andrew Kirk, *Theology and the Third World Church* (Downers Grove, IL: InterVarsity, 1983), 26, recognizes, "Sending countries maintained a rigid line of control over the beliefs and actions of the younger churches. Deviations from the official positions of the founding fathers were not tolerated." Thus theologically, "the children grew up as the mirror images of their parents." See also Conn, *Eternal Word*, 221–23.

30. Paul G. Hiebert, *Anthropological Insights for Missionaries* (Grand Rapids: Baker, 1985), 193–224.

of God in their regions as soon as possible. But little is said about the fourth self—self-theologizing. Do young churches have the right to read and interpret the Scriptures for themselves?"[31] Hiebert's answer was an emphatic *yes*. He contended, "To grow, spiritually young churches must search the Scripture themselves, and if—for fear that they will leave the truth—we do not allow them to do so, we condemn them to spiritual infancy and early death."[32] Since Hiebert's clarion call, many others have joined in advocating for such local theological development.[33]

While Western observers came to grips with the inadequacies of theological imposition, the rest of the world began reacting against it. One way in which Majority World Christians reacted against Western theology was through formal declarations.[34] For example, in the mid-1960s, the Christian Conference of Asia—an organization within the WCC comprising strictly Asian Christian churches and organizations—issued a statement urging a move beyond the long-standing pattern of

---

31. Hiebert, *Anthropological Insights*, 195–96.

32. Hiebert, *Anthropological Insights*, 208. He also adds, "It is important for a church to wrestle with the question of contextualizing the gospel in its own cultural setting. Every church must make theology its own concern, for it must face the challenges to faith raised by its culture. And when this happens, the results will be more profound and enduring" (214).

33. For example, the following monographs and compendiums all broach the topic of local theologizing beyond the gate of Western Christendom. Bevans and Schreiter, two of the foremost scholars on contextual theology, both do so from a Catholic perspective. See Stephen B. Bevans, *Models of Contextual Theology*, rev. and exp. ed. (Maryknoll, NY: Orbis, 2002); Stephen B. Bevans, *An Introduction to Theology in Global Perspective* (Maryknoll, NY: Orbis, 2009); Robert J. Schreiter, *Constructing Local Theologies* (Maryknoll, NY: Orbis, 1985); Robert J. Schreiter, *The New Catholicity: Theology Between the Global and the Local* (Maryknoll, NY: Orbis, 1997); Jeffrey P. Greenman and Gene L. Green, eds., *Global Theology in Evangelical Perspective: Exploring the Contextual Nature of Theology and Mission* (Downers Grove, IL: IVP Academic, 2012); Dean S. Gilliland, ed., *The Word Among Us: Contextualizing Theology for Mission Today* (Dallas: Word, 1989); Craig Ott and Harold A. Netland, eds., *Globalizing Theology: Belief and Practice in an Era of World Christianity* (Grand Rapids: Baker Academic, 2006); Matthew Cook et al., eds., *Local Theology for the Global Church: Principles for an Evangelical Approach to Contextualization* (Pasadena, CA: William Carey Library, 2010); William A. Dyrness, *Learning About Theology from the Third World* (Grand Rapids: Zondervan, 1990); William A. Dyrness, *Invitation to Cross-Cultural Theology: Case Studies in Vernacular Theologies* (Grand Rapids: Zondervan, 1992); William A. Dyrness and Oscar García-Johnson, *Theology Without Borders: An Introduction to Global Conversations* (Grand Rapids: Baker Academic, 2015).

34. One such formal statement is the 1982 Seoul Declaration, which this chapter will examine in a proceeding section.

Western theological imposition.[35] While expressing appreciation for the "great tradition" and its theological confessions which Asian churches had received from the West, it posited, "such formulations have been signposts and pointers to the truth, but we have often interpreted them, or had them interpreted to us, as the final word of truth."[36] As a result, "The Asian churches so far, and in large measure, have not taken their theological task seriously enough, for they have been largely content to accept the ready-made answers of Western theology or confessions."[37] The conference thus sharply contended, "Dogmatic theological statements from a church that stands on the sidelines as spectator or even interpreter of what God is doing in Asia can carry no conviction."[38]

In addition to such formal declarations, the development of indigenous theologies across the world has also served as a critique of Western theology and its supposed superiority. Regarding this supposition, Oscar García-Johnson asserts, "Western modernity/coloniality has occupied Western theologies and Christianity in a way that has projected an image of inferiority and codependency on the former colonies of Europe (occidentalism) in matters of doctrine, institutions, and social practices."[39] Out of this milieu, voices from the margins have risen to challenge such Western theological hegemony. R. S. Sugirtharajah—a

---

35. Jae Woong Ahn, "The Christian Conference of Asia and the Ecumenical Movement," *Church Soc.* 92.1 (2001) 8, provides an overview of the organization: "The Christian Conference of Asia, formed in 1957 in Prapat, Indonesia, is the region's first ecumenical organization. Its original name was the East Asia Christian Conference. However, in 1973, the Singapore General Assembly changed that name to the Christian Conference of Asia. It has made significant contributions in the ecumenical movement, especially in the fields of theological thinking, missiological endeavor, sociopolitical involvement, religious-cultural impact, providing leadership development, and more." For a detailed treatment of the organization's history, see Kim Hao Yap, *From Prapat to Colombo: History of the Christian Conference of Asia, 1957–1995* (Hong Kong: Christian Conference of Asia, 1995).

36. Christian Conference of Asia, "The Confessing Church in Asia and Its Theological Task," in *What Asian Christians Are Thinking: A Theological Source Book*, ed. Douglas J. Elwood (Quezon City, Philippines: New Day, 1978), 43.

37. Christian Conference of Asia, "Confessing Church in Asia," 44.

38. Christian Conference of Asia, "Confessing Church in Asia," 44. In a subsequent statement, the organization further develops some of the convictions posited in the first. See Christian Conference of Asia, "Confessing the Faith in Asia Today," in *What Asian Christians Are Thinking: A Theological Source Book*, ed. Douglas J. Elwood (Quezon City, Philippines: New Day, 1978), 7–15.

39. Oscar García-Johnson, "Transoccidentalism and the Making of Global Theology," in *Theology Without Borders: An Introduction to Global Conversations*, by William A. Dyrness and Oscar García-Johnson (Grand Rapids: Baker Academic, 2015), 9.

leading scholar in the field of postcolonial biblical studies—explains, "Third World theologies, especially the liberation variety, arose as a way of critiquing the universalistic, Eurocentric, individualistic, patriarchal and anti-environmental tendencies of . . . Western theologies."[40]

Scholars of the Majority World have also reacted against such imposition in the field of postcolonial biblical and theological studies— a discourse that seeks to counter various assumptions and aspects of Western theology. On a broader level, postcolonialism is, according to Sugirtharajah, "a resistant discourse which tries to write back and work against colonial assumptions, representations, and ideologies."[41] In the field of biblical and theological studies, such resistance has meant, in part, writing back against the universalization of Western theology and its hermeneutical methods.[42] Notable scholars in this developing field

---

40. R. S. Sugirtharajah, *Postcolonial Reconfigurations: An Alternative Way of Reading the Bible and Doing Theology* (St. Louis, MO: Chalice, 2003), 123; Simon Kwan, "Theological Indigenisation as Anti-Colonialist Resistance: A Chinese Conception of the Christian God as a Case Study," *Stud. World Christ.* 15.1 (2009) 22–50, points out that theological indigenization in China arose in the midst of anti-imperialist sentiment and served as a subtle means of resistance to Western missionary theology. Peter White, "Decolonising Western Missionaries' Mission Theology and Practice in Ghanaian Church History: A Pentecostal Approach," *Skriflig* 51.1 (2017) 2, similarly asserts that certain "African theologies came into African church history as a way of decolonizing the Western missionaries' mission theology and approach."

41. R. S. Sugirtharajah, *Asian Biblical Hermeneutics and Postcolonialism: Contesting the Interpretations* (Maryknoll, NY: Orbis, 1998), x.

42. Gene L. Green, "The Challenge of Global Hermeneutics," in *Global Theology in Evangelical Perspective: Exploring the Contextual Nature of Theology and Mission*, ed. Jeffrey P. Greenman and Gene L. Green (Downers Grove, IL: IVP Academic, 2012), 59–63.

of study include Sugirtharajah,[43] Pui-lan Kwok,[44] Fernando Segovia,[45] and Musa W. Dube.[46]

Within and beyond these avenues of critique lies substantial literature in which those from the Majority World react against Western theology and its imposition. For instance, Joseph Mitsuo Kitagawa,[47] Juan Luis Segundo,[48]

---

43. R. S. Sugirtharajah, ed., *Voices from the Margin: Interpreting the Bible in the Third World* (Maryknoll, NY: Orbis, 1995); Sugirtharajah, *Asian Biblical Hermeneutics*; R. S. Sugirtharajah, ed., *Vernacular Hermeneutics* (Sheffield: Sheffield Academic, 1999); Sugirtharajah, *Postcolonial Reconfigurations*; R. S. Sugirtharajah, *Postcolonial Criticism and Biblical Interpretation* (New York: Oxford University Press, 2009); R. S. Sugirtharajah, *The Bible and Asia: From the Pre-Christian Era to the Postcolonial Age* (Cambridge, MA: Harvard University Press, 2013).

44. Pui-lan Kwok, *Introducing Asian Feminist Theology* (Sheffield: Sheffield Academic, 2000); Pui-lan Kwok, *Discovering the Bible in the Non-Biblical World* (Eugene, OR: Wipf & Stock, 2003); Pui-lan Kwok, *Postcolonial Imagination and Feminist Theology* (Louisville, KY: Westminster John Knox, 2005); Pui-lan Kwok et al., eds., *Teaching Global Theologies: Power and Praxis* (Waco, TX: Baylor University Press, 2015).

45. Fernando F. Segovia, *Decolonizing Biblical Studies: A View from the Margins* (Maryknoll, NY: Orbis, 2000); Stephen D. Moore and Fernando F. Segovia, eds., *Postcolonial Biblical Criticism: Interdisciplinary Intersections*, The Bible and Postcolonialism (New York: T&T Clark International, 2007); Fernando F. Segovia and Mary Ann Tolbert, eds., *Teaching the Bible: The Discourses and Politics of Biblical Pedagogy* (Minneapolis: Fortress, 2009); Fernando F. Segovia and Mary Ann Tolbert, eds., *Reading from This Place*, Vol. 1: *Social Location and Biblical Interpretation in the United States* (Minneapolis: Fortress, 1995); Fernando F. Segovia and Mary Ann Tolbert, eds., *Reading from This Place*, Vol. 2: *Social Location and Biblical Interpretation in Global Perspective* (Minneapolis: Fortress, 2000).

46. Musa W. Dube, *Postcolonial Feminist Interpretation of the Bible* (St. Louis, MO: Chalice, 2000); Musa W. Dube and R. S. Wafula, eds., *Postcoloniality, Translation, and the Bible in Africa* (Eugene, OR: Pickwick, 2017); Musa W. Dube, "The Subaltern Can Speak: Reading the Mmutle (Hare) Way," *J. Afr. Relig.* 4.1 (2016) 54–75.

47. Joseph M. Kitagawa, *The Christian Tradition: Beyond Its European Captivity* (Philadelphia: Trinity Press International, 1992).

48. Juan Luis Segundo, *The Liberation of Theology*, trans. John Drury (Maryknoll, NY: Orbis, 1976); Juan Luis Segundo, *The Liberation of Dogma: Faith, Revelation, and Dogmatic Teaching Authority* (Eugene, OR: Wipf & Stock, 2004).

Hermeneutical Community

Choan-Seng Song,[49] Anri Morimoto,[50] John Mbiti,[51] and Aloysius Pieris[52] have all attempted to move, in various ways, beyond Western theological control over Christians and churches outside the West. Such Majority World theological literature, though not uniform in every respect, coalesces in its rejection of theological imposition and desire to promote local theologizing. As John Parratt summarizes, "Third World theologies have rejected the theological agendas which are set by the West. The agenda must come from the context in which Christians live; since Christians outside of Europe and North America must live their faith in different historical, political, socio-economic and religious contexts, the kinds of questions they are asking will be substantially different from those in the Western tradition."[53]

In light of the breadth of such literature, and in order to analyze Majority World reactions to Western theological imposition in a succinct manner, the remainder of this chapter will delimit its scope to several particular theological organizations, both ecumenical and evangelical.[54] First, it will examine formal theological discourses within the Ecumenical Association of Third World Theologians. Second, it will examine formal theological discourses within several related evangelical organizations,

---

49. Choan-Seng Song, "From Israel to Asia: A Theological Leap," in *Third World Theologies*, ed. Gerald H. Anderson and Thomas F. Stransky, Mission Trends 3 (New York: Paulist, 1976), 211–22; Choan-Seng Song, *Third-Eye Theology: Theology in Formation in Asian Settings* (Cambridge, UK: Lutterworth, 1980); Choan-Seng Song, "Let Us Do Theology with Asian Resources," *East Asia J. Theol.* 3.2 (1985) 202–8; Choan-Seng Song, "Theological Transpositions," *Theol. Cult.* 7.2 (2010) 10–28.

50. Anri Morimoto, "Contextualised and Cumulative: Tradition, Orthodoxy and Identity from the Perspective of Asian Theology," *Stud. World Christ.* 15.1 (2009) 65–80; Anri Morimoto, "Asian Theology in the Ablative Case," *Stud. World Christ.* 17.3 (2011) 201–15.

51. John S. Mbiti, "Theological Impotence and the Universality of the Church," in *Third World Theologies*, ed. Gerald H. Anderson and Thomas F. Stransky, Mission Trends 3 (New York: Paulist, 1976), 6–18.

52. Aloysius Pieris, *An Asian Theology of Liberation* (Maryknoll, NY: Orbis, 1988).

53. John Parratt, "Introduction," in *An Introduction to Third World Theologies*, ed. John Parratt (New York: Cambridge University Press, 2004), 8.

54. By delimiting this particular study to the following organizations and their bodies of literature, this chapter will be able to engage important discourses (e.g., liberation theology, postcolonial theological studies) as well as some of the most significant theological voices of the Majority World (e.g., Gustavo Gutiérrez, Leonardo Boff, René Padilla, John Mbiti, Byang Kato, Aloysius Pieris, Tite Tiénou, Bong Rin Ro, etc.). Also, because the following organizations incorporate diverse ecclesial and theological orientations, this delimitation allows this chapter to engage a wide variety of reactions within a narrower body of literature.

including the Latin American Theological Fraternity, the Association of Evangelicals of Africa, and the Asia Theological Association.

VOICES FROM THE MAJORITY WORLD

Majority World scholars and practitioners from across the theological spectrum have voiced concerns about the precedent of Western theological imposition. Representing one side of the spectrum is the Ecumenical Association of Third World Theologians (EATWOT), a network of scholars and practitioners around the world—mostly from Latin America, Africa, and Asia—seeking to develop contextually relevant theologies in collaboration with one another. The organization is ecumenical not in the sense of being a branch of the conciliar movement of the WCC, but rather in the sense that it includes Catholic, Protestant, and Orthodox members. From its beginning in the late 1970s, its stated aim was "the continuing development of Third World Christian theologies which will serve the church's mission in the world and witness to the new humanity in Christ expressed in the struggle for a just society."[55] The organization has since served as a platform for Majority World voices to develop progressive theologies in response to confronting realities like poverty and marginalization.[56]

EATWOT came into existence as new political and theological currents were churning across the world. Politically, two events helped set the stage for EATWOT's emergence: the meeting of leaders from newly independent African and Asian countries in Bandung, Indonesia, in 1955, and the establishment of the United Nations Conference on Trade and Development. M. P. Joseph posits, "The euphoria related to these two events enjoyed such a high momentum that the communities in the third world believed that a new dawn was imminent in global economic

---

55. EATWOT, "Communiqué: Ecumenical Dialogue of Third World Theologians, Dar es Salaam, August 12, 1976," in Torres and Fabella, *The Emergent Gospel: Theology from the Underside of History: Papers from the Ecumenical Dialogue of Third World Theologians, Dar es Salaam, August 5–12, 1976*, ed. Sergio Torres and Virginia Fabella (Maryknoll, NY: Orbis, 1978), 273.

56. M. P. Joseph, *Theologies of the Non-Person: The Formative Years of EATWOT* (New York: Palgrave MacMillan, 2015), ix–x, explains, "How do the poor and the marginalized, in the midst of their struggle to survive, encounter God? Manifold ramifications of doing theology arise from asking the questions that the invisible nonbeings silently raise through their life and death, questions that have marked a radical transposition in theological inquiry."

and political relations, in which the hegemony of the Western colonizers would be effectively checked."[57] Bandung 1955 exerted a formative influence on EATWOT, particularly in how it promoted Third World countries as subjects of their own lives and histories, rather than mere objects of Western foreign policy.[58] This recovery of local agency in political affairs inspired a similar such recovery in the realm of theology, which EATWOT exemplified—so much so that one European observer described EATWOT as the "Bandung of Theology."[59]

New theological currents also factored into the formation of EATWOT. In both Roman Catholicism and Protestant ecumenical circles, new vistas were opening for engaging with the realities facing Majority World churches. Within Catholicism, Vatican II loosened (to a degree) Rome's hierarchical grip over theology, recognizing a role for the laity and those outside the West to participate in theological reflection and expression.[60] Further, it called for the church to seek transformation among communities across the world, particularly among the poor. Similarly within the Protestant ecumenical movement, theologians and churches began embracing a broader understanding of the nature and scope of God's saving activity. At the WCC's world mission conference at Bangkok in 1973, ecumenicals moved to define salvation holistically and emphasized the need for the church to stand in solidarity with the poor and marginalized of the world.[61] According to Joseph, there thus existed in both circles a "shifting of the locus of attention from Europe to the third world."[62]

57. Joseph, *Formative Years of EATWOT*, 4–5.

58. Joseph, *Formative Years of EATWOT*, 4–5, 10. Joseph maintains, "By rejecting the Cold War deterrence theory, Bandung solidarity refused to accept the ethical claims of absolutism and created space for the poor and the marginalized nations to exercise their ability to make political and security decisions by themselves. . . . Bandung affirmed that each group of people should have the freedom to decide what is best for them, without any interference from other nations and groups" (13).

59. M. D. Chenu, quoted in Joseph, *Formative Years of EATWOT*, 5; K. C. Abraham, ed., "Latin American Report," in *Third World Theologies: Commonalities and Divergences: Papers and Reflections from the Second General Assembly of the Ecumenical Association of Third World Theologians, December 1986, Oaxtepec, Mexico* (Eugene, OR: Wipf & Stock, 2004), 78, notes, "When [Third World] countries became independent and their people started a process of self-development, Christians also stated their right to think their faith in the context of their own cultural and religious traditions."

60. Joseph, *Formative Years of EATWOT*, 17–18.

61. "Salvation and Social Justice: Report of Section II of the Bangkok Conference," *Int. Rev. Mission* 62.246 (1973) 198–201.

62. Joseph, *Formative Years of EATWOT*, 4.

In addition to theological changes taking place within the established structures of Catholicism and Protestant ecumenism, new theological developments and discussions from the Majority World also paved the way for EATWOT's emergence. Already in the 1960s, Latin American theologians were seeking to break away from Western theological assumptions to develop more contextually relevant theologies.[63] It was during this time that liberation theology began to take shape.[64] Then in the early 1970s, as liberation theology attracted more adherents, several important intercontinental dialogues occurred to facilitate conversation among those who sought to liberate theology from Western hegemony. These included a 1973 meeting in Geneva between Latin American and Black theologians, a 1974 conference in Ghana of Black American and African theologians, and a 1975 meeting in Detroit called "Theology in the Americas," in which Black theologians of the United States and Latin American liberation theologians recognized their common ground.[65] These developments and dialogues served as forerunners to the emergence of EATWOT, which would provide an ongoing forum for such theological activity.

EATWOT formally came into existence in 1976 at a conference of theologians in Dar es Salaam, Tanzania. The conference drew twenty-two participants—mostly from Latin America, Africa, and Asia—who sought to examine together the socio-political and ecclesial contexts of the three continents, and what bearing those might have on theological method.[66] The theologians present, seeing value in learning from one another, decided to form EATWOT as a platform for ongoing dialogue and theological development. Its stated objectives were as follows:

1. Sharing with one another the present trends of interpretation of the gospel in the different Third World countries, particularly bearing in mind the roles of theology in relation to other faiths and ideologies as well as the struggle for a just society;

---

63. Joseph, *Formative Years of EATWOT*, 20. Among these were Gustavo Gutiérrez and Emilio Castro.

64. For an overview of the historical development of liberation theology, see Enrique D. Dussel, "The Political and Ecclesial Context of Liberation Theology in Latin America," in Torres and Fabella, *The Emergent Gospel: Theology from the Underside of History*, 175–92.

65. Joseph, *Formative Years of EATWOT*, 24–29.

66. EATWOT, "Communiqué," 272.

2. Promoting the exchange of theological views through writings in the books and periodicals of Third World countries;

3. Promoting the mutual interaction between theological formulation and social analysis;

4. Keeping close contacts as well as being involved with action-oriented movements for social change.[67]

The organization was thus born with a progressive vision for theology.[68]

From its inception, EATWOT recognized and reacted against Western theological imposition. In its first formal statement, it noted that Western missionaries often thought of "the spread of Christianity in terms of transplanting the institutions of their Euro-American churches.... The liturgy was imported wholesale from the 'mother churches'; so were the ecclesiastical structures and theologies."[69] Further, it added,

> The theologies from Europe and North America are dominant today in our churches and represent one form of cultural domination. They must be understood to have arisen out of situations related to those countries, and therefore must not be uncritically adopted without our raising the question of their relevance in the context of our countries. Indeed, we must, in order to be faithful to the gospel and to our peoples, reflect on the realities of our own situations and interpret the word of God in relation to these realities. We reject as irrelevant an academic type of theology that is divorced from action. We are prepared for a radical break in epistemology which makes commitment the first act of theology and engages in critical reflection on the praxis of the reality of the Third World.[70]

67. EATWOT, "Communiqué," 273.

68. Joseph, *Formative Years of EATWOT*, 1–3, highlights the various narratives of EATWOT's emergence, including events leading up to the 1976 Dar es Salaam conference, and involving figures like Oscar K. Bimwenyi, François Houtart, Star Lourdusami, and Enrique Dussel. Joseph posits, "In these accounts EATWOT is presented as emerging from a collective recognition of three factors: first, the economic and theological conditions of the world's poor were the same across countries and cultures; second, the silencing of the theological voice of the world's poor was linked to their exploitation, if not, perhaps, a cause of their exploitation; and third, theologians in the third world needed to create solidarities across borders that may eventually strengthen their determination to make the poor the subjects of theology" (3).

69. EATWOT, "Final Statement: Ecumenical Dialogue of Third World Theologians, Dar es Salaam, August 12, 1976," in Torres and Fabella, *The Emergent Gospel: Theology from the Underside of History*, 265–66.

70. EATWOT, "Final Statement: Ecumenical Dialogue," 269.

EATWOT thus understood its own life as a movement against Western theological imposition.[71]

Although this rejection of Western hegemony over theology did not necessarily entail a wholesale dismissal of Western theology itself, it did involve confrontation. In his opening address to the 1976 Dar es Salaam conference, Sergio Torres noted that the gathering was actually part of a wider, ongoing conversation among First and Third World churches, and his hope was that Christians from both might ultimately labor together in theological formulation.[72] Nevertheless, he asserted, "There exists a healthy reaction against the theological imperialism of the West. We believe that we should face this challenge in a spirit of faith and solidarity—but with truth and honesty. This assumes dialogue and, at times, confrontation."[73]

Among those to confront such North Atlantic theology were voices from Latin America. The Latin American EATWOT constituents consciously sought to subvert Western theology by developing new methods for theological reflection in context. As Peruvian Catholic theologian Jorge Alvarez Calderón claimed, "This reflection, this theology, marks a break with the stage that had gone before, in which theological reflection was presented in terms of a European problematic."[74] EATWOT

---

71. Joseph, *Formative Years of EATWOT*, 42, explains, "In the mission fields, churches were made to believe that [Western] theological constructs were eternal and universal. Adherence to these theological models helped reproduce a system of domination that legitimized the alienation of the poor and the marginalized from any control of the construction of theological nuances. One of the primary concerns of EATWOT theology was to break away from these inherited models of theology." This breaking away became more pronounced in the years after EATWOT's inception. Following its initial conference in 1976 at Dar es Salaam, EATWOT held a series of regional conferences to explore relevant theological issues in its main constituent continents: Latin America (São Paulo, 1980), Africa (Accra, Ghana, 1977), and Asia (Sri Lanka, 1979). After spending several years exploring the theological contexts of each continent in depth, EATWOT again organized several broader general meetings in 1981 (New Delhi), 1983 (Geneva), 1986 (Oaxtepec, Mexico), and 1992 (Nairobi). The theological discourses stemming from these conferences demonstrate the frustrations that many Majority World scholars and practitioners maintained with Western theology and its presumed universality.

72. Sergio Torres, "Opening Address," in Torres and Fabella, *The Emergent Gospel: Theology from the Underside of History*, 5.

73. Torres, "Opening Address," 5.

74. Jorge Alverez Calderón, "Peruvian Reality and Theological Challenges," in Fabella and Torres, *Irruption of the Third World: Challenge to Theology: Papers from the Fifth International Conference of the Ecumenical Association of Third World Theologians, August 17-29, 1981, New Delhi, India*, ed. Virginia Fabella and Sergio Torres

members from Latin America also sought to subvert the normative universality projected by Western theology. The Latin American Report at the 1986 intercontinental EATWOT conference thus stated, "Western theology tries to establish limits on the theologies of the Third World, forgetting that it itself is limited. It pretends to be universal, and for this, it is dominating."[75]

The African EATWOT contingent was no less critical. In the words of Engelbert Mveng, a Jesuit priest and executive secretary of the Ecumenical Association of African Theologians, they were reacting against "the masters of Western theology, those who have monopolized Christ, the church, the faith, and the world, and who claim that their discourse is universal."[76] African EATWOT contributors decried the ongoing domination that such Western theological discourses exhibit. One African report group asserted,

> The influence of Western theology throughout the continent is a fact of its colonial heritage and cultural domination by the West. All, or nearly all, African theologians have been trained in Western schools of theology. . . . [T]he official churches exercise a perduring, albeit uneasy, control over the thought and work of African theologians. African churches are often faithful copies of their missionary mother churches, and so they refuse to admit any theological thought, any ecclesiology, or any church law but that developed in and sent here from the West.[77]

As a result, the African churches have relied on "second-hand theology"[78] and thus "pray with borrowed words, think by proxy, and operate by way of Rome, Paris, London, and other European capitals."[79]

(Maryknoll, NY: Orbis, 1983), 46.

75. Abraham, "Latin American Report," 77.

76. Engelbert Mveng, "A Cultural Perspective," in *Doing Theology in a Divided World: Papers from the Sixth International Conference of the Ecumenical Association of Third World Theologians, January 5–13, 1983, Geneva, Switzerland*, ed. Virginia Fabella and Sergio Torres (Maryknoll, NY: Orbis, 1985), 72.

77. African Report Group, "In Search of an African Theology," in Fabella and Torres, *Irruption of the Third World: Challenge to Theology*, 59–60.

78. Kwesi A. Dickson, "The African Theological Task," in Torres and Fabella, *The Emergent Gospel: Theology from the Underside of History*, 46.

79. Ngindu Mushete, "The History of Theology in Africa: From Polemics to Critical Irenics," in *African Theology en Route: Papers from the Pan African Conference of Third World Theologians, December 17–23, 1977, Accra, Ghana*, ed. Kofi Appiah-Kubi and Sergio Torres (Maryknoll, NY: Orbis, 1979), 26; Patrick A. Kalilombe, "Self-Reliance of the African Church: A Catholic Perspective," in Appiah-Kubi and Torres, *African Theology*

POST-COLONIAL REJECTION

African EATWOT members thus sought to counteract and move beyond this situation marked by Western theological control. Without mincing words, Ghanaian theologian Kofi Appiah-Kubi described this agenda: "We demand to serve the Lord in our own terms and without being turned into Euro-American or Semitic bastards before we do so. That the Gospel has come to remain in Africa cannot be denied, but now our theological reflections must be addressed to the real contextual African situations. Our question must not be what Karl Barth, Karl Rahner, or any other Karl has to say, but rather what God would have us do in our living concrete condition."[80] Many others joined Appiah-Kubi in this quest to wrest local theology out of Western hands and root it in African soil.[81]

---

en Route, 42–43, added, "The final obstacle to selfhood is that the local churches in the mission lands have usually been nothing more than imitations or 'carbon-copies' of the older churches of Europe and America. The way these mission churches exist and operate is not primarily determined by the local situation: the culture of the people, their needs, their problems, their possibilities, or their outlook. No, it is first and foremost pre-determined by customs, prescriptions, and standards coming from elsewhere, and only secondarily from the exigencies of the locality. 'The church' in the missions is usually a foreign reality, an imported organization."

80. Kofi Appiah-Kubi, "Preface," in Appiah-Kubi and Torres, *African Theology en Route*, viii. Similarly, Mushete, "History of Theology in Africa," 30, added, "Against the proponents of some universally valid theology, Africans assert the right and the necessity of a specifically African theology. Such a theology would not necessarily be based on Greek philosophy and its confreres. It would accept and value the cultural and religious experience of the African peoples, and it would attempt to reply to the questions raised by African society and its contemporary development."

81. See Charles Nyamiti, "Approaches to African Theology," in Torres and Fabella, *The Emergent Gospel: Theology from the Underside of History*, 45; Allan Boesak, "Coming In out of the Wilderness," in Torres and Fabella, *The Emergent Gospel: Theology from the Underside of History*, 82–83; Kalilombe, "Self-Reliance of the African Church," 38–45; Gabriel M. Setiloane, "Where Are We in African Theology?," in Appiah-Kubi and Torres, *African Theology en Route*, 61–62; Mercy Amba Oduyoye, "The Value of African Religious Beliefs and Practices for Christian Theology," in Appiah-Kubi and Torres, *African Theology en Route*, 110; Desmond Tutu, "The Theology of Liberation in Africa," in Appiah-Kubi and Torres, *African Theology en Route*, 168; Allan Boesak, "Liberation Theology in South Africa," in Appiah-Kubi and Torres, *African Theology en Route*, 169–75; Bonganjalo Goba, "Emerging Theological Perspectives in South Africa," in Fabella and Torres, *Irruption of the Third World: Challenge to Theology*, 20; Engelbert Mveng, "Third World Theology—What Theology? What Third World? Evaluation by an African Delegate," in Fabella and Torres, *Irruption of the Third World: Challenge to Theology*, 217–21; Emílio J. M. de Carvalho, "Hope for the Future," in Fabella and Torres, *Irruption of the Third World: Challenge to Theology*, 276–77; Emílio J. M. de Carvalho, "Opening Statement," in Fabella and Torres, *Doing Theology in a Divided World*, 5–8; Mercy Amba Oduyoye, "Who Does Theology? Reflections on the Subject of Theology," in Fabella and Torres, *Doing Theology in a Divided World*, 143–49; K. C. Abraham, ed., "African Report," in *Third World Theologies: Commonalities and Divergences*, 38–39, 45;

Hermeneutical Community

Highlighting the spread of cultural Western Protestantism, Gabriel M. Setiloane, a theologian from South Africa, maintained, "For almost two centuries this type of Christianity has been passed on to this continent. We have imbibed it all. But now can we not claim the right to expand our insights and interpretations? Our insights and our interpretations are based on our African-ness."[82] The African EATWOT contingent sought to do just that—expand theological reflection to incorporate African contexts, exigencies, and agents.

Asian members of EATWOT aimed for similar outcomes. According to Indonesian theologian Henriette Katoppo, "For a long time, Asians were denied the right to theologize. . . . Christianity had been the 'white man's burden' for so long that European and American theologians did not accept independent Asian thinking."[83] Tissa Balasuriya, a Catholic Priest in Sri Lanka, similarly highlighted this monopoly over local theological conviction:

> As we reflect from an Asian point of view on the Christian message and activities present and manifest today, we are struck by the extent to which they have been molded by the experience and interests of the Western peoples, especially of Europe and North America. While the Christian Faith is presented as universal, valid for all times and meant for all peoples, the content of its dogma, moral teachings, and pastoral orientations has been largely related to the needs, concerns, and interests of the Western peoples. It is as if Christianity, having converted Europe, had in turn been made European.[84]

Bernadette Mbuy-Beya, "African Spirituality: A Cry for Life," in *Spirituality of the Third World: A Cry for Life: Papers and Reflections from the Third General Assembly of the Ecumenical Association of Third World Theologians, January, 1992, Nairobi, Kenya*, ed. K. C. Abraham and Bernadette Mbuy-Beya (Eugene, OR: Wipf & Stock, 2005), 66.

82. Setiloane, "Where Are We?," 61.

83. Henriette Katoppo, "Asian Theology: An Asian Woman's Perspective," in *Asia's Struggle for Full Humanity: Towards a Relevant Theology: Papers from the Asian Theological Conference, January 7-20, 1979, Wennappuwa, Sri Lanka*, ed. Virginia Fabella (Maryknoll, NY: Orbis, 1980), 140.

84. Tissa Balasuriya, "Towards the Liberation of Theology in Asia," in Fabella, *Asia's Struggle for Full Humanity: Towards a Relevant Theology*, 18. An Asian Report Group, "Toward a Relevant Theology in Asia," in Fabella and Torres, *Irruption of the Third World: Challenge to Theology*, 75, added, "The official mainstream theology of the Christian churches everywhere in Asia continues to be a Western theology, focusing on Western concerns, with little relevance to the Asian reality. Such a theology is alienated and alienating. Asian theology needs to be liberated from the colonial bondage in which it finds itself."

POST-COLONIAL REJECTION

This Western orientation of theology in Asia led to the perception that the church throughout the continent is but "an extension of Western Christianity," according to Jesuit priest Aloysius Pieris of Sri Lanka.[85]

The Asian constituency thus advocated a break from the Western theological tradition. For them, the concerns that occupied Western theology remained irrelevant and meaningless in the contexts of Asia.[86] Sebastian Kappen, a Jesuit priest in India, asserted, "Asian theology will come into its own only when it will have made a complete break with the rationalism of Western theology and evolve a new manner of discourse about God drawn from the life of God and God's people."[87] Balasuriya added, "For Asian Christians to be able to relate meaningfully to the aspirations of our people and the vast changes taking place in our countries we need a freeing of our theology from many categories imposed from abroad and by the past. For theology to be helpfully connected with struggle for liberation, theology itself needs to be liberated."[88] Merely parroting theology from the West or using it as a starting point for Asian theological expression did not suffice for Asian EATWOT contributors.[89]

The emerging theologies of EATWOT thus constituted a clear rejection of the historic pattern of Western theological imposition. Such theologies, according to one EATWOT report,

> are a sign of rebellion and protest against white domination and against models of Western development. At the same time they express a new way of doing theology arising from painful experiences. They are signs of the vitality of the young churches of the Third World. For this reason, they are not a carbon copy of European theology. They accept and recognize the authentic tradition of Jesus of Nazareth kept alive in the different

---

85. Aloysius Pieris, "Towards an Asian Theology of Liberation: Some Religio-Cultural Guidelines," in Fabella, *Asia's Struggle for Full Humanity: Towards a Relevant Theology*, 89.

86. Virginia Fabella, "An Introduction," in Fabella, *Asia's Struggle for Full Humanity: Towards a Relevant Theology*, 4; Peter K. H. Lee, "Between the Old and the New," in Torres and Fabella, *The Emergent Gospel: Theology from the Underside of History*, 133; Balasuriya, "Towards the Liberation," 26–27.

87. Sebastian Kappen, "Orientations for an Asian Theology," in Fabella, *Asia's Struggle for Full Humanity: Towards a Relevant Theology*, 119–20.

88. Balasuriya, "Towards the Liberation," 20.

89. Carlos H. Abesamis, "Doing Theological Reflection in a Philippine Context," in Torres and Fabella, *The Emergent Gospel: Theology from the Underside of History*, 120; Carlos H. Abesamis, "Faith and Life Reflections from the Grassroots in the Philippines," in Fabella, *Asia's Struggle for Full Humanity: Towards a Relevant Theology*, 128.

confessions, but at the same time they want to reread the event of the Jews in the light of their own scriptures and native religious experiences.[90]

According to José Míguez-Bonino, a Methodist theologian from Argentina, EATWOT focused from the beginning on "the affirmation of a 'theological autonomy' in relation to the theologies of the Northern world."[91] And while such autonomy does not necessarily entail a complete break from all Western theological influence, it does entail a recognition that no theology—Western or otherwise—can lay claim to universal normativity. Accordingly, EATWOT constituents refused to "submit *a priori* to tests of excellence developed in the academic theologies of the West."[92]

Instead, Majority World ecumenicals argued that true theology is praxiological in method, holistic in nature, liberative in effect, relevant in content, and local in its derivation. Their explicit aim was to promote such theology in the face of ongoing Western theological dominance. According to Torres, "They are engaged in a new way of doing theology. Western theology has read the Scriptures from the point of view of the dominant classes. The new theologies of the oppressed and the poor are looking at the event of Jesus Christ from their oppression and poverty, from the underside of history."[93] Thus EATWOT voices from across the world sought to counter Western theology both in principle and in light of its perceived weaknesses.

Yet the ecumenicals of EATWOT were not the only ones to react against Western theological imposition; in the latter half of the twentieth century, evangelicals of the Majority World likewise began speaking out.[94] Although they represented the other side of the theological spectrum

90. Abraham, "Latin American Report," 78.

91. José Míguez-Bonino, "Commonalities: A Latin American Perspective," in Abraham, *Third World Theologies: Commonalities and Divergences*, 110.

92. Míguez-Bonino, "Commonalities," 110.

93. Sergio Torres, "Introduction," in Torres and Fabella, *The Emergent Gospel: Theology from the Underside of History*, xv.

94. The three evangelical organizations which this chapter highlights stated the nature of their evangelical conviction in a joint statement called "The Seoul Declaration: Toward an Evangelical Theology for the Third World," *Int. Bull. Mission Res.* 7.2 (1983) 64–65, which declares, "We all hold fast to the authority and inspiration of the Bible and to basic evangelical convictions such as the personality, love and justice of our sovereign God, the uniqueness and finality of Jesus Christ, the regenerating and empowering of the Holy Spirit, the sinfulness and lostness of the human race, the need for repentance and faith, the life and witness of the church, and the personal return of Jesus Christ" (65).

and did not share every theological conviction with those associated with EATWOT, they did express misgivings about the precedent of theological imposition from the West as well as the character and outworking of Western theology.

Such evangelical objections surfaced clearly in a 1982 consultation in Seoul, Korea, the central theme of which was "Theology and the Bible in Context." Three major evangelical theological organizations jointly arranged the conference. These included the Asia Theological Association, the Theological Commission of the Association of Evangelicals in Africa, and the Latin American Theological Fraternity.[95] The conference drew eighty-two delegates from the Majority World, including a number of prominent evangelical theologians.[96] Their expressed aim was fourfold:

1. to deal with theological issues which are vitally related to evangelism and church growth and which are common to churches in developing countries,

2. to exchange ideas and information among evangelical theologians in the Third World,

3. to encourage fellowship and cooperation among these theologians, and

4. to learn from the church in Korea, which is one of the fastest growing churches in the world.[97]

In pursuit of these aims, they also articulated critiques of the Western theological enterprise.[98]

---

95. For an overview of the history of the Latin American Theological Fraternity, see Ruth Padilla DeBorst, "Who Sets the Table for Whom? Latin American Congresses on Evangelization (CLADE) 1969–2012: A Revision with Eyes Toward a New Celebration," *J. Lat. Am. Theol.* 5.2 (2010) 107–24. For a history of the Association of Evangelicals in Africa, see Christina M. Breman, *The Association of Evangelicals in Africa: Its History, Organization, Members, Projects, External Relations, and Message* (Zoetermeer, Netherlands: Boekencentrum, 1996). For an overview of the history of the Asia Theological Association, see Saphir Athyal, "A History of the Asia Theological Association," in *Voice of the Church in Asia: Report of Proceedings, Asia Theological Association Consultation (Hong Kong, December 27, 1973—January 4, 1974)*, ed. Bong Rin Ro (Singapore: Asia Theological Association, 1975), 1–6.

96. "Seoul Declaration," 64. Prominent evangelicals offering papers for the conference included Samuel Escobar, René Padilla, Tokunboh Adeyemo, and Tite Tiénou.

97. "Seoul Declaration," 64.

98. The main evangelical source for this chapter—the 1982 Seoul consultation—was an isolated event that was not part of a wider, overarching organization encompassing theologians across the world. Accordingly, the main evangelical literature which the

This conference—including its associated essays and final statement—thus serves as a valuable source for discerning evangelical reactions to Western theological imposition. Unlike the situation on the ecumenical side, where EATWOT served as an encompassing forum for theological voices across the world, there existed no prominent global organization within which Majority World evangelical theologians could discourse. The Seoul consultation therefore became a significant opportunity for evangelicals across Latin America, Africa, and Asia to meet and discuss theology from their respective contextual viewpoints.

Evangelicals, though less sharply critical of the Western tradition than the ecumenicals of EATWOT, have likewise rejected the precedent of Western theological imposition. For example, without dismissing Western theology wholesale, Latin American evangelicals have critiqued the imposition of such theology on churches throughout the continent.[99] Emilio Antonio Núñez C., a theology professor in El Salvador, asserted that paternalistic missionaries had long held to "the idea that the evangelicals in [Latin American] countries are still children unable to think for themselves and to express the Christian faith within the context of their own culture."[100] This attitude had resulted in long-standing theological immaturity in Latin America. Núñez claimed, "We suffer from a theological underdevelopment which is largely a product of our theological dependence. Many of us have been satisfied to receive an imported theology."[101] J. Norberto Saracco, former Lausanne International deputy director for Latin America, added that despite evangelicalism's general adherence to the doctrine of the priesthood of all believers, "what

---

following sections explore is understandably less than that which stems from the many gatherings of EATWOT. In cases where salient critiques remain underdeveloped in the literature published from the Seoul consultation, this section draws from other sources associated with the constituent organizations in order to present such critiques more fully.

99. Evangelicals of Latin America have expressed appreciation for aspects of Western theology from which they have benefited and recognized the need to interact with historical theology in a constructive manner. For example, see Ismael E. Amaya, "A Latin American Critique of Western Theology," *Evang. Rev. Theol.* 7.1 (1983) 17; Emilio Antonio Núñez C., "Towards an Evangelical Latin American Theology," *Evang. Rev. Theol.* 7.1 (1983) 124; C. René Padilla, "Biblical Foundations: A Latin American Study," *Evang. Rev. Theol.* 7.1 (1983) 86; Valdir Steuernagel, "The Relevance and Effects of European Academic Theology on Theological Education in the Third World," *Evang. Rev. Theol.* 27.3 (2003) 205.

100. Núñez C., "Towards an Evangelical," 123.

101. Núñez C., "Towards an Evangelical," 123.

happens in practice is that evangelicals and Protestants are obligated to assimilate and accept a pre-packaged theology."[102]

Such theological parroting remained unacceptable to evangelicals of Latin America. Núñez thus claimed that Latin American theology "should not be merely a reproduction made by Latin Americans of evangelical thought imported from other latitudes."[103] This kind of theological reproduction, moreover, inhibits local ownership of the faith.[104] Ismael Amaya of Argentina therefore argued, "It is the responsibility of each generation to declare the Christian truth within the framework of its own time and situation."[105] This sentiment found wide support among evangelicals of Latin America.

According to René Padilla, theologian from Ecuador, Majority World Christians must opt for developing their own theological convictions. He declared, "Christians in the Two-thirds World have two alternatives before them when they come to the question of their theological task: (1) to import a brand of Western theology such as Reformed, Dispensationalist, Lutheran and at most making an attempt to 'adapt' it to their own situation; (2) to struggle for a theology with a biblical foundation in the wider sense—a theology resulting from the merging of the horizons of their own situation and the horizons of the biblical text."[106] For Padilla and other Latin American evangelicals, the second alternative is the only legitimate way forward. He explained, "If theology is to have a biblical foundation, nothing less than a contextual approach to Scripture will do. Western theologies may be useful as preliminary expositions of the Christian faith, but must never be allowed to take the place of Scripture."[107] In other words, Latin American Christians must take up the hermeneutical task and bring God's word to bear on the issues confronting them in their contexts—something which Western theology has largely failed to do.

102. J. Norberto Saracco, "Search for New Models of Theological Education," in *New Alternatives in Theological Education*, ed. C. René Padilla (Oxford: Regnum, 1988), 34.

103. Núñez C., "Towards an Evangelical," 130.

104. C. René Padilla, "The Contextualization of the Gospel," in *Readings in Dynamic Indigeneity*, ed. Charles H. Kraft and Tom N. Wisley (Pasadena, CA: William Carey Library, 1979), 301, stated, "Have we made the Christian faith really *ours* while we limit ourselves to repeating doctrinal formulas worked out in other latitudes?" (emphasis original).

105. Amaya, "Latin American Critique," 26.

106. Padilla, "Biblical Foundations," 85–86.

107. Padilla, "Biblical Foundations," 86.

African evangelicals took up a similar stance. According to ma Djongwé Daïdanso of Chad, "African Christian theologians rightly feel that, so far, they have lived a theology which they have not reflected on by themselves, but which the missionaries thought for them and brought 'ready baked' from their homes."[108] Tite Tiénou, theologian from Burkina Faso, similarly declared, "Theology as we experience it in Africa is basically of European origin. It may at best have been recooked in Africa, or maybe only rewarmed."[109] Western theology has thus dominated the life of the African church, which has in turn decried this precedent as a form of paternalism.[110]

One factor contributing to such foreign theological imposition in Africa was the power that foreign agencies maintained. Tiénou explained, "The theological task facing evangelicals in Africa is very complicated because mission agencies and denominations, by allocation of money and other means of power, seek to foster their own brands of theology in our continent.... The continued real power of foreign Christian agencies is indeed one of the factors which contribute to our junior-partner mentality in African Christianity."[111] Tiénou contended that the proliferation of Western theological education contributed much to the African church's dependence on Western theology. From his perspective, "The Western ethos of theological education in Africa is accentuated by the large number of foreigners teaching in the continent's theological institutions.... The models of theological education in Africa as well as the people who implement them contribute, sadly, to the theological void in the continent."[112]

Evangelicals of Africa thus sought a day in which the African church would no longer remain beholden to the West for its theological convictions. In this regard, Tiénou posited, "The most pressing challenge

---

108. ma Djongwé Daïdanso, "An African Critique of African Theology," *Evang. Rev. Theol.* 7.1 (1983) 66.

109. Tite Tiénou, *The Theological Task of the Church in Africa*, 2nd rev. and exp. ed., Theological Perspectives in Africa 1 (Achimota, Ghana: Africa Christian Press, 1990), 46.

110. Billy K. Simbo, "An African Critique of Western Theology," *Evang. Rev. Theol.* 7.1 (1983) 32, added, "On the mission field, western theology has tended to be very paternalistic. It has failed to adapt to life situations and often makes unreasonable demands on people, rewarding only those who break away from their culture and become 'westernized.'"

111. Tiénou, *Theological Task*, 41.

112. Tite Tiénou, "Indigenous African Christian Theologies: The Uphill Road," *Int. Bull. Mission. Res.* 14.2 (1990) 76.

for evangelical theology in Africa is the requirement to serve fully the needs of Christians and churches in Africa without being an appendix to Western or other theologies and also without being an exotic mixture of Christianity and African cultures or religions. Ultimately, African Christian theology is not about crafting new doctrines; it is rather about stating the Christian teaching in language and thought forms understandable to Africans in their contemporary situations."[113] Such a task is, according to Nigerian theologian Byang H. Kato, a means of "safeguarding biblical Christianity in Africa," and therefore of great importance.[114]

Like their Latin American and African compatriots, Asian evangelicals had faced the reality of Western theological imposition throughout their continent. Wilson W. Chow, theologian from China, claimed, "What we have inherited, as a result of missionary activities and theological training in the West, are western theological traditions."[115] Ken Gnanakan and Sunand Sumithra, theologians both from India, similarly observed, "Unfortunately, we have still depended on handed down packages of theology which we feel can universally communicate whether in America or Asia."[116] Chinese theologian Jonathan T'ien-en Chao pointed out, similarly to Tiénou, that this reality stemmed largely from the control that Western missionary bodies maintained over local theological education, which remained beholden to Western theological standards.[117]

Over time, evangelicals of Asia challenged this precedent. For Rodrigo D. Tano, theologian from the Philippines, "The situational character of theology . . . indicates that no theological formulations should be transported into another period or culture without creative

---

113. Tite Tiénou, "Evangelical Theology in African Contexts," in *The Cambridge Companion to Evangelical Theology*, ed. Timothy Larsen and Daniel J. Treier (Cambridge, UK: Cambridge University Press, 2007), 221.

114. Byang H. Kato, *Theological Pitfalls in Africa* (Kisumu, Kenya: Evangel, 1975), 181.

115. Wilson W. Chow, "Biblical Foundations: An East Asian Study," *Evang. Rev. Theol.* 7.1 (1983) 102.

116. Ken Gnanakan and Sunand Sumithra, "Theology, Theologization and the Theologian," in *Biblical Theology in Asia*, ed. Ken Gnanakan (Bangalore, India: Theological Book Trust, 1995), 44.

117. Jonathan T'ien-en Chao, "Development of National Faculty for Asian Theological Education," in *Voice of the Church in Asia: Report of Proceedings, Asia Theological Association Consultation (Hong Kong, December 27, 1973–January 4, 1974)*, ed. Bong Rin Ro (Singapore: Asia Theological Association, 1975), 95–98.

Hermeneutical Community

reinterpretation and recontextualizing."[118] In a similar vein, theologian Chris Marantika of Indonesia declared,

> The time has come for Asian theologians to think and to speak about God without depending on other theologians in other parts of the world. Asian theologians should free themselves from the shadows of the post-apostolic writers, from the corruption of medieval scholasticism, and even from the western theology of the Protestant Reformation, as good as it may be. Asian theologians should also stop being the trumpets of western liberalism and neo-orthodoxy.... [T]hey should begin to search the Scriptures, master God's revealed truth, and express it through the vehicle of their oriental thinking. Hard as it may be, this task can no longer be postponed.[119]

For Hwa Yung, bishop emeritus of the Methodist Church in Malaysia, the Asian church should become self-theologizing. He contends, "It must be able to define theologically its own sense of identity in Christ and understanding of the gospel, instead of finding it in some other group of Christians or alien form of Christianity."[120] This task does not necessarily entail a rejection of the Western theological tradition.[121] Rather, it entails direct study of the Scriptures on the part of Asian Christians, without having to go through the Western tradition to do so. As Tano claimed, "Christian communities in the Third World can come to the text directly with their questions, needs and aspirations, and allow the text to speak to them."[122]

---

118. Rodrigo D. Tano, "Toward an Evangelical Asian Theology," *Evang. Rev. Theol.* 7.1 (1983) 157.

119. Chris Marantika, "Towards an Evangelical Theology in an Islamic Culture," in *Biblical Theology in Asia*, ed. Ken Gnanakan (Bangalore, India: Theological Book Trust, 1995), 181.

120. Hwa Yung, "The Integrity of Mission in the Light of the Gospel: Some Reflections from Asian Christianity," *Sven. Mission.* 93.3 (2005) 342.

121. Despite leveling significant critiques at Western theology, Asian evangelical theologians did not generally reject the Western tradition wholesale. For example, Sunand Sumithra, "Towards Evangelical Theology in Hindu Cultures," in *Biblical Theology in Asia*, ed. Ken Gnanakan (Bangalore, India: Theological Book Trust, 1995), 151, claimed, "Not only does the West need the East, and the North need the South, but we from the two-thirds world need our brethren from the one-third world! Evangelical theology in any culture needs henceforth to restate itself in the light of the above inter-contextual factors." See also Chow, "Biblical Foundations," 103; Tano, "Toward an Evangelical Asian Theology," 156.

122. Tano, "Toward an Evangelical Asian Theology," 156.

Ultimately, according to Asian evangelicals, the well-being of the church in Asia rests, in part, on this local theological task. Gnanakan and Sumithra explained, "The Church in Asia today will only be able to stand against opposing forces both from inside and outside, only as it manifests maturity in theology and theologisation."[123] Saphir Athyal of India thus declared, "We should not shut ourselves in certain straight-jacket theologies manufactured by certain developments in the Church in the west generations ago. We should endeavor to develop true Asian Biblical scholarship by struggling with the task of proper exegesis and application of the Bible, standing under its final authority in all matters relating to belief and life."[124] In other words, the imposition of Western theology will not suffice for churches in the Majority World. With this general sentiment, ecumenicals and evangelicals across the world readily agree, a fact to which the frequency and similarity of the forgoing claims testify.

ARGUMENTS AGAINST THEOLOGICAL IMPOSITION

Beyond the more general critiques noted above, though, Majority World voices on both sides of the theological spectrum have expressed specific misgivings with Western theology and its imposition on local believers and churches across the world. Several such critiques come to the fore in literature associated with EATWOT and the various evangelical organizations that helped formulate the Seoul Declaration. Significant among these critiques are a rejection of (1) theological dualism, (2) theological disengagement from relevant social issues, (3) theological support for injustice, (4) theological method, and (5) a precedent of denying theological agency to locals—all of which Majority World theologians view as besetting the Western theological enterprise. Although not every one of these contentions received equal treatment among ecumenical and evangelical literature explored here, there does appear an underlying unity in perspective in most cases.

Against Western Theological Dualism

One of the most clear and consistent critiques of Western theology from the Majority World concerns its dualistic nature. EATWOT voices

---

123. Gnanakan and Sumithra, "Theology, Theologization and the Theologian," 39.
124. Athyal, "History of the Asia Theological Association," 1.

across Latin America, Africa, and Asia have leveled this critique. Beatriz Melano Couch, a theology professor in Argentina, explained regarding Western theology, "The stress is on the otherworldliness of Christianity and on a dualism expressed in a strict differentiation between world and church, body and soul, worldly and spiritual matters, evil and the kingdom of God (interpreted in eschatological terms as the kingdom to come in the other life, or in the other world)."[125] Such dualism leads to an individualistic and moralistic understanding of conversion and also tends to dislodge new believers from their cultural heritage—because it belongs to the material world. "In summary," Couch posited, "the new converts do not belong to this world, which is under the power of evil; therefore they do not associate with the people 'of the world,' nor with politics and social matters, which are considered 'dirty business' in the realm of evil."[126] Couch believed that such dualism remained a formative and unfortunate influence on the church in Latin America.[127]

Pablo Richard, theologian from Chile, discerned roots of such theological dualism in the early history of Western civilization. He claimed, "From its origins in Hellenistic and Greco-Latin civilization, passing through colonial Christendom and into its modern liberal development, Western civilization has been based on a distinction between soul and body; it has asserted that the soul must have dominion over the body—ultimately showing contempt for the body."[128] This theoretical framework helped to legitimize Western colonial conquest of the New World. As a notorious example of this legitimation, Richard pointed to Juan Ginés de Sepúlveda, who claimed that Western domination over "uncultured and inhuman" barbarians of the New World was both for their own good and in keeping with Natural Law. Sepúlveda asserted, "It is . . . right, by natural law, that matter should obey form, the body the soul, appetite reason, brute beasts human beings, the wife her husband, children a father, the imperfect the perfect, the worse the better, for the universal good of all things."[129] Richard noted that in response to such

---

125. Beatriz Melano Couch, "New Visions of the Church in Latin America: A Protestant View," in Torres and Fabella, *The Emergent Gospel: Theology from the Underside of History*, 194.

126. Couch, "New Visions of the Church," 195.

127. Couch, "New Visions of the Church," 211.

128. Pablo Richard, "A Theology of Life: Rebuilding Hope from the Perspective of the South," in Abraham and Mbuy-Beya, *Spirituality of the Third World: A Cry for Life*, 105.

129. Juan Ginés de Sepúlveda, *Tratado Sobre las Justas Causas de la Guerra Contra*

dualistic claims, many in the Majority World endeavor to "subvert this Hellenistic-Western-colonial framework."[130]

This dualistic theological framework led to a devaluation of material life in this world, according to EATWOT voices. Ngindu Mushete, theology professor in Zaire, asserted, "Fashioned on the basis of a dualistic anthropology, this particular theology ran the dangerous risk of disregarding the concrete, historical dimension of the integral salvation brought by Christ."[131] Kodwo E. Ankrah, a theologian from Ghana, added, "The message was expressed in terms that gave the impression that what really mattered was eternal life, and, therefore, what really counted most was to lead a life that prepared us for eternal life."[132] In other words, because of its dualistic nature, Western Christianity tended to be apolitical, focusing more on eternal, transcendent matters than on concrete historical transformation.[133]

EATWOT constituents also discerned a reductionistic view of evangelism within this dualistic theological framework. According to them, the work of evangelization ought to be concerned with more than just the salvation of individual souls. Orlando P. Carvajal, theologian from the Philippines, asserted that within the dualistic theology of the North Atlantic, however,

> salvation becomes a private, individual affair in the worst sense of the term. If the human body is material, then it is worthless and meaningless. It can only be the source of evil. Only the soul, which belongs to the spiritual world, has value. It is the source of good in people. Hence the object of salvation is the soul. The church, therefore, as the society entrusted with human salvation, can only be responsible for the soul. It is not to meddle in politics and economics because these are considered secular, material, and have relevance only to the body.[134]

---

los Indios, quoted in Richard, "Theology of Life," 105.

130. Richard, "Theology of Life," 105.

131. Mushete, "History of Theology in Africa," 24.

132. Kodwo E. Ankrah, "Church and Politics in Africa," in Appiah-Kubi and Torres, *African Theology en Route*, 157.

133. Goba, "Emerging Theological Perspectives," 24; Frank Chikane, "Spirituality of the Third World: Conversion and Commitment," in Abraham and Mbuy-Beya, *Spirituality of the Third World: A Cry for Life*, 176.

134. Orlando P. Carvajal, "The Context of Theology," in Torres and Fabella, *The Emergent Gospel: Theology from the Underside of History*, 106–7.

Ronaldo Muñoz, a Catholic theologian from Chile, yet argued, "Authentic evangelization is a proclamation of, and a radical impetus to, liberation for human beings and concrete peoples. This liberation is not just within each individual or aimed solely at the salvation of the individual's soul. It is meant to cover the totality of human and societal life. It is not solely aimed at complete fulfillment and happiness in the eschatological future; it is to be operative right now, generating a new human being and a new society in history."[135] For Muñoz and others within EATWOT, the church must labor to liberate not just what is spiritual (i.e., human souls), but also what is concrete and historical (i.e., human society).

Western theological dualism was not only incompatible with the prevailing worldviews in the Majority World, it was also out of step with authentic Christianity, according to EATWOT constituents.[136] South African theologian Allan Boesak, from the Dutch Reformed tradition, maintained, "Blacks detest the way western theology has departmentalized life and brought into our thinking the western dualistic pattern of thought—which is completely foreign to the biblical mentality and to African traditional thought."[137] Far from diverting Christians away from the material realm and its social and political dimensions, authentic Christianity presses them in to that concrete historical arena to promote liberation and wholeness of life. Boesak explained, "When we believe in Jesus Christ it does not make us immigrants out of history. In fact it places us right back within the world, in the middle of history, and that is the place where we have to proclaim his name."[138]

In sum, EATWOT discerned within the Western theological tradition an unwarranted disjunction between the sacred and the secular.

---

135. Ronaldo Muñoz, "Ecclesiology in Latin America," in *The Challenge of Basic Christian Communities: Papers from the International Ecumenical Congress of Theology, February 20–March 2, 1980, São Paulo, Brazil*, ed. Sergio Torres and John Eagleson (Maryknoll, NY: Orbis, 1981), 151.

136. Oduyoye, "Value of African Religious Beliefs," 111–12, noted that in African thought, there is a "sense of *wholeness of the person*," which contradicts the dualism of Western theology. She believed theological contributions from Africa can serve as a corrective to such dualism. Takatso Mofokeng, "Response from South Africa," in Abraham and Mbuy-Beya, *Spirituality of the Third World: A Cry for Life*, 138, also highlighted the "unacceptability of duality" for Africans. Regarding the incompatibility of dualism with Christianity, Abesamis, "Faith and Life Reflections," 131, argued that the concern of biblical faith "is not just the salvation of the soul for heaven but of total persons, societies, nations, and the whole of creation for total life."

137. Boesak, "Coming In," 82.

138. Boesak, "Liberation Theology in South Africa," 175.

Western theology tends to bifurcate reality into separate spiritual and material realms, while focusing predominantly on the former as the locus for true Christian spirituality.[139] It dwells largely on the vertical dimension of the Christian faith (i.e., the spiritual relationship between God and humanity) while neglecting its horizontal dimensions (i.e., the gospel's communal and social aspects), according to EATWOT voices.[140] An Asian EATWOT report aptly summarized the ecumenical view: "Human life is no longer just a period of trial to be rewarded or punished in an afterlife; it has value in its own terms and opposes whatever is dehumanizing in this life. Salvation is no longer simply eternal bliss and beatific vision for the disembodied soul in heaven above, but a new world of justice, resurrection, and life in a future that challenges us to make something of that future actual today."[141] Thus, in contradistinction to the dualism they perceived in Western theology, EATWOT members advocated a theology that is more holistic in its understanding of salvation and Christian witness—one that makes liberative praxis part and parcel of the Christian life.[142]

Evangelicals of the Majority World similarly critiqued such dualism within the Western theological tradition. According to René Padilla, "The individualism that characterizes Western culture has clouded the social dimension of the Gospel in the eyes of the majority of Christians in the Western world."[143] Regarding the aforementioned incompatibility between theological dualism and worldviews of the Majority World, Tokunboh Adeyemo, theologian from Nigeria, claimed, there is "no dichotomy between the sacred and the secular to the African mind."[144]

---

139. Carvajal, "Context of Theology," 103–8.

140. Balasuriya, "Towards the Liberation of Theology," 24, posited, "Since a good deal of theological thinking is individualistic in orientation, the social aspects of the kingdom of God, sin, conversion, and salvation are neglected. Sometimes these social aspects are considered merely human, humanitarian, horizontal, and natural as if they were not related to the spiritual, to God."

141. Asian Report Group, "Toward a Relevant Theology," 74, emphasis original.

142. See also D. S. Amalorpavadass, "The Indian Universe of a New Theology," in Torres and Fabella, *The Emergent Gospel: Theology from the Underside of History*, 148; Samuel Rayan, "Theological Priorities in India Today," in Fabella and Torres, *Irruption of the Third World: Challenge to Theology*, 36; Mary John Mananzan, "Response from the Philippines," in Abraham and Mbuy-Beya, *Spirituality of the Third World: A Cry for Life*, 182–83; Jon Sobrino, "The Witness of the Church in Latin America," in Torres and Eagleson, *The Challenge of Basic Christian Communities*, 163, 181.

143. Padilla, "Contextualization," 291.

144. Tokunboh Adeyemo, "The African Church and Selfhood," *Evang. Rev. Theol.*

Moreover, such a dichotomy remains at odds with biblical Christianity. Washington Padilla, another theologian from Ecuador, argued, "God's Word views life as a totality; in it there is no artificial separation between spiritual life and physical life, private life and social life, religious life and secular life."[145]

While ecumenicals critiqued those who overemphasized the spiritual side of this duality, evangelicals have criticized the way modern liberal theology demythologizes the spiritual side. In this regard, Asian evangelicals have been especially critical of Western theology's subservience to the Enlightenment—a seventeenth- and eighteenth-century philosophical movement in Europe. Yung explains, "Western Christianity, at least among the more educated, in the twentieth century has been largely controlled by a naturalistic and mechanistic view of the world. Within such a worldview, the supernatural tends to be rejected, whether it is about miracles, demons or, ultimately, God. This worldview is largely rooted in the Enlightenment with its narrow empiricism and skeptical rationalism."[146] According to Han Chul-Ha, theologian from South Korea, modern Western theology capitulated to this rationalism and opted to reinterpret core tenets of Christianity accordingly instead of embracing the literal teaching of the Scriptures.[147] South Korean theologian Kim Ki-Hong thus declared, "The Bible as the traditional source of truth gradually lost its authority as the ultimate truth, and the scientific method based on discovery of natural laws through experimental research became a new foundation of truth."[148] Asian evangelicals have decried such theological domestication and captivity to the Enlightenment.[149]

5.2 (1981) 41.

145. Washington Padilla, "Non-Formal Theological Education," in *New Alternatives in Theological Education*, ed. C. René Padilla (Oxford: Regnum, 1988), 130.

146. Yung, "Integrity of Mission," 328–29. Yung also notes, "The western worldview tends to be dualistic, separating soul and body, spirit and matter," (343); see also Lorenzo Bautista et al., "The Asian Way of Thinking in Theology," in *Biblical Theology in Asia*, ed. Ken Gnanakan (Bangalore, India: Theological Book Trust, 1995), 124.

147. Han Chul-Ha, "An Asian Critique of Western Theology," *Evang. Rev. Theol.* 7.1 (1983) 34, 44–45. In view here for the author were theologians like Karl Barth, Paul Tillich, Friedrich Schleiermacher, Albrecht Ritschl, Pierre Teilhard de Chardin, Rudolf Bultmann, Wolfhart Pannenberg, and Jürgen Moltmann.

148. Kim Ki-Hong, "Key Theological Issues in Asia: Influence of Modern Western Theology in the Asian Church," in *Biblical Theology in Asia*, ed. Ken Gnanakan (Bangalore, India: Theological Book Trust, 1995), 92.

149. Yung, "Integrity of Mission," 343–44.

For modernists in the wake of the Enlightenment, the natural world assumes priority of importance, while the supernatural, spiritual world recedes to the background, if acknowledged at all. Chul-Ha explained, "The modern scientific worldview created a secularistic spirit, and so modern man has lost scope of the larger world beyond the visible world."[150] Western theology has not escaped the influence of this bifurcated outlook on reality.[151] Yung thus contends, "Asian Christians must begin to learn to read and understand the Bible from within their own contexts, shorn of dualistic and Enlightenment presuppositions."[152]

Such theological dualism proves harmful to both the church and society, according to Majority World evangelicals. Tiénou believed that the evangelical church in Africa is in danger of succumbing to an ahistorical view of faith, which theological dualism tends to engender. He asserted that threatening "the church's theological task is a lack of proper historical perspective: faith and religion are lived in an a-historical manner and this can lead to all kinds of distortions and misconceptions.... The lack of historical perspective imprisons people in a superficial and shallow faith."[153] Moreover, according to Washington Padilla, when theology separates private life from public life and focuses inordinately on the former, it essentially displaces God from the public sphere, which then falls under the tyranny of false gods.[154]

This theological dualism has also led to distorted understandings of salvation, a claim which EATWOT members similarly made. On one hand, some modernist theologians of the West—influenced by Enlightenment rationalism and empiricism—tended to confine salvation strictly to the material world. Ki-Hong asserted, "They have rejected, or at least ignored, the supernatural realm. Therefore, their concept of salvation is not supernatural but limited entirely to this physical world. The pleasures and benefits of this life are substituted for the reality of spiritual salvation—things such as love, reason, autonomy, freedom, utopia, authentic existence, ethics, peace, equality, affluence, democracy, socialism and so

---

150. Chul-Ha, "Asian Critique of Western Theology," 39.

151. Chul-Ha, "Asian Critique of Western Theology," 37, contended, "Because of the secularistic spirit of modern western theology, it has completely lost the spiritual dimension of the biblical faith, that is, the major portion of the reality in the divine economy of creation and redemption."

152. Hwa Yung, *Mangoes or Bananas? The Quest for an Authentic Asian Christian Theology*, 2nd ed. (Maryknoll, NY: Orbis, 2014), 177.

153. Tiénou, *Theological Task*, 37–38.

154. Padilla, "Non-Formal Theological Education," 131.

on."[155] On the other hand, others in the West have exclusively emphasized the spiritual dimension of salvation. For them, as Yung explains, "Salvation . . . is both other-worldly and individualistic, with primary emphasis given to the redemption of the soul rather than to the reconciliation of the world."[156] Both of these positions stand in contrast to the more holistic outlook common to people of the Majority World.[157]

Thus, both ecumenicals and evangelicals have decried the theological dualism they perceive in the Western tradition. They reject as unwarranted the disjunction between the sacred and the secular and the way that disjunction had led to an overly privatized understanding of the Christian faith.[158] They promote a more holistic theology that recognizes God's reign over both public and private life, a theology which guides Christians to live as faithful witnesses of the gospel in their contexts.

Against Western Theological Disengagement from Society

Implicit in this rejection of Western theological dualism is a recognition that Western theology—despite its often presumed universality—fails to address pertinent cultural and contextual issues facing Majority World Christians. In other words, Western theology imported into other contexts had often been socially disengaged, focused more on the future eschatological kingdom of God than its contemporary outworking in society. According to Peruvian priest and theologian Gustavo Gutiérrez, "Gradually bourgeois Europe unraveled Christianity from its social fabric and made it a personal and private matter."[159] As a result, Western theology often leaves pressing social issues unaddressed.

155. Ki-Hong, "Key Theological Issues in Asia," 93.

156. Yung, "Integrity of Mission," 343.

157. Jonathan Tien-En Chao, "Some Ideas on the Direction of Chinese Theological Development," *Occas. Bull.* 20.6 (1969) 4, with particular reference to the Chinese context, added, "This separation of Christian faith as a personal religious faith from the total demands and implications of the gospel upon their whole life as Chinese within the Chinese cultural context must be regarded as a key factor in deadening the desire for applying the Christian faith to the intellectual life of the Chinese student community."

158. Peter F. Savage, "The 'Doing of Theology' in a Latin American Context," *Theol. Stud. Fellowsh. Bull.* 5.4 (1982) 4–5, maintained, "There is both a division between the saving work of Jesus Christ and his lordship as Sovereign over all things, and a division between the private life of the individual and one's social involvement in society." Along with this belief, "there has been 'escapism' which rationalizes that the world is the territory of Satan and the church is the territory of God" (5).

159. Gustavo Gutiérrez, "Two Theological Perspectives: Liberation Theology and

This lacuna gave rise in Latin America to "base ecclesial communities"—small groups of believers engaging in liberative praxis within contexts of poverty and marginalization.[160] From the perspective of the Latin American EATWOT contingent, these small communities were engaging theologically their own contemporary contexts, which imported Western theology had failed to do. Endorsing such grassroots communities, Leonardo Boff, a Franciscan priest from Brazil, argued, "Faith does not alienate us from the world. It does not create a community set apart from the rest of humanity. It is a leaven of invincible hope and love, which stakes everything on the strength of the weak and on the infallibility of the cause of justice and community. Concern for heaven does not cause us to forget the earth. On the contrary, heaven depends on what we do on earth, what we do with the earth."[161] In other words, Christian faith and theology must be socially engaged; they must not remain relegated to and isolated within a separate spiritual realm, a precedent that tends only to legitimize existing structures of oppression (a claim which constitutes another major critique of Western theology).[162] Rather, true spirituality is holistic, engaging even the material realm in all its specificity.[163]

Other EATWOT contributors have lodged similar critiques. African constituents argued that traditional Western theology does not adequately address the contemporary African situation. This reality derived

---

Progressivist Theology," in Torres and Fabella, *The Emergent Gospel: Theology from the Underside of History*, 231.

160. For an overview of such base ecclesial communities, see Sergio Torres and John Eagleson, eds., *The Challenge of Basic Christian Communities: Papers from the International Ecumenical Congress of Theology, February 20–March 2, 1980, São Paulo, Brazil* (Maryknoll, NY: Orbis, 1981).

161. Leonardo Boff, "Theological Characteristics of a Grassroots Church," in Torres and Eagleson, *The Challenge of Basic Christian Communities*, 143.

162. Sergio Torres, "The Irruption of the Third World: A Challenge to Theology," in Fabella and Torres, *Irruption of the Third World: Challenge to Theology*, 10, posited, "Theology, not only in the North, but also in seminaries and divinity schools of Third World countries, is ahistorical. . . . Because theology is ahistorical it can become part of oppressive systems and structures." See also Luis A. Gómez de Souza, "Structures and Mechanisms of Domination in Capitalism," in Torres and Eagleson, *The Challenge of Basic Christian Communities*, 16, 20–21; Gustavo Gutiérrez, "The Irruption of the Poor in Latin America and the Christian Communities of the Common People," in Torres and Eagleson, *The Challenge of Basic Christian Communities*, 110, 113–14; Boff, "Theological Characteristics of a Grassroots Church," 128–30.

163. Sergio Torres and John Eagleson, eds., "Final Document: International Ecumenical Congress of Theology, February 20–March 2, 1980, São Paulo, Brazil," in Torres and Eagleson, *The Challenge of Basic Christian Communities*, 240–42.

from the fact that Western theology is itself a situational theology—one rooted in and influenced by the context of the North Atlantic world.[164] Western theology thus bore marks of its locale. Charles Nyamiti, a Catholic theologian from Tanzania, explained, "Each theology has its particular themes of preference; and these normally coincide with the values or problems prominent in the community for whom the particular theology is intended."[165] Moreover, Kwesi A. Dickson, Methodist theologian from Ghana, asserted that Western theology—being conditioned by its context—can tend to overlook important theological issues in the Bible. He maintained that Christian doctrine is often "the result of biblical truth being interpreted in a western way, which interpretation may obscure some aspect of the faith or indeed omit reference to matters which are taken account of in the Scriptures, but which are not part of the active, living experience of western theologians."[166]

The social disengagement of Western theology thus led African EATWOT contributors to seek a more authentic and relevant theology for the context of Africa.[167] Boesak, reflecting on the Dutch Reformed tradition in which he grew up, explained, "This tradition never gave us an understanding of ourselves, and, therefore, there was never room to ask the vital kinds of existential and theological questions that should be asked if we want to say something theologically that would make sense of our situation."[168] Thus, African theologians ought not feel constrained to do theology according to the categories and frameworks of the West, as if these were immutable.[169] Rather, according to the African contingent,

---

164. Tutu, "Theology of Liberation," 165, claimed, "All theology is provisional and cannot lay claim to a universal validity, for any relevant theology must accept the scandal of its particularity, which, after all, is the price of its relevance. And no theology can easily transcend the limitations and conditioned-ness of those who theologize."

165. Nyamiti, "Approaches to African Theology," 37.

166. Dickson, "African Theological Task," 49.

167. Boesak, "Liberation Theology in South Africa," 171–72, contended, "It is theological foolishness . . . to say that what is good for the situation in Germany as discovered by a good German Reform theologian is also good for the situation in North America and therefore also good for the situation in South Africa. Each theological concept develops within a particular context, and our theological thinking . . . has everything to do with what we eat and how many times a day we eat, what salary we earn, whether we own a home, whether we live happily with our family, and so on. The situation in which we live, the context in which we live, profoundly influences the way we do our theology."

168. Boesak, "Liberation Theology in South Africa," 169.

169. Dickson, "African Theological Task," 49.

African theology should embrace its context and explain Christian truth in light of and in response to the cultural, political, and socio-economic themes prevalent in Africa.[170]

The Asian EATWOT contingent similarly contested the abstract character of theology emanating from the West. Kappen asserted that theology ought not be "an attempt to flee from the concrete world of praxis to the world of sterile abstractions."[171] In this view, it is not in abstraction that one encounters God or the knowledge of him, but rather in the concrete exigencies of history. However, the Western theological tradition—influenced as it was by Greek philosophy—has tended to dwell on such abstraction. Carlos H. Abesamis, a Jesuit from the Philippines, argued, "Theology cannot stop at reflection. It must lead to action. . . . [O]ur long association with Greek metaphysics has conditioned us to regard theology as abstruse speculation. Now, praxis, analysis, and the faith all conspire to make us see that for theology, too, the point is not to contemplate or explain the world but to change it."[172] Thus, for the Asian contributors, true theology must move away from or at least beyond abstraction to a place in which it catalyzes social change.[173]

This theological disconnect from the exigencies of context and culture was not lost on Majority World evangelicals either. Amaya claimed that North Atlantic theology often failed to deal with social issues in its own continent.[174] Further, the importing of such theology into Latin America by missionaries compounded the disconnect. René Padilla explained,

> Western missionaries have often assumed that their task is simply to extract the message directly from the biblical text and to transmit it to hearers in the "mission field" with no consideration of the role of culture in the whole interpretive process. . . . As a result, in many parts of the world Christianity is regarded as an ethnic religion—the white man's religion. The Gospel has a foreign sound, or no sound at all, in relation to many of the dreams and anxieties, problems and questions, values and

---

170. Nyamiti, "Approaches to African Theology," 36–45.
171. Kappen, "Orientations for an Asian Theology," 110.
172. Abesamis, "Faith and Life Reflections," 135.
173. J. Russell Chandran, "Development of Christian Theology in India: A Critical Survey," in Torres and Fabella, *The Emergent Gospel: Theology from the Underside of History*, 171.
174. Amaya, "Latin American Critique," 24–26.

customs of people. The Word of God is reduced to a message that touches life only on a tangent.¹⁷⁵

As such, Western theology remained disconnected from the social realities with which the Latin American church had to grapple.¹⁷⁶

For Latin American evangelicals, one of the root causes of that disconnect in their continent was a dependence on theological curricula from the North Atlantic. Núñez posited, "We also have curriculum that imitates that found in other latitudes. This is due in part to the problem of our theological dependency. We copy both the theology and the manner in which it is taught. In some cases the curriculum committee has brought to the worktable samples of curricula 'made in U.S.A.,' without taking into consideration the particular needs of the country in which the theological institution fulfills its ministry."¹⁷⁷ According to Valdir Steuernagel, a theologian from Brazil, such curricula remained "out of touch with the life of the church and the challenges of the society."¹⁷⁸ Washington Padilla thus raised the question, "Who determines 'the agenda' (the curriculum) of our theological education: God's Word as the answer to the problems and needs that arise as the people of God in Latin America attempt to accomplish their mission in this continent or some 'agendas' foreign to us and imposed upon us, leaving great gaps in our knowledge of God's Word?"¹⁷⁹ For evangelicals of Latin America, the former should displace the latter as the pattern for theological education.

African evangelicals likewise contended that Western theology did not address the issues that confront African Christians and churches. For Billy K. Simbo, theologian from Sierra Leone, this disengagement from social realities was evident even in the West, as Amaya claimed. He maintained, "Western Christians and their theology have, on the whole,

---

175. C. René Padilla, "The Interpreted Word: Reflections on Contextual Hermeneutics," *Themelios* 7.1 (1981) 23.

176. C. René Padilla, "Evangelical Theology in Latin American Contexts," in *The Cambridge Companion to Evangelical Theology*, ed. Timothy Larsen and Daniel J. Treier (New York: Cambridge University Press, 2007), 268, claimed that for many North American missionaries, "the mission of the church was defined exclusively in terms of 'saving souls' and planting churches. One of the consequences of this view has been the common lack of concern for human needs on the part of evangelical Christians in Latin America."

177. Emilio A. Nuñez C., "The Problem of Curriculum," in *New Alternatives in Theological Education*, ed. C. René Padilla (Oxford: Regnum, 1988), 75–76.

178. Steuernagel, "Relevance and Effects," 206.

179. Padilla, "Non-Formal Theological Education," 126.

failed to apply Christian principles to their societies."[180] Theology in the West remains a matter of intellectual assent, and "does not necessarily produce life-changing commitment."[181] The imposition of such theology in Africa only compounded that problem. According to Daïdanso, as the church spreads throughout the continent, it "is sometimes confronted with social and theological problems specific to Africa which need answers which may not always be apparent in a theology developed for the needs of another people or continent."[182]

Theology must, according to evangelicals of Africa, engage such local contextual issues. Simbo argued, "Our faith *must* confront the issues of our society. Western theology has often lead to an 'Ivory-Tower' mentality among theologians who live in their own world in the clouds while the real world struggles with problems as to what to eat, wear, and drink."[183] More specifically, Kato asserted, "The African problems of polygamy, family structure, spirit world, liturgy, to mention a few, need to be tackled by evangelical African theologians and Biblical answers presented."[184] African evangelicals pushed for such theological engagement with social realities, in part, because they recognized the danger of syncretism should those confronting questions not receive biblical answers. According to Tiénou, the African church "can develop monstrous heresies because of its lack of grappling with the pressing issues."[185] Thus for them, Western theology's failure to address social realities remained unacceptable.

From Asia, evangelicals similarly criticized Western theology's irrelevance to the issues that confront Asian Christians. According to Tano, "Western theology is basically abstract and almost a-historical."[186] This characteristic is one reason that Western theology generally failed to address contextual issues. Yet another is the fact, as noted by others, that Western theology developed from a different set of historical

180. Simbo, "African Critique of Western Theology," 28.
181. Simbo, "African Critique of Western Theology," 30.
182. Daïdanso, "African Critique of African Theology," 66.
183. Simbo, "African Critique of Western Theology," 31.
184. Kato, *Theological Pitfalls in Africa*, 182.
185. Tite Tiénou, "The Church and Its Theology," *Evang. Rev. Theol.* 7.2 (1983) 246; Tokunboh Adeyemo, "Contemporary Issues in Africa and the Future of Evangelicals," *Evang. Rev. Theol.* 2.1 (1978) 7, added, "The theological deficiency of churches in Africa has led to the rise of many sects, heresies, cults and numerous other false movements all over the continent."
186. Tano, "Toward an Evangelical Asian Theology," 156.

circumstances.[187] Bong Rin Ro, theologian from South Korea, explained, "The West has its own theological formulations derived from its own cultural background.... Yet in Asia the historical and cultural background is quite different from that of the West and demands careful attention from Asian Christians to their own cultures in order to make the gospel relevant to their life situation."[188] Ro notes that some of the contextual challenges necessitating biblical reflection in Asia include "Communism, poverty, overpopulation, hunger, suffering, war, demon possession, bribery, cheating, idolatry, ancestor worship, caste system, secularism, and the resurging Asian religions of Buddhism, Islam and Hinduism. Asian theologians must grapple with these issues and produce Asian theology that wrestles with these problems, yet being faithful to the historic teachings of the Scriptures over the centuries."[189] Thus, for these Asian evangelicals and many others across the world, the church must move beyond Western theology and its silence in reference to local exigencies.

Against Western Theological Support for Social Injustice

As an extension of their critique of Western theological dualism and the silence of Western theology in the face of pressing social realties, Majority World voices have maintained that such theology has served to implicitly or explicitly endorse social injustices. Tracing this logic from an evangelical perspective, Simbo noted how theology from the West—focused predominantly on spiritual matters of faith—often fails to affect the lives of Christians. He claimed, "Christian principles do not actually dictate how most of these people live. Rather, secular culture shapes their lives and values. In most cases, western Christianity has generally conformed to secular culture. To a Third World person, this dichotomizing of personality is a major problem. This dichotomy often separates Christianity from western political, economic and social life."[190] As a result, "Western theology either became a silent by-stander or in many instances, such as

---

187. Bong Rin Ro, *Train Asians in Asia: A New Mission Strategy*, Asian Perspective 35 (Taichung, Taiwan: Asia Theological Association, 1987), 11, posited, "Because of the political, economic and cultural differences between Asia and the West, Asian theological students studying in the West often discover that much of what they learn is irrelevant to their own Asian contexts."

188. Bong Rin Ro, "Theological Trends in Asia," *Themelios* 13.2 (1988) 57.

189. Ro, "Theological Trends in Asia," 57.

190. Simbo, "African Critique of Western Theology," 31.

slavery, racism, apartheid, economic and social exploitation and oppression, it was used to justify the status quo."[191]

EATWOT contributors pressed further in their critique. Those from Africa claimed that theology emanating from the West has historically served as ideological support for the oppression of natives. Boesak pointed out that Western theology—being dualistic in nature—had embraced an eschatology which locates Christian hope wholly in the future, thus engendering a "waiting-patiently-upon-the-Lord kind of attitude" that is reticent to challenge contemporary patterns of oppression.[192] This type of eschatology, according to Ankrah, amounts to "an ideological legitimation of the status quo."[193] He posited, "By ignoring this world and its activities, the church indirectly blessed the operative social, economic, and political structures."[194]

The African EATWOT contingent sharply condemned Western theology on this point. Boesak asserted that the Christianity promoted by whites has often been a "racist ideology," a "'slave religion' designed for the oppression of the poor."[195] For Bonganjalo Goba, a theologian from South Africa, Western theology was a "theology of white supremacy," a "theology of oppression that has promoted our systematic dehumanization."[196] Mercy Amba Oduyoye, a Methodist theologian from Ghana, went so far as to claim that the brand of Christianity often promoted by the West "is nothing short of the demonic."[197] Accordingly, African EATWOT members sought to subvert this type of Christianity, believing that theirs maintained a stronger continuity with historic Christian orthodoxy.[198]

191. Simbo, "African Critique of Western Theology," 31.

192. Boesak, "Coming In," 89.

193. Ankrah, "Church and Politics in Africa," 157.

194. Ankrah, "Church and Politics in Africa," 157.

195. Boesak, "Coming In," 76.

196. Bonganjalo Goba, "A Black South African Perspective," in Fabella and Torres, *Doing Theology in a Divided World*, 57–58.

197. Mercy Amba Oduyoye, "Commonalities: An African Perspective," in Abraham, *Third World Theologies: Commonalities and Divergences*, 101.

198. Boesak, "Coming In," 82, asserted that Black and African theology is "an essential correction on traditional western theological thinking." Further, he added, "Liberation theology reclaims the Christian heritage and reinterprets the gospel to place it within its authentic perspective, namely, liberation. In so doing, it questions the historical role of the Christian church, the alliances of the church with 'the powers that be,' and insists on a true church, i.e., a church that takes the liberating gospel seriously" (90).

Hermeneutical Community

Similar contentions came from Asia. Abesamis explained, "We see how the a-historical, individualistic, other-worldly kind of theology of the Christian churches has functioned as a nonliberating factor, giving legitimation to an unjust social order."[199] Indian theologian J. Russell Chandran claimed that stemming from such an interpretation of the Christian faith, "some powerfully organized evangelistic movements use the gospel to support the status quo and keep Christians insensitive or blind to the injustices of political and economic structures."[200] The Asian constituency thus categorically rejected any theology—Western theology included—perceived as an ally of exploitation and accomplice to the undermining of human dignity.[201]

Among evangelicals, Latin American theologians were perhaps the most vocal concerning the notion that Western theology has implicitly sanctioned social injustices. Amaya maintained, "One of the problems with western theology is that because it has developed within the democratic system and it is congenial with it, it has developed a theological 'near-sightedness' which has prevented it from detecting [certain] evils and therefore it has not let its prophetic voice be heard on these issues."[202] This same kind of near-sightedness infiltrated the theological enterprise in Latin America as well and led to theological silence on social justice issues throughout the continent.

Washington Padilla explained that by accepting Western theological dualism—and its concomitant silence on social issues—the Latin American church indirectly legitimated injustice and oppression. He asserted, "One of the most regrettable features of Latin American evangelical Christianity is its wrongly called *apoliticism*. When this apoliticism is critically and historically analyzed, it is discovered that it is simply support for the unjust and oppressive system in which our people live; it is just 'conformity to the world' which has never tried to understand God's Word wholistically and 'has swallowed' one of the most insidious and anti-Christian myths of modern secularism."[203] That myth, ac-

---

199. Abesamis, "Faith and Life Reflections," 134.

200. J. Russell Chandran, "A Methodological Approach to Third World Theology," in Fabella and Torres, *Irruption of the Third World: Challenge to Theology*, 85.

201. See also Balasuriya, "Towards the Liberation," 20, 24; Kappen, "Orientations for an Asian Theology," 114–18; Carvajal, "Context of Theology," 107, 111; Chandran, "Development of Christian Theology," 171; Rayan, "Theological Priorities in India," 34.

202. Amaya, "Latin American Critique," 21.

203. Padilla, "Non-Formal Theological Education," 130.

cording to Padilla, is the dualistic worldview of the Enlightenment that compartmentalizes life instead of treating it holistically. He continued, "In accepting this doctrine of modern secularism, a good part of Latin American evangelical Christianity is simply 'conformed to the world' and consciously or unconsciously gives its support to 'the established order,' no matter how criminal and diabolical it may be."[204]

Thus, both ecumenicals and evangelicals alike trace Western theology's dualistic character to its tacit support for injustices within society. Though EATWOT contributors are more disparaging in their rhetoric, both camps reject this characteristic of the Western theological tradition. They perceive injustice to be an unfortunate status quo in many places across the Majority World and reject any theology which appears—explicitly or implicitly—to endorse that status quo.

Against Western Theological Method

Yet another reason why some in the Majority World have rejected the imposition of Western theology has to do with theological method. Latin American and Asian members of EATWOT were most critical of the Western tradition on this point. Various Latin American contributors advocated a theological method that sought to subvert that of Western theology. First, they perceived much of Western theology as unduly tied to a fixed scriptural text.[205] That is, they argued that God's revelation is not static (i.e., fixed and closed in the text of the Bible), but rather is dynamic—discernible within the concrete events of history. For Carlos Mesters, a Catholic theologian from Brazil, this meant that "the word of God has moved in a certain sense from the Bible to real life."[206] Further, the salvation history of the Bible is not the sole instance of God's salvific activity; rather, the Bible's presentation of God's saving work is merely a "model experience"—an exemplary case in which God works to save and liberate humanity. Following this, Mesters maintained, "Every single people has *its own* history of salvation."[207] For history itself, according to

---

204. Padilla, "Non-Formal Theological Education," 132.

205. J. Severino Croatto, "Biblical Hermeneutics in the Theologies of Liberation," in Fabella and Torres, *Irruption of the Third World: Challenge to Theology*, 162–63; Carlos Mesters, "The Use of the Bible in Christian Communities of the Common People," in Torres and Eagleson, *The Challenge of Basic Christian Communities*, 197–210.

206. Mesters, "Use of the Bible," 208.

207. Mesters, "Use of the Bible," 208, emphasis original. Croatto, "Biblical

Gutiérrez, "is the concrete locale of human encounter with the Father of Jesus Christ."[208]

This claim that God's revelation is ongoing rather than locked into the biblical text is central to Latin American liberation theology.[209] Gutiérrez argued, "God is a liberating God, revealed only in the concrete historical context of liberation of the poor and oppressed."[210] J. Severino Croatto, a Catholic theologian from Argentina, rooted this conviction in the notion that God reveals himself fundamentally through events, prior to any revelation through words.[211] Thus he asked rhetorically, "Is God saying nothing new in the struggles of oppressed peoples, in the processes of liberation, in the contribution of the social sciences to knowledge of human beings, their problems, and their real situations of structural oppression?"[212] Indeed he is speaking through such historical events, per Croatto. He asserted, "There is no closure of God's revelation in history. It is likewise nonsense to pretend to transform the Bible into a closured 'deposit,' from which one need only to 'draw.'"[213]

Second, Latin American EATWOT members criticized Western theology's penchant for highly critical, academic hermeneutical methodologies which focused primarily on past theological meaning. Such methodologies, they believed, remained disconnected from the plight

---

Hermeneutics," 162–63, concurs. He claims, "The Bible is the faith reading of paradigmatic events of salvation history, and the paradigmatic reading of an unfinished salvation history. The Bible, as paradigmatic and normative, does not exclude its own rereading in the light of new events. It is nonsense to think that there will be no more salvation events."

208. Gutiérrez, "Liberation Theology and Progressivist Theology," 248.

209. Concerning the biblical text, the Latin American Report presented at the 1986 EATWOT conference in Oaxtepec, Mexico, states, "The Bible constitutes the great code for reading the oppressions suffered and also the source of inspiration for liberation and life." See Abraham, "Latin American Report," 72.

210. Gutiérrez, "Liberation Theology and Progressivist Theology," 247.

211. Croatto, "Biblical Hermeneutics," 162, maintains, "It is above all a matter of his revealing himself in events, and as he does so, his epiphany ought to generate a hermeneutic process that will produce its word—the faith discourse, in all its modalities and variations, such as prayer, creeds, proclamation, theology, and so on. And this word will be new. It will not simply be 'light shed on' present history from behind (from the biblical text). It will be a seeing of the face of God precisely as he enters the present history of men and women. The Bible orientates the reading of God within the events of the world and teaches us to recognize him as he manifests himself right now—not as a repetition of the past. Human history is constant novelty, and so is the presence of God accompanying it."

212. Croatto, "Biblical Hermeneutics," 162.

213. Croatto, "Biblical Hermeneutics," 163.

of the present poor and marginalized masses.[214] Reacting against these perceived emphases, the Latin American constituency promoted an alternate locus and method for theology.

Opposed to the notion that the knowledge of God rests with those employing critical theological methods, the Latin American EATWOT constituency believed that it is the poor and marginalized of the world who maintain a privileged epistemological and hermeneutical position when it comes to theological reflection.[215] That is, the poor serve as the locus for discerning divine revelation, for it is they who experience firsthand God's revelatory work in the midst of concrete history. Gutiérrez explained, "We are coming to realize in a new way that God is revealed in history and that God is revealed through the poor. It is to them that God's love is revealed. It is they who accept, understand, and proclaim God's message. . . . [They] are not just the privileged addressees of the gospel message. They are also its bearers by the very fact of who they are."[216] For Gutiérrez, the kingdom teaching of Jesus in the Gospel of Matthew underscores the poor's privileged position of understanding and interpreting the word of God. Jesus' teaching ministry commences with a blessing of the poor (Matt 5:3) and concludes with an illustration that one truly encounters Christ by standing in solidarity with the poor

---

214. For example, Croatto, "Biblical Hermeneutics," sought to highlight a way beyond such methodologies, and offered this essay as a philosophical and hermeneutical legitimation of liberation theology and its methodology. He contended, "[A] concern to safeguard the truth of the spiritual sciences has so preoccupied the Western world over these last centuries that the West has concentrated its attention on the literal meaning as the 'historical' one (as the expression 'historical-critical' betrays). This is a form of reductionism and exaggerates the importance of 'the intention of the sacred writer' in the analysis of such or such a passage. Ultimately the danger is that we can turn to the Bible as a 'deposit,' with a closed meaning coinciding with the thought of the redactor, or even of the preredactors of the actual text" (141–42). Further, he argued against the Western theological notion that exegesis can be thoroughly objective in its reading and interpreting the text. He posited, "The exegete's claim to have isolated the objective, *historical*, meaning of the biblical text is illusory" (153). Regarding an overly academic approach to theology, Gustavo Gutiérrez, "Reflections from a Latin American Perspective: Finding Our Way to Talk About God," in Fabella and Torres, *Irruption of the Third World: Challenge to Theology*, 224–25, asserted, "We must avoid an academic theology dissociated from grassroots work, where the 'first act' of theology is taken. . . . Such a dissociation is ruled out, not just because we want to elaborate a committed theology, but even more importantly because we want to develop a discourse on faith that will respond to the real questions raised by the contemporary world and the Christian community living in it."

215. See Torres and Eagleson, "Final Document," 234–38, particularly sections 25, 26, 42, and 43.

216. Gutiérrez, "Irruption of the Poor," 120.

Hermeneutical Community

and acting on their behalf (Matt 25:31–46). Thus, "the teaching of Jesus is framed in a context that moves *from the poor to the poor*.... The poor and the Kingdom are linked realities. It is in their relationship that the Father's gratuitous love is revealed."[217]

Based on these two convictions—that God reveals himself in history and among the poor—theological reflection necessarily starts with praxis—i.e., concrete, liberative action on behalf of and alongside of the poor and marginalized. In other words, because God reveals himself most fundamentally through the concrete events of history, and because God is centrally concerned with the liberation of the poor and oppressed, it stands to reason that one cannot truly theologize without being an active participant in God's contemporary liberative work in society.[218] It is primarily there that God reveals himself—revelation which then becomes the source of all theologizing.[219] Gutiérrez summarized, "Active commitment to liberation comes first and theology develops from it. Theology is critical reflection on and from within historical praxis, and the historical praxis of liberation theology is to accept and live the word of God through faith."[220] Thus theology remains a "second act," one which follows praxis rather than precede it.[221]

By locating God's revelation in the concrete, liberative events of history and urging that theological reflection begin not with the biblical text but rather with liberative praxis in society, the Latin American constituency turned traditional Western theological method on its head. That is, theological method does not flow from theory to action (i.e., orthodoxy to orthopraxy), but from action to theory (i.e., orthopraxy to orthodoxy).

---

217. Gutiérrez, "Irruption of the Poor," 121, emphasis original; Boff, "Theological Characteristics of a Grassroots Church," 135, added, "It is the poor who are the natural bearers of the utopia of God's kingdom. It is they who bear the torch of hope, and the future belongs to them."

218. In fact, the final document from the Latin American continental EATWOT conference stated, "Christ can be encountered only in concrete actions that redeem the poor from their condition of exploitation, oppression, hunger, that is, of being stripped of their human dignity as children of God (Matt 25:31–40)." See Torres and Eagleson, "Final Document," 235.

219. Accordingly then, the social sciences assume an important role in liberation theological method. See Couch, "New Visions of the Church," 206–7; Gutiérrez, "Liberation Theology and Progressivist Theology," 240–41; Croatto, "Biblical Hermeneutics," 165, went so far as to claim, "Are not the social sciences themselves part of God's contextualized message?"

220. Gutiérrez, "Liberation Theology and Progressivist Theology," 247.

221. Gutiérrez, "Reflections from a Latin American," 225–26.

Ultimately, the shifted locus of revelation precipitated this reversal in theological method.

Asian EATWOT constituents also leveled a significant critique against what they perceived as the dominant method for Western theology. First, like their Latin American colleagues, they contested Western theology's tendency to fix the locus of God's revelation in the text of the Bible. According to Balasuriya, "Traditional theology . . . accentuated deduction from first principles known from scripture or an accepted philosophy."[222] Instead, the Asian contingent embraced a more dynamic understanding of revelation—one that isn't exclusively tied to the Bible.[223] D. S. Amalorpavadass, Catholic theologian from India, explained, "The revelation and realization of God's universal plan of salvation for humankind is older than the church; it is wider than the narrow, linear, and limited Judeo-Christian history of four thousand years."[224] Further, he argued, "[God's] presence and action . . . are universally operative and effective both in time and space, hence before the foundation of the institutional church by Christ and outside it too today. Thus the religions of the world and the realities of the temporal order must be viewed as included in God's universal saving plan and its historical fulfillment."[225]

Beyond the Bible, Asian EATWOT constituents posited two major sources of divine revelation—concrete history and ancient religions. Regarding history, they too argued that one encounters God primarily in contemporary liberative movements, for it is in such events that God reveals himself.[226] Indian Jesuit priest Samuel Rayan explained, "Truth is not words and books. Truth is people, their lives, their minds, their self-understanding. If the gospel is directly addressed to the poor, they are the ones likely to have the best grasp of its intent and meaning. It is in their praxis that the gospel becomes an historical force for transformation, and thus acquires historical truth. We do well in going to them to encounter revelation that is being made in their midst."[227] Thus, theological method

---

222. Tissa Balasuriya, "A Third World Perspective," in Fabella and Torres, *Doing Theology in a Divided World*, 199.

223. K. C. Abraham, ed., "Asian Report," in *Third World Theologies: Commonalities and Divergences*, 26, recommended "accepting pluriform sources of revelation."

224. Amalorpavadass, "Indian Universe of a New Theology," 138.

225. Amalorpavadass, "Indian Universe of a New Theology," 138.

226. Kappen, "Orientations for an Asian Theology," 109–10; Rayan, "Theological Priorities in India," 36–37.

227. Samuel Rayan, "Reflections on a Live-In Experience: Slumdwellers," in Fabella, *Asia's Struggle for Full Humanity: Towards a Relevant Theology*, 55.

ought to begin not with a scriptural text, but with praxis—committed action to restore human dignity to the poor and oppressed. According to Abesamis,

> The underlying theological persuasion for making history the source and material of our theological reflection is the conviction-in-faith that the God we believe in is a God who acts and speaks very especially in concrete events in history. God speaks the challenges of today through the sufferings and hopes of people today, and God acts out salvation in and through human efforts and movements towards a more human world. God's salvific acts are concretized in our time and in our Third-World Asia; the Asian theologians will accordingly search there for these raw materials of their theology.[228]

In other words, history is the primary locus for discerning divine revelation.

Additionally, ancient religions like Hinduism and Buddhism serve as sources of divine revelation, according to the Asian EATWOT constituents. This tenet is a logical outgrowth of their presupposition that God decisively reveals himself among and on behalf of the poor. Rayan elaborated, "The poor of Asia are mainly non-Christian. To meet God in the poor is to meet God in the non-Christian poor, to meet God in their beliefs, hopes, and symbols, in their traditions and in their religiousness."[229] Pieris added, "The vast majority of God's poor perceive their ultimate concern and symbolize their struggle for liberation in the idiom of non-Christian religions and cultures. Therefore, a theology that does not speak to or speak through this non-Christian peoplehood is an esoteric luxury of a Christian minority. Hence we need a theology of religions that will expand the existing boundaries of orthodoxy as we enter into the liberative streams of other religions and cultures."[230] In other words, if God's preferential option for the poor is the primary axiom of divine revelation, then one is obliged to recognize such revelation among the poor regardless of their religious persuasion. Thus Asia's ancient religions, many of whose adherents are poor, become valid sources for discerning God's self-revelation.

228. Abesamis, "Faith and Life Reflections," 129.

229. Samuel Rayan, "Reconceiving Theology in the Asian Context," in Fabella and Torres, *Doing Theology in a Divided World*, 140.

230. Aloysius Pieris, "The Place of Non-Christian Religions and Cultures in the Evolution of Third World Theology," in Fabella and Torres, *Irruption of the Third World: Challenge to Theology*, 113–14.

Moreover, among such non-Christian religions, God is universally present and active, according to the Asian constituency.[231] Sri Lankan Anglican bishop Lakshman Wickremesinghe, for example, maintained, "Other nations with their religious cultures are viewed as guided by God, and in the end they share in the inheritance of his kingdom without the intervention of Israel or the Christian church. Adherents of other religions are seen as illuminated by God, who indwells them within their religious commitments."[232] Furthermore their scriptural texts, according to Rayan, have long been "the word of God for Asian peoples" and thus an important resource for theology.[233]

In addition to critiquing the revelational locus common to Western theology, the Asian contingent also subverted its common method of elaborating theology. Along with the Latin American EATWOT group, they maintained that theological method begins not with the fixed text of the Bible—as is the case in much of Western theology—but with committed participation with the oppressed in their struggle for liberation and full humanity.[234] They further affirmed Latin American liberation theology vis-à-vis "social analysis as an indicator of the signs of the times" and "the process of doing theology by action-reflection-action."[235] Accordingly, Rayan asserted, "Asian theology will be a process of discovering and joining God as God lives and works with Asian peoples."[236]

However, not only did Asian EATWOT contributors embrace the subversive theological method of the Latin Americans, they also added to it an emphasis on dialogue with other religious traditions.[237] Such an emphasis makes sense in light of their belief that God reveals himself through non-Christian religions. That is, if other religions are legitimate sources of divine revelation, then one must enter into dialogue with them

---

231. Amalorpavadass, "Indian Universe of a New Theology," 138–43.

232. Lakshman Wickremesinghe, "Christianity in the Context of Other Faiths," in Fabella, *Asia's Struggle for Full Humanity: Towards a Relevant Theology*, 34.

233. Rayan, "Reconceiving Theology in the Asian Context," 133.

234. EATWOT, "The Final Statement," in Fabella, *Asia's Struggle for Full Humanity: Towards a Relevant Theology*, 156; Chandran, "Methodological Approach to Third World Theology," 84.

235. Abraham, "Asian Report," 19.

236. Rayan, "Reconceiving Theology in the Asian Context," 139.

237. Abraham, "Asian Report," 26; Asian Report Group, "Toward a Relevant Theology," 76; Amalorpavadass, "Indian Universe of a New Theology," 143–45; Wickremesinghe, "Christianity in the Context," 31–33; Chandran, "Development of Christian Theology," 166–68.

in order to more fully encounter and discern the message of God for people today. Balasuriya explained, "Interreligious dialogue is considered a *source of theology*. Through it we can know better God's self-manifestation to humanity. It is one means of listening to God, contemplating the divine or the absolute, and participating in the transformative action to realize the design of God for humanity."[238] This approach countered the common theological method of Western theology, which proceeds more narrowly from the biblical text and Christian tradition.

Against Western Denial of Local Theological Agency

Finally, various ecumenical and evangelical voices have criticized the Western theological stance that does not permit locals to contribute to the development of theology and theological conviction. For example, the African EATWOT constituency decried the way in which the imposition of Western theology robbed Africans of their own theological agency. That is, Western missionaries regarded Africans merely as recipients of theology rather than agents of their own convictions. In the wake of this precedent, many African Christians became "tired of being advised,"[239] and "tired of being regarded as objects by their white missionary leaders."[240] Takatso Mofokeng, theologian from South Africa, recognized such relegation in the broader sweep of European expansionism. He argued,

> We have been coerced, albeit partially, into the ideological universe of our subjugators. In cases where that insertion into the world of ideas, thought forms and spiritual experience of our conquerors has succeeded, our absorption has only given us the status of being perpetual junior partners in the perception, definition, development and articulation of that universe of ideas and emotionality. In other words, those of us who have succumbed to that coercion exist and operate as junior Christians in the Christian community that is dominated by their oppressors.[241]

---

238. Tissa Balasuriya, "Divergences: An Asian Perspective," in Abraham, *Third World Theologies: Commonalities and Divergences*, 115, emphasis original.

239. John Mbiti, "The Biblical Basis for Present Trends in African Theology," in Appiah-Kubi and Torres, *African Theology en Route*, 91.

240. Constance Baratang Thetele, "Women in South Africa: The WAAIC," in Appiah-Kubi and Torres, *African Theology en Route*, 150.

241. Mofokeng, "Response from South Africa," 136.

POST-COLONIAL REJECTION

The African contingent rejected this junior partnership status and the control that outsiders have exerted over local theological conviction. Regarding such outside control in South Africa, Boesak explained, "We have lived through a theological tradition that, although it was our own, was really never our own. It has always been controlled by people who also control the political parties, the economic and social situation, our very lives."[242] Underlying such foreign theological control, according to Catholic bishop Patrick A. Kalilombe of Malawi, was an "unconscious but extremely repulsive presumption of 'knowing better than the natives,' knowing what is best for them, or assuming the duty of thinking, feeling, and deciding for them."[243]

To counteract this trend, Manas Buthelezi, a Lutheran bishop in South Africa, called for Africans to become the subjects of their own theology. He characterized the historical approach to theological indigenization in Africa as "ethnographical," an approach by which Western outsiders sought to articulate an indigenous theology that corresponded with their reconstruction of the traditional African worldview.[244] In contrast, Buthelezi argued for an "anthropological approach," in which "the point of departure for indigenous theology is not an ethnographically reconstructed worldview, but African people themselves."[245] In other words, the point of indigenous theology is not to distinguish a local worldview from that of the West as fodder for theological reflection. Such an approach allows outsiders to continue controlling the local theological enterprise.[246]

---

242. Boesak, "Liberation Theology in South Africa," 169.

243. Kalilombe, "Self-Reliance of the African Church," 39.

244. Manas Buthelezi, "Toward Indigenous Theology in South Africa," in Appiah-Kubi and Torres, *African Theology en Route*, 56–65.

245. Buthelezi, "Toward Indigenous Theology," 65.

246. Buthelezi, "Toward Indigenous Theology," 66–67, claimed, "Indigenous theology . . . means more than just a theology that treats as its object 'indigenous' problems and issues, that is, *res indigenae*. . . . The virtually exclusive concern with *res indigenae* tends to locate the problems that indigenous theology has to resolve at the point of the conflict between two worldviews: the European and the African. The human factor recedes to the background, if recognized at all. It then becomes a problem of epistemological entities, of fixed impersonal data—things 'out there,' the body of categories for interpreting the universe. These categories are static entities which form something that can be located, studied, and defined—thanks to ethnography. Hence, [Placide] Tempels can confidently say: 'It is we [Europeans] who will be able to tell them [Africans], in precise terms, what their inmost concept of being is. They will recognize themselves in our words and will acquiesce, saying, "You understand us, you know us completely."'"

Hermeneutical Community

Rather, the point of indigenous theology is for local believers to become the agents of theological reflection in their own contexts. Thus for Buthelezi, local Africans are not "'third person' entities: persons who are talked about and discussed and whose 'minds' are analyzed and systematized, who become important simply because their problems provide fruitful material for specialists."[247] Instead, Africans are to operate in the "first person," as subjects of theology rather than its objects.

A similar critique came from Latin American evangelicals. The theological enterprise in Latin America—following the precedent of the North Atlantic world—had remained overly professionalized and inaccessible to the majority of Christians. René Padilla asserted, "Theology in the West has all too frequently been conceived as an academic discipline in which only a few intellectually qualified experts, who may or may not participate in the life of the church, are able to engage."[248] Amaya thus claimed that Western theology was an "ivory-tower theology."[249] It was a professional enterprise in which scholars maintained a monopoly on interpreting the faith.[250] "As a result," claimed Padilla, "theology is divorced from the church and the Bible is assumed to be a book closed to ordinary people."[251]

Such an approach to theology denied theological agency to Latin American Christians. That is, Latin Americans served merely as receptors of theology rather than producers of it. According to Washington Padilla, this problem stemmed partially from a theological education system characterized by "monologism"—the "unidirectional communication . . . from the preacher or the teacher who knows to the listener or student who does not know."[252] Such a system "does not give the opportunity for the student to discover truth by himself or herself so that he/she may really appropriate God's Word."[253] The theological professional simply relays theological content to passive recipients.

Evangelicals of Latin America balked at such a precedent. For example, Washington Padilla argued that theological education should not just impart information, but should aid students in developing "instruments

---

247. Buthelezi, "Toward Indigenous Theology," 66.
248. Padilla, "Biblical Foundations," 81.
249. Amaya, "Latin American Critique," 24.
250. Saracco, "Search for New Models," 33–34.
251. Padilla, "Biblical Foundations," 81.
252. Padilla, "Non-Formal Theological Education," 128.
253. Padilla, "Non-Formal Theological Education," 124.

of assimilation" by which they can apply theological truth.[254] In other words, theological education is not just about teaching theology; it is also about teaching people to think theologically—to develop in students what Núñez called a "theological mentality."[255] However, according to Núñez, "Foreign models still seek to impose themselves without attempting a profound consideration of the problems and challenges that confront us in Latin America."[256] As a result, the local theological enterprise tended to produce "decontextualized thinkers or theologians"—those who are unable to bring the Scriptures to bear on the issues that confront them in context.[257]

To counteract this pattern, René Padilla advocated a "hermeneutical community" approach to theological development. He explained, "The Christian community is the place where the Word of God finds its home and releases its transforming power.... The gathered community of believers is meant to be the organ through which the Word of God takes up a fresh meaning in relation to a concrete historical situation."[258] It is "the place where the interpretation of Scripture is an ongoing process."[259] Further, Saracco maintained, "It is impossible to understand biblical theology apart from the basic fact that it is a product of a community that experienced God through its own history. The Word of God was revealed to a community, transmitted through a community, and canonized by a community."[260]

In this communal understanding of biblical hermeneutics, local believers have a vital role to play. Far from accepting pre-packaged theological answers and formulae wholesale from the North Atlantic world, Latin American Christians assume the role of theological agents who interpret the Scriptures in community and in relation to their context. Washington Padilla asserted, "All the members of the Body of Christ, no matter how humble or 'ignorant' they may be according to this world's criteria, have

---

254. Padilla, "Non-Formal Theological Education," 125–26. Padilla drew here from the work of Paulo Freire and Jean Piaget.

255. Núñez C., "Problem of Curriculum," 76.

256. Núñez C., "Problem of Curriculum," 76.

257. Núñez C., "Problem of Curriculum," 76.

258. Padilla, "Biblical Foundations," 81.

259. Padilla, "Biblical Foundations," 82. Here Padilla quoted from a previous essay of his entitled "Hermeneutics and Culture: A Theological Perspective," which he delivered at Lausanne's 1978 Willowbank Consultation.

260. Saracco, "Search for New Models," 34.

something to contribute to our understanding of the truth of God."²⁶¹ Such a participatory approach to theology, according to him, "is part of the very essence of the Church and of the function of the diverse gifts . . . of the Spirit."²⁶² Thus for these Latin American evangelicals, and others, the denial of local theological agency to local Christians remained unacceptable, both practically and biblically.

COMMONALITIES OF CONTENTION

The redundancy of the foregoing critiques underscores the depth and breadth of anti-colonial theological sentiment across continents and theological orientations. That is, ecumenicals and evangelicals across the world have offered similar appraisals of Western theology and its imposition on Majority World churches. They have critiqued Western theology's dualism, its irrelevance to social issues outside the West, its service as ideological support—whether explicitly or implicitly—for injustice, and the way its imposition throughout the world has left locals without a voice in theological reflection.²⁶³

---

261. Padilla, "Non-Formal Theological Education," 129.

262. Padilla, "Non-Formal Theological Education," 128–29. Padilla rooted this conviction in the "Rule of Paul" from 1 Cor 14:29.

263. EATWOT, "The Irruption of the Third World: Challenge to Theology: Final Statement of the Fifth EATWOT Conference, New Delhi, August 17–29, 1981," in Fabella and Torres, *Irruption of the Third World: Challenge to Theology*, 197, formally summarized, "Official mainstream theology of the Christian churches continues to be Western, with little relevance to our Third World situation. Though this traditional theology has provided an impetus for personal spirituality and for tremendous missionary expansion, it has been incapable of responding to the social problems of the First World and to the challenges of the Third World. For the Third World, this theology has been alienated and alienating. . . . It has remained highly academic, speculative, and individualistic, without regard for the societal and structural aspects of sin." Evangelicals associated with the 1982 Seoul Conference offered a similar conclusion in their Seoul Declaration. They argued in the "Seoul Declaration," 64, "Western theology is by and large rationalistic, moulded by western philosophies, preoccupied with intellectual concerns, especially those having to do with the relationship between faith and reason. All too often, it has reduced the Christian faith to abstract concepts which may have answered the questions of the past, but which fail to grapple with the issues of today. It has consciously or unconsciously been conformed to the secularistic worldview associated with the Enlightenment. Sometimes it has been utilised as a means to justify colonialism, exploitation, and oppression, or it has done little to nothing to change these situations. Furthermore, having been wrought within Christendom, it hardly addresses the questions of people living in situations characterised by religious pluralism, secularism, resurgent Islam or Marxist totalitarianism. We have recognized that if Evangelical theology is to fulfill its task in the Third World it must be released

POST-COLONIAL REJECTION

Perhaps the key point of difference between Majority World ecumenicals and evangelicals in their appraisal of Western theology lies in the issue of theological method. As previous sections have shown, ecumenicals of EATWOT typically adhered to a liberationist theological method which locates divine revelation in historical events and thus grants primacy to praxis over biblical exegesis in theological reflection. Evangelicals reject such a method. The Seoul Declaration explained,

> We have found that some of the presuppositions, sources, and hermeneutics of theologies such as ethnotheologies, syncretistic theologies and liberation theologies are inadequate. Ethnotheologies are often politically motivated and do little or no justice to the Scriptures. Syncretistic theologies often accommodate biblical truth to cultural variables. Several liberation theologies have raised vital questions which we cannot ignore. But we reject their tendency to give primacy to a praxis which is not biblically informed in the doing of theology. Likewise we object to their use of a socioeconomic analysis as the hermeneutical key to the Scriptures. . . . We unequivocally [sic] uphold the primacy and authority of the Scriptures.[264]

Thus, theological method has become a major source of disagreement between Majority World ecumenicals and evangelicals.

Nevertheless, theologians of the Majority World have been united in their insistence that theological reflection take place from within their contexts rather than being imposed from without. Both ecumenicals and evangelicals outside of the North Atlantic argue that theology must aid Majority World churches as they navigate environments that are far different from the Christendom context which has prevailed for centuries in Europe and North America, where many of Christianity's most prominent theological formulations developed. In order for theology to serve this function, local Christians and churches must embrace the task of theological reflection rather than outsource their convictions to the West and its theological standards.

---

from captivity to individualism and rationalism of Western theology in order to allow the Word of God to work with full power. . . . We urgently need an Evangelical theology which is faithful to Scripture and relevant to the varied situations in the Third World."

264. "Seoul Declaration," 64.

EVALUATION OF THEOLOGICAL IMPOSITION

In reconsidering the precedent of Western theological imposition from an evangelical point of view, several deficiencies of this approach surface. These deficiencies have led some in the direction of missionary moratorium—the withdrawal of Western outsiders from involvement with local churches. Other Majority World voices, however, still recognize value in an ongoing role for missionaries among local believers and churches. Yet even among those who affirm an ongoing role for outsiders, that role in local theological development remains unclear.

Deficiencies

One deficiency of the colonial pattern of theological imposition is that it fails to apprehend the contextual nature of all theology—Western theology included.[265] It often proceeds under an assumption that theology emanating from the West is cross-culturally normative, or "supracultural."[266] In reality, western theological formulations—far from offering universally normative truth—remain conditioned by the categories which they employ. As Donald Grigorenko points out, "We do not begin the task of theological formulation with a conceptual blank slate. We have conceptions of reality and how it works already installed as a kind of conceptual operating system."[267] Throughout much of church history, Western theology has drawn its conceptual categories from the field of philosophy—particularly Greek philosophy.[268] Shenk argues that the use of such

---

265. For a helpful overview of how context shapes theology, see Steve Strauss, "The Role of Context in Shaping Theology," in *Contextualization and Syncretism: Navigating Cultural Currents*, ed. Gailyn Van Rheenen, Evangelical Missiological Society Series 13 (Pasadena, CA: William Carey Library, 2006), 99–128.

266. David J. Bosch, *Transforming Mission: Paradigm Shifts in Theology of Mission* (Maryknoll, NY: Orbis, 1991), 448.

267. Donald Grigorenko, "Reconceiving Theology: Influencing Factors to the Formation of Theology," *Int. J. Front. Missiology* 35.2 (2018) 65.

268. Grigorenko, "Reconceiving Theology," 65, traces this relationship with philosophy from Clement of Alexandria to Augustine to Thomas Aquinas, noting that each drew heavily from the conceptual resources of either Plato or Aristotle. He posits, "Although we can debate the appropriateness of Augustine and Aquinas resting their theology on Platonic or Aristotelian foundations as they did, the fact remains that they did, and theology today owes much of its color to those beginnings with those conceptual resources."

"Hellenic categories and formulations . . . has encouraged development of theology as a set of abstractions organized into doctrinal systems."[269]

Yet not only does the character of theology reflect the context in which it develops, the process of its development also betrays its contextual rootedness. That is because the task of hermeneutics—including exegesis—is inevitably contextual. One exegetes Scripture not from a vacuum, but from specific social, economic, and political circumstances which invariably affect the process.[270] Westerners have been slow to recognize this reality. Harvey Conn maintains, "Often missing in evangelical trumpeting of 'objective' exegesis is an awareness of certain hidden presuppositions, established and reinforced over the centuries. Exegesis has remained essentially a skill exercised by the Westerner, carried on in a basically Western-oriented, monocultural mindset. It moves within a 'Constantinian cultural captivity.'"[271] Thus, from scriptural exegesis to formal expression, the reality of context bears heavily on theology. Accordingly, one must recognize with Bosch that "there is no eternal theology, no *theologia perennis* which may play the referee over 'local theologies.' In the past, Western theology arrogated to itself the right to be such an arbitrator in respect to Third-World theologies."[272] Today that practice appears illegitimate.

A second deficiency in the colonial practice of theological imposition—and one that follows from the first—is that such an approach fails to address issues relevant to the local context. Walls explains, for example, that because many Western theologies operate within an Enlightenment worldview,

> they have nothing useful to say on issues involving such things as witchcraft or sorcery, since these do not exist in an Enlightenment universe. Nor can Western theology usefully discuss ancestors, since the West does not have the family structures that raise the questions. Western theology has difficulty coping with principalities and powers, whether in relation to their grip on the universe or to Christ's triumph over them on the cross. The reason is that it is hard for Western consciousness to treat them

---

269. Shenk, "Theology and the Missionary Task," 296.

270. Bosch, *Transforming Mission*, 423, explains, "Interpreting a text is not only a literary exercise; it is also a social, economic, and political exercise. Our entire context comes into play when we interpret a biblical text. One therefore has to concede that all theology . . . is, by its very nature, contextual."

271. Conn, *Eternal Word*, 185.

272. Bosch, *Transforming Mission*, 456.

as other than abstractions. So Western theology has difficulty in relating personal sin and guilt and structural and systemic evil and sometimes offers different gospels for dealing with each or quarrels as to which has priority.[273]

Mbiti adds that traditional Western theology "is largely ignorant of, and often embarrassingly impotent in the face of, human questions in the churches of Africa, Latin America, parts of Asia, and the South Pacific."[274] This shortcoming leads to yet other deficiencies.

Third, the colonial approach also stunts the maturation of local churches. Such arrested development occurs, in part, because the ready-made theological answers imported from the West often fail to address important local questions, as noted above. Local churches are then left with few resources with which to think about and respond biblically to the contextual issues they face.[275] Moreover, the colonial approach stunts maturation because it inhibits local believers and church leaders from exercising important hermeneutical muscles. According to Hiebert, "A church only grows spiritually if its members learn to apply the teachings of the gospel to their own lives."[276] Failure to entrust this theological task to local churches is therefore to "condemn them to spiritual infancy and early death."[277] René Padilla similarly contends, "This imposition of Western cultural molds, often supported by economic power, cannot but retard indefinitely the growth of indigenous churches, rooted in their own culture and capable of making their own theological contribution."[278] In other words, local believers must learn to bring the Scriptures to bear on the issues that confront them; unfortunately, the colonial pattern of theological imposition prevents them from growing in this ability.

A fourth problem of colonial theological imposition is that it leaves the local Christian community susceptible to syncretism. Finding no answers in Western theology to the real and existential issues that people face, local believers are left to look outside of Christianity and its

---

273. Andrew F. Walls, "Globalization and the Study of Christian History," in *Globalizing Theology: Belief and Practice in an Era of World Christianity*, ed. Craig Ott and Harold A. Netland (Grand Rapids: Baker Academic, 2006), 76.

274. Mbiti, "Theological Impotence," 8.

275. Oosthuizen, *Theological Discussions*, 162–63.

276. Hiebert, *Anthropological Insights*, 185.

277. Hiebert, *Anthropological Insights*, 208.

278. Padilla, "Contextualization," 299.

Scriptures for solutions.[279] There is thus an unfortunate irony to the claim that one should avoid contextualizing theology so as to avoid syncretism. René Padilla explains, "Those who object to the contextualization of the Gospel out of fear of syncretism must take into account that precisely when there is no conscious reflection as to the form that obedience to the lordship of Jesus Christ must take in a given situation, quite easily conduct is determined by the culture instead of being controlled by the Gospel.... [S]yncretism will enter through the back door and product [sic] a 'culture Christianity' that simply assimilates the values of the surrounding culture."[280] In other words, when local Christians have no clear scriptural answers to the contextual questions that confront them, many will resort to the resources of their former worldview to make sense of what lies before them. Thus, even the best of Western theology, when imposed on Majority World Christians, can inadvertently create conditions in which syncretism can easily develop.

Fifth, the colonial approach operates with a suspicion toward the ability of locals to contribute to the task of theology. Conn contends that this suspicion is the result of a blinding ethnocentrism that emerged in the monocultural context in which Reformation theology developed. "This same blindness," he claims, "creates in the missionary and Western-trained churchman an ecclesiastical parochialism that keeps us from seeing any good coming from the Nazareths of the Third World church's struggle with its own culture. It contributes to the fossilization of the progress of dogma at the seventeenth- or eighteenth-century stage."[281] Consequently, local believers and church leaders remain perpetual recipients of theology rather than agents, and they thus fail to grow in their ability to apply biblical truth to the issues they face.

Finally, the colonial approach of controlling local theological conviction serves to perpetuate foreign control over younger churches and

---

279. Dean E. Flemming, *Contextualization in the New Testament: Patterns for Theology and Mission* (Downers Grove, IL: InterVarsity, 2005), 303.

280. Padilla, "Contextualization," 303. He also adds, "If the gospel is not contextualized, the Word of God is a *logos asarkos* (unincarnate word), a message that touches our lives only on a tangent. This is precisely one of the most tragic consequences of the lack of theological reflection among us—that the Gospel still has a foreign sound, or no sound at all, in relation to many of the dreams and anxieties, problems and questions, values and customs in the Third World.... This is why the African, underneath all the doctrinal structure that he accepts at the conscious level, can maintain intact his traditions and customs, whether or not they are congruent with Biblical faith."

281. Conn, *Eternal Word*, 186-87.

inhibit ecclesial indigeneity. As long as churches and believers in other parts of the world remain yoked to Western theological convictions, the West will continue to exert—however implicitly—some measure of authority over Majority World churches, an authority which many in the Majority World deem illegitimate.[282] Moreover, though some missionary outsiders may emphasize the classic marks of indigeneity (i.e., self-supporting, self-governing, self-propagating) in their work, if that logic does not extend to the theological enterprise (i.e., self-theologizing), Majority World churches will fall short of true indigeneity.[283]

Thus, even if this colonial approach derived from altruistic motives (e.g., a concern to safeguard sound doctrine), its clear deficiencies render it untenable. Recognizing these deficiencies, Majority World theologians have cried out for the space to develop their own theologies. As René Padilla poignantly asserts,

> A xeroxed copy of a theology made in Europe or North America can never satisfy the theological needs of the Church in the Third World. Now that the Church has become a world community, the time has come for it to manifest the universality of the Gospel in terms of a theology that is not bound by a particular culture but shows the many-sided wisdom of God. . . . The theological task can no longer be regarded as the task of one sector of the Church; it must be viewed as the task of the whole Church in search for "the unity of faith and the knowledge of the Son of God."[284]

As this chapter has shown, similar claims have reverberated among theologians throughout the world.

Toward Moratorium

What then is one to make of the outsider's role in local theological development? In light of the preceding evaluation and contentions from Majority World ecumenicals and evangelicals, it remains unclear what

---

282. This chapter, in its exploration of ecumenical and evangelical reactions from the Majority World to theological imposition, has shown that many perceive such theological control over local churches as illegitimate.

283. Dean S. Gilliland, "Contextual Theology as Incarnational Mission," in *The Word Among Us: Contextualizing Theology for Mission Today*, ed. Dean S. Gilliland (Dallas: Word, 1989), 13–15.

284. Padilla, "Contextualization," 305.

role, if any, outsiders should play in that task. What is clear is that the colonial pattern of theological imposition is not a viable option, particularly in the wake of post-colonial critiques.[285] There is too much at stake for churches across the world to rely solely on outsourced theological convictions that do not adequately penetrate the worldviews of local believers. Nevertheless, there exists no clear road ahead for outsider involvement in local theological development. Some, reacting strongly to theological paternalism, see little to no role at all for outsiders. Others embrace a more mediating position that recognizes value in outsider contributions. Yet even within such mediating views, the outsider's role remains unclear.

Various spokespersons have moved toward the opposite extreme from colonial theological imposition—the removal of all Westerners from missionary service overseas. For example, Emerito Nacpil, a Methodist bishop from the Philippines, claimed that Western missionaries are often "a symbol of the universality of Western imperialism among the rising generations of the Third World."[286] Thus he asserted, "I believe that the present structure of modern missions is dead. And the first thing we ought to do is to eulogize it and then bury it."[287] The result will be "a charter of freedom and life for the younger churches. In other words, the most missionary service a missionary under the present system can do today in Asia is to go home!"[288]

This view found a home among advocates of Western missionary moratorium. Discussions regarding the withdrawal of missionaries from foreign lands gained momentum in the early 1970s after John Gatu of the Presbyterian Church of East Africa began advocating for such a moratorium.[289] He stated, "I . . . argue that the time has come for the withdrawal of foreign missionaries from many parts of the Third World, that the churches of the Third World must be allowed to find their own identity, and that the continuation of the present missionary movement

---

285. The preceding section has sought to substantiate this claim.

286. Emerito Nacpil, "Mission but not Missionaries," *Int. Rev. Mission* 60.239 (1971) 359.

287. Nacpil, "Mission but not Missionaries," 359.

288. Nacpil, "Mission but not Missionaries," 360.

289. For an overview of the issue of moratorium in missiological circles, see Gerald H. Anderson, "A Moratorium on Missionaries?," *Christ. Century* 91.2 (1974) 43–45; Additionally, see Robert Reese, "John Gatu and the Moratorium on Missionaries," *Missiology* 42.3 (2014) 245–56, who highlights the way different people understood moratorium in different ways.

is a hindrance to this selfhood of the church."²⁹⁰ Others joining Gatu in this conviction included Paul Verghese,²⁹¹ José Míguez-Bonino,²⁹² Patrick A. Kalilombe,²⁹³ and various members of the All Africa Conference of Churches (AACC).²⁹⁴ The Commission on World Mission and Evangelism of the WCC also recognized value in moratorium claims at its 1973 conference at Bangkok on "Salvation Today."²⁹⁵

Although the moratorium issue focused mostly on foreign funding and personnel, which inhibited Majority World churches from authentic growth, the prospect of moratorium also carried theological implications. That is, moratorium meant that Westerners would no longer remain in control over local theology. For instance, the AACC's promotion of moratorium stemmed partially from a desire to see African churches liberated from "theological conservatism, so that we can understand, interpret, apply and experience the message of the Gospel afresh."²⁹⁶ Further, a report from the 1974 AACC Lusaka Assembly, which advocated for moratorium, declared, "Christianity in Africa should not only be self-reliant in finance and personnel, but it should also find both its own 'self-awareness' and its own African expression of the Gospel message."²⁹⁷ In other words, for moratorium advocates, the removal of outsiders was not just a means for Majority World churches to become self-supporting,

---

290. John Gatu, "Missionary, Go Home," *IDOCInternational Doc.* 63 (1974) 70; while Gatu's sentiment appeared to many as radical and unevangelical, Reese, "John Gatu and the Moratorium," 251–55, demonstrates that Gatu was more evangelical than some imagined and less radical than his claims led some to believe.

291. Quoted in Anderson, "Moratorium on Missionaries?," 43, Verghese posits, "Today it is economic imperialism or neocolonialism that is the pattern of missions. Relief agencies and mission boards control the younger churches through purse strings. Foreign finances, ideas and personnel still dominate the younger churches and stifle their spontaneous growth.... So now I say, 'The mission of the church is the greatest enemy of the gospel.'"

292. José Míguez-Bonino, "The Present Crisis in Mission," *IDOCInternational Doc.* 63 (1974) 74–78.

293. Kalilombe, "Self-Reliance of the African Church."

294. Burgess Carr, "Internationalizing the Mission," *IDOCInternational Doc.* 63 (1974) 72–74; "All Africa Conference of Churches and the Lusaka Assembly," *AFER* 16.2 (1974) 329–34.

295. "Churches Renewed in Mission: Report of Section III of the Bangkok Conference," *Int. Rev. Mission* 62.246 (1973) 223.

296. AACC report quoted in Luckio O. Otieno, "Theological Developments in the All Africa Conference of Churches—1958–1978" (MA thesis, University of Nairobi, 1983), 108–9.

297. "All Africa Conference of Churches," 331.

self-governing, and self-propagating; it was also a means of becoming self-theologizing. In each of these areas—finance, polity, mission, and theology—moratorium advocates sought to bring churches of the Majority World out from under the heavy-handed control of Western missionaries.

While advocates of moratorium did not generally reject Westerners wholesale, they remained leery of Western missionary involvement in the life of local churches, including theological development.[298] As Nacpil explained, "The selfhood of the church means that a church is fully responsible for managing its own life. . . . Should there be those who feel compelled to travel from their home country to another in response to a 'Macedonian call,' they are to serve within the imperatives of this selfhood."[299] Likewise Míguez-Bonino left the door open for outsiders to continue playing a role in the life of Majority World churches.[300] However, he claimed, "If . . . they want to impose on us a way of understanding in witnessing to Christ that is not related to our struggle, to what we feel is the call of God to us, we will have to tell them, 'Stay home, go home; we must do our task before God and take our responsibility alone.'"[301]

Toward Hermeneutical Community

Others actively promote a communal approach to theological development, in which multiple voices and perspectives contribute to the task. Majority World Christians have conceived of such an approach in different ways. For some, the focus of a communal approach is to recognize that communities of lay believers—particularly the poor and oppressed—serve as primary agents of theology, while theological professionals serve in auxiliary roles. This view has come to dominate much of the liberation

---

298. Various moratorium advocates saw the move as a means of abolishing unhealthy existing relationships with missionaries in order to establish new, more equitable ones. Thus, for many such advocates, moratorium was not necessarily a move toward total isolation from the West. In fact, Gatu later clarified his intention to avoid such isolation and to ultimately build constructive relationships between national churches and foreign missionary agents. See Reese, "John Gatu and the Moratorium," 251–55; see also "All Africa Conference of Churches," 31; Otieno, "Theological Developments," 121.

299. Nacpil, "Mission but Not Missionaries," 360–61.

300. Míguez-Bonino, "Present Crisis in Mission," 78.

301. Míguez-Bonino, "Present Crisis in Mission," 78.

Hermeneutical Community

theology movement and its emphasis on base ecclesial communities.[302] It finds further support in the WCC's Programme on Theological Education, which published a compendium entitled *Theology by the People: Reflections on Doing Theology in Community* that highlights various ways that theology develops in community.[303]

Some theologians, particularly on the ecumenical side, claim that theology should develop in conversation with those of other faiths. The final statement of EATWOT's 1981 New Delhi conference thus declared, "Christian theology must be open to learn from other religions. In the Third World, theology must develop in deep communion with the religions and cultures of the people."[304] Further, it argued, "Adherents of other religions and beliefs also reveal some aspects of the will and message of God for our times.... [W]e must learn to discern God's presence among the oppressed of other faiths as they struggle for full humanity in the Third World today. Their sacred scriptures and traditions are also a source of revelation for us."[305] According to this view, interfaith dialogue is a necessary part of theological method because God reveals himself in and through other religions. Thus, the community in which these ecumenical theologians theologize includes even adherents of other faiths.

While evangelicals typically reject such interfaith community as a requisite for theological development, many evangelicals of the Majority World promote the incorporation of different (Christian) voices in the development of local theology—even those from the West.[306] For example,

---

302. See, for example, the essays of Torres and Eagleson, *Challenge of Basic Christian Communities*.

303. Samuel Amirtham and John S. Pobee, eds., *Theology by the People: Reflections on Doing Theology in Community* (Geneva: World Council of Churches, 1986); see Samuel Amirtham and John S. Pobee, eds., "Introduction," in *Theology by the People: Reflections on Doing Theology in Community* (Geneva: World Council of Churches, 1986), 1–26, for a helpful overview of this understanding of communal theologizing.

304. EATWOT, "Irruption of the Third World," 201.

305. EATWOT, "Irruption of the Third World," 202.

306. David K. Clark, *To Know and Love God: Method for Theology* (Wheaton, IL: Crossway, 2010), 61, explains that for evangelicals, "[The Bible] alone is the unique, written revelation of God, a permanent, meaningful, and authoritative self-expression by God of his nature and will." Owing to this belief, evangelicals usually reject the notion that God reveals himself in and through other religions, as well as the progressive contention that theology should develop in communion with those of other faiths. For example, while recognizing that theological dialogue with those of other faiths can be helpful in several ways, Saphir F. Athyal, "Toward an Asian Christian Theology," in *What Asian Christians Are Thinking: A Theological Source Book*, ed. Douglas J. Elwood

Paul Siu contends, "There are rich resources in the church history of the West as there are in the spiritual history of the East. In formulating an adequate local theology in the East Asian perspective, it would be imprudent not to consult the insights of those theological giants in the West and learn from them. We ignore their theological acumen to our own impoverishment."[307] Yung offers a similar assessment. He asserts, "The very fact that Asians approach truth more via relationship and experience, and westerners more via their rational faculties, is enough to demonstrate to us our need for each other to help us to come to a greater and more wholesome perception of the wonder and majesty of God. This and much more remind us that it is much more fruitful for East and West to learn from one another."[308] Majority World evangelicals thus tend to recognize value in having Western voices contribute to local theologizing.[309]

The term which perhaps best describes this communal evangelical approach to theological development is "hermeneutical community." The Seoul Declaration promoted this term, stating, "A biblical foundation for theology presupposes the church as the hermeneutical community."[310] René Padilla, who clearly influenced the Seoul Declaration, further explains, "The task of interpreting Scripture is the task of the whole Church. The biblical foundation for theology in the Two-thirds World presupposes a church that functions as the 'hermeneutical community'—the place where the Gospel is received not as a human word, but as it actually is, the living Word of God."[311]

(Quezon City, Philippines: New Day, 1978), 76, nevertheless contends, "In all the pious admonitions we hear today from around us that we as Christians ought to be teachable, humble, genuinely loving, and open to what Christ has to say to us through our fellow-believers in other religions, there is a failure to distinguish between the truth as revealed in Christ and institutional Christianity. When it comes to the revealed truth and the gospel of Christ, there is no more searching except for further clarity of what is revealed." Further, "Inter-religious dialogue can be quite valuable in several respects. . . . But in fundamental aspects of the Christian faith which really matter, no common ground is found with other religions for fruitful dialogue" (77).

307. Paul Siu, "Theologizing Locally," in *Local Theology for the Global Church: Principles for an Evangelical Approach to Contextualization*, ed. Matthew Cook et al. (Pasadena, CA: William Carey Library, 2010), 161.

308. Yung, *Mangoes or Bananas?*, 190.

309. See also Kwame Bediako, "The Willowbank Consultation Jan 1978: A Personal Reflection," *Themelios* 5.2 (1980) 31.

310. "Seoul Declaration," 64.

311. Padilla, "Biblical Foundations," 82.

Hermeneutical Community

For advocates of this approach, the hermeneutical and theological task thus involves multiple participants—from theological professionals to lay believers—and also incorporates insights from those outside of one's immediate local context. As René Padilla claims, Majority World Christians, in their effort to contextualize the gospel, should not

> ignore the results of long years of work in the field of Biblical research carried on by theologians in Europe or North America. It would be ridiculous to think that we in the Third World must start at the beginning, erasing the contributions that others have made to our thinking. What is necessary, on the other hand, is a theology that, taking advantage of that which is of value in any study, whatever its source, shows the relevance of Biblical revelation to our culture, the relation between the Gospel and the problems that the Church is facing in our society.[312]

Yet even with these "hermeneutical community" affirmations, the role of outsiders remains somewhat ambiguous. Padilla and others leave the door open for outsiders to play a role in local theological development, but do not explain clearly what that role might be. The burden of the following chapters is to outline such a role (with due regard for critiques lodged by Majority World theologians toward Western theological imposition) by demonstrating what "hermeneutical community" means, exploring how this approach developed, highlighting its biblical moorings, and showing how it might frame the outsider's role in local theological development.

CONCLUSION

Over the latter part of the twentieth century, many in the Majority World reacted against the colonial pattern of Western theological imposition. Both ecumenicals and evangelicals have articulated reasons for their rejection of this colonial precedent. Though evangelicals have not followed ecumenicals in their convictions concerning biblical revelation and theological method, they have expressed other objections similar to those of EATWOT. That is, they have critiqued Western theology's dualism, its irrelevance to social issues outside the West, its service as ideological support—whether explicitly or implicitly—for injustice, and the

---

312. Padilla, "Contextualization," 302–3.

way its imposition throughout the world has left locals without a voice in theological reflection.

In light of the case studies in chapter 2 and the post-colonial reactions here in this chapter, several deficiencies in the colonial pattern of theological imposition have surfaced. First, Western theology has not adequately recognized the contextual nature of all theology. Second, the imposition of Western theology has left local cultural issues unaddressed. Third, this pattern stunts local church maturation. Fourth, it leaves local churches susceptible to syncretism. Fifth, colonial theological imposition operates with an illegitimate suspicion toward the ability of locals to contribute to the task of theological reflection. Finally, it serves to perpetuate foreign control over local churches while inhibiting their indigeneity.

These deficiencies have rendered the outsider's role in local theological development unclear. Some have moved in the direction of the opposite extreme—the withdrawal of outsiders from local churches and their theological development. Others who likewise reject theological imposition nevertheless affirm a role for outsiders in the life of local churches. However, such affirmations have not clarified the nature of the outsider's role, particularly in reference to local theological development. The following chapters thus aim to provide clarity regarding the outsider's role and will do so by employing the concept of hermeneutical community.

4

Hermeneutical Community for Local Theological Development

HERMENEUTICAL COMMUNITY AS AN approach to local theological development charts a path between the theological pitfalls of colonial practice and post-colonial sentiment. What follows is a survey of different conceptions of hermeneutical community, an assessment of its biblical-theological moorings, a case for its relevance in light of historic missiological practice, and a consideration of its function in local theological development.

CONCEPTIONS OF HERMENEUTICAL COMMUNITY

The notion of hermeneutical community has developed in different fields of thought, including early Anabaptist ecclesiology, philosophical hermeneutics, theological hermeneutics (i.e., Theological Interpretation of Scripture), postliberal hermeneutics, Pentecostal hermeneutics, and ecumenical hermeneutics within the World Council of Churches. The following sections will explore these fields of discourse, highlighting the concept of hermeneutical community in each before finally proposing an evangelical understanding of hermeneutical community.[1]

---

1. Further, because those within the Anabaptist tradition have been the most explicit in advocating for a hermeneutical community approach to theology, the section on Anabaptist hermeneutics will also consider implications of its hermeneutical vision for contemporary local theological development.

Anabaptist Hermeneutics

One arena in which the notion of hermeneutical community has developed is Anabaptist ecclesiology. The Anabaptist tradition grew out of the early sixteenth-century Reformation movement in continental Europe, after various supporters of Ulrich Zwingli in Switzerland became increasingly dissatisfied with some of his theological convictions.[2] They ultimately broke away from Zwingli and established a church of their own—the Swiss Brethren.[3] The establishment of this small church marked the birth of Anabaptism.[4] The resulting Anabaptist movement, in contradistinction to both state-sponsored Protestantism and Catholic traditionalism, emphasized the priority of the local, gathered church in theological formation.[5] In doing so, Anabaptists embraced a communal approach to hermeneutics that challenged both Protestant and Catholic conventions.

Early Anabaptists affirmed the right of individual Christians to develop theological convictions directly from the text of Scripture, yet insisted that such individual activity remain accountable to the community of believers. Stuart Murray, a scholar on Anabaptists, explains, "Anabaptists were committed to the right of all believers to read and interpret Scripture, but from the movement's earliest years their understanding of community would have made it unthinkable for this right to be exercised in isolation or not be subject to testing in congregational meetings."[6] Their understanding of community included the conviction that the church served as the proper locus for developing theological understanding. According to Mennonite theologian Adolf Ens, "The church as a whole, rather than individuals within it or the clergy or the scholars, was thus seen as being responsible for scriptural interpretation."[7]

For Anabaptists, the church thus operated as a hermeneutical community—a community in which the Spirit was at work to illuminate the Scriptures and impart an understanding of their meaning. Individuals

---

2. William R. Estep, *The Anabaptist Story* (Nashville: Broadman, 1963), 8–9.

3. Estep, *Anabaptist Story*, 9–10.

4. Estep, *Anabaptist Story*, 10.

5. Stuart Murray, *Biblical Interpretation in the Anabaptist Tradition*, Studies in the Believers Church Tradition 3 (Kitchener, Ontario: Pandora, 2000), 157–83.

6. Murray, *Biblical Interpretation*, 157.

7. Adolf Ens, "Theology of the Hermeneutical Community in Anabaptist-Mennonite Thought," in *The Church as Theological Community: Essays in Honour of David Schroeder*, ed. Harry Huebner (Winnipeg: CMBC Publications, 1990), 81.

brought their own understandings of Scripture to the gathering of believers, who then weighed each contribution, assessing its value in light of the revealed truth of Scripture. As David Schroeder, a Mennonite professor of New Testament and philosophy, posits, "The interpretation of a Scripture passage is not something that can be worked out individually, mechanically, or in separation from the Spirit of God and the community of faith. The Holy Spirit works not only through the individual but also through the community of believers, the church, to give us an understanding of God's will. We must therefore, bring the interpretation of Scripture that we come to in our reading and study to the larger community of faith for its consideration and response."[8] Thus the task of theology became congregational, allowing "each person to share insights the Spirit gave to all believers," according to Murray.[9] He adds, "Discussing these insights together and seeking a consensus would help them to discard unreliable and erroneous interpretations, as well as confirming those that seemed helpful and trustworthy."[10]

This hermeneutical community approach to theology paved a third way between Catholic traditionalism and Protestant individualism. That is, within theology, it checked the overextended authority of tradition in Catholicism as well as the pitfalls of interpretation isolated from the church—to which Protestant reformers were prone. Mennonite scholar Antonio González explains, "In contrast to both Catholic institutional mediation and Protestant individualism, the Anabaptists understood that there existed a third possibility, one characterized precisely by the fact that the following of Jesus is a communitarian process, one in which a fraternal group . . . relates itself to the Lord collectively and directly."[11] The reality that the church relates *directly* to God limits the role of tradition in theological development, while the reality that the church relates *collectively* to God challenges those who attempt to theologize apart from intimate involvement in the life of God's people.

---

8. Quoted in William Klassen, "The Voice of the People in the Biblical Story of Faithfulness," in *The Church as Theological Community: Essays in Honour of David Schroeder*, ed. Harry Huebner (Winnipeg: CMBC Publications, 1990), 141.

9. Murray, *Biblical Interpretation*, 179.

10. Murray, *Biblical Interpretation*, 179.

11. Antonio González, "Anabaptist Hermeneutics and Theological Education," *Mennon. Q. Rev.* 84.2 (2010) 214–15; see also John Howard Yoder, "The Hermeneutics of Peoplehood: A Protestant Perspective on Practical Moral Reasoning," *J. Relig. Ethics* 10.1 (1982) 48–49.

In other words, Anabaptists relocated theological authority. They recognized that such authority rested neither in Rome nor the Reformers' studies, but in the community of believers.[12] As John Howard Yoder maintains, this relocated authority implied that "the congregation must not be bound by tradition or former creedal statements, nor by the supervision of government authority."[13] Further, this relocation "takes the authority away from specialized theologians or hierarchical authorities, in whom the church up until then had placed ultimate intellectual authority."[14]

The Anabaptists' move to locate interpretive authority in the gathered community of believers was radical and novel in the sixteenth century. Murray asserts, "Designating the congregation as the locus of interpretation may not have been uniformly practiced by sixteenth-century Anabaptist groups, but the suggestion itself remains one of the most radical and provocative components of Anabaptist hermeneutics. We can regard the interpreting community as the focal point of Anabaptist hermeneutics, the context for the hermeneutical enfranchisement of every believer, and the setting for their reliance on the Spirit as interpreter and commitment to the contemporary application of Scripture."[15] Thus, for Anabaptists, the task of hermeneutics was thoroughly ecclesial.

Development of Hermeneutical Community Approach

While no systematic explication of hermeneutical community exists from the sixteenth-century Anabaptist movement, there does exist a clear precedent. It might strike one as surprising that such a theological and historical precedent would come from Anabaptists—known, in part, for their lack of formal theological expression.[16] Yet as Ens explains, "There was a remarkably pervasive consensus among most of the leaders of the movement in the sixteenth century about the importance of all members of the church studying the scriptures and participating in the process

---

12. Murray, *Biblical Interpretation*, 157–59.

13. John Howard Yoder, "The Hermeneutics of the Anabaptists," *Mennon. Q. Rev.* 41.4 (1967) 301.

14. Yoder, "Hermeneutics of the Anabaptists," 303.

15. Murray, *Biblical Interpretation*, 249; see also John Driver, *Community and Commitment* (Scottdale, PA: Herald, 1976), 23.

16. Ens, "Theology of the Hermeneutical Community," 69.

Hermeneutical Community

of understanding their meaning in and for the contemporary church."[17] This precedent continues even today among the denominational heirs of the Anabaptist tradition.[18]

A prominent early advocate of this hermeneutical community approach was Balthasar Hubmaier. In 1524, Hubmaier entered into a debate with John Eck, a debate which laid groundwork for an Anabaptist communal hermeneutic. Hubmaier proposed that prior to their disputation, both men should lay out their convictions before the congregation, which would then be able to consider whose beliefs were more in line with Scripture.[19] The plan itself thus involved a communal hermeneutic. Moreover, Hubmaier's theses against Eck clarified his congregational approach. In his first thesis, Hubmaier declared, "Every Christian is obligated to give account of his hope and thereby of the faith which is in him to whoever desires it (1 Peter 3:15)."[20] In the fifth, he stated, "Further, the decision which of two understands it more correctly is conceived in the church by the Word of God and born out of faith. When you come together, etc., the others should judge (1 Corinthians 14:30)."[21]

Hubmaier's theses clarified a framework for hermeneutical community, one which other Anabaptists embraced. Ens explains, "Two underlying assumptions in these statements are: that every member of the church must have a sufficient understanding of the faith to be personally able to defend it, and that the gathered community was the appropriate body to discern the right interpretation."[22] Others joining Hubmaier in this embrace of congregational hermeneutics included Conrad Grebel, Michael Sattler, Pilgram Marpeck, Dirk Philips, and Menno Simons.[23] Ens thus asserts, "Interpretation by the congregation was in fact a widely accepted principle in the sixteenth-century Anabaptist movement."[24]

---

17. Ens, "Theology of the Hermeneutical Community," 69.

18. For example, a hermeneutical community approach remains operative in the Mennonite tradition. See Doug Heidebrecht, "Community Hermeneutics in Practice: Following the Interpretive Path Together," *Direction* 49.2 (2020) 123–40; Bradley G. Siebert, "Tested in the Faith Community: The Congregational Hermeneutics of the Mennonites" (paper presented at the 48th Annual Meeting of the Conference on College Composition and Communication, Phoenix, AZ, March 12–15, 1997).

19. Yoder, "Hermeneutics of the Anabaptists," 300–301.

20. Quoted in Ens, "Theology of the Hermeneutical Community," 76.

21. Quoted in Ens, "Theology of the Hermeneutical Community," 76.

22. Ens, "Theology of the Hermeneutical Community," 76.

23. Ens, "Theology of the Hermeneutical Community," 77–80.

24. Ens, "Theology of the Hermeneutical Community," 80.

LOCAL THEOLOGICAL DEVELOPMENT

This emphasis on communal hermeneutics developed, in part, out of necessity. Anabaptists were radical reformers who defied the theological conventions of both Catholicism and state-sponsored Protestantism. According to Bradley Siebert, "Such defiance made the early Anabaptists both heretics and insurrectionists in the eyes of the established churches and their sponsoring states, respectively, and led to a history of persecution, flight, and martyrdom."[25] This situation rendered formal theological training difficult. Siebert thus contends, "Because they were hunted by both church and state, they had little access to seminary-trained leaders, except those who risked conversion after training. This secured the lay tradition and the practices of congregational hermeneutics in the Anabaptist movement."[26]

Yet Anabaptists employed a hermeneutical community approach more out of conviction than necessity. One conviction undergirding such congregational hermeneutics was their anti-clericalism—their suspicion and rejection of church models in which authority remains vested in higher church leadership. Murray maintains that in light of this stance, "it stands to reason that alternative practices regarding the interpretation of Scripture, one of the key clerical responsibilities, should have emerged. . . . Anticlerical action aimed at empowering church members to read and interpret the Bible would have foundered if the only alternative was individual study."[27] In other words, hermeneutical community became the preferred option in the face of a clergy-dominated theological enterprise.[28]

In addition to their anti-clericalism, Anabaptists recognized the danger that a multiplicity of individual readings might present to the theological task. Their insistence that all church members assume a role in theologizing could lead to conflicting interpretations of Scripture. They sought to overcome this challenge by adopting a hermeneutical community approach. Ens explains, "The Anabaptists realized the danger of antinomianism inherent in simply allowing everyone to interpret a passage in accordance with some internal impulse ascribed to the

---

25. Siebert, "Tested in the Faith Community," 3.
26. Siebert, "Tested in the Faith Community," 4.
27. Murray, *Biblical Interpretation*, 171–72.
28. Regarding the dominance of clergy in theology, Ens, "Theology of the Hermeneutical Community," 73, asserts, "Since access to scripture had for so long been denied to the membership of the church, its interpretation had naturally been taken over (or retained) by the clergy and the scholars."

Holy Spirit. Hence, the need arose for some kind of 'testing the spirits' to ensure that the one Spirit would not appear to be giving occasion for conflicting interpretations of the Word. The congregation became the locus for that kind of testing."[29] In other words, Anabaptists believed that the gathered community of believers served as a check and balance to individual interpretation on both the clerical and lay sides.[30] Thus for Anabaptists, hermeneutical community was not just a contextual necessity; it was a conscious preference.

Rationale for Hermeneutical Community Approach

Further, Anabaptists recognized biblical and theological rationale for a hermeneutical community approach. Biblically, the "Rule of Paul"—derived from 1 Cor 14:29—undergirded such congregational hermeneutics.[31] Yoder asserts that Zwingli first identified 1 Cor 14:29 as the "Rule of Paul."[32] In the broader passage, the apostle Paul addresses the issue of orderly worship as it relates to the exercising of spiritual gifts in church gatherings. Regarding prophesy, he states, "Let two or three prophets speak, and let the others weigh what is said" (1 Cor 14:29). According to Mennonite theologian John Driver, "The function of prophets was to expound the will of God as it had been revealed to them in the Scriptures. . . . The function of the rest of the congregation was to hear the message of the prophets, and then weigh or discern the message over against the other criteria at their disposal."[33] Accordingly, the congregation acted as a hermeneutical community.

In addition to the Rule of Paul, Anabaptists recognized the "Rule of Christ"—derived from Matt 18:15-20—as a basis for hermeneutical community. In this passage, Jesus explains to his community of disciples

---

29. Ens, "Theology of the Hermeneutical Community," 75–76.

30. González, "Anabaptist Hermeneutics and Theological Education," 214, adds, "By insisting on the need of a communitarian hermeneutical process, the Anabaptists . . . implicitly acknowledged that the Scriptures were susceptible to different interpretations, some of which did not necessarily lead to following Jesus. For that reason, the initial clarity of the Scriptures yielded to a process that went beyond any individual reading, including that of a specialist."

31. Murray, *Biblical Interpretation*, 174, claims, "This passage was fundamental to the ordering of Anabaptist congregations and . . . was the basis for fierce criticisms of the state churches."

32. Yoder, "Hermeneutics of the Anabaptists," 301.

33. Driver, *Community and Commitment*, 23.

LOCAL THEOLOGICAL DEVELOPMENT

how to address individual sin within the corporate body and how to restore wayward members. Driver explains the significance of this passage for congregational hermeneutics: "The presence of the Spirit of Christ is promised when the congregation assembles to discern the will of God so that it can make ethical decisions in obedience to Christ."[34] This important theological concern—practical moral reasoning—occupies the attention of the assembly; it was not strictly a private matter.[35] As such, the church operates as a "discerning" (i.e., hermeneutical) community.[36]

Anabaptists and their successors have pointed to yet other biblical texts in support of a congregational approach to theological development. William Klassen, for example, points to Rom 12:2 and its admonition to test and discern the will of God as being a corporate responsibility.[37] Further, he highlights Rom 12:16,[38] Rom 15:5,[39] 1 Cor 1:10,[40] and 2 Cor 13:11[41] as but a few passages teaching the importance of church members agreeing with one another.[42] Klassen contends that in such passages, "Paul directs himself to those who have confidence in their own abilities to make choices and assume that they have the right to do as they feel is right. Thus, the correct way can be determined only by listening to one another and finding ways of conversing with one another."[43] Further, those in the Anabaptist tradition find in the Jerusalem Council of Acts 15 a biblical precedent for their hermeneutical community approach.[44]

---

34. Driver, *Community and Commitment*, 24.

35. Yoder, "Hermeneutics of Peoplehood," 50–52.

36. Arthur G. Gish, *Living in Christian Community* (Scottdale, PA: Herald, 1979), 93–132; James Wm. McClendon Jr., *Systematic Theology*, vol. 2: *Doctrine* (Nashville: Abingdon, 1994), 142–45.

37. Klassen, "Voice of the People," 155. Elsewhere he adds, "In Paul's basic appeal in Romans 12:2 he calls for a renewed mind which searches more intensely for the will of God in the context of communal existence within the church" (158).

38. "Live in harmony with one another. Do not be haughty, but associate with the lowly. Never be wise in your own sight."

39. "May the God of endurance and encouragement grant you to live in such harmony with one another, in accord with Christ Jesus."

40. "I appeal to you, brothers, by the name of our Lord Jesus Christ, that all of you agree, and that there be no divisions among you, but that you be united in the same mind and the same judgment."

41. "Finally, brothers, rejoice. Aim for restoration, comfort one another, agree with one another, live in peace; and the God of love and peace will be with you."

42. Klassen, "Voice of the People," 156.

43. Klassen, "Voice of the People," 156.

44. Heidebrecht, "Community Hermeneutics in Practice," 133; Siebert, "Tested in the

Hermeneutical Community

Theologically, Anabaptists held convictions concerning the nature of the church and its members that led them to embrace a communal hermeneutic. Murray highlights three such convictions: a radical commitment to the priesthood of all believers (which he refers to as the "theologian-hood of all believers"), a belief in the centrality of the church in redemptive history, and a strong conviction that the Holy Spirit is especially operative in the gathered community of believers.[45] From this last conviction, Anabaptists viewed the church as a charismatic[46] community, and, according to Murray, "the confidence Anabaptist leaders placed in it was rooted in their expectancy that the Spirit would operate there in a way he would not within individuals alone."[47] That is, they believed the Spirit would lead the church into a deeper understanding of truth when its members are gathered to discern the Scriptures together. Their pneumatology—along with their ecclesiology—therefore led them to a hermeneutical community approach.

Thus, the Anabaptist hermeneutical community approach developed in the sixteenth century as a new and conscious theological method. It was conscious in that it developed more out of conviction than need. As Murray concludes, "Locating hermeneutical authority in the congregation thus seems to have been a preferred option, not a counsel of necessity."[48] This preference stems from the fact that their theological convictions "logically required a communal approach to biblical interpretation."[49] Further, this theological method was new in that it

---

Faith Community," 19; Klassen, "Voice of the People," 162, adds that such hermeneutical community characterized the early church at large. He claims, "What appears evident is that theologizing . . . was closely related to community life. The main purpose for the gathering of the community was to engage in this kind of theologizing. The apostolic concern focused on conversation among the various members of the church. . . . The early church was then in the most fundamental sense a hermeneutical community in which the apostolic message was repeatedly tested and checked out over against other understandings of Christ's significance in the world." Yoder, "Hermeneutics of the Anabaptists," 304, summarizes, "Anabaptists considered themselves quite clearly in the succession of the early church's process of decision making: 'It seemed good to the Holy Spirit and to us.'"

45. Murray, *Biblical Interpretation*, 175–76.

46. The term "charismatic community" here refers simply to a community of believers whom the Holy Spirit indwells, not to contemporary churches that affirm an ongoing role for certain spiritual gifts, like speaking in tongues, in the life of the church.

47. Murray, *Biblical Interpretation*, 176.

48. Murray, *Biblical Interpretation*, 173.

49. Murray, *Biblical Interpretation*, 157.

broke away from Catholic institutionalism and Protestant individualism and upheld the church as the locus for biblical interpretation.[50]

Implications of Hermeneutical Community Approach

This Anabaptist conception of hermeneutical community can shed valuable light on theological development in a post-colonial world. First, it provides a helpful framework for mitigating the extremes of local theological autonomy and foreign theological imposition. Mennonite scholar Lydia Harder notes that within a hermeneutical community approach, "All members of the congregation are responsible for discerning the meaning of the Bible for both their personal and their communal lives. Neither hierarchical authority, nor specialized theologians are to be the final judges of the Bible's meaning. There is no privilege of the powerful. Accountability is to the whole community of faithful followers. The congregation discovers the guidance of the Spirit through mutual dialogue and counsel."[51] That is, the established tradition and its representative specialists are not to impose theology on the group.[52] Yet, neither are the individual local members exempt from accountability to the wider group—which would lead to total theological autonomy.

Contra foreign theological imposition, an Anabaptist hermeneutical community approach recognizes the importance of local church members discerning scriptural truth and thus developing their own theological convictions. As Doug Heidebrecht, professor at Mennonite Brethren Biblical Seminary, claims, "The joy of discovering the Bible's meaning should not just be a second-hand experience."[53] González adds, "In the Anabaptist perspective, the believing people are not just the object, but

---

50. Yoder, "Hermeneutics of the Anabaptists," 301, claims, "It is a basic novelty in the discussion of hermeneutics to say that a text is best understood in a congregation. This means that the tools of literary analysis do not suffice; that the Spirit is an interpreter of what a text is about only when Christians are gathered in readiness to hear it speak to their current needs and concerns."

51. Lydia Harder, "Discipleship Reexamined: Women in the Hermeneutical Community," in *The Church as Theological Community: Essays in Honour of David Schroeder*, ed. Harry Huebner (Winnipeg: CMBC Publications, 1990), 203.

52. Murray, *Biblical Interpretation*, 226, asserts, "A key element in Anabaptist hermeneutics particularly relevant in post-Christendom settings is its enfranchisement of all believers as interpreters."

53. Heidebrecht, "Community Hermeneutics in Practice," 131.

also the first agent of theological education."[54] This helps to ensure that the issues which local theological training addresses are pertinent to the believers of that context.[55] Further, it incorporates the theological wisdom of locals who, as fellow members in the body of Christ, have insight to offer.[56]

When outsiders fail to recognize the role of locals in theological development and instead consolidate theological authority in themselves, however, what results is local theological subservience—something Anabaptists vehemently challenge. For example, González contends,

> Ignorance of, contempt for or a denial of the theological wisdom of the believing community frustrate the hermeneutical experience, for *they undermine its very starting point,* which is the hermeneutical horizon of those who are interpreting. Without that starting point, educated individuals will experience something like a "brainwashing," which obliges them to situate themselves in a different intellectual horizon, one in which their categories stop functioning.... It can only result in some people imposing their ideas on others and in "lay people" being trained as intellectual clones of the theologians.[57]

Anabaptists thus insist that theology develop from within the local church rather than be imposed from without.

Conversely, Anabaptists insist that local believers remain accountable to the wider body of Christ for their theological convictions. In other words, even though they promote the right of all believers to participate in theological reflection, they do not permit total theological autonomy on the part of individuals. Rather, as Murray shows, the Anabaptists sought "to balance the right of private interpretation, on which they insisted, with the exercise of this right in fellowship with others."[58] Thus, this framework can help course correct the historic role of outsiders in local theological development, while also guarding against the post-colonial extreme of total local autonomy in theologizing—precisely because all involved in theological development remain accountable to a wider community.

54. González, "Anabaptist Hermeneutics and Theological Education," 222.
55. González, "Anabaptist Hermeneutics and Theological Education," 222.
56. González, "Anabaptist Hermeneutics and Theological Education," 222.
57. González, "Anabaptist Hermeneutics and Theological Education," 222–23, emphasis original.
58. Murray, *Biblical Interpretation,* 159.

This broad understanding of communal hermeneutics in the Anabaptist tradition finds a corollary in several contemporary discourses—one of which is philosophical hermeneutics.[59] That is, various concerns that have occupied Anabaptists and their heirs from a theological perspective have also occupied recent scholars from a philosophical perspective. Harder explains, "A shift from a focus on the individual interpreter in her/his subjectivity to an emphasis on the interpretive community can be recognized in writings on hermeneutics" within philosophical studies.[60]

Philosophical Hermeneutics

Unlike early Anabaptist hermeneutics, which was mainly concerned with interpreting the Bible, philosophical hermeneutics focuses more on the hermeneutical nature of human reality. González explains, "In contrast to the traditional idea of hermeneutics as simply a stock of methods that the specialized interpreter can use to find the true meaning of a text, contemporary philosophy understands hermeneutics to be a universal process in which we are all involved by the sheer fact of being human beings."[61] In other words, from the perspective of philosophical hermeneutics, the process of understanding and interpretation (i.e., hermeneutics) is central to human existence. González adds, "Interpretation takes place even in our modest perceptions, since any meaning we attribute to things already involves some interpretation of the things. But such interpretation is not done through the use of the static, universal categories that every subject possesses *qua* subject. Rather, we are actually constituted as human by being inserted into a cultural, historical horizon, from which we receive the basic categories for understanding one another and the world that surrounds us."[62] Thus, in contemporary philosophical perspective, hermeneutics is an interpretive process that pervades human life.

---

59. González, "Anabaptist Hermeneutics and Theological Education," 217–19.

60. Lydia Harder, "A Hermeneutics of Discipleship: Toward a Mennonite/Feminist Approach to Biblical Authority" (ThD diss., Toronto School of Theology, 1993), 14. She cites Stanley Fish, Richard Bernstein, and Paul Ricoeur as philosophers who exemplify this shift (15–16).

61. González, "Anabaptist Hermeneutics and Theological Education," 217.

62. González, "Anabaptist Hermeneutics and Theological Education," 217.

Hans-Georg Gadamer

The chief exponent of such contemporary philosophical hermeneutics is Hans-Georg Gadamer.[63] Stanley E. Porter and Jason C. Robinson observe, "Whereas Friedrich Schleiermacher (1768–1834) is often credited with the birth of modern hermeneutics, it is Gadamer who championed its twentieth-century development. His name has become synonymous with philosophical hermeneutics."[64] Gadamer—born in Germany in 1900—completed his doctoral studies under eminent philosopher Martin Heidegger and then, over the course of his career, held professorships at the Universities of Leipzig, Frankfurt, and Heidelberg.[65] Gadamer became renowned in his own right with his publication in 1960 of *Truth and Method*,[66] which was, according to Porter and Robinson, a "monumental work that influenced the entire course of interpretive thought in the last third of the twentieth century."[67]

Gadamer challenges interpretive methodologies of the Enlightenment that feign objective epistemological certainty.[68] He observes, "The fundamental presupposition of the Enlightenment [is] that methodologically disciplined use of reason can safeguard us from all error."[69] Enlightenment rationalism refused to grant authority to tradition, for doing so would introduce prejudices that impede the pursuit of objective knowledge through disciplined human reasoning. Rather, the Enlightenment, as Gadamer notes, "takes tradition as an object of critique, just as

---

63. For an overview of Gadamer's life and work, see Robert J. Dostal, "Gadamer: The Man and His Work," in *The Cambridge Companion to Gadamer*, ed. Robert J. Dostal (Cambridge, UK: Cambridge University Press, 2002), 13–35.

64. Stanley E. Porter and Jason C. Robinson, *Hermeneutics: An Introduction to Interpretive Theory* (Grand Rapids: Eerdmans, 2011), Kindle, loc. 1103.

65. Porter and Robinson, *Hermeneutics*, loc. 1122.

66. Hans-Georg Gadamer, *Truth and Method*, 2nd rev. ed. (New York: Continuum, 2004).

67. Porter and Robinson, *Hermeneutics*, loc. 1116. So influential has been the work of Gadamer, that Porter and Robinson claim, "The field of philosophical hermeneutics owes its very origins to the work of Gadamer" (loc. 1108).

68. Georgia Warnke, *Gadamer: Hermeneutics, Tradition and Reason* (Oxford: Polity, 1987), 6, explains, "For Gadamer, the development of hermeneutics extending from Schleiermacher, through the Historical School of Ludwig von Ranke and Johann Gustav Drovsen to Dilthey himself unfolds a positivistic misconception that equates understanding with a methodologically secured, 'Cartesian certainty.'"

69. Gadamer, *Truth and Method*, 279.

the natural sciences do with the evidence of the senses."[70] In so doing, Enlightenment philosophers, like Wilhelm Dilthey, sought to liberate the pursuit of knowledge from the confines of traditional dogma.[71] The scientific method of the natural sciences therefore became the gold standard for processes of understanding and interpretation—even within the human sciences—because it championed reason as authoritative over traditional knowledge.[72]

Contrary to this Enlightenment pursuit of epistemological objectivity through detached observation and reasoning, Gadamer argues that the interpretive methods of the Enlightenment are not truly objective, but instead remain inevitably subjective.[73] He contends, "The idea of an absolute reason is not a possibility for historical humanity. Reason exists for us only in concrete, historical terms—i.e., it is not its own master but remains constantly dependent on the given circumstances in which it operates."[74] In other words, Gadamer challenged the long-held belief that one could arrive at objective knowledge through detached hermeneutical reasoning.[75] For him, one cannot reduce the pursuit of knowledge to methodological procedures.[76]

Emerging from Gadamer's critique of such Enlightenment sensibilities are several major hermeneutical emphases. First, Gadamer emphasizes that prejudices and tradition inevitably influence the hermeneutical process. The term "prejudice" here simply means "pre-judgment," or as philosophical hermeneutics scholar Georgia Warnke describes, "a

---

70. Gadamer, *Truth and Method*, 274.

71. Warnke, *Gadamer*, 5–6.

72. Gadamer, *Truth and Method*, 3–8, 274–85.

73. Warnke, *Gadamer*, 77, explains, "Against the Enlightenment he argues that no understanding is objective in a Cartesian sense; all understanding rather involves projections of meaning that arise out of one's own situation and go beyond the observable 'facts.'"

74. Gadamer, *Truth and Method*, 277.

75. Charles Taylor, "Gadamer on the Human Sciences," in *The Cambridge Companion to Gadamer*, ed. Robert J. Dostal (Cambridge, UK: Cambridge University Press, 2002), 128, explains, "Gadamer does not believe that the kind of knowledge that yields complete intellectual control over the Object is attainable, even in principle, in human affairs. It may make sense to dream of this in particle physics, even to set this as one's goal, but not when it comes to understanding human beings."

76. Jean Grondin, *The Philosophy of Gadamer*, trans. Kathryn Plant (Montreal: McGill-Queen's University Press, 2003), 20, claims, "[Gadamer] never challenges science, but only the fascination which emanates from it and which threatens to reduce the understanding to an instrumental process."

judgment made before all the evidence has been adequately assessed."[77] Regarding the influence of such prejudices, Gadamer contends, "History does not belong to us; we belong to it. Long before we understand ourselves through the process of self-examination, we understand ourselves in a self-evident way in the family, society, and state in which we live.... *That is why the prejudices of the individual, far more than his judgments, constitute the historical reality of his being.*"[78] In other words, prejudices are unavoidable, because one cannot detach oneself from the historical milieu and traditions in which he or she was born, and which prejudice understanding.[79] Because of this, rather than seek to rise above prejudices and tradition, one must acknowledge and account for them in the hermeneutical process.[80] Gadamer asserts, "We have to recognize the element of tradition in historical research and inquire into its hermeneutic productivity."[81] Moreover he claims that such prejudices, stemming from tradition, are "conditions of understanding."[82]

For Gadamer, this reality of prejudices does not necessarily impede the hermeneutical process, but can contribute positively to the task.[83] Philosopher Richard E. Palmer explains this sentiment of Gadamer concerning presuppositions and their potentially positive relationship to hermeneutics:

> If there can be no presuppositionless understanding ... then we must reexamine our relationship to our heritage. Tradition and authority need no longer be seen as the enemies of reason and rational freedom as they were in the Enlightenment and the Romantic period, and into our day. Tradition furnishes the

77. Warnke, *Gadamer*, 76.

78. Gadamer, *Truth and Method*, 278, emphasis original.

79. Richard E. Palmer, *Hermeneutics: Interpretive Theory in Schleiermacher, Dilthey, Heidegger, and Gadamer* (Evanston, IL: Northwestern University Press, 1969), 182–83.

80. Here Gadamer stands in opposition to Enlightenment hermeneutics, which emphasizes the need for one to dissociate from tradition and its prejudices in order to arrive at true understanding through methods of inquiry. Warnke, *Gadamer*, 75, explains, "In the perspective of the Enlightenment prejudices arise from two sources: first from a reliance on traditional views and refusal to employ one's own reason and second from an over-hasty, unmethodical use of that reason where it is employed. In achieving an adequate understanding of a subject-matter, reason and method are allied with one another against prejudice and authority. In opposition to this view, Gadamer argues that prejudice and tradition are essential to understanding."

81. Gadamer, *Truth and Method*, 284.

82. Gadamer, *Truth and Method*, 278.

83. Gadamer, *Truth and Method*, 278–91.

> stream of conceptions within which we stand, and we must be prepared to distinguish between fruitful presuppositions and those that imprison and prevent us from thinking and seeing. In any event, there is no intrinsic opposition between the claims of reason and those of tradition; reason stands always within tradition. Tradition even supplies reason with the aspect of reality and history with which it will work.[84]

Thus for Gadamer, tradition impacts all knowledge and understanding, the recognition of which can help hermeneuts avoid seeking the mirage of pure, objective knowledge.

Second, Gadamer argues that the hermeneutical process is dialogical. In fact, he claims that human experience itself is dialogical, set within a question-and-answer framework: "It is clear that the structure of the question is implicit in all experience. We cannot have experiences without asking questions. Recognizing that an object is different, and not as we first thought, obviously presupposes the question whether it was this or that."[85] More specifically, Gadamer likens the interpretation of a text to a conversation.[86] W. Alan Smith explains, "In place of the Enlightenment procedure of making the text an object to be studied coldly and dispassionately, as one might study an object under scientific investigation, Gadamer claims hermeneutics takes place between two partners in dialogue."[87]

In this dialogical process, a text acts not as a mere object of study, but as a subject which addresses the interpreter.[88] In other words, the process of hermeneutics is inter-subjective,[89] and therefore one cannot understand the meaning of a text by treating it as an object to be analyzed through methodological procedures. Porter and Robinson explain, "Coming-to-understand a text is not about merely peering into the historical past and reconstructing the intent and tradition of the author, summarizing meaning as it is constructed. On the contrary, we are perpetually attempting to reinterpret the question the text is possibly answering and doing so in response to a living question we have in mind.

---

84. Palmer, *Hermeneutics*, 183.
85. Gadamer, *Truth and Method*, 356.
86. Gadamer, *Truth and Method*, 370.
87. W. Alan Smith, "Intersubjectivity and Community: Some Implications from Gadamer's Philosophy for Religious Education," *Relig. Educ.* 88.3 (1993) 381.
88. Gadamer, *Truth and Method*, 363.
89. Smith, "Intersubjectivity and Community," 381.

Understanding is more than merely re-creating another's meaning."[90] Arriving at true understanding involves a conversation between subjects, whether those subjects are human or textual.[91]

Third, corresponding to his understanding of hermeneutics as dialogical, Gadamer maintains that the hermeneutical process involves a fusion of horizons.[92] By "horizon," he means "the range of vision that includes everything that can be seen from a particular vantage point."[93] For Gadamer, true understanding happens when one's horizon collides and fuses with the horizon of another. Palmer explains, "The horizon of meaning within which a text or historical act stands is questioningly approached from within one's own horizon; and one does not leave his own horizon, but broadens it so as to fuse it with that of the act or text."[94] Porter and Robinson add, "Gadamer argues that the world is encountered in such a way that our mere subjectivities alone cannot grasp it, nor the ideals of objectivism see it. Truth emerges only when our individual horizons and the horizons of the other (e.g., text, person, work of art) fuse, bringing different worlds together in surprising new ways."[95] Thus for Gadamer, hermeneutics involves multiple subjects coming together in a process of dialogue and exchange, thereby expanding horizons of understanding.

Communal Hermeneutics

While Gadamer does not employ the term "hermeneutical community," the aforementioned emphases within his work point to a hermeneutical process that is inevitably communal in nature. The notion that tradition conditions hermeneutics underscores the reality that multiple voices (e.g., classical texts, traditional rituals, authoritative spokespersons) contribute to the process of understanding. Likewise the notion that this process of understanding is dialogical and proceeds by way of fusing horizons highlights the necessity of incorporating multiple voices in the task. One cannot expand his or her horizon of understanding apart from encountering other horizons of understanding.

90. Porter and Robinson, *Hermeneutics*, loc. 1485.
91. Gadamer, *Truth and Method*, 352–70.
92. Gadamer, *Truth and Method*, 303–6.
93. Gadamer, *Truth and Method*, 301.
94. Palmer, *Hermeneutics*, 201.
95. Porter and Robinson, *Hermeneutics*, loc. 1296.

In other words, the hermeneutical process that Gadamer conceives necessarily involves multiple participants. If one cannot arrive at true understanding through methods which isolate the subject and object of inquiry, then one has to broaden the process through conversation with other subjects. Warnke explains that, for Gadamer, understanding involves "integrating the tradition or opinions of others into one's search for 'truth,' treating them as equal partners in dialogue and attempting to come to some kind of position that both they and we can support."[96] Smith adds, "[Gadamer] does not understand hermeneutics as the production of meaning from misunderstanding as a result of expert application of sound method. Instead, he claims partners, fellow subjects engaged in dialogue around a common subject matter, are encountered by the meaning that emerges out of that dialogue."[97] Thus for Gadamer, hermeneutics is a communal endeavor.

Granted, evangelicals will rightly object to the way Gadamerian hermeneutical approaches undermine biblical authority by allowing the reader—rather than the author—to determine the meaning of a text.[98] In

---

96. Warnke, *Gadamer*, 102.

97. Smith, "Intersubjectivity and Community," 393.

98. Grant R. Osborne, *The Hermeneutical Spiral: A Comprehensive Introduction to Biblical Interpretation*, rev. and exp. ed. (Downers Grove, IL: IVP Academic, 1991), 358–61, locates Gadamer at the heart of contemporary hermeneutics' shift away from the author toward more reader-centric approaches to understanding texts. Regarding this shift, he posits, "The focus of interest has thus shifted from the text to the self, and the significance of this shift is still being explored. The result is that the reader is now seen as the creator of meaning rather than the text, and the act of 'coming to understanding' has become an individual self-discovery more than a process of decoding textual meaning. The author is now seen as entirely removed from the text or the discovery of meaning" (358–59). Regarding Gadamer's work in particular, Osborne claims, "Gadamer's aesthetic hermeneutic moves from the author and the text to a union of text and reader, with roots in the present rather than in the past. Gadamer has correctly seen the place of the reader in the hermeneutical process and the fact that the subject is always present in the study of the object. His 'fusion of horizons' is an important correction to the psychologist school. Yet there are several weaknesses inherent to this theory. As is true also of the New Hermeneutic, it is not so clear how Gadamer avoids the danger of subjective interpretation. For him there are two controls against subjectivity—the past horizon of the text and the present community of the interpreters (the 'tradition' that challenges subjective interpretations). However, there are no clear criteria for avoiding subjectivism. In fact, each moment of reading can produce a new and innovative understanding" (361). Kevin J. Vanhoozer, *Is There a Meaning in This Text? The Bible, the Reader, and the Morality of Literary Knowledge* (Grand Rapids: Zondervan, 2009), 113, adds that the hermeneutical approach of Gadamer (and others) "abandon[s] the ideal of objective literary knowledge by acknowledging that meaning is largely the product of historically situated ways of reading or decoding."

Gadamer's view, interpretation does not seek to ascertain the intent of a text's author, but rather seeks a dialogue between reader and text that, as Porter and Robinson explain, generates "a living truth and meaning that transcends them both without being fixed and permanent."[99] When applied to the Bible—as with, for example, the "new hermeneutic" of Gerhard Ebeling and Ernst Fuchs—such an approach leaves little to no objective basis for Christian truth.[100] As D. A. Carson maintains, "The new hermeneutic pursues 'what is true for me' at the expense of 'what is true.' Theology proper becomes impossible. . . . [I]f the new hermeneutic denies that writers, including God, have intent and can convey meaning, it is but another faddish aberration in theology."[101] For evangelicals, such a move away from authorial intent remains out of bounds.[102]

However, the import of Gadamer's work for the church as a hermeneutical community lies not in reader-centric interpretive theory vis-à-vis the biblical text, but in the recognition that all interpreters of

---

99. Porter and Robinson, *Hermeneutics*, loc. 1476.

100. Gadamer, *Truth and Method*, 379n91, views Ebeling and Fuchs' hermeneutical approach within theology as similar to what he advocates.

101. D. A. Carson, "Hermeneutics: A Brief Assessment of Some Recent Trends," *Themelios* 5.2 (1980) 15–16; J. I. Packer, "Infallible Scripture and the Role of Hermeneutics," in *Scripture and Truth*, ed. D. A. Carson and John D. Woodbridge (Grand Rapids: Baker, 1992), 344, adds, "Fuchs really has left us to sink in the swamps of subjectivist subjectivity, with no available criteria of truth and value at all for the language-events that came our way. The new hermeneutic is in truth the end of the Schleiermacherian road. Its denial of the reality of revealed truth, linked with its rejection of the subject-object frame of reference for knowledge of God through Scripture, produces a state of affairs beyond which there is nowhere to go. Logically, the new hermeneutic is relativism; philosophically, it is irrationalism; psychologically, it is freedom to follow unfettered religious fancy; theologically, it is unitarianism; religiously, it is uncontrolled individualistic mysticism; structurally, it is all these things not by accident but of necessity. We leave it, and move on."

102. As Carl F. H. Henry, *God, Revelation and Authority*, vol. 4: *God Who Speaks and Shows* (Waco, TX: Word, 1979), 313, claims, "It is imperative to rescue the field of hermeneutics from those literary critics who in establishing the meaning of any given text reject the importance of an author's own cognitive intention. An author's meaning is now widely abandoned as the normative ideal of exegesis; any objective foundation for textual criticism in an earnest philological pursuit of authorial meaning is disowned." Further, "We must therefore repudiate the notion that the interpreter's present-day self-understanding, experience or response is decisive for the meaning and truth of the text, and shun an existential rather than rational approach to the literary documents; we must champion the indispensable importance of historical and philological exegesis in identifying the content of the scripturally given revelation, and must acknowledge that authorial cognitive intention is ultimately definitive for textual meaning" (314–15).

Scripture remain limited in perspective and can thus benefit from interpreting alongside others in the church. David K. Clark rightly asserts, "It is a descriptive fact that readers bring preunderstandings to the Bible, and evangelical theologians simply must acknowledge this fact and reflect on its implications. It is simplistic to think that we are *tabulae rasae* as we interpret the Bible and develop theological convictions."[103] Yet one need not remain beholden to such pre-understandings. As Gadamer claims, although horizons limit one's perspective, one can arrive at deeper understandings through the integration of feedback and insights from multiple perspectives. Churches ought then to pursue and assess their theological convictions not in isolation, but in conjunction with others.[104] As Warnke claims, "It is precisely in confronting other beliefs and other presuppositions that we can both see the inadequacies of our own and transcend them."[105] Those churches which therefore articulate theology in conversation with others—particularly those of other cultures and contexts—might ultimately arrive at a fuller, deeper understanding of biblical truth.[106]

Theological Hermeneutics

One area in which the communal aspect of philosophical hermeneutics has taken root in the church is the emerging discourse on Theological Interpretation of Scripture (TIS).[107] TIS is a hermeneutical approach that

103. David K. Clark, *To Know and Love God: Method for Theology* (Wheaton, IL: Crossway, 2010), 108.

104. Clark, *To Know and Love God*, 114, offers a dialogical model for theological contextualization that seeks to do just that, while also remaining committed to the priority of Scripture in the process.

105. Warnke, *Gadamer*, 172.

106. Merold Westphal, *Whose Community? Which Interpretation? Philosophical Hermeneutics for the Church* (Grand Rapids: Baker Academic, 2009), 143, contends, "The (ongoing) formation of pastors should include learning the hermeneutical humility that recognizes the limits of one's own traditions by learning to recognize and treasure the resources to be found in other traditions. . . . If carried out in a spirit of friendship and mutual respect, they might discover more common ground than they suspected, and even if this does not happen, they might learn from one another. But the double conversation with the biblical text and with other traditions cannot be the exclusive task of an ecclesiastical elite, namely, theologians and pastors. If we take seriously the Reformation theme of the priesthood of all believers, we will have to acknowledge the hermeneutical conversation is the privilege and responsibility of the laity as well."

107. For an introduction and brief evaluation of TIS, see Gregg R. Allison, "Theological Interpretation of Scripture: An Introduction and Preliminary Evaluation," *South.*

emphasizes the value of reading and interpreting the Bible in the context of Christian tradition.[108] According to Joel B. Green, TIS is not a "carefully defined method," but rather "is identified more by certain sensibilities and aims."[109] Daniel J. Treier identifies three such common aims: (1) recovering pre-modern biblical interpretation that consciously sought to read the Bible as God's self-revelation to his people, (2) promoting interpretation within the "Rule of Faith," and (3) locating the task of interpretation within the community of faith—the church.[110]

This interpretive approach contrasts sharply with modern historical-critical methods, which seek to isolate the interpreter from his or her theological tradition to prevent one's preunderstandings from derailing objective interpretation.[111] Proponents of TIS point out that Enlightenment presuppositions that undergird such historical-critical methodologies have fallen into disrepute, and that the promise of objective certainty and interpretive neutrality through the application of

---

Baptist J. Theol. 14.2 (2010) 28–37. The field of TIS has grown in recent years, of which one finds evidence in the *Journal of Theological Interpretation*, as well as volumes like Kevin J. Vanhoozer, ed., *Dictionary for Theological Interpretation of the Bible* (Grand Rapids: Baker, 2005); A. K. M. Adam et al., eds., *Reading Scripture with the Church: Toward a Hermeneutic for Theological Interpretation* (Grand Rapids: Baker Academic, 2006); Kevin J. Vanhoozer et al., eds., *Theological Interpretation of the Old Testament: A Book-by-Book Survey* (Grand Rapids: Baker Academic, 2008); Kevin J. Vanhoozer et al., eds., *Theological Interpretation of the New Testament: A Book-by-Book Survey* (Grand Rapids: Baker Academic, 2008).

108. J. Todd Billings, *The Word of God for the People of God: An Entryway to the Theological Interpretation of Scripture* (Grand Rapids: Eerdmans, 2010), xii, asserts, "In brief, the theological interpretation of Scripture is a multifaceted practice of a community of faith in reading the Bible as God's instrument of self-revelation and saving fellowship. It is not a single, discrete method or discipline; rather, it is a wide range of practices we use toward the goal of knowing God in Christ through Scripture. Reflection on our theological hermeneutic involves examining the theology that we bring to Scripture and investigating how our theologies operate as we read Scripture in the midst of worshiping communities. It also involves patient attention to the biblical text, various forms of biblical criticism, and a critical engagement with the Christian tradition through history—in a variety of cultural contexts."

109. Joel B. Green, *Practicing Theological Interpretation: Engaging Biblical Texts for Faith and Formation* (Grand Rapids: Baker Academic, 2011), 2.

110. Daniel J. Treier, *Introducing Theological Interpretation of Scripture: Recovering a Christian Practice* (Grand Rapids: Baker Academic, 2008), 34–35.

111. For overviews of historical criticism and its relationship to TIS, see Stephen E. Fowl, *Theological Interpretation of Scripture*, Cascade Companions (Eugene, OR: Cascade, 2009), 15–24; Treier, *Introducing Theological Interpretation*, 12–14; Green, *Practicing Theological Interpretation*, 43–50.

rationalistic methods has become more illusion than assurance.[112] Thus J. Todd Billings contends, "The theological interpretation of Scripture is, in many ways, simply the church's attempt to read Scripture again after the hubris and polarities of the Enlightenment have begun to fade."[113]

Theological Tradition

While historical criticism eschews tradition, TIS consciously enfranchises tradition as a formative voice in biblical interpretation. On one level, this interpretive moves flows from an acknowledgment that theological preunderstandings are inevitable. Green asserts, "We live out our lives or engage in biblical interpretation not as 'generic Christians' but as followers of Christ embedded in particular faith communities and theological traditions."[114] This contextual embeddedness then affects how interpreters view and understand the Bible. As Billings claims, "There is no context-free interpretation.... All scriptural interpretation is shaped, to some extent, by the social and cultural location of the interpreter."[115]

The work of TIS involves acknowledging such theological preunderstandings and bringing them to the surface rather than letting them operate sight unseen. Green maintains, "The central question becomes whether we are able and willing to recognize our commitments since failure to do so does not keep us from having those commitments but rather increases the probability that we will unwittingly regard our commitments as simply the way things are for all people in all places and ... as simply 'the plain meaning of Scripture.'"[116] In other words, theological preunderstandings remain operative in biblical interpretation whether or not the interpreter is conscious of them. Therefore, it behooves interpreters to account for them so that such preunderstandings do not exert an uncritical influence on the interpretive process.[117]

---

112. Treier, *Introducing Theological Interpretation*, 34; Green, *Practicing Theological Interpretation*, 47.

113. Billings, *Word of God*, 224.

114. Green, *Practicing Theological Interpretation*, 10.

115. Billings, *Word of God*, 105.

116. Green, *Practicing Theological Interpretation*, 102.

117. Billings, *Word of God*, 17, contends, "Scripture never simply comes to us in a flatly biblical way. It always comes to us within a community of shared faith and mediated by certain theological presuppositions and assumptions. We can hope that these assumptions will themselves be biblical, and that they will be open to being *reshaped* by the Bible—as it is read in light of Christ, by the Spirit's power. But until we admit that

Further, TIS proponents maintain that theological preunderstandings—stemming from various Christian traditions—can exert a positive influence on biblical interpretation. As Treier claims, "Presuppositions can preserve perspectives from outside our time and place and personal subjectivity, bringing them to bear on interpretation perhaps in spite of ourselves."[118] Accordingly, granting theological preunderstandings a seat at the interpretive table can even guard against unhealthy subjectivity in theology. Billings adds, "Belonging to a tradition is not about blind obedience to its norms; it is about making use of legitimate preunderstandings that have shown themselves useful and productive over time."[119] Thus following Gadamer, advocates of TIS seek to incorporate theological tradition and preunderstanding into the hermeneutical task rather than seek to move beyond them.[120]

Communal Hermeneutics

The rationale for this interpretive move implies a need for communal discernment in hermeneutics. Treier explains, "If we replace the ideal of neutral objectivity with constructively critical use of interpreters' presuppositions and perspectives, then Scripture study must not be the province of isolated individuals."[121] Rather, proper hermeneutics requires reading the Bible in the context of both theological tradition and the community of faith. This incorporation of other voices past (i.e., theological tradition) and present (i.e., contemporary church) is necessary because, as Treier claims, "None of us can see comprehensively, with the God's-eye point of view that universal reason would require."[122]

Thus for TIS proponents, the proper locus of biblical interpretation is the church. This conviction stems not just from necessity, but also from the belief that the church was both the recipient of God's revelation in

---

we always bring a map of faith to the biblical text, we cannot make progress in even assessing whether that map is biblical," (emphasis original).

118. Treier, *Introducing Theological Interpretation*, 202.

119. Billings, *Word of God*, 47.

120. Billings, *Word of God*, 46, contends, "Thus, if preunderstandings are simply inescapable, and if they can actually help the process of understanding emerge from the text, then we should not make the normative move of trying to get beyond those preunderstandings."

121. Treier, *Introducing Theological Interpretation*, 34.

122. Treier, *Introducing Theological Interpretation*, 35.

Scripture and—by way of the Spirit—that which gave shape to the canon of Scripture. As Stephen E. Fowl and L. Gregory Jones claim, "Scripture is addressed principally to communities constituted and reconstituted by the Triune God."[123] Further, regarding the development of the biblical canon, Richard D. Thompson adds, "To speak of Christian canon was and is to understand the Christian faith community as the location both for the reading and theological interpretation of these texts in formative ways as part of that community's worship and practice."[124] Thus it is the church, rather than the biblical-critical scholarly guild, which serves as the rightful and primary context for scriptural interpretation.[125]

This conviction concerning the centrality of the church for biblical interpretation also stems from the church's pneumatological character. That is, the church is the context in which the Holy Spirit is at work to illuminate the Scriptures for those seeking to discern God's voice therein. Thus, biblical interpretation necessitates an ecclesial context. Billings explains the rationale:

> 1) The Spirit works to bind together believers into a community held together in oneness rooted in Jesus Christ, and through Christ given "access in one Spirit to the Father" (Eph. 2:17). 2) The Spirit brings fruit manifested in community and witness. . . . 3) As a covenant community, the church is in the sphere of the Spirit's special influence, having moved from being "aliens" and "strangers to the covenants of promise" to being a people joined together into "a holy temple in the Lord," "built together in the Spirit into a dwelling place for God" (Eph. 2:12, 21–22). 4) The Spirit bears witness to Jesus Christ: the teachings, commands, and confession of Jesus Christ (John 14:23–26; 16:12–15; 1 Cor. 12:3).[126]

From this logic, Billings contends, "Through all of these works of the Spirit, we see how God uses the Christian community of the church as

---

123. Stephen E. Fowl and L. Gregory Jones, *Reading in Communion: Scripture and Ethics in Christian Life* (Eugene, OR: Wipf & Stock, 1998), 56.

124. Richard P. Thompson, "Scripture, Christian Canon, and Community: Rethinking Theological Interpretation Canonically," *J. Theol. Interpret.* 4.2 (2010) 265.

125. Thompson, "Scripture, Christian Canon, and Community," 266, notes, however, that "the formative aspect of the biblical-interpretive task in the context of the Christian church has typically been a subject bracketed out of contemporary biblical-critical scholarship."

126. Billings, *Word of God*, 132–33.

Hermeneutical Community

part of the discernment process of hearing what the Spirit speaks through Scripture."[127]

From the perspective of TIS, such hermeneutical community includes the church of past ages. That is, the theological convictions of Christians from previous centuries ought to inform how Christians today interpret the Bible. Billings again highlights the rationale for this conviction: "If we are to believe God's promise through Scripture to send the Spirit to the church to lead her into all truth, to bind together the church as Christ's body, to give her gifts and bear fruit through the Spirit's power—then we should expect to see the Spirit's work in past Christian communities."[128] In other words, the presence and work of the Holy Spirit in the church from Pentecost onward engenders a high view of theological tradition. Such tradition is not dead orthodoxy but a witness to the Spirit's theological guidance. Historical theology therefore has a role to play in contemporary biblical interpretation.[129]

TIS advocates thus adhere to the ancient "Rule of Faith" as a formative part of hermeneutics. The Rule of Faith was an early summary account of core Christian beliefs that served to guide biblical interpretation.[130] According to Fowl, this summary—and its development in early creeds—"provides the framework within which the diversity of Scripture can be rightly ordered."[131] Billings adds, "The rule of faith is a communal, received account of the central story of Scripture that helps identify the center and the boundaries of a Christian interpretation of Scripture."[132] In adhering to the Rule of Faith, TIS proponents seek to incorporate voices of the past into present biblical interpretation as checks and balances. As Green contends, "The measure of validity for Christian theological interpretation cannot be taken apart from the great creeds of the church,

---

127. Billings, *Word of God*, 133.

128. Billings, *Word of God*, 134.

129. Billings, *Word of God*, 134, notes, "For both Roman Catholics and most Protestants in the sixteenth and seventeenth centuries, the creeds and teachings of the ancient church were standards of discerning the Spirit even though they emerged from cultural and historical circumstances that were vastly different from their own. Instead of assuming that these cultural differences made attention to the ancient church irrelevant, a trust in the Spirit's work in the Christian community through time made them draw upon ancient creeds, councils, and teachings as a check and balance for their own time."

130. Fowl, *Theological Interpretation of Scripture*, 29.

131. Fowl, *Theological Interpretation of Scripture*, 29.

132. Billings, *Word of God*, 28–29.

a concern with the Rule of Faith, and the history of Christian interpretation and its embodiment in Christian lives and communities."[133]

The hermeneutical community that TIS envisions also includes the present, worldwide church. That is, biblical interpreters must take into account the interpretive conclusions of Christians in other contexts and cultures, for they too are part of God's church—the community of the Spirit. Treier thus claims, "Thanks to the Holy Spirit, non-Western voices can no longer be marginal as they once were. We must listen."[134] Kevin J. Vanhoozer adds, "No one interpretive community can mine all the treasures of the Word of God by itself. If biblical interpretation is indeed the soul of theology, then theologians had better attend the global conversation."[135]

Conversation in such a cross-cultural hermeneutical community aids theological development by helping interpreters transcend their cultural limitations. Billings explains,

> Since all cultures have idols resistant to God's transforming work through Scripture, how are we to discern them? Cultural exegesis is notoriously difficult. Culture is like the water that fish swim in; it's just "the way things are," the lens through which we see the world. Because of this, one of the most effective ways of coming to know one's own culture is to encounter another culture. We don't realize that we have been swimming in a stream until we encounter a pond or an ocean! This cross-cultural encounter provides both illumination and criticism of how one receives the Bible in one's own culture.[136]

In other words, a cross-cultural hermeneutical community can help interpreters overcome their cultural blind spots to more adequately understand God's word. Cultural variance in theology can thus be a gift to the church as it seeks to interpret the Scriptures.[137]

TIS proponents thus seek to foster global theological conversation as a formative aspect of theological development. Michael A. Rynkiewich

---

133. Green, *Practicing Theological Interpretation*, 127.

134. Treier, *Introducing Theological Interpretation*, 186.

135. Kevin J. Vanhoozer, "One Rule to Rule Them All? Theological Method in an Era of World Christianity," in *Globalizing Theology: Belief and Practice in an Era of World Christianity*, ed. Craig Ott and Harold A. Netland (Grand Rapids: Baker Academic, 2006), 122.

136. Billings, *Word of God*, 137.

137. Billings, *Word of God*, 107.

raises an important question: "As local churches begin to do local theology, how will the church as a whole resist parochialism and nihilism?"[138] One way is for the church to engage other theological perspectives. Rynkiewich explains, "With the majority of Christians now in the south and east, perhaps it is time to work toward a mutuality in which equal partners enter a round-table discussion, bringing gifts of hermeneutical principles, in order to do theology together."[139] Acknowledging the fact that every community is prone to misread Scripture by projecting cultural assumptions onto it, Thompson adds, "Thus, not only do these various interpretive communities need the diversity of voices at their own table, but they also need to be conversant at other tables, listening to other faith communities, divergent voices, and even dissenters who may see and interpret things differently."[140]

Ultimately, advocates of TIS view the past and present church as valuable checks and balances within the task of theology. Such a hermeneutical community that spans time and space serves, in Vanhoozer's words, to keep theology "in bounds."[141] While the church is not the final standard for truth and theology—but rather sits under the Bible as the supreme norm for life and faith—the church, as a hermeneutical community filled with the Spirit, nevertheless serves as a valuable source of discernment for theological development.[142] Thus, for TIS proponents, theology is a task for the church, by the church, and within the church.

Postliberal Hermeneutics

A similar movement to TIS came in the form of postliberal theology, which developed out of Yale Divinity School in the late twentieth century.[143] The similarity between these two approaches to theology owes partially to the mutual influence of Karl Barth. Treier cites Barth as a

---

138. Michael A. Rynkiewich, "Mission, Hermeneutics, and the Local Church," *J. Theol. Interpret.* 1.1 (2007) 60.

139. Rynkiewich, "Mission, Hermeneutics, and the Local Church," 60.

140. Thompson, "Scripture, Christian Canon, and Community," 268.

141. Vanhoozer, "One Rule to Rule Them All?," 116.

142. Billings, *Word of God*, 132–35.

143. Daniel J. Treier, "What Is Theological Interpretation? An Ecclesiological Reduction," *Int. J. Syst. Theol.* 12.2 (2010) 144–61, highlights similarities between the two movements and considers postliberalism a "hermeneutical cousin" of TIS (159).

pioneer and inspiration for contemporary theological interpretation,[144] while Gary Dorrien claims, "The postliberal movement is essentially a Barthian project."[145] Such Barthian roots also help explain, to some extent, why advocates of TIS and theological postliberalism both embrace a kind of communal, ecclesial hermeneutic. Barth himself located the pursuit of biblical understanding within the context of the church. He argued, "Theology is not a private subject for theologians only. Nor is it a private subject for professors. . . . Nor is theology a private subject of study for pastors. Fortunately, there have repeatedly been congregation members, and often whole congregations, who have pursued theology energetically while their pastors were theological infants or barbarians. Theology is a matter for the Church. . . . In the Church there are really no non-theologians."[146] He also recognized the value of pursuing theological understanding in conversation with other past and present voices within the church.[147] With such roots in Barth, postliberalism grew into a major movement in theological studies and beyond toward the end of the twentieth century.[148]

Postliberal theology serves as a reaction to modern theological liberalism, which tends to domesticate biblical truth by seeking to make the

---

144. Treier, *Introducing Theological Interpretation*, 14–20.

145. Gary J. Dorrien, "A Third Way in Theology? The Origins of Postliberalism," *Christ. Century* 118.20 (2001) 16; Treier, "What Is Theological Interpretation?," 150, yet cautions against "loading the entire genealogy" of both TIS and, by extension, postliberal theology on the shoulders of Karl Barth, and highlights other additional sources from which the movements developed (150–53).

146. Karl Barth, *God in Action: Theological Addresses*, trans. E. G. Homrighausen and Karl J. Ernst (New York: Round Table, 1936), 56–57. It is not surprising then that Karl Barth, "No Boring Theology!," *South East Asia J. Theol.* 11.1 (1969) 5, later encouraged leaders of the church in Asia, saying, "Now it is your task to be Christian theologians in your new, different and special situation with heart and head, with mouth and hands. . . . [S]ay that which you have to say as Christians for God's sake, responsibly and concretely with your own words and thoughts, concepts and ways! . . . You truly do not need to become 'European', 'Western' men, not to mention 'Barthians', in order to be good Christians and theologians. You may feel free to be South East Asian Christians."

147. Barth, *God in Action*, 54, insists that the task of dogmatics "is to carry on a comprehensive investigation of the entire Church's language, concepts, phrases, and way of thinking in the present. It must keep in living contact with biblical exegesis, and it must make critical comparison of the conclusions of older and newer interpreters, preachers, and teachers of the Church, and thereby constantly inquire after 'the dogma.'"

148. For an overview of the rise (and subsequent decline) of theological postliberalism, see Paul J. DeHart, *The Trial of the Witnesses: The Rise and Decline of Postliberal Theology* (Malden, MA: Blackwell, 2006), 1–56.

Bible intelligible and relevant within modern society. Postliberal theologians believe that such liberal theology has undermined the witness of the Scriptures. They instead aim to develop theology that allows the Scriptures to speak on their own terms rather than treat them as mere references to historical events or expressions of some deeper religious experience. Postliberal theology, however, defies a clear, bounded definition.[149] Sam Houston, a religious studies scholar, observes that theological postliberalism did not feature "one unified set of conceptual tools that marked its approach to theological doctrine and biblical hermeneutics."[150] George Hunsinger notes that it "represents a loose coalition of interests, united more by what it opposes or envisions than by any common theological program."[151]

Accordingly, it is perhaps easier to define postliberalism negatively—in reference to what it stands against. Paul J. DeHart thus defines theological postliberalism as "the attempted construction of a distinct approach to Christian theology's basic procedures and self-understanding which self-consciously and systematically opposes itself to specific and identifiable concepts and methods of academic theology (putatively dominant since at least the beginning of the nineteenth century) which are labeled 'liberal,' 'modernist,' or 'revisionist' and which are seen as covertly threatening or undermining the basic theological task of enabling Christian witness."[152] For example, early postliberals expressed dissatisfaction at how modern liberal theologians locate the meaning of Scripture outside the text—whether in its historical referent or in the supposed universal religious experience it evokes—and sought to counter this tendency in various ways.

At the forefront of this emerging postliberal movement were George Lindbeck and Hans Frei—colleagues on the theological faculty at Yale. In *The Eclipse of Biblical Narrative: A Study in Eighteenth and*

---

149. Kevin W. Hector, "Postliberal Hermeneutics: Narrative, Community, and the Meaning of Scripture," *Expo. Times* 122.3 (2010) 105–16; Michael Root, "What Is Postliberal Theology? Was There a Yale School? Why Care?," *Pro Eccles.* 27.4 (2018) 401, notes that part of the difficulty in defining postliberalism lies in the fact that "there was never a manifesto stating what postliberal theology was about or for."

150. Sam Houston, "Narrative and Ideology: The Promises and Pitfalls of Postliberal Theology," *Relig. Theol.* 23 (2016) 161.

151. George Hunsinger, "Postliberal Theology," in *The Cambridge Companion to Postmodern Theology*, ed. Kevin J. Vanhoozer (Edinburgh: Cambridge University Press, 2003), 42.

152. DeHart, *Trial of the Witnesses*, 1–2.

Nineteenth Century Hermeneutics, Frei demonstrates how both liberal and conservative theologians failed to adequately interpret the genre of "realistic narrative" in the Bible.[153] Frei outlined a third (intratextual)[154] way for understanding such passages, a move that became a harbinger of the kind of postliberal reaction against theological liberalism that was to come.[155] On the heels of Frei's landmark work, Lindbeck's publication of *The Nature of Doctrine: Religion and Theology in a Postliberal Age* in 1984 crystallized postliberal misgivings with liberal theology and provided contours for the emerging theological movement.[156] Others—particularly those scholars who studied and taught at Yale—also joined the fray and began developing theology along postliberal lines.[157]

Cultural-Linguistic Theory

One particular move that helped launch theological postliberalism was Lindbeck's application of cultural-linguistic theory within social sciences to ecumenical challenges related to Christian doctrine. He notes, "It has become customary in a considerable body of anthropological, sociological, and philosophical literature . . . to emphasize neither the cognitive nor the experiential-expressive aspects of religion; rather,

---

153. Hans W. Frei, *The Eclipse of Biblical Narrative: A Study in Eighteenth and Nineteenth Century Hermeneutics* (New Haven, CT: Yale University Press, 1974).

154. Frei did not directly appeal in *Eclipse of Biblical Narrative* to the concept of "intratextuality," which developed later through the work of Lindbeck. Yet Frei's hermeneutical approach was essentially intratextual, in that he believed the Bible sets the context for its own meaning. William C. Placher, "Paul Ricoeur and Postliberal Theology: A Conflict of Interpretations?," *Mod. Theol.* 4.1 (1987) 38, explains this hermeneutical notion of intratextuality that Frei and Lindbeck ultimately shared: "The Bible creates a linguistic world, and one understands it not by seeking its reference to religious experience or to historical events but by seeing the rules of language it sets out and exemplifies." In other words, the Bible's true meaning is not located somewhere outside of the text; it is located in the text itself, constituted by the content and shape of the narrative.

155. Frei, *Eclipse of Biblical Narrative*, 1–16, 245–66, 307–24; Hans W. Frei, "The 'Literal Reading' of Biblical Narrative in the Christian Tradition: Does It Stretch or Will It Break?," in *Theology and Narrative: Selected Essays*, by Hans W. Frei, ed. George Hunsinger and William C. Placher (New York: Oxford University Press, 1993), 147–48.

156. George A. Lindbeck, *The Nature of Doctrine: Religion and Theology in a Postliberal Age* (Louisville, KY: Westminster John Knox, 1984).

157. Dorrien, "Third Way in Theology," 16, cites James J. Buckley, J. A. DiNoia, Garrett Green, Stanley Hauerwas, George Hunsinger, Bruce D. Marshall, William Placher, George Stroup, Ronald Thiemann, and David Yeago as scholars who followed Frei and Lindbeck in the development of theological postliberalism.

emphasis is placed on those respects in which religions resemble languages together with their correlative forms of life and are thus similar to cultures (insofar as these are understood semiotically as reality and value systems—that is, as idioms for the constructing of reality and the living of life)."[158] Scholars have increasingly come to view cultural forms and languages not as the expressions or outworking of some inner reality of culture (however conceived), but rather as the very components that constitute and sustain a culture. That is, culture exists only as those forms and languages exist. Lindbeck's approach to theology and doctrine thus drew from the work of scholars like Emile Durkheim, Ludwig Wittgenstein, and Clifford Geertz.[159]

Lindbeck's aim in developing a cultural-linguistic approach to Christian doctrine was to provide a plausible basis for unity across branches of Christianity which have heretofore maintained seemingly incompatible doctrinal beliefs. Being heavily involved in global ecumenical discussions, Lindbeck was dissatisfied with the lack of "adequate categories" for understanding the nature and function of doctrines.[160] He thus sought a way of reconceptualizing doctrine that would explain the possibility of Christian unity without forcing various branches of Christianity to compromise or relinquish their long-held doctrinal convictions.[161]

This approach countered both "cognitive-propositional" and "experiential-expressivist" views of doctrine and religion, which Lindbeck viewed as inadequate for fostering Christian ecumenism. The cognitive-propositional view of religion and doctrine, according to Lindback, "stresses the ways in which church doctrines function as informative propositions or truth claims about objective realities."[162] The experiential-expressive view—prominent within theological liberalism—"interprets doctrines as noninformative and nondiscursive symbols of inner feelings, attitudes, or existential orientations."[163] Lindbeck contends that both views of doctrine undermine "the possibility of doctrinal reconciliation without capitulation."[164]

---

158. Lindbeck, *Nature of Doctrine*, 17–18.
159. Lindbeck, *Nature of Doctrine*, 20.
160. Lindbeck, *Nature of Doctrine*, 7.
161. Lindbeck, *Nature of Doctrine*, 15–17.
162. Lindbeck, *Nature of Doctrine*, 16.
163. Lindbeck, *Nature of Doctrine*, 16.
164. Lindbeck, *Nature of Doctrine*, 16.

Lindbeck's alternative aimed to promote ecumenism by reframing the nature and function of doctrine according to cultural-linguistic views of religion in contemporary anthropological, sociological, and philosophical studies.[165] He notes that within a cultural-linguistic approach, religions serve as *a priori* "comprehensive interpretive schemes . . . which structure human experience and understanding of self and world."[166] He further explains,

> A religion can be viewed as a kind of cultural and/or linguistic framework or medium that shapes the entirety of life and thought. . . . It is not primarily an array of beliefs about the true and the good (though it may involve these), or a symbolism expressive of basic attitudes, feelings, or sentiments (though these will be generated). Rather it is similar to an idiom that makes possible the description of realities, the formulation of beliefs, and the experiencing of inner attitudes, feelings and sentiments. Like a culture or language, it is a communal phenomenon that shapes the subjectivities of individuals rather than being primarily a manifestation of those subjectivities."[167]

In other words, religions resemble languages. Just as language and cultural frameworks serve as the prior realities that enable one to communicate and experience life, so also religions serve as prior frameworks which condition one's beliefs and experiences.

Drawing on the linguistic analogy, Lindbeck claims that in a cultural-linguistic approach, religious doctrines function like grammar rather than vocabulary.[168] While vocabulary is variable, grammatical rules remain constant. Linking the nature of doctrine to that of grammar within language, Lindbeck thus contends, "It is the framework and the medium within which Christians know and experience, rather than what they experience or think they know, that retains continuity down through the centuries. . . . To the degree that religions are like languages, they can obviously remain the same amid vast transformations of affirmation and experience."[169] Moreover, from this cultural-linguistic point of view, doc-

---

165. Lindbeck, *Nature of Doctrine*, 17–18.
166. Lindbeck, *Nature of Doctrine*, 32.
167. Lindbeck, *Nature of Doctrine*, 33.
168. Lindbeck, *Nature of Doctrine*, 80–81.
169. Lindbeck, *Nature of Doctrine*, 84.

trines function as "communally authoritative rules of discourse, attitude, and action."[170]

Accordingly, Lindbeck maintains that this cultural-linguistic understanding of doctrine is more capable of uniting factions of the Christian church because it recognizes doctrines not as fixed theological truth claims or expressive symbols but simply as the rules that regulate the life and faith of the church.[171] Lindbeck asserts, "Rules, unlike propositions or expressive symbols, retain an invariant meaning under changing conditions of compatibility and conflict."[172] Thus, "to the degree that doctrines function as rules ... there is no logical problem in understanding how historically opposed positions can in some, even if not all, cases be reconciled while remaining in themselves unchanged. Contrary to what happens when doctrines are construed as propositions or expressive symbols, doctrinal reconciliation without capitulation is a coherent notion."[173] According to Lindbeck, as the "cultural-linguistic system" (i.e., doctrine) interacts with new and variable contextual realties, it will lead to new theological formulas and expressions.[174] Yet those diverse formulas and expressions can remain united in a common doctrinal grammar that undergirds them all.[175]

---

170. Lindbeck, *Nature of Doctrine*, 18.

171. Lindbeck, *Nature of Doctrine*, 84. Lindbeck thus also refers to his proposal as "regulative" or "rule" theory (18). Moreover, he recognizes that the contention that doctrines function as a means of regulating life and faith is not new: "The notion of *regulae fidei* goes back to the earliest Christian centuries, and later historians and systematic theologians have often recognized in varying degrees that the operational logic of religious teachings in their communally authoritative (or, as we shall simply say, doctrinal) role is regulative. They have recognized, in other words, that at least part of the task of doctrines is to recommend and exclude certain ranges of—among other things—propositional utterances or symbolic activities" (18–19). Yet Lindbeck asserts, "What is innovative about the present proposal is that this becomes the only job that doctrines do in their role as church teachings" (19).

172. Lindbeck, *Nature of Doctrine*, 18.

173. Lindbeck, *Nature of Doctrine*, 18.

174. Lindbeck, *Nature of Doctrine*, 39.

175. Lindbeck, *Nature of Doctrine*, 95, posits, "If the same rules that guided the formation of the original paradigms are operative in the construction of new formulations, they express one and the same doctrine." Lindbeck highlights the creedal formulations of Nicaea and Chalcedon to explain his point (94–96). Regarding them, he contends, "Though the ancient formulations may have continuing value, they do not on the basis of rule theory have doctrinal authority. That authority belongs rather to the rules they instantiate. If these rules, as we earlier suggested, are such regulative principles as monotheism, historical specificity and Christological maximalism, it is at least plausible to claim that Nicaea and Chalcedon represent historically conditioned

This "regulative" approach to doctrine helped establish postliberal theology as a third option in light of what Lindbeck saw as an impasse between both the cognitive-propositional approach (among conservative theologians) and experiential-expressivist approach to theology (among adherents to modern theological liberalism). Lindbeck notes, "What propositionalists with their stress on unchanging truth and falsity regard as faithful, applicable, and intelligible is likely to be dismissed as dead orthodoxy by liberal experiential-expressivists. Conversely, the liberal claim that change and pluralism in religious expression are necessary for intelligibility, applicability, and faithfulness is attacked by the propositionally orthodox as an irrationally relativistic and practically self-defeating betrayal of the faith."[176] Lindbeck countered both approaches by launching a new one. He explains, "A postliberal might propose to overcome this polarization between tradition and innovation by a distinction between abiding doctrinal grammar and variable theological vocabulary."[177]

Lindbeck was not alone in seeking such a postliberal third way; Frei—his colleague at Yale—was equally instrumental in the rise of postliberal theology. Frei not only anticipated this cultural-linguistic turn in his earlier work on hermeneutics, he also developed a deep appreciation for Lindbeck's landmark proposal.[178] Frei describes Christianity along similar cultural-linguistic lines:

> Christianity is a religion, a social organism. Its self-description marks it typically as a religion in ways similar to those given by sociologists of religion or cultural anthropologists. It is a community held together by constantly changing yet enduring structures, practices, and institutions . . . and by a set of rituals—preaching, baptism, the celebration of communion, common beliefs and attitudes, all of these linked—again typical of a religion—with a set of narratives connected with each other in the sacred text and its interpretive tradition. All of these are, for

---

formulations of doctrines that are unconditionally and permanently necessary to mainstream Christian identity. Rule theory, in short, allows (though it does not require) giving these creeds the status that major Christian traditions have attributed to them, but with the understanding that they are permanently authoritative paradigms, not formulas to be slavishly repeated" (96).

176. Lindbeck, *Nature of Doctrine*, 113.

177. Lindbeck, *Nature of Doctrine*, 113.

178. Frei, "Literal Reading," 146–47; Charles L. Campbell, *Preaching Jesus: New Directions for Homiletics in Hans Frei's Postliberal Theology* (Eugene, OR: Wipf & Stock, 2006), 68, maintains, "It is difficult to overestimate the significance of this cultural-linguistic turn for Frei's approach to biblical narrative."

social scientist and theologian ... not the *signs* or *manifestations* of the religion, rather they *constitute* it, in complex and changing coherence.[179]

From this understanding of Christianity, Frei contends—along with Lindbeck—that "Christian doctrinal statements are understood to have a status similar to that of grammatical rules implicit in discourse."[180] This cultural-linguistic approach became, for Frei and Lindbeck, a central means of moving theology beyond cognitive-propositional and liberal theology. While postliberal theology is not without its shortcomings,[181] it became a powerful and popular alternative in the late twentieth century.

Communal Hermeneutics

An implication of this postliberal cultural-linguistic approach to doctrine is that hermeneutics and theology become communal endeavors. Just as language is always socially embodied and constituted, so too is doctrine in this view. Lindbeck highlights this communal aspect in his discussion of the infallibility of doctrine. He asserts that it is the *consensus fidelium* (or *consensus ecclesiae*) that is "most nearly infallible in grammatical and, by transference, doctrinal matters."[182] That is, the church—the community of the faithful—serves, according to Lindbeck, as the trustworthy arbiter of whether theological formulations are faithful. He explains, "Just as the contemporary linguist tests technical grammatical formulations by seeing whether their ordinary-language consequences are acceptable or unacceptable to competent speakers of the language being investigated, so the student of a religion submits the consequences of

---

179. Hans W. Frei, "Theology and the Interpretation of Narrative: Some Hermeneutical Considerations," in *Theology and Narrative: Selected Essays*, by Hans W. Frei, ed. George Hunsinger and William C. Placher (New York: Oxford University Press, 1993), 96–97, emphasis original.

180. Hans W. Frei, *Types of Christian Theology*, ed. George Hunsinger and William C. Placher (New Haven, CT: Yale University Press, 1992), 4. Frei makes this assertion in reference to a type of theology he associates with Karl Barth, for whom he maintained a strong affinity. A driving question for Frei in this work is "What kind of theology is most nearly hospitable to the literal sense of Scripture?" (18). For Frei, it was the theology which Barth typified (44).

181. For criticisms of postliberal theological sentiment, see Houston, "Narrative and Ideology"; Carl F. H. Henry, "Narrative Theology: An Evangelical Appraisal," *Trinity J.* 8.1 (1987) 3–19.

182. Lindbeck, *Nature of Doctrine*, 99.

doctrinal formulations to the judgment of competent practitioners of that religion."[183] In this view, "the locus of [doctrinal] infallibility . . . is the whole community of competent speakers of a language."[184] Theology and hermeneutics are thus communal pursuits, not isolated practices. Accordingly, Lindbeck envisions a day in which "communities of interpretation come into existence in which pastors, biblical scholars, theologians, and laity together seek God's guidance in the written word for their communal as well as individual lives."[185]

In addition to Lindbeck, Frei explores this communal aspect of theology and hermeneutics in his writing on the literal sense of Scripture. While his early work focused heavily on the biblical genre of "realistic narrative" and how narrative passages in Scripture have historically been interpreted,[186] his hermeneutical focus later turned toward the notion of Scripture's *"sensus literalis."*[187] Frei had previously argued that scriptural meaning rests in the text itself and is discernible through literary analysis (rather than critical appeals to references outside of the text). As his hermeneutical thought developed over the years following *Eclipse of Biblical Narrative*, he became dissatisfied with its more narrow focus on text and analytic procedure and sought to broaden the scope of biblical hermeneutics, which he did through his explication of Scripture's literal sense.

Frei locates the literal sense of Scripture within a communal context. He contends, "The *sensus literalis* is the way the text has generally been used in the community."[188] Scripture's literal sense, according to Frei, "belongs first and foremost into the context of a sociolinguistic community, that is, of the specific religion of which it is part, rather than into a literary ambience."[189] The meaning of the text, in other words, is what it means within the community that recognizes the text as sacred.

183. Lindbeck, *Nature of Doctrine*, 99.

184. Lindbeck, *Nature of Doctrine*, 102.

185. George A. Lindbeck, "Scripture, Consensus, and Community," in *Biblical Interpretation in Crisis: The Ratzinger Conference on Bible and Church*, ed. Richard John Neuhaus (Grand Rapids: Eerdmans, 1989), 99.

186. Frei, *Eclipse of Biblical Narrative*.

187. Frei, *Types of Christian Theology*, 14–18; Frei, "Theology and the Interpretation," 102–14.

188. Frei, "Theology and the Interpretation," 104. He asserts that the literal sense is "deeply embedded in the Christian interpretive tradition of its sacred text, and in that way embedded in the self-description of the Christian religion as a social complex," which "shows the convergence of interpretation and communal self-description" (110).

189. Frei, "Literal Reading," 143–44.

Hermeneutical Community

With such claims, Frei intends to show that one finds biblical meaning in and through the traditioned interpretation of Scripture by the Christian community, rather than in external, historical realities to which Scripture refers or through formal literary analysis of the text itself. Charles L. Campbell summarizes Frei's conviction here regarding the communal nature of scriptural interpretation: "Christians learn to interpret Scripture not by learning general hermeneutical or literary theories, but by being trained to apply the informal rules and conventions for the use of Scripture that are embodied in the language and practices of the Christian community."[190]

Insofar as Frei embodies basic hermeneutical sentiments within postliberalism, hermeneutics in this approach is thus properly communal. Charles M. Wood, who completed his doctoral studies at Yale and later influenced Frei's understanding of Scripture's literal sense, brings clarity to this point. He asserts that biblical knowledge

> is more readily achieved when one approaches it not as a solitary reader before an isolated text but as a *member of a community* in which the text already has a life. The interpreter who first hears the text as living voice, who witnesses that voice being heard by others, and whose own identity is formed or reformed in interaction with those for whom this text is the word of life, is in a different position from that of the interpreter who sits alone before a strange, mute document with the task of teasing some meaning from it. To the first, the text already says something; in its articulation and hearing there has already been interpretation. But, more important still, this interpreter has been given a way of using the text, and has been initiated into the conceptual skills and capacities that mark an existence nourished on these writings. The value of this sort of preparation is not so much that one has been furnished an interpretation of the text—that can be a mixed blessing indeed—but that one has been equipped to make use of the text.... [T]he interpreter who actually has the use of the text may be in a far better position to hear the text afresh than someone who comes to it without that sort of readiness.[191]

---

190. Campbell, *Preaching Jesus*, 84.

191. Charles M. Wood, *The Formation of Christian Understanding: Theological Hermeneutics* (Valley Forge, PA: Trinity Press International, 1993), 42, emphasis added. Wood's contention here underscores the point that even within a hermeneutical community approach to local theological development—one that seeks, as the subsequent chapter will show, to mitigate the imposition of foreign doctrinal systems on local

LOCAL THEOLOGICAL DEVELOPMENT

In other words, membership in a community of interpreters (e.g., the church) is a necessary part of Christian scriptural understanding.[192]

A danger of this postliberal understanding of communal hermeneutics, however, is that it can subsume the authority of Scripture under the consensus of the community. Lindbeck's proposal appears to do just that,[193] as does the work of Stanley Hauerwas,[194] a fellow postliberal theologian who claims that the Bible "should only be made available to those who have undergone the hard discipline of existing as part of God's people."[195] That is, it should be taken out of the hands of individuals and entrusted to the church, for only in the context of the church can one experience the kind of spiritual and moral transformation requisite for understanding Scripture's message.[196] More pointedly, Hauerwas maintains (via Stanley Fish) that "texts only exist in a continuing web of interpretive practices" and have "no 'real' meaning" in themselves.[197] Rather, it is the church that determines the meaning and sense of scriptural texts.[198] Such a construal locates authority not in the text but in the interpreting community, a move which evangelicals will decry (even while recognizing the reality and inevitability of traditioned interpretation, which Gadamer and advocates of TIS have noted).

---

believers—the outsider still inevitably brings preunderstandings to the theological process. Yet this reality does not necessarily impede the work of theological development among local churches, so long as outside voices actively promote the voices of locals as fellow hermeneutical community members. Indeed, as Wood claims, such traditioned interpretation of the text by one formed within a specific interpretive community can even be a fruitful way of "hearing the text afresh," in ways that might be unavailable to those who read from a different tradition. Wood's contention here displays a clear affinity with both Gadamerian hermeneutics and the TIS movement. Moreover, these points further underscore the need to read and interpret Scripture in community, to broaden one's conceptual horizons and identify theological blind spots of one's traditioned understanding.

192. Wood, *Formation of Christian Understanding*, 45–46, thus laments the kind of scholarly specialization in biblical interpretation that has alienated the task of theology from the local church.

193. Lindbeck, *Nature of Doctrine*, 98–104.

194. Hauerwas completed his doctoral work at Yale in the late 1960s, during which postliberal sentiments were taking shape among the theological faculty of the divinity school.

195. Stanley Hauerwas, *Unleashing the Scripture: Freeing the Bible from Captivity to America* (Nashville: Abingdon, 1993), 9.

196. Hauerwas, *Unleashing the Scripture*, 15.

197. Hauerwas, *Unleashing the Scripture*, 20.

198. Hauerwas, *Unleashing the Scripture*, 23, 27.

Nevertheless, postliberal theological discourse has served as a key area in which the notion of communal hermeneutics has developed. Some will rightly contend with the tendency of postliberal scholars to locate hermeneutical authority and infallibility in the believing community. Yet, as James Callahan explains, "Postliberals wish to resuscitate the practice of Bible reading within the Christian community rather than sacrifice it to the reproaches of the intellectually and critically elite."[199] Evangelicals can certainly appreciate this emphasis that the Bible is a book belonging to the church and is properly read and understood in community.

Pentecostal Hermeneutics

Another area in which communal hermeneutics has found a home is Pentecostal theology.[200] Yet as William Atkinson, a scholar in Pentecostal and charismatic studies, asserts, "It would be wrong to assume . . . that there is just one hermeneutical approach common to all Pentecostals, or that Pentecostals typically use hermeneutics which are unique to them. There are, rather, tendencies which are common among Pentecostals."[201] One common tendency is to approach the hermeneutical task through the triadic relationship between the Bible, the Holy Spirit, and the church, as the community of faith. Marius Nel, a scholar on Pentecostalism, explains, "The three main elements of a Pentecostal hermeneutics can thus be described as: The interrelationship between the *Holy Spirit* as the One animating the *Scriptures* and empowering the *believing community*."[202]

---

199. James Callahan, "The Bible Says: Evangelical and Postliberal Biblicism," *Theol. Today* 53.4 (1997) 463.

200. For a detailed history of Pentecostal hermeneutics, see Kenneth J. Archer, *A Pentecostal Hermeneutic: Spirit, Scripture and Community* (Cleveland, TN: CPT, 2005), 47–211; for more brief surveys, see Sam Hey, "Changing Roles of Pentecostal Hermeneutics," *Evang. Rev. Theol.* 25.3 (2001) 210–18; Kenneth J. Archer, "Pentecostal Hermeneutics: Retrospect and Prospect," *J. Pentecostal Theol.* 8 (1996) 63–81.

201. William Atkinson, "Worth a Second Look? Pentecostal Hermeneutics," *Evangel* 21.2 (2003) 49.

202. Marius Nel, "Attempting to Define a Pentecostal Hermeneutics," *Scriptura* 114 (2015) 6, emphasis original.

Hermeneutical Triad of Word, Spirit, and Community

This triad of the Scriptures, the Spirit, and the community of faith has become increasingly germane to Pentecostal hermeneutics in recent years.[203] Those advocating or utilizing this "threefold framework"[204] include Steven J. Land,[205] Rick D. Moore,[206] John Christopher Thomas,[207] Kenneth J. Archer,[208] and Amos Yong.[209] Accordingly, Archer claims that this triad has "become the primary rubric for discussing a critical and constructive pentecostal hermeneutic."[210] Further, Thomas roots such a triadic approach to hermeneutics in Acts 15 and points out that the components of this hermeneutical triad—"the community, the activity of the Spirit, and the Scripture"—were all present in the Jerusalem Council narrative, in which multiple interlocutors sought to discern the will of God.[211]

Each component of this hermeneutical triad plays a unique, yet interdependent role in the process of interpretation. Pentecostal scholar Melissa L. Archer explains, "Although theoretically each element of the rubric stands on its own, the reality is that Scripture, community, and

---

203. Mark J. Cartledge, "Text-Community-Spirit: The Challenges Posed by Pentecostal Theological Method to Evangelical Theology," in *Spirit and Scripture: Exploring a Pneumatic Hermeneutic*, ed. Kevin L. Spawn and Archie T. Wright (New York: T&T Clark International, 2012), 134, posits, "The most recent Pentecostal scholarship has articulated its theological method in terms of an interrelation between 'text-community-Spirit.' That is, the inspired text of Scripture functions normatively within the community of faith, the church, as the Holy Spirit mediates between the horizon of the text and the horizon of the community."

204. Lee Roy Martin, "Introduction to Pentecostal Hermeneutics," in *Pentecostal Hermeneutics: A Reader*, ed. Lee Roy Martin (Leiden: Brill, 2013), 9.

205. Steven J. Land, "A Passion for the Kingdom—Revisioning Pentecostal Spirituality," *J. Pentecostal Theol.* 1 (1992) 39.

206. Rick D. Moore, "Canon and Charisma in the Book of Deuteronomy," *J. Pentecostal Theol.* 1 (1992) 75–76.

207. John Christopher Thomas, "Reading the Bible from Within Our Traditions: A Pentecostal Hermeneutic as Test Case," in *Between Two Horizons: Spanning New Testament Studies and Systematic Theology*, ed. Joel B. Green and Max Turner (Grand Rapids: Eerdmans, 2000), 108–22; John Christopher Thomas, "Women, Pentecostalism, and the Bible: An Experiment in Pentecostal Hermeneutics," in *Pentecostal Hermeneutics: A Reader*, ed. Lee Roy Martin (Leiden: Brill, 2013), 81–94.

208. Archer, *Pentecostal Hermeneutic*.

209. Amos Yong, *Spirit-Word-Community: Theological Hermeneutics in Trinitarian Perspective* (Eugene, OR: Wipf & Stock, 2002).

210. Kenneth J. Archer, "Pentecostal Hermeneutics and the Society for Pentecostal Studies: Reading and Hearing in One Spirit and One Accord," *Pneuma* 37.3 (2015) 328.

211. Thomas, "Women, Pentecostalism, and the Bible," 90.

Spirit are so integrated into the ethos of Pentecostalism that it is difficult to separate them into distinct categories. The Scriptures are a product of the Spirit; the community is formed by the Spirit and shaped by both the Scriptures and the Spirit. Nevertheless, there are important ideas that Pentecostals affirm about Scripture, the community, and the Holy Spirit."[212] Thomas likens the interpretive process to a conversation: "In a Pentecostal hermeneutic the concrete activity of the Spirit in the community is placed into conversation with the biblical text to discern one's way forward on any number of issues."[213]

In this triadic conversation, the Scriptures play an essential role. Generally, Pentecostals highly regard the Bible.[214] Per Kenneth Archer, "The Holy Scripture in its final canonical form provides the primary arena in which the Pentecostal community desires to understand God."[215] Further, the Scriptures serve as an avenue for experiencing God. As Keith Warrington claims, "Pentecostals believe that the main purpose of the Bible is to help them develop their experience of and relationship with God, to be more available to the ministry of the Spirit and to be drawn closer to Jesus."[216] In addition to serving as a means of understanding and experiencing God, the Scriptures also play a corrective role. Scott A. Ellington explains, "Within Pentecostal and charismatic circles, the Bible is the basic rule of faith and practice and supplies the corrective and interpretive authority for all religious experience."[217]

Alongside the Scriptures, the Holy Spirit also plays an important role in the hermeneutical process. According to Kenneth Archer, "The role of the Holy Spirit in the hermeneutical process is to lead and guide the community in understanding the present meaningfulness of

---

212. Melissa L. Archer, "'I Was in the Spirit on the Lord's Day': A Pentecostal Engagement with Worship in the Apocalypse" (PhD diss., Bangor University, 2013), 36.

213. John Christopher Thomas, "'What the Spirit Is Saying to the Church': The Testimony of a Pentecostal in New Testament Studies," in *Spirit and Scripture: Exploring a Pneumatic Hermeneutic*, ed. Kevin L. Spawn and Archie T. Wright (New York: T&T Clark International, 2012), 129.

214. Archer, "'I Was in the Spirit,'" 36, claims, "Pentecostals hold to a high view of Scripture; that is, the Bible is God's written revelation given to humanity, second only to the revelation of Jesus Christ."

215. Archer, *Pentecostal Hermeneutic*, 221.

216. Quoted in Archer, "'I Was in the Spirit,'" 36n29.

217. Scott A. Ellington, "Pentecostalism and the Authority of Scripture," in *Pentecostal Hermeneutics: A Reader*, ed. Lee Roy Martin (Leiden: Brill, 2013), 154.

Scripture."[218] Chris E. W. Green calls the Holy Spirit "Scripture's definitive interpreter,"[219] while Mark J. Cartledge contends, "Pneumatology provides the link between text and community, since the Spirit has both inspired the original text and inspires the reading of the text today."[220] Yet in Pentecostal perspective, the Spirit speaks not just through the Scriptures, but also through the community of believers.[221] Accordingly, the church assumes a vital role in the process of interpretation.[222]

Community as a Component of Hermeneutical Triad

For Pentecostals, the community of faith serves as the proper location for interpreting God's revelation. Kenneth Archer explains, "Pentecostals believe that it is in the context of the believing community that Scripture should be interpreted. The Scripture is not subordinate to the community. The Scripture is a precious gift of God's grace to the community, God's words to them, which is Spirit and truth. The goal of the community is to come to an understanding of what the Spirit is saying presently to the community in and through the biblical text(s) and in and through their cooporate [sic] experiences of the Holy Spirit."[223] Arden C. Autry, professor at Oral Roberts University, adds, "Biblical interpretation is a community task, just as edification, obedience and growth are community responsibilities and functions."[224]

Pentecostals locate the rationale for such communal hermeneutics in the presence of the Holy Spirit within the church. Autry reasons, "If the church is indeed Christ's body and his Spirit indwells the church, I should certainly expect to learn something of him through attention

---

218. Archer, *Pentecostal Hermeneutic*, 248; Archer, "'I Was in the Spirit,'" 37, adds, "Scripture is made alive through the Spirit, who aids both the individual reader and the community in understanding, discerning, and applying it."

219. Chris E. W. Green, "Foretasting the Kingdom: Toward a Pentecostal Theology of the Lord's Supper" (PhD diss., Bangor University, 2012), 189.

220. Cartledge, "Text-Community-Spirit," 141.

221. Archer, *Pentecostal Hermeneutic*, 247–51.

222. Archer, "'I Was in the Spirit,'" 42, posits, "The Spirit is closely connected with the worshipping community for Pentecostals fully expect to encounter the Spirit of God when they are gathered together."

223. Archer, *Pentecostal Hermeneutic*, 252.

224. Arden C. Autry, "Dimensions of Hermeneutics in Pentecostal Focus," *J. Pentecostal Theol.* 1.3 (1993) 45.

to the church."[225] As Robby Waddell claims, "Within Pentecostalism, the Spirit is not limited to the leaders, but all who believe experience the presence and the power of the Spirit. In addition to enabling the revelation and inspiring the reading of scripture, the Spirit also plays a vital role in inspiring the testimonies of the believers."[226]

The church community—being the community of the Spirit—serves as an important safeguard within the task of interpretation. Autry explains, "The subjectivity inherent in personal religious experience is best kept on track not simply through comparison with objective data in the text (important as that is) but also through the sharing of experiences in a community of believers. The multiplication of vantage points provides greater likelihood (if not a guarantee) that self-deception or distortion of the text will be detected and corrected."[227] Similarly, Atkinson declares, "The safeguards are simply that pneumatic exegesis must not be 'cut free' from careful grammatico-historical exegesis, and that the pneumatic exegesis suggested by an individual must be offered to the believing community for evaluation."[228] Such a communal safeguard helps to prevent what Jackie David Johns and Cheryl Bridges Johns call "privatized subjectivism on the one hand and totalitarian objectivism on the other."[229]

---

225. Autry, "Dimensions of Hermeneutics," 45–46.

226. Robby Waddell, "Hearing What the Spirit Says to the Churches: Profile of a Pentecostal Reader of the Apocalypse," in *Pentecostal Hermeneutics: A Reader*, ed. Lee Roy Martin (Leiden: Brill, 2013), 201.

227. Autry, "Dimensions of Hermeneutics," 45; Craig S. Keener, "The Spirit and Biblical Interpretation: Spirit Hermeneutics," *Asian J. Pentecostal Stud.* 23.2 (2020) 141, however, cautions against appealing to this community criterion in isolation. He claims that the Spirit-filled community "is certainly part of the biblical safety net. . . . Awareness of interpretive communities also help us guard against prejudices that reflect a single interpretive location's biases." Yet it is also true that such communities can be wrong in their convictions. Further, group consensus on interpretive issues can often prove elusive. Keener thus contends, "Simply designating one subgroup of Christians as the reliable community of interpretation without argument begs the question of how such a group should be identified, unless we tautologically pre-identify them as 'the best interpreters'" (142–43).

228. Atkinson, "Worth a Second Look?," 52. However, the historical-grammatical approach to biblical hermeneutics, which Atkinson mentions, remains a source of contention within some circles of Pentecostalism. For example, see Kenneth J. Archer, "Spirited Conversation About Hermeneutics: A Pentecostal Hermeneut's Response to Craig Keener's Spirit Hermeneutics," *Pneuma* 39 (2017) 179–97.

229. Jackie David Johns and Cheryl Bridges Johns, "Yielding to the Spirit: A Pentecostal Approach to Group Bible Study," *J. Pentecostal Theol.* 1 (1992) 116.

Pentecostals also recognize that the community of the Spirit transcends time and space—a reality which is leading Pentecostals to see value in engaging with historical theology as well as theology from other cultures. Pentecostal scholar Howard M. Ervin contends,

> The Scriptures are now read within the pneumatic continuity of the faith community, and that community is much larger than the post-Reformation communities of the West. There is a growing sense of accountability to and for the cumulative deposit of the faith once for all delivered. Part of Jesus' promise of the Holy Spirit to the Church is that "he will teach you all things and bring to your remembrance all that I have said unto you . . . he will guide you into all the truth" (John 14:27; 16:13). Thus it seems, at least to this writer, that the hermeneutical enterprise must entertain seriously the insight of the Church. The creeds are not Scripture, but neither are they the memorabilia of a dead past. They are the warp and woof of a living hermeneutical tradition.[230]

In other words, because the Spirit indwelled churches of the past, contemporary churches—communities of that same Spirit—would do well to consider the theological input of historic churches as well as those from different cultures.[231] Autry adds, "Private interpretation of the Bible should be open to being informed by the understanding of others and should be concerned for the needs of others. This openness and concern should be local and world-wide, contemporary and historical in scope."[232]

The Pentecostal community thus recognizes value in adopting a communal approach to hermeneutics. The task of biblical interpretation requires more than just the biblical text and a solitary interpreter; it requires a dialogic relationship among the word of God, the Spirit of God, and the community of God. Thus in Pentecostal perspective, the absence

---

230. Howard M. Ervin, "Hermeneutics: A Pentecostal Option," *Pneuma* 3.1 (1981) 23.

231. Autry, "Dimensions of Hermeneutics," 46–47, follows Ervin's notion of continuity, arguing, "We do not merely share a faith; we share a relationship—to God as 'Abba, Father,' to Christ as Lord, to one another as members of the same body—by the work of the Holy Spirit. We can speak, then, not only of historical, temporal or organizational continuity but also of a spiritual or 'pneumatic continuity,' a continuity of experience with believers of all places and all times, including the very first generation of Christians."

232. Autry, "Dimensions of Hermeneutics," 45.

of any component of this hermeneutical triad significantly undermines the work of discerning and interpreting God's revelation.

Ecumenical Hermeneutics

The notion of communal hermeneutics has also developed within the global ecumenical movement. According to the Faith and Order Commission of the World Council of Churches, "Ecumenical hermeneutics take as its starting point the reality that conversations aiming at greater unity are carried out by representatives of the various churches and that their contributions are mediated through particular ecclesial, cultural, social, economic, geographical and historical backgrounds."[233] Its emphasis on theological conversation between equal partners underscores the communal nature of the ecumenical movement's hermeneutical vision.

This vision for communal hermeneutics became even clearer after the Faith and Order Commission's fifth world conference at Santiago de Compostela in 1993. Following the conference, the commission sought to clarify hermeneutical issues that were troubling ecumenical dialogue on baptism, the eucharist, and the church's ministry.[234] After three further consultations and two draft meetings, the commission published *A Treasure in Earthen Vessels: An Instrument for an Ecumenical Reflection on Hermeneutics*.[235] While this work does not exhaust the ecumenical movement's vision for hermeneutics, it does offer a clear picture of the role of community in the task of theology. Thus, the following sections will focus mainly on this text and its hermeneutical vision.

Hermeneutical Community

According to *A Treasure in Earthen Vessels*, the church is a hermeneutical community. It declares,

> The Church, whether embodied in a local congregation, episcopal diocese, or a Christian World Communion, is called to interpret texts, symbols and practices so as to discern the Word of

---

233. *A Treasure in Earthen Vessels: An Instrument for an Ecumenical Reflection on Hermeneutics*, Faith and Order Paper 182 (Geneva: World Council of Churches, 1998), 34.

234. *Treasure in Earthen Vessels*, 11–12.

235. *Treasure in Earthen Vessels*.

God as a word of life amid ever-changing times and places. This hermeneutical task undertaken by the Church, with the guidance of the Holy Spirit, is a condition for apostolic mission in and for the world. To speak of the Church as an hermeneutical community is also to say that this community is a proper locus for the interpretation and the proclamation of the Gospel.[236]

Further, it advocates for the participation of all members of the community in biblical interpretation:

> Hermeneutics, perhaps especially ecumenical hermeneutics, is not the work of specialists. Ecumenical hermeneutics, in the pursuit of visible church unity, is first and foremost the work of the whole people gathered in believing communities in diverse contexts. Believers, pastors, theologians, and biblical exegetes, each have distinctive gifts to bring to the hermeneutical task. These gifts are most appropriately brought together and exercised within the various settings in which the Church carries out its work as an hermeneutical community.[237]

In this vision for hermeneutical community, theological development must account for theology emanating from church history and tradition. According to this ecumenical text, there exists continuity between the "one Tradition" and the "many traditions" of the church. It explains, "The 'one Tradition' signifies the redeeming presence of the resurrected Christ from generation to generation abiding in the community of faith, while the 'many traditions' are particular modes and manifestations of that presence."[238] Accordingly, "conciliar teaching, the writings of the early church, and the witness of saints and martyrs" are all "testimonies to the apostolic faith [which] disclose the faithful and fruitful interpretation of God's word through Christian history."[239] It therefore behooves interpreters today to consider such theological tradition as they aim to more faithfully embody the "one Tradition."[240]

Moreover, the hermeneutical community of the church also includes contemporary voices across the world. *A Treasure in Earthen Vessels* explains,

---

236. *Treasure in Earthen Vessels*, 33.
237. *Treasure in Earthen Vessels*, 33.
238. *Treasure in Earthen Vessels*, 23.
239. *Treasure in Earthen Vessels*, 33.
240. *Treasure in Earthen Vessels*, 24.

> As the churches engage in dialogue in the growing communion of churches in the ecumenical movement, a further and wider hermeneutical community is created. As it engages in ecumenical dialogue each church and tradition opens itself to being interpreted by other churches and traditions. To listen to the other does not necessarily mean to accept what other churches say, but to reckon with the possibility that the Spirit speaks within and through the others. This might be called "*hermeneutics of confidence.*" A hermeneutics for unity should entail an ecumenical method whereby Christians from various cultures and contexts, as well as different confessions, may encounter one another respectfully, always open to a *metanoia* which is a true "change of mind" and heart.[241]

In other words, churches and Christians from across the world constitute a broad hermeneutical community in which theological development proceeds by way of dialogue. In such conversation, churches "learn to appreciate mutually each other's gifts, as well as to challenge limited or false understandings of what God expects churches to be and to do in the world."[242]

Theological Foundations

A Treasure in Earthen Vessels roots this ecumenical vision for hermeneutical community in several biblical passages. For one, it points to Rom 15:7, in which the apostle Paul declares, "Therefore receive one another, as Christ also has received us, to the glory of God" (NKJV). It adds, "The hermeneutical implications of this reception of one another are manifold and bear upon the way churches relate to one another's traditions of texts, symbols, rites and practices."[243] The text also points to the Jerusalem Council of Acts 15 as an example of theological dialogue[244] and to 1 Pet 2:9, which pictures all believers as priests who, according to this ecumenical paper, participate in the "active reception of the gospel."[245]

Further, this vision for hermeneutical community draws from the theological conviction that the church is catholic, in the sense that it is

---

241. *Treasure in Earthen Vessels*, 10, emphasis original.
242. *Treasure in Earthen Vessels*, 24.
243. *Treasure in Earthen Vessels*, 39.
244. *Treasure in Earthen Vessels*, 38.
245. *Treasure in Earthen Vessels*, 39.

a united whole. The text declares, "Churches are called to grow in God's gift of catholicity by engaging one another in collegial structures, by mutual accountability to the Gospel, and by prayer for the eschatological work of the Holy Spirit."[246] It further explains the benefit of such growth in catholicity:

> Interpretation of the Gospel has to be relevant to particular believing communities in particular contexts in order to be both pastoral and prophetic. But no interpretation can claim to be absolute. All must be aware of the limitations of any perspective or position. The catholicity that binds communities together makes possible this awareness of limitation as well as mutual acknowledgment of contribution to one another's interpretation. In this way, catholicity enables communities to free one another from one-sidedness or from over-emphasis on only one aspect of the gospel. Catholicity enables communities to liberate one another from being blinded or bound by any one context and so to embody across and among diverse contexts the solidarity that is a special mark of Christian *koinonia*.[247]

That is, the oneness of the church across the world allows for and encourages mutual exchange of theological insight across diverse contexts and cultures.

Pneumatological convictions also undergird the notion of hermeneutical community in *A Treasure in Earthen Vessels*. It maintains that within the church, the presence of the Holy Spirit grants hermeneutical capacity to each member: "The Holy Spirit empowers each one to understand more fully the revealed Word of God and to apply it more fruitfully to the concrete situations of daily life."[248] Accordingly, the text asserts, "The Church as an hermeneutical community is responsible for the faithful transmission of the inherited Gospel in different times and places. In that process the Holy Spirit guides the churches in discerning, receiving and communicating the will of God in the ever-changing circumstances of life."[249]

From these theological convictions, *A Treasure in Earthen Vessels* urges churches across the world to embrace hermeneutical community

---

246. *Treasure in Earthen Vessels*, 31.

247. *Treasure in Earthen Vessels*, 31–32.

248. *Treasure in Earthen Vessels*, 39. See also 26 for an overview of "the ecclesial capacity of *receiving* revelation" under the power of the Holy Spirit.

249. *Treasure in Earthen Vessels*, 35.

as they reflect on the Scriptures. It declares, "Churches are encouraged to increase their consultation with other churches, at all levels, regarding important questions of faith and discipline. Any church which is not prepared to listen to the voices of other churches runs the danger of missing the truth of the Spirit as it operates in the other churches."[250] In sum, this ecumenical paper views the church as a community of "co-responsible persons," who have both the capacity and responsibility to bring the Word of God to bear on their contexts and to share such theological convictions with other churches beyond their context, for the theological enrichment of all.[251]

Toward Evangelical Hermeneutical Community

As the foregoing sections have demonstrated, the notion of hermeneutical community has developed in different fields of discourse, and as a result, its development has been neither linear nor uniform. Anabaptists have stressed the importance of the gathered church as a safeguard for biblical interpretation. Philosophical hermeneutics has emphasized the dialogical process of understanding, which proceeds by way of fusing the horizons of various subjects. Theological hermeneutics has sought to retrieve the import of Christian tradition and emphasizes the need to interpret Scripture in conversation with the past and present church. Postliberals have sought to locate Scripture's literal sense in the context of the church. Pentecostal hermeneutics has emphasized the importance of the believing community within the hermeneutical triad of the Spirit of God, the word of God, and the community of God. Finally, ecumenical hermeneutics has argued for hermeneutical community as means of guarding and enriching theological understanding. Although these discourses overlap in various emphases, their aims sometimes differ, and the extent to which they have explicitly drawn from one another remains unclear.

Further, not every hermeneutical community approach remains congenial to evangelical theological conviction. For example, the promotion of reader-response criticism by some advocates of communal hermeneutics might understandably raise among evangelicals a suspicion toward allocating a prominent role for the community in the

---

250. *Treasure in Earthen Vessels*, 37.
251. *Treasure in Earthen Vessels*, 35.

hermeneutical task.[252] Additionally, evangelicals will rightly decry any move that places the authority of the biblical text underneath the consensus of the community.[253] However, without falling into such errors, the evangelical community—and particularly evangelical missionaries—can benefit from embracing a hermeneutical community approach.

From an evangelical missiological perspective, hermeneutical community is an approach to local theological development in which multiple participants together interpret the Bible—as their supreme, authoritative norm for life and faith—in order to bring it to bear on the issues they face in context. It envisions participants as theological agents, rather than mere recipients of ready-made theologies. That is, rather than adopting wholesale the theological convictions of others, each participant contributes to the process of discerning biblical truth and articulating biblically rooted theological convictions. Further, participants in such a process can include voices from the past as well as those from the contemporary church worldwide.

This approach aligns with the vision that evangelicals laid out in the 1978 Willowbank Report. It declares, "The task of understanding the Scriptures belongs not just to individuals but to the whole Christian community, seen as both a contemporary and historical fellowship."[254] In

---

252. See for example Archer, *Pentecostal Hermeneutic*, 233–47; Stanley Fish, *Is There a Text in This Class? The Authority of Interpretive Communities* (Cambridge, MA: Harvard University Press, 2000).

253. For example, Stephen E. Fowl, *Engaging Scripture: A Model for Theological Interpretation* (Malden, MA: Blackwell, 1998), 113–26, appears to set the community over the Scriptures in his treatment of Acts 10–15; Treier, *Introducing Theological Interpretation*, 90–91, critiques this move. He notes, "Fowl finds [in Acts 10–15] a possible analogy for the full inclusion in contemporary churches of those who engage in homosexual behavior. On this reading, the force of the biblical law must sometimes be set aside in light of the Holy Spirit's present work, as Fowl believes it was in the case of the Gentiles, and this might serve as a pattern for setting aside certain proscriptions regarding homosexual acts—if through friendship the church hears narratives of the Spirit's activity in the lives of persons who engage in that behavior. Although Fowl's discussion of this controversial analogy is tentative, it apparently manifests the extent of his hermeneutical focus on the Spirit and community relative to the direct content of biblical texts." In a more explicit move to place the biblical text under the authority of the community, Mennonite scholar Klassen, "Voice of the People," 163, contends, "We must, under the guidance of our communities and the Holy Spirit, have the courage to point out areas in which writers of Holy Scripture have been unfaithful in their handing on of God's word to us."

254. Lausanne Theology and Education Group, "The Willowbank Report," in *Down to Earth: Studies in Christianity and Culture*, ed. Robert T. Coote and John R. W. Stott (Grand Rapids: Eerdmans, 1980), 317.

such community, outsiders and locals labor together in the hermeneutical task: "By common prayer, thought and heart-searching, in dependence on the Holy Spirit, expatriate and local believers may learn together how to present Christ and contextualize the gospel with an equal degree of faithfulness and relevance. . . . [W]e believe that fresh creative understandings do emerge when the Spirit-led believing community is listening and reacting sensitively to both the truth of Scripture and the needs of the world."[255] The report summarizes, "A church's theology should be developed by the community of faith out of the Scripture in interaction with other theologies of the past and present, and with the local culture and its needs."[256]

Ultimately, hermeneutical community is an approach that promotes doing theology together, rather than in isolation. As Stephen B. Bevans contends, theology is not just "faith seeking understanding," as Augustine and Anselm maintained,[257] but "faith seeking understanding *together*."[258] In such a hermeneutical community approach, theological conviction is neither imposed from without nor isolated from within. Rather, theology in hermeneutical community is the outcome of multiple believers seeking to discern and interpret the truth of Scripture together in order to remain faithful to it and bring it to bear on the issues they face in context.

BIBLICAL FOUNDATIONS FOR HERMENEUTICAL COMMUNITY

While the Bible does not explicitly reference such hermeneutical community, various passages lay a foundation for it by demonstrating that both *theological authority* (i.e., the right to theologize) and *theological agency* (i.e., the responsibility to theologize) reside with all members of the church, rather than a select few. In particular, Acts 15:1–35 provides a unique opportunity for readers to explore the issue of theological authority as it relates to theological concerns in the church. Further, 1 Cor 14:26–33, 1 Pet 3:15, Rom 15:14, and 1 Pet 2:9 all underscore the notion

---

255. Lausanne Theology and Education Group, "Willowbank Report," 320.

256. Lausanne Theology and Education Group, "Willowbank Report," 334.

257. Donald K. McKim, ed., *"fides quaerens intellectum,"* in *Westminster Dictionary of Theological Terms* (Louisville, KY: Westminster John Knox, 1996), 104.

258. Stephen B. Bevans, *An Introduction to Theology in Global Perspective* (Maryknoll, NY: Orbis, 2009), 61, emphasis original.

of theological agency among all members of the church. While the following sections offer merely a brief, non-exhaustive sketch of biblical foundations for hermeneutical community, it should reveal a consistency between this approach to theological development and the witness of Scripture.

Theological Authority (Acts 15:1–35)

The account of the Jerusalem Council in Acts 15 serves not only as a major turning point in the broader narrative of Acts, but also as an example of how the early church developed theological convictions.[259] Luke Timothy Johnson explains, "The prophetic witness of the Acts 15 *narrative* is critical to the theological reflection of the church because it gives the fullest picture in the New Testament of the *process* by which the church reaches decision. . . . Only here do we have so explicit a picture of the church as church articulating its faith in response to new and threatening circumstances."[260] In other words, Acts 15 provides an important precedent for the process of theological development, even for the church today.

Further, the Jerusalem Council narrative provides a unique opportunity for readers to consider the issue of theological authority in the early church. That is, it presents a behind-the-scenes look at how the church developed theology and who it considered authorized to contribute to that process and formalize its outcome. In particular, it demonstrates that final theological authority within the Christian movement rested neither with the mother church in Jerusalem nor the esteemed leaders therein. Rather, in various ways, the narrative suggests that the Jerusalem church

---

259. Luke Timothy Johnson, *Scripture and Discernment: Decision-Making in the Church* (Nashville: Abingdon, 1996), 89–90, posits, "The importance of the decision is shown by the placement of the account and the close attention it receives. Chapter 15 is the principal turning point in the book of Acts. Before it, the Jerusalem mission dominates; after it, attention is almost exclusively focused on Paul's preaching all the way to Rome. The significance of the turning point can be grasped, however, only when Acts 15 is recognized as the climax to a story beginning in Acts 10. Nowhere else in Luke's writing do we find such painstaking attention to minute detail at each stage of the action. His narrative elsewhere moves lightly and rapidly. Here, it pauses, recapitulates, and reinterprets itself. The author does not want the reader to miss the meaning of these events."

260. Johnson, *Scripture and Discernment*, 78, emphasis original.

stopped short of exerting authority over believers in Antioch concerning the theological matter which precipitated the council.

Overview

At the beginning of Acts 15, theological debate concerning the requirements for salvation envelops the gentile church at Antioch and ultimately leads to a theological council with the apostles and elders of the church in Jerusalem. Some believers from Jerusalem, who belonged to the party of the pharisees, had come to Antioch and were teaching gentile believers there that in order to be saved, one must be circumcised and keep the law of Moses (Acts 15:1, 5). After Paul and Barnabas became embroiled in debate with them over this issue, the church decided to send Paul, Barnabas, and others to Jerusalem to confer with the apostles and elders of the church there (Acts 15:2–5). Upon their arrival, the apostles and elders received them and "were gathered together to consider this matter" (Acts 15:6).

Acts 15 then presents two speeches at the council that were influential in settling this issue. In the first, Peter relays his prior experience of witnessing gentiles coming to faith apart from circumcision and the keeping of the law. After significant deliberation at the gathering, Peter declared,

> Brothers, you know that in the early days God made a choice among you, that by my mouth the Gentiles should hear the word of the gospel and believe. And God, who knows the heart, bore witness to them, by giving them the Holy Spirit just as he did to us, and he made no distinction between us and them, having cleansed their hearts by faith. Now, therefore, why are you putting God to the test by placing a yoke on the neck of the disciples that neither our fathers nor we have been able to bear? But we believe that we will be saved through the grace of the Lord Jesus, just as they will. (Acts 15:7–11)

For Peter, this experience of ministry among gentiles had demonstrated to him that the Holy Spirit can—and indeed has—come upon gentiles who receive the gospel in faith. Further, the indwelling of the Spirit within them indicates that such gentiles have been saved apart from keeping the law. Following Peter's speech, the council becomes silent as it listens to further testimony from Paul and Barnabas on their experience of God working among gentiles (Acts 15:12).

James then delivers the second recorded speech of Acts 15. Quoting Amos 9:11–12, he declares before the council, "Brothers, listen to me. Simeon has related how God first visited the Gentiles, to take from them a people for his name. And with this the words of the prophets agree, just as it is written, 'After this I will return, and I will rebuild the tent of David that has fallen; I will rebuild its ruins, and I will restore it, that the remnant of mankind may seek the Lord, and all the Gentiles who are called by my name, says the Lord, who makes these things known from of old'" (Acts 15:13–18). For James, the Scriptures confirm the experience and testimony of Peter (i.e., "Simeon") that gentiles have gained salvation along with the remnant of Israel. He then encourages the gathering not to "trouble" gentile converts (Acts 15:19) by laying on them unnecessary burdens like the requirements of circumcision and keeping the law, since both the witness of the Spirit and the witness of the word together indicate the gentiles are saved "through the grace of the Lord Jesus" (Acts 15:11). Instead, James asserts that gentile converts would do well—as a matter of witness—simply to abstain from several practices: sexual immorality, eating that which has been strangled, and consuming food either with blood or that which has been polluted through idolatry (Acts 15:20–21).

Following James's speech, the assembly reaches an agreement and decides to send a letter to the church at Antioch in order to clarify and help resolve the issue at hand and encourage them in the faith. According to their letter, the gathering agrees to James's resolution because it "seemed good to the Holy Spirit and to us" (Acts 15:28). The apostles, the elders, and the church at Jerusalem then send Paul, Barnabas, Judas (called Barsabbas), and Silas to Antioch to deliver the letter to the brothers and sisters there. As a result, "when they had read it, they rejoiced because of its encouragement" (Acts 15:31).

Implications

This account of the Jerusalem Council in Acts 15 provides a clear precedent for communal theological reflection. Throughout the narrative, the author highlights the involvement of multiple participants in theological conversation. He records Paul and Barnabas (Acts 15:2), others from

Hermeneutical Community

Antioch (Acts 15:2), the Jerusalem church (Acts 15:4), Judaizers (Acts 15:1, 5), apostles and elders (Acts 15:6, 23)—particularly Peter and James (Acts 15:7, 13)—the "assembly" (Acts 15:12), and "the whole church" (Acts 15:22) as part of the deliberation. Moreover, each appears to have a voice in the process of theological reasoning.

Although commentators are split on whether the main assembly from Acts 15:6–21 included the larger body of believers or just the apostles and elders,[261] the fact remains that multiple stakeholders participated in the conversations. As Eckhard Schnabel asserts, whether in separate gatherings or all together in one large assembly, "It is indeed the whole body of believers in Jerusalem, as well as leading missionaries such as Barnabas and Paul, who are involved in the debate and its outcome."[262] With the author consciously highlighting this example of communal theological discernment for his readers, Acts 15 provides a valuable precedent for later generations.

Yet before drawing implications from this account in support of hermeneutical community, one must consider whether the author, Luke, intends for the narrative to serve as a model for such communal theologizing. Timothy Wiarda offers three reasons for why one should hesitate to attach paradigmatic significance to the narrative. First, he contends that the temporal closeness of the council to the unique events of Jesus' life, death, and resurrection should dissuade one from viewing Acts 15 as a kind of model for theological development.[263] However, Wiarda does

---

261. For example, the following commentators maintain that select leaders deliberated in a separate council meeting apart from the rest of the assembly: Luke Timothy Johnson, *The Acts of the Apostles*, SP 5 (Collegeville, MN: Liturgical, 1992), 261; Eckhard J. Schnabel, *Acts*, ZECNT (Grand Rapids: Zondervan, 2012), 632, 647; Craig S. Keener, *Acts: An Exegetical Commentary*, 4 vols. (Grand Rapids: Baker Academic, 2012–15), 3:2230–31, 3:2280. Conversely, the following commentators believe that the council included the larger gathering of the believers, among whom the leaders conversed: Ernst Haenchen, *The Acts of the Apostles: A Commentary* (Philadelphia: Westminster, 1971), 441, 451; John B. Polhill, *Acts*, NAC 26 (Nashville: Broadman, 1992), 302; Ben Witherington III, *The Acts of the Apostles: A Socio-Rhetorical Commentary* (Grand Rapids: Eerdmans, 1998), 453; David G. Peterson, *The Acts of the Apostles*, PNTC (Grand Rapids: Eerdmans, 2009), 424, 436.

262. Schnabel, *Acts*, 647.

263. Timothy Wiarda, "The Jerusalem Council and the Theological Task," *J. Evang. Theol. Soc.* 46.2 (2003) 238, posits, "Given the intimate connection between the issue brought before the Council and the unique events of messianic fulfillment that shortly preceded it, it might be wise to think twice before attempting to replicate the Council's process of theological decision-making today. In other words, the Spirit's hermeneutical guidance, fresh and context-related though it was, may have been decisively tied to the eschatological change brought about by the once-for-all (all times and all

not adequately demonstrate how this observation concerning temporal closeness establishes his exhortation against seeing Acts 15 as exemplary. His contention appears to rest on a logical fallacy that derives how something "ought" to be from an observation about what something "is."[264] In other words, one cannot move directly from an observation of the uniqueness of that time period to an exhortation that therefore one "ought" not to follow a pattern emanating from that period. Thus, it remains unclear how temporal closeness to Jesus undermines the prospect of Acts 15 serving as a model for communal theological development.

Second, Wiarda argues that the presence of the apostles and "near-apostles" at the council should likewise deter one from attaching paradigmatic significance to the narrative.[265] This argument carries more weight than the first, but still lacks force. One could turn this argument on its head and claim that Acts 15 has paradigmatic value precisely because the apostles employed such a method for theological discernment. In other words, if the apostles saw value in such a communal process, then Christians today might do well to follow their lead. Additionally, nothing in the narrative suggests that these unique first-century leaders relied on special apostolic knowledge or powers of discernment as they engaged the assembly. Rather, they reasoned theologically from the

---

communities) work of Christ."

264. David Hume, *Treatise of Morals: And Selections from the Treatise of the Passions*, ed. James H. Hyslop (Boston, 1893), 115, famously dealt with this distinction between "is" and "ought." Max Black, "The Gap Between 'Is' and 'Should,'" *Philos. Rev.* 73.2 (1964) 166, refers to the logical separation of "is" and "ought" as "Hume's Guillotine." See also D. C. Yalden-Thomson, "Hume's View of 'Is-Ought,'" *Philosophy* 53.203 (1978) 89–93.

265. Wiarda, "Jerusalem Council," 238–39, states, "The named speakers [in the council] are Peter, Barnabas, Paul, and James. Does this heavy presence of apostles or near-apostles encourage an easy correlation between the theological decision-making done at the Council and that carried out by Christians and churches today? Are the chief characters portrayed in Acts 15 exemplary disciples or uniquely authoritative figures? In the narrative leading up to the Council episode the apostles are shown to occupy a special position that includes bearing witness to the resurrection of Jesus, giving authoritative teaching, and making decisions (1:2, 15–16; 2:14, 42; 6:2–4; 8:14). This might well suggest that the leading figures depicted in Acts 15 are something other than typical Christians, or even typical church teachers. . . . An emphasis on apostleship, authority, and revelation runs throughout this section, in fact, with little to suggest that Paul wishes to hold himself up as an example for the churches to emulate. The effectiveness of a model depends on the degree of analogy between the original example and the later situations to which it is applied. That being so, the gap between the apostles and us, and between their time and our own, is a matter that must not be overlooked."

Hermeneutical Community

Scriptures and the witness of the Holy Spirit—both of which the church still possesses today. Thus again, it remains unclear how the presence of apostles undermines the value of the Jerusalem Council for contemporary theological reflection.

Finally, Wiarda asserts that the narrative shape of Acts 15 focuses more attention on the theological outcome of the deliberations than the process.[266] Wiarda is certainly correct in his contention that Luke's main purpose in recounting the Jerusalem Council is not to offer a model for theological development, but rather to demonstrate that gentiles do not have to adhere to Jewish law in order to be saved—a theological conclusion of great magnitude.[267] Yet, Wiarda still leaves very little room for seeing Acts 15 as exemplary.[268] At most, he claims, the Jerusalem Council serves as an example that churches today can and should resolve problems harmoniously.[269]

---

266. Wiarda, "Jerusalem Council," 244, contends, "Those who make use of scriptural models will . . . need to be sensitive to the dynamics of narrative interpretation. An important starting point is to recognize that biblical narratives—certainly NT narratives—are *rhetorically shaped*. They are not neutral accounts. If they describe events, they also guide the reader to see the significance of those events. . . . All this means that the most powerful and reliable biblical paradigms will be those that follow the shaping of the texts from which they are derived" (emphasis original). With regard to Acts 15, Wiarda states, "Is the text about the mechanics of decision-making, or does it focus attention on the truth that uncircumcised Gentiles are freely accepted by God? My assessment is that the narrative forcefully highlights the theological message, that God's purpose for the Gentiles is salvation without circumcision. . . . In other words, the narrative directs the reader first and foremost to the content and truth of the Council's decision" (245).

267. Wiarda, "Jerusalem Council," 245.

268. In contrast, Johnson, *Scripture and Discernment*, 78, contends, "Perhaps the theological significance of the Council rests on the principles communicated by some of its participants, such as that spoken by Peter in 15:11: 'We shall be saved through the grace of the Lord Jesus, just as they will.' This is a statement of great importance. Taken with the still sharper sayings of Paul on the radical breakdown of human distinctions in Christ (e.g., 1 Cor 7:7–24; 12:13; Gal 3:27–29; Eph 2:11–22; Col 3:11), it stands as an enduring norm against which the church can measure itself. The principle, however, is found elsewhere, and, abstracted from the narrative, represents only a fraction of the passage's meaning."

269. Wiarda, "Jerusalem Council," 245, asserts, "At the same time, however, I believe the narrative does make a secondary paradigmatic point. One reason for saying this is that Acts presents readers with a whole series of scenes depicting church life. Some of these show a positive picture of fellowship and worship, some show the church overcoming problems, and one even portrays disobedience, but they all seem to serve as examples, setting down a pattern for Christian life in the church. The narrative of the Jerusalem Council to some extent fits within this series of scenes. If that is so, what is it designed to exemplify? Perhaps it is not a process for decision-making, but rather the

However, the narrative shape of Acts 15 focuses more attention on the process of theological discernment than Wiarda acknowledges. As Johnson claims, "The structure of the story calls our attention . . . to the dynamics of decision-making in the Church. This formal gathering of the Church (*ekklēsia*) is called in order to respond to a crisis that not only threatens the peace of the community but raises fundamental questions concerning the community's identity and the grounds for its fellowship. The attention Luke gives to *how* the Church makes the decision required of it is an intrinsic part of his narrative message."[270] The narrative consistently highlights elements of the church's process for theological reasoning. Luke shows characters in the story seeking counsel from others (Acts 15:2), intentionally gathering (Acts 15:6), listening to and considering different viewpoints (Acts 15:4, 6, 12), debating (Acts:15:2, 7), sharing experiences (Acts 15:4, 7–9, 12), interpreting experiences (Acts 15:10–11), reflecting on Scripture (Acts 15:15–17), remaining sensitive to the Holy Spirit (Acts 15:28), and arriving at theological convictions together (Acts 15:22, 25, 28).

Elements of process thus pervade the narrative, which suggests that Luke intentionally brings these to light. As Lyle Story claims, "Luke tells the story of how the various points of conflict are resolved and he does so in a persuasive way to instruct the early communities of how they should go about seeking the communal will of God."[271] Moreover, the detail which Luke gives concerning this theological process becomes even more salient when one considers that its resolution appears as a foregone conclusion earlier in Acts (and even in the Gospel of Luke). Johnson explains, "Luke has shown the reader from the beginning of his composition that God intended the salvation of the Gentiles. . . . The standpoint of the storyteller, which is shared with the reader, makes the event appear inevitable. It is the more striking, then, that Luke is so concerned to show the *human process* of coming to recognize and affirm God's intention."[272]

Thus Acts 15 appears to have some level of instructive value when it comes to theological discernment and development within the church. For Johnson, Luke "provides a model for making decisions within this

---

fact that church problems can and should be resolved in a harmonious way."

270. Johnson, *Acts of the Apostles*, 270–71, emphasis original.

271. Lyle Story, "Luke's Instructive Dynamics for Resolving Conflicts: The Jerusalem Council," *J. Biblic. Pneumatological Res.* 3 (2011) 100.

272. Johnson, *Scripture and Discernment*, 90, emphasis original.

people constituted by faith."²⁷³ Story likewise argues, "Luke intends his readers to understand and embrace the story as a model for the nascent church."²⁷⁴ He explains,

> Through the story, Luke invites his readers to experience and feel the various points of tension, to see how the conflict was managed and, indeed, advanced the Christian message—to be changed and then return to their own communities with this instructive paradigm. He helps the community to live and relive the event and its nuances and thereby, adopt and embrace his point of view in changing thoughts, attitudes and behavior as to how the church ought to discern the will of God as it encounters fresh challenges.²⁷⁵

Although terms like *model* and *paradigm* might be too strong, Acts 15 at minimum serves as an instructive account for the process of theological development.²⁷⁶

Particularly instructive is the narrative's portrayal of theological authority in the early church. That is, it illustrates the dynamics of how the church wrestled with a serious theological issue—who contributed to the process, how they arrived at a conclusion, and on what authority the stakeholders promulgated that conclusion. Further, the council is perhaps even more instructive when one views it from within the context of cross-cultural missions, since it portrays a mother church (Jerusalem) in theological conversation with one of its daughter churches (Antioch). An understanding of how the mother church postures itself toward its

---

273. Johnson, *Acts of the Apostles*, 279. Elsewhere, Johnson, *Scripture and Discernment*, 78–79, claims, "Acts 15 witnesses to the church concerning the way it reaches decisions, not by prescription, but by way of a paradigmatic story. The church is not challenged by its hearing of this witness to imitate mechanically the steps taken by the characters in the story. The narrative, rather, invites us to consider the dynamics of decision making themselves, and to use this consideration when reflecting on the practice of the church wherever it exists."

274. Story, "Luke's Instructive Dynamics," 99.

275. Story, "Luke's Instructive Dynamics," 118.

276. David K. Strong and Cynthia A. Strong, "The Globalizing Hermeneutic of the Jerusalem Council," in *Globalizing Theology: Belief and Practice in an Era of World Christianity*, ed. Craig Ott and Harold A. Netland (Grand Rapids: Baker Academic, 2006), 128, assert, "If we are to remain faithful to the intent of the narrative, therefore, we can only secondarily derive lessons from the council's actions. Having acknowledged this, the approach used by the Jerusalem Council reveals one successful way in which diverse Christian communities with different theological concerns achieved consensus. . . . Thus, while not paradigmatic, the theological process employed at the council points a way forward in mediating between local and global theologies."

daughter church might prove instructive for local theological development today, particularly for Western churches and mission agencies seeking to plant and nurture churches overseas.

Some scholars have viewed Jerusalem and its church as the seat of theological authority.[277] Richard Bauckham, for example, argues this case historically.[278] Others argue from the text of Acts that Luke himself views the Jerusalem church as authoritative. For instance, Ernst Haenchen asserts that for Luke, "wherever Christianity is implanted, the town or region concerned is in one way or another subordinated to the capital of Judaea."[279] Further, "The Apostles and elders are the supreme court of authority to which Antioch sends Paul and Barnabas. They do not deal with the Apostles on equal footing but receive their commands."[280] Similarly, F. F. Bruce maintains that the Jerusalem Council demonstrates "the desire of the Jerusalem church to maintain control over the extension of the Christian way and Luke's understanding of its authority."[281]

Alex T. M. Cheung presses these claims further, arguing that Luke intentionally shapes the story to communicate that no authority exists independent of Jerusalem.[282] One way Luke does this, according to Cheung, is by not recording approval from the Antioch church of Paul and Barnabas's report following their first missionary journey (Acts 14:27).[283] Cheung claims, "Their response is suppressed by Luke because

---

277. For example, see Haenchen, *Acts of the Apostles*, 461–62; F. F. Bruce, "The Church of Jerusalem in the Acts of the Apostles," *Bull. John Rylands Univ. Libr. Manch.* 67.2 (1985) 653–55; Alex T. M. Cheung, "A Narrative Analysis of Acts 14:27–15:35: Literary Shaping in Luke's Account of the Jerusalem Council," *Westminst. Theol. J.* 55.1 (1993) 145–46; Richard Bauckham, "James and the Jerusalem Church," in *The Book of Acts in Its Palestinian Setting*, ed. Richard Bauckham (Grand Rapids: Eerdmans, 1995), 450–51; Witherington, *Acts of the Apostles*, 451, 469.

278. Bauckham, "James and the Jerusalem Church," 450–51. With regard to Acts 15, Bauckham argues, "The Jerusalem council presupposes the authority of Jerusalem to decide the issue of Gentile Christians' obedience to the Law (Acts 15). Its decision binds not only Antioch and its daughter churches (15:22–31), but also the churches founded by Paul and Barnabas (16:4)" (450). Yet in response to Bauckham, Peterson, *Acts of the Apostles*, 424, contends that "such an authority structure is not really evident in the relationship between Jerusalem and the Gentile churches in the preceding narratives."

279. Haenchen, *Acts of the Apostles*, 461.
280. Haenchen, *Acts of the Apostles*, 462.
281. Bruce, "Church of Jerusalem," 653.
282. Cheung, "Narrative Analysis," 145.
283. Cheung, "Narrative Analysis," 145.

what matters is Jerusalem's approval, not Antioch's!"[284] Further, he adds, "Antioch's enthusiastic response might actually convey the impression that the authorization of the Gentile mission comes from there and not Jerusalem, thus undermining both the authority of Jerusalem and the unity of the Jewish and Gentile churches."[285] Yet Cheung's argument here does not account for the fact that already in the book of Acts, Luke has recorded authorization for Paul's mission, both in the narrative of his conversion (Acts 9:1–19) and in the Antioch church's releasing of Paul and Barnabas for the work to which the Holy Spirit had called them (Acts 13:1–3). Cheung does not deal with these texts and ultimately contends that Luke believes "any Gentile mission undertaken independent of Jerusalem's authority is inconceivable."[286]

However, a closer look at the text of Acts 15 suggests that the Jerusalem church did not wield final theological authority over the church at Antioch. Granted, the church in Jerusalem maintained some level of authority by virtue of it being a hub of apostles and leaders who had spent time directly with Jesus.[287] Yet several aspects of the Jerusalem Council narrative challenge the notion that the Jerusalem church—with its apostles and elders—served as the seat of theological authority within the early Christian movement.

First, while some might point to Antioch's sending of a delegation to Jerusalem as tacit acceptance of the Jerusalem church's authority, the text supplies a more immediate explanation for the delegation. That is, the reason the Antioch church looks *to* Jerusalem is the fact that the Judaizers who were troubling the Antioch church came *from* Jerusalem. As David G. Peterson claims, "Jerusalem is the place where this issue must be decided because the problem emerged from that context."[288] Further, it is possible that the delegation from Antioch served to challenge the theology that appeared to be emanating from Jerusalem. Johnson asserts, "The sending of a delegation from Antioch . . . is something of a confrontation. Jerusalem had once approved this community, but now

---

284. Cheung, "Narrative Analysis," 145.

285. Cheung, "Narrative Analysis," 146.

286. Cheung, "Narrative Analysis," 153.

287. Pieter G. R. de Villiers, "Communal Discernment in the Early Church," *Acta Theol.* 17 (2013) 139, highlights the prominent role that the apostles and elders played in the Jerusalem church. He contends, "The authority of the church in Jerusalem is, therefore, especially linked with the presence of the apostles and the elders."

288. Peterson, *Acts of the Apostles*, 424.

those who came from Judea were disturbing it. Was Jerusalem going back on its word and breaking fellowship?... The Antiochian group is therefore going to the source of the trouble, to call the Jerusalem Church to account."[289] If Johnson is right, Antioch's sending of a delegation is far from an act of theological self-subordination.

Second, the narrative in Acts 15 clearly pictures a decision-making process featuring group deliberation and consensus rather than unilateral action from authoritative spokespersons. Luke highlights debate (Acts 15:6), listening (Acts 15:12), and consideration (Acts 15:6) among a gathering of multiple participants. Further, the passage three times reports that the conclusion of the theological deliberation "seemed good" to all who were involved (Acts 15:22, 25, 28) and also that the participants came "to one accord" (Acts 15:25). In other words, the theological process incorporated multiple voices, jointly pursuing a resolution for the matter at hand.

Such conversation and consensus would have been largely superfluous had the apostles and elders in Jerusalem reserved for themselves the right to prescribe theological conviction. The implication here is that the mother church in Jerusalem did not control the theological outcome, but participated in a deliberation that included multiple stakeholders, both from Jerusalem and Antioch. Thus, as James D. G. Dunn observes, Luke presents the decision of the council "as a genuine consensus and not as a power play by one faction dictating its will to the rest."[290]

Third, while the "requirements" (Acts 15:28) of the final decision appear in some respect authoritative, the authority behind them rested not in the Jerusalem elite, but in the fact that the assembly derived its conclusion from the witness of both the Holy Spirit and the Scriptures—central authorities for the church. In his speech at the council, Peter testifies to the work of the Spirit in his ministry among gentiles, claiming, "God, who knows the heart, bore witness to them, by giving them the Holy Spirit just as he did to us, and made no distinction between us and them, having cleansed their hearts by faith" (Acts 15:8–9). James then corroborates this precedent by demonstrating from Scripture that the "words of the prophets agree" with Peter's testimony (Acts 15:15–17).

Luke, not coincidentally, records the final consensus of the council immediately after James's corroborating exposition of Scripture, which

---

289. Johnson, *Scripture and Discernment*, 100.

290. James D. G. Dunn, *The Acts of the Apostles* (Valley Forge, PA: Trinity Press International, 1996), 208.

established the basis—and authority—for the theological conclusion that followed.[291] Thus Luke pictures theological authority as resting in the Spirit and the word, rather than in a select few leaders. Any authority the letter from Jerusalem possessed derived not from James's stature or the status of Jerusalem as the mother church, but from the assembly's sensitivity to the Spirit and exposition of the word in the process of coming to a decision.

A fourth indication that the Jerusalem church did not assert authority over the believers in Antioch lies in the language and content of its letter to them (Acts 15:23–29).[292] The letter's praise of Paul and Barnabas, as "beloved" brothers "who have risked their lives for the name of our Lord Jesus Christ" (Acts 15:25–26), serves to strengthen fellowship between the two churches.[293] The letter also serves to make amends with the Antioch church. Johnson explains, "Although the Jerusalem Church denies responsibility for the activity of the troublemakers, it grants that they came 'from us,' and, by acknowledging that they had unsettled the

---

291. Arthur A. Just Jr., "The Apostolic Councils of Galatians and Acts: How First-Century Christians Walked Together," *Concordia Theol. Q.* 74.3–4 (2010) 287–88, quoting Bauckham, posits, "Although Peter, Paul, and Barnabas testified about the truth of the gospel as it was being expressed in the Gentile mission through either an apocalyptic vision from God or the signs and wonders accompanying the mission, it was the clear word of the Scriptures as presented by James that carried the day.... The reason that various parties gave 'the fullest possible authority to the council's decisions' is, undoubtedly, due to the council's use of the authoritative Scriptures in coming to a consensus."

292. Story, "Luke's Instructive Dynamics," 105, points out that the letter contains only one imperative—"farewell" (*errōsthe*)—which comes at the end (Acts 15:29). Further, in reference to the four prohibitions, the letter states that "if" the gentile Christians in Antioch abstain from such things, "then" they will do well (Acts 15:29). He thus concludes, "The decision is set within the context of politeness, respect and fairness." However, this observation alone is not strong enough to prove the congeniality of the letter. As F. F. Bruce, *The Book of the Acts*, rev. ed., NICNT (Grand Rapids: Eerdmans, 1988), 298–99, asserts, "Significance has been attached to the fact that none of the Greek verbs of commanding is used when the council's directives are conveyed. But the form of words that is used, 'it has been resolved,' is authoritative enough: it was a form widely used in the wording of imperial and other government decrees." Further, Frederick W. Danker, "Reciprocity in the Ancient World and in Acts 15:23–29," in *Political Issues in Luke-Acts*, ed. Richard J. Cassidy and Philip J. Scharper (Maryknoll, NY: Orbis, 1983), 49–58, highlights commonalities between civic declarations in the Greco-Roman world, which feature strong overtones of benefaction and reciprocity, and the letter to the Antioch church in Acts 15. This commonality could potentially portray the Jerusalem church in Acts 15 as a benefactor issuing authoritative demands. Yet even if there are similarities between Greco-Roman civic decrees and the letter from Jerusalem, the broader context of the passage seems to mitigate such a conclusion.

293. Johnson, *Scripture and Discernment*, 105.

minds of the believers at Antioch, effectively apologizes for the harm they did."[294] Further, by acknowledging the Holy Spirit's guidance within the council, the letter roots its prohibitions in divine direction rather than human fiat. Thus, the letter does not appear to be an extension of the Jerusalem church's theological authority. Rather, according to Johnson, it demonstrates the Jerusalem church showing "great pastoral concern for those whom, wittingly or not, it has harmed. It works strenuously to renew fellowship."[295]

The letter thus appears to be more of an encouragement to believers in Antioch than an act of theological control over them. According to Peterson, "The letter which is sent to the churches (15:23–9) has a hortatory rather than a legislative tone."[296] It comes across as an encouragement to respected brethren, not a mandate to subordinates. Thus, Hinne Wagenaar refers to the letter from Jerusalem not as an "Apostolic Decree," as is common among scholars,[297] but rather as a "Pastoral Letter."[298] He reasons, "Though it is an important Pastoral Letter whose requirements need to be kept for living harmoniously, it is not pronounced as an imposition from above, from the centre of the church to the periphery."[299]

Finally, one might even understand the letter from Jerusalem as an endorsement of the Antioch church's prior theological convictions. For instance, over and against the Judaizers, the final conclusion of the council implicitly commends Paul and Barnabas's theological position on the issue. The council does not necessarily come to a new conclusion as much as it backs the prior theological reasoning of Paul and Barnabas with the authority of the Spirit and the Scriptures. Moreover, according to Schnabel, the Antioch church's joyful response to the letter appears to indicate "that the four stipulations were not regarded as a burden by the Gentile Christians, but as regulations to which they had already committed themselves."[300] If this is true, then the letter would serve as an endorsement of previously held theological conviction within the church at Antioch.

---

294. Johnson, *Scripture and Discernment*, 105–6.

295. Johnson, *Scripture and Discernment*, 106.

296. Peterson, *Acts of the Apostles*, 424.

297. See for example, Dunn, *Acts of the Apostles*, 208; Polhill, *Acts*, 305–6.

298. Hinne Wagenaar, "'Stop Harassing the Gentiles': The Importance of Acts 15 for African Theology," *J. Afr. Christ. Thought* 6.1 (2003) 51.

299. Wagenaar, "Stop Harassing the Gentiles," 51.

300. Schnabel, *Acts*, 651.

In sum, the Jerusalem Council narrative of Acts 15 demonstrates that the mother church (Jerusalem) did not wield theological authority over its daughter church (Antioch). Rather, Luke presents the Jerusalem church and its leaders as participants in theological reflection with constituents from Antioch. The narrative thus vests neither the right nor responsibility for theological reflection in merely a select few. Instead, it demonstrates that the authority and capability for theological reflection remain diffused throughout those who are "saved through the grace of the Lord Jesus" (Acts 15:11), whether they reside at Jerusalem, Antioch, or the "end of the earth" (Acts 1:8). This diffusion of theological authority coheres with Jesus' entrusting of the Holy Spirit—the one who teaches and guides the believing community into all truth (John 16:13)—to all believers (John 14:16–17, 26; 15:26; Ezek 36:27; 37:14; Eph 5:18).

Theological Agency

Beyond addressing theological authority in the early church (i.e., the right to theologize), New Testament scriptures also shed light on the issue of theological agency (i.e., the responsibility to theologize). That is, rather than present believers as passive *recipients* of theology, various passages indicate that followers of Christ are *agents* of theological conviction. In other words, all believers maintain the capability and responsibility to reason theologically and articulate theological convictions. Passages undergirding this assertion include 1 Cor 14:26–33 (Rule of Paul), 1 Pet 3:15 (readiness to testify), Rom 15:14 (responsibility to instruct), and 1 Pet 2:9 (royal priesthood of all believers).

Rule of Paul (1 Cor 14:26–33)

The Rule of Paul refers to the apostle Paul's admonition to the Corinthian church to evaluate prophesies which church members offer in the context of corporate worship.[301] He urges, "When you come together, each one has a hymn, a lesson, a revelation, a tongue, or an interpretation. Let all things be done for building up" (1 Cor 14:26). Further, Paul states that, as part of such edification, "Let two or three prophets speak, and let the others weigh what is said" (1 Cor 14:29). An exploration of the gift of

---

301. Yoder, "Hermeneutics of the Anabaptists," 301, asserts that Ulrich Zwingli first identified 1 Cor 14:29 as the "Rule of Paul."

prophecy and the role of prophets lies outside the scope of this work; the relevant point here is that Paul pictures church members as having the ability and responsibility to reason theologically from the Scriptures as they "weigh" given prophecies. Members do not passively receive prophecy, but rather evaluate what they hear as active agents of theological conviction.

The verb which Paul uses in 1 Cor 14:29 for *weigh* (*diakrinō*) here means to "judge" or to "evaluate by paying careful attention to" the object under consideration.[302] New Testament scholar Paul Gardner explains, "This 'judgment' is probably an assessment made by 'others' concerning, first, whether this is truly of the Lord and, second, how the word delivered by the prophet should be applied to those present."[303] Additionally, *diakrinō* often means to "make a distinction" or "differentiate."[304] Anthony Thiselton describes the distinguishing process of which 1 Cor 14:29 speaks: "The authentic is to be sifted from the inauthentic or spurious, in the light of the OT scriptures, the gospel of Christ, the traditions of all the churches, and critical reflections. Nowhere does Paul hint that preaching or 'prophecy' achieves a privileged status which places them above critical reflection in the light of the gospel, the Spirit, and the scriptures. *It is never infallible.*"[305] The appraisal of such infallible prophecies given in corporate worship thus requires theological reasoning on the part of the appraisers. That is, Paul expects appraisers not to passively receive prophesies at the behest of the prophets, but to actively sift such prophesies as agents of theological conviction.

---

302. BDAG, s.v. "διακρίνω."

303. Paul Gardner, *1 Corinthians*, ZECNT (Grand Rapids: Zondervan, 2018), 627.

304. BDAG, s.v. "διακρίνω." Wayne A. Grudem, *The Gift of Prophecy in 1 Corinthians* (Washington, DC: University Press of America, 1982), 64, notes, "Although the word has a quite wide range of meanings, it very frequently carries a sense of separating, distinguishing, or making careful distinctions among related things or ideas." He also adds, "This sense of 'making distinctions' or 'carefully evaluating' makes διακρίνω an appropriate word in 1 Cor. 14.29 if Paul had meant to speak of a process whereby every member of the congregation would listen carefully and evaluate each statement, distinguishing what he felt to be good from the less good, what he [felt] to be helpful from the unhelpful, what he felt to be true from the false. Now since this is not the only possible meaning for διακρίνω, one cannot say on lexical grounds alone that it absolutely requires this sense in 1 Cor. 14.29. But it fits very well in the context and is a common meaning for διακρίνω" (64–65).

305. Anthony C. Thiselton, *The First Epistle to the Corinthians: A Commentary on the Greek Text* (Grand Rapids: Eerdmans, 2000), 1140, emphasis original.

Hermeneutical Community

Further, this responsibility to *weigh* or *evaluate* likely rested on the whole community of believers. Regarding the "others" to which this passage refers, C. K. Barrett notes,

> *The others* may mean "the other prophets, who do not on this occasion prophesy," or "the other members of the church." The latter is more probable; Paul gives us no ground for thinking that only prophets were capable of testing prophetic messages, and the whole church appears to be involved in passages such as 1 Thess. v. 21; compare also 1 John iv. 1; *Didache* xi. 2–7. Indeed, the long section on spiritual gifts, which began in chapter xii, proceeds on the assumption that all spiritual manifestations must be tested, and the test provided in xii. 3 is one that can be applied by any Christian, whether himself a prophet or not.[306]

In other words, Paul expects each member of the community to participate in this discernment process.[307] This passage therefore indicates that theological agency resides in every member of the church, not just a select few leaders or spokespersons. Further, New Testament scholar Mark Taylor adds, "Paul does not specify exactly what the others must discern and by what criteria it is measured, but we can assume that such genuine prophetic speech resonated with the Scriptures and with the gospel as given through the apostles."[308] Paul thus expects Corinthian church members to be able to reason theologically from the Scriptures and the gospel and to apply their theological convictions in the evaluation of prophecies.

While promoting theological agency among all church members, this passage simultaneously indicates that the task of theology does not remain exclusively in the domain of church leaders. Considering that

---

306. C. K. Barrett, *A Commentary on the First Epistle to the Corinthians* (New York: Harper & Row, 1968), 328.

307. Thomas R. Schreiner, *1 Corinthians: An Introduction and Commentary*, TNTC (Downers Grove, IL: IVP Academic, 2018), 294, adds, "It is difficult to know if the *others* refers to other prophets or to the entire congregation. If we use verse 30 as our guide, the 'another' (*allō*) there refers to another prophet. On the other hand, in . . . 1 John 4 and 1 Thess 5 . . . the entire community is called upon to test false prophets and prophecies. Furthermore, the gift of distinguishing spirits is not given to the same people who have the gift of prophecy; thus it seems preferable to see a reference to the whole community here." Others who contend that the whole congregation is in view here for Paul include David E. Garland, *1 Corinthians*, BECNT (Grand Rapids: Baker Academic, 2003), 663; Grudem, *Gift of Prophecy*, 62, 66.

308. Mark Taylor, *1 Corinthians*, NAC 28 (Nashville: Broadman & Holman, 2014), 351.

LOCAL THEOLOGICAL DEVELOPMENT

others take part in the process of discernment in church gatherings, David E. Garland asserts, "The assumption is that the prophets do not speak with unquestionable authority.... Prophets must allow the content of their revelation to be tested in the community and may need reminding that their 'prophecy' is only partial and temporary (13:9–10)."[309] That is, Paul here undercuts the prospect of certain leaders controlling theological conviction for the wider body of believers. Garland explains, "Paul's intention seems to be to bring prophets down a notch to the level of the community. They are not to regard themselves as infallible and unanswerable to the church body."[310]

The picture which 1 Cor 14:29 presents is thus one in which church members are active agents of theology, not beholden to a select few who control theological conviction for the group. Paul expected Corinthian church members to evaluate prophecies before receiving them, which required them to be competent to interpret the Scriptures and to articulate their theological convictions within the gathering of believers. Further, by promoting such theological agency among church members, Paul's instruction challenges church leaders who might suppose they possess exclusive authority in prophesying. As Garland claims, "In 14:37–38, Paul expects those who consider themselves to be prophets or spiritual to be the most likely to object to what he says. His instructions would prevent the 'specialists' from dominating and monopolizing the worship."[311] In other words, the Rule of Paul here demonstrates that the whole church possesses theological agency, not just the spiritual elite.[312]

---

309. Garland, *1 Corinthians*, 662.

310. Garland, *1 Corinthians*, 662–63.

311. Garland, *1 Corinthians*, 663.

312. First Corinthians 14:31 might also support this notion of theological agency among all church members. While it is not entirely clear who "all" refers to in Paul's contention that "you can all prophesy one by one," Gordon D. Fee, *The First Epistle to the Corinthians*, rev. ed. (Grand Rapids: Eerdmans, 2014), 768–69, argues that Paul is referencing the whole congregation. He explains, "Some have argued, on the basis of an earlier moment (12:28), that 'prophets' [in 14:29] refers to the special group of authoritative persons in the community who have been given this gift. 'The others' in this case would mean 'the other prophets,' so that the whole text is intended to regulate the activities of the prophets, vis-à-vis regulating 'prophecies' per se. But nearly everything else in the argument stands over against such a view. (a) The argument from the outset (v. 1) has been in the second plural, addressing the entire community. He urges all of them 'eagerly [to] desire gifts of the Spirit, especially that *you* prophesy,' without a hint that this gift is limited to the 'prophets.' (b) So with the rest of the argument; for example, later (v. 12) he exhorts, 'Since you are eager for gifts of the Spirit [referring to their collective enthusiasm for tongues], try to excel in those that build up the church

Readiness to Testify (1 Pet 3:15)

Another passage which underscores theological agency among the whole church is 1 Pet 3:15, in which Peter declares, "In your hearts honor Christ as holy, always being ready to make a defense to anyone who asks you for a reason for the hope that is in you." Peter offers this exhortation as part of his broader encouragement to Christians facing persecution for their faith. In pagan contexts, Christians would encounter questions from non-believers who could see that the Christian way of life was different but could not understand the nature of that difference. Peter urges believers in such cases to be ready to respond with an account of the faith that has transformed them. In I. Howard Marshall's words, such interest from non-Christians "should gladly be grasped as an opportunity for a positive, reasoned presentation of the gospel."[313]

The context for Peter's admonition to "make a defense" suggests that all believers—not just a select few—are to be capable and ready to testify. The Greek word for "make a defense" (*apologian*) often serves as a legal term associated with a courtroom context.[314] However, it can also assume a more general sense, referring to the act of defending oneself before others among whom one lives.[315] Scholars generally believe Peter has the latter use in view here.[316] As Thomas R. Schreiner explains, "Persecution in 1 Peter was sporadic and informal and does not represent the kind of

---

[meaning esp. the gift of prophecy].' (c) The evidence in the preceding paragraph (v. 24), even though hypothetical, is especially telling. As before (v. 23), Paul implies a situation that could conceivably occur, namely that 'all prophesy,' so that the unbeliever is convicted by *all* and judged by *all*. (d) So also in the coming final sentence (v. 31) he urges orderliness, 'for you may *all* prophesy in turn so that *all* may learn and *all* be encouraged/exhorted.' It is completely gratuitous to suggest that the first 'all' means 'all the prophets' while the next two refer to the whole community" (emphasis original). If Fee is correct, this not only would imply that each member of the congregation could potentially prophesy (even apart from possessing the gift of prophecy), but would also underscore the notion that each member acts as a theological agent—someone who actively develops and maintains theological convictions rather than relying solely on others to tell them what to believe. For the one who prophesies acts, by default, as an agent of theology.

313. I. Howard Marshall, *1 Peter*, IVPNTC (Downers Grove, IL: InterVarsity, 1991), 116.

314. BDAG, s.v. "ἀπολογία."

315. BDAG, s.v. "ἀπολογία."

316. For example, see J. N. D. Kelly, *A Commentary on the Epistles of Peter and of Jude* (New York: Harper & Row, 1969), 142–43; Peter H. Davids, *The First Epistle of Peter* (Grand Rapids: Eerdmans, 1990), 131; J. Ramsey Michaels, *1 Peter*, WBC 49 (Grand Rapids: Zondervan, 1988), 188.

state-sponsored persecution under Pliny and Trajan.... Hence, the text does not address primarily formal legal situations. It envisions instead informal circumstances when believers are asked spontaneously about their faith. This interpretation is supported by the words 'everyone who asks you' (*panti tō aitounti hymas*), suggesting that believers respond to a wide variety of people, not exclusively in court situations."[317] Thus, it is not just those who face formal persecution who must give a defense; rather, all believers must be ready to respond in the informal occasions in which non-believers inquire about the Christian faith. Further, Peter's audience includes "elect exiles of the Dispersion in Pontus, Galatia, Cappadocia, Asia, and Bithynia" (1 Pet 1:1). That is, Peter was not speaking simply to church leaders, but to the myriad of scattered Christians who must remain capable and ready to testify to the faith that has distinguished them from their pagan surroundings.

Peter calls the faith to which Christians must testify the "hope that is in you" (1 Pet 3:15). J. N. D. Kelly asserts, "Hope is for the writer a conception of primary importance, expressing as it does a cardinal aspect of the gospel."[318] Marshall maintains that "hope" serves as Peter's "synonym for faith."[319] What Peter thus envisions is every believer having the ability to articulate basic Christian theological conviction in response to the inquiries of others. Peter does not urge them to redirect such inquiries to respected Christian spokespersons; he urges them to understand, own, and articulate the Christian faith themselves.

In other words, 1 Pet 3:15 pictures all believers as agents of theology. New Testament scholar Karen H. Jobes explains, "According to Peter, believers must be able to relate the Christian faith to unbelievers by addressing their questions in terms they find meaningful."[320] Schreiner adds, "This does not mean, of course, that every Christian is to be a highly skilled apologist for the faith. It does mean that every believer should grasp the essentials of the faith and should have the ability to explain to others why they think the Christian faith is true."[321] Thus in urging believers who are scattered abroad "to make a defense to anyone who asks you for a reason for the hope that is in you" (1 Pet 3:15), Peter

---

317. Thomas R. Schreiner, *1, 2 Peter, Jude*, NAC 37 (Nashville: Broadman & Holman, 2003), 174.
318. Kelly, *Commentary on Peter and of Jude*, 143.
319. Marshall, *1 Peter*, 115.
320. Karen H. Jobes, *1 Peter*, BECNT (Grand Rapids: Baker Academic, 2005), 230–31.
321. Schreiner, *1, 2 Peter, Jude*, 175.

Responsibility to Instruct (Rom 15:14)

The book of Romans presents yet another instance in which the NT presents all believers as agents of theological conviction. In Rom 15:14, the apostle Paul declares, "I myself am satisfied about you, my brothers, that you yourselves are full of goodness, filled with all knowledge and able to instruct one another." Here Paul states his confidence that his fellow believers in Rome are competent to *instruct*—or, according to other translations (NASB, KJV), to *admonish*—each other in the church. Such ability to instruct presupposes theological agency. That is, Roman believers were not mere recipients of theology, but rather they had the ability to articulate theological insight to others in order to instruct or admonish.

The Greek word here for *instruct* (*nouthetein*) often means "to counsel about avoidance or cessation of an improper course of conduct."[322] Such counsel required of Paul's audience an understanding of scriptural truth (i.e., what is right and wrong according to God's standard) and an ability to apply it to issues facing the church.[323] The word also appears in connection with the teaching ministry of church leaders. For example, Paul uses the same word in Acts 20:31 in declaring to the Ephesian elders that he "did not cease night or day to *admonish* every one with tears" (emphasis added). Likewise in Col 1:28, he employs this word as he asserts, "Him we proclaim, *warning* everyone and teaching everyone with all wisdom, that we may present everyone mature in Christ" (emphasis added). Further, in 1 Thess 5:12, Paul urges believers to honor church leaders who regularly "admonish" the congregation.

The Scriptures, however, do not reserve this right to *instruct* or *admonish* only for apostles and elders. In Col 3:16, the word appears as an expected practice among church members: "Let the word of Christ dwell in you richly, teaching and *admonishing* one another in all wisdom"

---

322. BDAG, s.v. "νουθετέω."

323. C. E. B. Cranfield, *A Critical and Exegetical Commentary on the Epistle to the Romans*, 2 vols., ICC (Edinburgh: T&T Clark, 1979–80), 2:753n3, explains regarding the word νουθετέω, "What is denoted is the earnest attempt by words spoken (or written) to correct what is wrong in another, to encourage him to do what is right and to refrain from what is evil." This act thus presupposes theological agency and acumen on the part of the person instructing.

(emphasis added). Further, Paul urges believers in the Thessalonian church to "admonish the idle" (1 Thess 5:14). A cognate of this Greek word also appears in Eph 6:4, in which Paul encourages fathers to raise children "in the discipline and *instruction* of the Lord" (emphasis added). In these cases, the instructors—the ones admonishing others with theological insight—are not necessarily church leaders.

The context of Rom 15:14 likewise indicates that theological instruction is a responsibility of all believers. For one, Paul's audience here includes "all those in Rome who are loved by God and called to be saints" (Rom 1:7).[324] He is not speaking only to respected church leaders. Rather, he is speaking to all the saints, implying that each one—being "filled with all knowledge" (Rom 15:14)—is able to instruct others with theological insight. Further, Paul implies theological agency on the part of church members by expecting them to encourage him when he visits. He states at the outset of his letter, "For I long to see you, that I may impart to you some spiritual gift to strengthen you—that is, that we may be mutually encouraged by each other's faith, both yours and mine" (Rom 1:11–12).[325] Paul views believers in Rome as theological agents from whom he can learn and receive encouragement.[326] In other words, he promotes theological mutuality. Colin G. Kruse explains, "Paul does not want his audience to think that the benefits of his intended visit will flow in one direction only."[327]

Thus in Rom 15:14, Paul recognizes and endorses Roman believers' capacity to do theology—to bring the word of God to bear on the life of the church. He did not reserve only for himself this right to teach and

324. Grant R. Osborne, *Romans*, IVPNTC (Downers Grove, IL: IVP Academic, 2004), 34, comments, "He is writing to *all in Rome*, probably all the house churches in the city. His usual practice is to greet 'the church' in the city, so this unusual form may indicate that there are too many to meet in one place and perhaps that he is addressing the factions in the city as a whole group" (emphasis original).

325. Robert H. Mounce, *Romans*, NAC 27 (Nashville: B&H, 1995), 67, explains, "The apostle was not at this point speaking of spiritual gifts such as those listed in 1 Corinthians 12. He was concerned that believers in Rome become increasingly established in their faith. To this end he wanted to share with them some spiritual insight or gift he had received from the Spirit. His visit with them would provide the opportunity to accomplish that purpose."

326. Mounce, *Romans*, 68, comments, "In this aside Paul revealed a genuine sense of appreciation for the spiritual life of others. Although he was an apostle, sent by God to proclaim the good news throughout the known world, he valued and would profit from the faith of other believers."

327. Colin G. Kruse, *Paul's Letter to the Romans*, PNTC (Grand Rapids: Eerdmans, 2012), 102.

instruct, but expected local believers in Rome to embrace this task as well. Grant R. Osborne comments that, according to this text, these Roman believers "are *complete in knowledge*, meaning they have a comprehensive knowledge of God and the gospel truths, including all Paul has talked about in this letter. As a result, they are *competent to instruct one another*, certainly referring to the problem of the strong and the weak in the previous section but going beyond that to general instruction in the Christian faith."[328] Robert H. Mounce adds, "The believers in Rome were expected to help one another toward spiritual maturity.... None were so wise that they had nothing more to learn, and none were so inept that they had nothing of value to share. Spiritual insight is by no means the sole prerogative of those with high intelligence."[329] Thus for Paul, these Roman believers were agents of theology, not just recipients.[330]

Royal Priesthood of All Believers (1 Pet 2:9)

Another foundational warrant for local theological agency rests in the doctrine of the royal priesthood of all believers.[331] Theologian Hank Voss defines the doctrine as "the believer's sharing in the Son's royal priesthood through faith and baptism resulting in participation in the *missio Dei* and spiritual sacrifices of Worship, Work, and Witness."[332] A foundational component of most Protestant ecclesiologies, this doctrine finds its most common support in 1 Pet 2:4–9, in which Peter declares, "But you are a chosen race, a royal priesthood, a holy nation, a people for his own possession, that you may proclaim the excellencies of him who called you out of darkness into his marvelous light" (v. 9). This doctrine also holds deep roots in other parts of the biblical narrative, including the call of Israel to be a kingdom of priests (Exod 19:6), Isaiah's portrayal of the

---

328. Osborne, *Romans*, 387, emphasis original.

329. Mounce, *Romans*, 266.

330. Charles Brock, *Indigenous Church Planting: A Practical Journey* (Neosho, MO: Church Growth International, 1994), 92–93, appeals to Rom 15:14 in arguing that indigenous churches should be "self-teaching."

331. This section was previously published in the *Great Commission Baptist Journal for Missions*. See C. S. Barefoot, "Local Ownership of the Theological Task," *Great Comm. Bapt. Journ. Missions* 2.2 (2023) 1–16.

332. Hank Voss, *The Priesthood of All Believers and the Missio Dei: A Canonical, Catholic, and Contextual Perspective* (Eugene, OR: Pickwick, 2016), 6. See also Uche Anizor and Hank Voss, *Representing Christ: A Vision for the Priesthood of All Believers* (Downers Grove, IL: IVP Academic, 2016).

royal-priestly Servant and his seed (Isa 40–66), the apostolic interpretation of Melchizedekian priesthood in Ps 110 (e.g., Hebrews), Matthew's narrative portrayal of Jesus as the royal priest-king, and John's picture of an eschatological kingdom of priests (Rev 1:6; 5:10).[333]

In the Old Testament, priests served as mediators between God and the people, a role that included the task of instruction in God's Law. Voss explains, "One of the priests' original responsibilities was to serve as oracular spokespersons. They were to inquire of the Lord, and to speak his Word to the people."[334] The prophet Malachi rebuked Israelite priests in his day for failing in this task (Mal 2:1–9). They had not upheld the standard that God established with the Levitical priesthood: "For the lips of a priest should guard knowledge, and people should seek instruction from his mouth, for he is the messenger of the Lord of Hosts" (Mal 2:7). Pointing to this verse, Voss asserts, "The importance of the priests' responsibility to know the Word of God so as to be ready to teach remained throughout Israel's history."[335]

The events of the New Testament radically broadened this priesthood. The tearing of the temple veil at Jesus' crucifixion (Matt 27:51) and the subsequent descending of the Holy Spirit through tongues of fire (Acts 2:1–13) symbolize the new reality that all followers of Christ now share the same priestly access to God that Old Testament priests had maintained. Moreover, this access carries with it the priestly responsibility for all believers to serve as heralds of the faith. No longer does the responsibility to declare and teach rest solely upon a select caste of clergy; it rests on all those who name and follow Jesus as Lord and Savior.

This broadening of the priesthood to include all believers carries significant implications for theologizing. It signifies that disciples of Christ are agents of theology—priests with access to Truth and an ability to discern and teach that Truth. For example, as previously noted, the apostle Paul praised the Roman church because its members were "full of goodness, filled with all knowledge and able to *instruct* one another" (Rom 15:14, emphasis added). Read in light of Malachi's rebuke of Israelite priests, this passage indicates that these Roman Christians were faithfully upholding the theological standard to which those priests had failed to adhere. The recipients of Malachi's warning had dishonored

---

333. For an excellent biblical theology of the priesthood of all believers, see Voss, *Priesthood of All Believers*, 25–99.

334. Voss, *Priesthood of All Believers*, 226.

335. Voss, *Priesthood of All Believers*, 227.

God's name (Mal 2:2), corrupted the covenant (Mal 2:8), and failed to guard or instruct the people in theological knowledge (Mal 2:7–8). These Roman believers, however, were carrying out their priestly duty to embody sound theology and instruct one another in it.

In other words, the call to priesthood is a call to local theologizing. Stuart Murray, a mission practitioner and scholar on Anabaptism, thus refers to the "priesthood of all believers" also as the "theologian-hood" of all believers.[336] He contends, "'Trickle-down' theology, disseminated by academic theologians via graduates from theological institutions to passive congregations, must be replaced by theological reflection on the frontiers of mission and partnerships between those who know what questions matter and those who can offer biblical, historical, and theological resources."[337] Earlier in the twentieth century, Barth similarly and rightly declared, "In the Church there are really no non-theologians."[338]

In sum, various biblical passages lend credence to a hermeneutical community approach to theological development. The Jerusalem Council episode of Acts 15, by showing how the mother church in Jerusalem refrained from asserting final authority over the younger church in Antioch, demonstrates that theological authority resides in the whole community of believers. Further, 1 Cor 14:26–33, 1 Pet 3:15, Rom 15:14, and 1 Pet 2:9 each promote theological agency among all members of the church. Thus, the notion of hermeneutical community maintains roots in biblical truth.

RELEVANCE OF HERMENEUTICAL COMMUNITY

Such a hermeneutical community approach to theological development can serve as a way forward between the extremes of both colonial and post-colonial theological development. On one hand, it seeks to avoid the kind of theological imposition common among missionaries in the colonial era. Robert J. Schreiter explains that during this period, it was "assumed that the younger churches are not in a position to understand their own questions or that their questions are really not as they might believe. The older churches impose a solution to their questions, knowing

---

336. Stuart Murray, *Post-Christendom: Church and Mission in a Strange New World*, 2nd ed. (Eugene, OR: Cascade, 2018), 220.

337. Murray, *Post-Christendom*, 220.

338. Barth, *God in Action*, 57.

much better what the younger church needs or would ask for if it could properly speak."[339] On the other hand, hermeneutical community guards against the post-colonial prospect of outsiders withdrawing from the process of local theological development.[340]

The Willowbank Report elucidates this need to avoid both theological imposition and theological withdrawal by outsiders:

> Cross-cultural witnesses must not attempt to impose a ready-made theological tradition on the church in which they serve, either by personal teaching or by literature or by controlling seminary and Bible college curricula. For every theological tradition both contains elements which are biblically questionable and have been ecclesiastically divisive and omits elements which, while they might be of no great consequence in the country where it originated, may be of immense importance in other contexts. At the same time, although missionaries ought not to impose their own tradition on others, they also ought not to deny them access to it (in the form of books, confessions, catechism, liturgies and hymns), since it doubtless represents a rich heritage of faith. Moreover, although the theological controversies of the older churches should not be exported to the younger churches, yet an understanding of the issues, and of the work of the Holy Spirit in the unfolding history of Christian doctrine, should help to protect them from unprofitable repetition of the same battles.[341]

In other words, outsiders should neither control local theology and theological conviction nor withdraw from the process of local theological development altogether. Instead, as the Willowbank Report states, "We should seek with equal care to avoid theological imperialism or theological provincialism."[342]

---

339. Robert J. Schreiter, *Constructing Local Theologies* (Maryknoll, NY: Orbis, 1985), 99.

340. While not arriving fully at this position, many advocates for "moratorium" in missions moved in this direction. For more on the topic of missionary moratorium, see Emerito Nacpil, "Mission but not Missionaries," *Int. Rev. Mission* 60.239 (1971) 356–62; John Gatu, "Missionary, Go Home," *IDOCInternational Doc.* 63 (1974) 70–72; Gerald H. Anderson, "A Moratorium on Missionaries?," *Christ. Century* 91.2 (1974) 43–45; Byang H. Kato, "Another Look at Moratorium," *Christ. Today* 20.7 (1976) 41–42; Robert Reese, "John Gatu and the Moratorium on Missionaries," *Missiology* 42.3 (2014): 245–56.

341. Lausanne Theology and Education Group, "Willowbank Report," 333–34.

342. Lausanne Theology and Education Group, "Willowbank Report," 334.

Hermeneutical Community

Hermeneutical community can help navigate past these extremes by delineating a role for outsiders in which they are neither controlling nor absent, but rather *conversant*. A key concept that animates this approach is that of dialogue, or conversation. A hermeneutical community approach establishes a conversation between the existing Christian tradition from other parts of the world and the emerging Christian tradition within a local context. Rather than theological imposition from without or theological isolation from within, the task of theology in hermeneutical community recognizes the need for outside and local sources to remain in conversation with one another. As Paul Siu claims, "We must do our utmost to guard against cultural imperialism on the one hand, and arrogant provincialism of the other. Our basic premise of genuine dialogue is that each culture of the world should have a place at the table and should have a right to speak."[343]

This conversational dynamic of the hermeneutical community approach counteracts the colonial trend of theological imposition by incorporating local voices into a broader theological conversation, one in which the existing Christian tradition acts not as king, but as a respected dialogue partner. Theological imposition during the colonial era muted the voices of local believers and churches and thereby jettisoned a valuable source of theology—locals who, by virtue of their location in culture, are far more able to bring scriptural truth to bear on contextual issues. The hermeneutical community approach counteracts this colonial pattern by incorporating those local voices into the process of theological development.

Additionally, the hermeneutical community approach guards against theological parochialism, in which local theologizing becomes secluded from the wider, historic Christian tradition. Charles R. Taber asserts, "It is becoming increasingly evident that working within a single intellectual frame of reference . . . makes anyone, willy-nilly, parochial. . . . A hermeneutic worked out exclusively within one civilization and history will have its strong points and its clear insights, but it will also have its inevitable weaknesses, errors, and blind spots."[344] Parochialism, or provincialism, refers here to the isolation of theological reflection from realities and conversations outside of its immediate context. A

---

343. Paul Siu, "Theologizing Locally," in *Local Theology for the Global Church: Principles for an Evangelical Approach to Contextualization*, ed. Matthew Cook et al. (Pasadena, CA: William Carey Library, 2010), 151.

344. Charles R. Taber, "Missiology and the Bible," *Missiology* 11.2 (1983) 240.

conversational approach helps to prevent such provincialism in theology by allowing different voices and traditions to contribute to theological development in positive ways.

The hermeneutical community approach can thus chart a path beyond both colonial and post-colonial approaches to local theology. Central to this communal approach is an emphasis on the catholicity of the church in its reading of Scripture. As Vanhoozer claims, "Understanding the Bible involves more than exegesis; it involves our engagement in a catholic conversation about its meaning/significance and our active participation in some performance tradition. Doing theology in an era of world Christianity ultimately means taking part in a worldwide conversation about how best to understand—to perform—the biblical text."[345] This catholic conversation neither grants hegemony to Western outsiders nor isolates them from local theologizing, but rather incorporates them in limited but valuable ways.[346]

Accordingly, the notion of communal hermeneutics has garnered wide support in recent years.[347] The concept has become a growing topic

---

345. Vanhoozer, "One Rule to Rule Them All?," 116.

346. Charles E. Van Engen, "The Glocal Church: Locality and Catholicity in a Globalizing World," in *Globalizing Theology: Belief and Practice in an Era of World Christianity*, ed. Craig Ott and Harold A. Netland (Grand Rapids: Baker Academic, 2006), 174, adds, "To view doing theology as the construction of one monolithic theology superimposed on all Christians everywhere violates the truth that God's revelation took place 'at many times and in various ways' (Heb. 1:1) and has always been received within the categories of specific cultural contexts. On the other hand, the atomization of a plurality of local theologies violates the oneness of the church, the unity of the Holy Spirit, the singularity of the gospel, and the unity of all Christians who read the same Bible. Thus, neither monolithic uniformity nor atomized pluriformity are satisfactory approaches to doing theology in a globalizing world. Therefore, the challenge before us is to find a way to know God in context, that is, to do critical theologizing in a glocal fashion through reading the same Bible in the midst of multiple cultures."

347. Examples abound, as already evident in the preceding chapters. For instance, Clark, *To Know and Love God*, 114, offers a contextual theological method in keeping with this dialogical, conversational emphasis. In his method, "Christians in one culture discuss their findings with theologians in another culture, either in time or in space. Maybe the 'other culture' is a distant era of time. Theologians from the past who struggled with parallel questions might have wisdom to offer. Maybe the 'other culture' is a far-off place. Theologians from the other side of the world who grapple with similar issues could suggest ways to interpret the Bible more faithfully or resolve the questions more authentically." Charles R. Taber, "The Limits of Indigenization in Theology," in *Readings in Dynamic Indigeneity*, ed. Charles H. Kraft and Tom N. Wisley (Pasadena, CA: William Carey Library, 1979), 395, argues for "dialogue with the Church in the broadest sense. I believe it is important to maintain in a proper balance both the autonomy of indigenous theologians in working out their indigenous theologies, and

Hermeneutical Community

of conversation in Western theological and missiological discourse, as theologians and missionaries have sought to makes sense of the emerging plurality of contextual theologies toward the end of the twentieth century. David J. Bosch acknowledges, "We are beginning to realize that all theologies, including those in the West, need one another; they influence, challenge, enrich, and invigorate each other—not least so that Western theologies may be liberated from the 'Babylonian captivity' of many centuries."[348] Charles Van Engen is representative of this recognition on the part of Westerners when he asserts,

> Christians from everywhere need to share with other Christians how they are coming to know God in context. Each step forward, each 'translation' of the gospel offers the possibility of discovering something about God as revealed in the Bible that no one has previously seen.... But this deepening and enriching of our understanding of God's revelation in the Bible are possible only if there is an ongoing conversation between the local congregations and churches and the church globally by way of a mutually enriching process of critical theologizing.[349]

Beyond the North Atlantic world, Majority World theologians likewise recognize value in such a communal approach to theology. For example, V. E. Devadutt, a theologian from India, asserts, "There is no virtue in a heresy, but it is desirable that the Indian Church should enter into a theological heritage arising from its own grappling with the problems of our Faith, without of course losing contact with all that comes to her through the age-long wisdom of the Church Universal."[350] Others, in-

---

the interdependence of all parts of the Body for the enrichment of all." See also Matthew Cook, "Contextual but Still Objective?," in *Local Theology for the Global Church: Principles for an Evangelical Approach to Contextualization*, ed. Matthew Cook et al. (Pasadena, CA: William Carey Library, 2010), 86–88; Paul G. Hiebert, *Anthropological Reflections on Missiological Issues* (Grand Rapids: Baker, 1994), 102–3.

348. David J. Bosch, *Transforming Mission: Paradigm Shifts in Theology of Mission* (Maryknoll, NY: Orbis, 1991), 456.

349. Van Engen, "Glocal Church," 175.

350. V. E. Devadutt, "What Is an Indigenous Theology?," in *Readings in Dynamic Indigeneity*, ed. Charles H. Kraft and Tom N. Wisley (Pasadena, CA: William Carey Library, 1979), 316–17.

cluding Hwa Yung,[351] René Padilla,[352] Simon Chan,[353] and Paul Siu,[354] similarly maintain that Majority World churches should not withdraw from interaction with the West and its theology.

FUNCTION OF HERMENEUTICAL COMMUNITY

Hermeneutical community thus functions in several important ways. First, it provides a valuable means of critique. In some cases, the critique of the hermeneutical community serves as a safeguard against theological error. As Schreiter claims, "Any theological formulation can be subject to human failing, to a less than complete fidelity to the message of Jesus. For this reason it needs to be tested against the experience of other Christian communities, both present and past."[355] For example, if a local theology has denied the bodily resurrection of Christ, then the theological witness of others in the global hermeneutical community can rightly point out such an error. Thus, the collective convictions of other groups of Christians—both past and present—in hermeneutical community help to provide and give shape to parameters around authentic Christian theology.[356] Chan rightly notes, "For a local theology to be authentically

---

351. Hwa Yung, *Mangoes or Bananas? The Quest for an Authentic Asian Christian Theology*, 2nd ed. (Maryknoll, NY: Orbis, 2014), 190.

352. Padilla, "The Contextualization of the Gospel," in *Readings in Dynamic Indigeneity*, ed. Charles H. Kraft and Tom N. Wisley (Pasadena, CA: William Carey Library, 1979), 302–3, contends, "Even less would we wish a theology that, in an effort to 'contextualize' the Gospel, superciliously ignores the results of long years of work in the field of Biblical research carried on by theologians in Europe or North America. It would be ridiculous to think that we in the Third World must start at the beginning, erasing the contributions that others have made to our thinking. What is necessary, on the other hand, is a theology that, taking advantage of that which is of value in any study, whatever its source, shows the relevance of Biblical revelation to our culture, the relation between the Gospel and the problems that the Church is facing in our society."

353. Simon Chan, *Grassroots Asian Theology: Thinking the Faith from the Ground Up* (Downers Grove, IL: InterVarsity, 2014), 7, maintains that grassroots Asian theology, "cannot be derived solely from Asian cultural resources. Any authentic theology must be developed in light of the larger Christian tradition. The appeal to Christian tradition is not simply a matter of preference but essential to our theological quest. If the Asian church is truly a part of the church catholic, the accumulated contributions of the past and present are essential to moving the church forward wherever it is found."

354. Siu, "Theologizing Locally," 161.

355. Schreiter, *Constructing Local Theologies*, 34.

356. Bevans, *Introduction to Theology*, 89; Benno van den Toren, "Can We See the Naked Theological Truth?," in *Local Theology for the Global Church: Principles for an*

Christian, it must have substantial continuity with the larger Christian tradition."[357]

A second function of hermeneutical community is to illuminate and challenge cultural blind spots in local theological conviction. Any given context can provide unique vantage points for understanding Scripture, thereby highlighting certain features in the text; yet it can also serve to blind the interpreter to other features. Steve Strauss contends, "Context both increases and decreases theologians' awareness of aspects of the biblical text. . . . Because their context will both open their eyes and blind them to aspects of the biblical text, theologians from every context need one another. Listening to theologians from other cultures helps theologians see what they may have missed because of their own cultural, theological, or historical biases. It helps them make sure their theology reflects as many implications of the biblical text as possible."[358] Interaction within a hermeneutical community can thus broaden the perspectives of local theological agents.

Western theology itself stands to benefit from such a broadening of perspective. Jeffrey Greenman notes, "Western academic theology arises from a particular cultural context, operates with a particular set of assumptions and seeks to answer a particular set of questions. Like any other form of theology, it has its share of blind spots."[359] It would do well then to engage and learn from theologies from other locales, which could help illuminate those Western cultural blind spots. The same goes for theologies arising from the Majority World. The reality is, as Greenman contends, "Any monocultural theology will need supplementation. This means that Western theology needs the challenges and correctives of non-Western theology just as much as non-Western theology needs the challenges and correctives of Western theology."[360]

Evangelical Approach to Contextualization, ed. Matthew Cook et al. (Pasadena, CA: William Carey Library, 2010), 105–6.

357. Chan, *Grassroots Asian Theology*, 11.

358. Steve Strauss, "Creeds, Confessions, and Global Theologizing: A Case Study in Comparative Christologies," in *Globalizing Theology: Belief and Practice in an Era of World Christianity*, ed. Craig Ott and Harold A. Netland (Grand Rapids: Baker Academic, 2006), 153.

359. Jeffrey P. Greenman, "Learning and Teaching Global Theologies," in *Global Theology in Evangelical Perspective: Exploring the Contextual Nature of Theology and Mission*, ed. Jeffrey P. Greenman and Gene L. Green (Downers Grove, IL: IVP Academic, 2012), 238.

360. Greenman, "Learning and Teaching Global Theologies," 245.

A third function of a hermeneutical community approach—one which derives from the previous two—is to provide an arena in which believers and theologies from different contexts can mutually enrich one another. As the community pools insight and perspective, it gains a deeper, broader, and richer understanding of and appreciation for the God of the Bible and the redemptive history in which he is ever at work. According to Bengt Sundkler, "As the given Gospel is preached in new languages and the Church planted in new soil, there may appear hitherto forgotten or hidden treasures of truth which will enrich the Church as a whole."[361] Strauss expounds this idea:

> When local theologians are developing new, locally appropriate forms to communicate biblical meaning, their insights will contribute to a richer, fuller understanding of biblical truth for the global church. As they understand why a form has proven unacceptable locally, they prod the worldwide church to more closely examine its own theology. As they develop new forms, they add color to the multihued tapestry of the worldwide church's understanding of the meaning of Scripture. Global theologizing—the sharing of local theologies from around the world—enhances the theology of the worldwide church.[362]

This type of mutual enriching has become desirable in the eyes of many theologians and church leaders across different contexts.[363]

These functions of the hermeneutical community help to chart a path beyond both the colonial and post-colonial approaches to local theologizing. In a hermeneutical community approach, there is neither local privilege nor foreign hegemony. Rather, as William Dyrness and Oscar

---

361. Bengt Sundkler, "Towards a Christian Theology in Africa," in *Readings in Dynamic Indigeneity*, ed. Charles H. Kraft and Tom N. Wisley (Pasadena, CA: William Carey Library, 1979), 507.

362. Strauss, "Creeds, Confessions, and Global Theologizing," 152.

363. For example, see Andrew F. Walls, *The Cross-Cultural Process in Christian History: Studies in the Transmission and Appropriation of Faith* (Maryknoll, NY: Orbis, 2002), 46–47; Devadutt, "What Is an Indigenous Theology?," 319–24; Clark, *To Know and Love God*, 122, adds, "While African dialogical theology neither mimics Western theology nor seeks a supracultural theology, it does benefit from dialogue with the world church. Theologians need to develop a sensitivity to their own cultural, denominational, and individual blind spots. This is one benefit of using a multiple-perspective approach, seeking mutual critique and enrichment, and in the end integrating perspectives. Dialogical theology coheres with the hermeneutical idea of a fusion of horizons. Theologians are initially limited by their cultural horizons. By opening themselves to new horizons, dialogue enables them to see things they may have missed before."

García-Johnson claim, there exists "a conversation among many voices contributing to the enlarging and developing understanding of Christianity—a transoccidental conversation."[364] Such a conversation is needed because the gospel always proceeds through particular theological traditions, which inevitably impact—sometimes positively, sometimes negatively—people's reception of the message. Dyrness and García-Johnson thus contend, "The traditioning of the gospel message—centered on the reality of Jesus Christ—though indispensable for Christian existence, is at the same time subject to human manipulation and misinterpretation and is constantly in need of the historically situated discernment of the Christian community and the guidance and correction of the Holy Spirit."[365] In other words, Christians today would do well to theologize in the midst of a hermeneutical community.

CONCLUSION

The notion of hermeneutical community—though it has developed in different fields of thought—serves as a framework by which evangelicals laboring in local theological development can do so without succumbing to a pattern of theological imposition or settling for theological withdrawal. It provides a structure for theological development that is not only biblically sound, but can also delineate a constructive role for outsiders in the process. The following chapter will consider how such a hermeneutical community approach might thus shape the outsider's role in local theological development.

---

364. William A. Dyrness and Oscar García-Johnson, *Theology Without Borders: An Introduction to Global Conversations* (Grand Rapids: Baker Academic, 2015), 66.

365. Dyrness and García-Johnson, *Theology Without Borders*, 100.

5

Outsider Role in Local Theological Development

A HERMENEUTICAL COMMUNITY APPROACH to local theological development recasts the outsider's role in the process. In such an approach, no longer does the outsider remain in control of local theological conviction and expression, as was the case during much of the Modern Missionary Movement.[1] Yet, neither does the outsider retreat from local theological development, which may seem like a necessary measure from a post-colonial perspective.[2] Rather, the outsider operates as one voice among others—predominantly local believers—in the process of reading Scripture and bringing it to bear on local exigencies.[3]

Accordingly, the outsider's role in a hermeneutical community approach serves as a way forward between the extremes of foreign control over and foreign withdrawal from local theological development. In the following sections, this chapter will reflect on what warrant outsiders have for participating in local theological development, consider metaphors for understanding the outsider's role in a hermeneutical community approach to local theology, and propose core practices for the outsider in

---

1. Chapter 2 has highlighted this pattern of colonial theological control on the part of outsiders. See also Harvie M. Conn, *Eternal Word and Changing Worlds: Theology, Anthropology, and Mission in Trialogue* (Grand Rapids: Zondervan, 1984), 247.

2. Chapter 3 has surveyed post-colonial responses to the pattern of foreign theological imposition and highlighted the potential of post-colonial sentiment leading toward outsider withdrawal from local theological development.

3. Chapter 4 has explored and defended this "hermeneutical community" approach to local theological development.

such an approach. Finally, this chapter will examine several examples in which outsiders have adopted a similar role. Such precedents are valuable because, as Michael A. Rynkiewich notes, "Despite all the talk in missiology over the last two decades about the local hermeneutical community doing critical contextualization, we have few examples."[4]

WARRANT FOR THE OUTSIDER

The characteristics and functions of hermeneutical community which chapter 4 highlighted establish a general degree of validity to the prospect of outsider involvement in local theologizing. However, evident shortcomings of outsider involvement in the past and the legitimate concerns of post-colonial voices warrant a deeper apologetic. William A. Dyrness raises this issue by asking, "To what extent can we use Western theology in constructing global theology if Western theology itself has been part of the problem for non-Western theologians? Can it free itself of its colonial, imperial core?"[5] Considering that Western missionaries operate, in some ways, as extensions of the Western theological tradition, and considering the ways in which that tradition intermingled with colonialism, such questions are reasonable.

Another concern is whether it is even possible for an outsider—a non-participant of a given culture—to do authentic local theology in that context. For Stephen B. Bevans, the answer is both *yes* and *no*. On one hand he claims, "[A] person who does not fully share one's experience is not to be fully trusted to speak of God in that person's context.... Try as they might, nonparticipants ultimately bring their own feelings, perceptions, experiences, and privilege into a situation, and however slightly, this foreignness works to distort theology in the other context."[6] On the other hand, Bevans contends that there remains a limited role in which the outsider can contribute to local, contextual theology: "To a certain extent and in limited ways, people who do not fully share the experience

---

4. Michael A. Rynkiewich, "Mission, Hermeneutics, and the Local Church," *J. Theol. Interpret.* 1.1 (2007) 57. This claim is nearly two decades old at this point, but his observation is nonetheless important.

5. William A. Dyrness, "Doing Theology out of a Western Heritage: Gains and Losses," in *Theology Without Borders: An Introduction to Global Conversations*, by William A. Dyrness and Oscar García-Johnson (Grand Rapids: Baker Academic, 2015), 33.

6. Stephen B. Bevans, *Models of Contextual Theology*, rev. and exp. ed. (Maryknoll, NY: Orbis, 2002), 19.

of the other can contribute to the development of a contextual theology."[7] This ambivalence, as well as the historic association of Western outsiders with colonialism, necessitates an apologetic that might more clearly establish the legitimacy of outsiders playing a role in local theological development.

Bevans offers three reasons for maintaining an outsider role in local theologizing. First, he points out that "a person can participate in another context to some degree."[8] In other words, an outsider maintains the ability to engage and understand other cultures in a meaningful way. Such participation, which involves the intentional learning of and immersing oneself in a local context, carves out a space—albeit a limited one—for the outsider to contribute to local theological development. Moreover in some contexts, the local church and its members "were formed in their Christianity and theology in an era when culture and cultural expression was taken little into consideration."[9] As a result, their theologies can remain acontextual in nature, disconnected from the deeper theological concerns and questions of the context, as well as the positive aspects of the local culture. In such places, outsiders today can actually play a valuable role in reversing that trend and helping the local believing community to recognize important aspects of the context which their previous theological formation may have neglected. As Bevans maintains, "In a limited but never complete way, the nonparticipant can help in developing a theology that is culturally and socially sensitive to the context by sharing his or her insights as a stranger into the culture."[10]

Second, outsiders can sometimes illuminate cultural blind spots and shortcomings more clearly than locals of a given context. According to Bevans, "the nonparticipant in a context can provide a kind of counterpoint by his or her critique of a particular culture or situation."[11] He explains, "In the same way that the outsider can gain insights into the positive aspects of a context and can serve it by pointing these aspects out, so also the outsider can be more aware than those who share in a context what its weak, negative, or inconsistent aspects might be. . . . A person who has no stake in a culture can often more easily and effectively bring out the 'shadow side' of culture than one who lives within it;

7. Bevans, *Models of Contextual Theology*, 19.
8. Bevans, *Models of Contextual Theology*, 19.
9. Bevans, *Models of Contextual Theology*, 19.
10. Bevans, *Models of Contextual Theology*, 19–20.
11. Bevans, *Models of Contextual Theology*, 20.

in this way, the nonparticipant can help spot areas in a culture that are dehumanizing and ideological."[12] This ability to highlight cultural blind spots lends credence to the notion of outsiders contributing to local theologizing.[13] As Bevans contends, "If participants in a culture or situation are honest and open, they can learn a lot from the stranger in their midst, and in this way the stranger can do a great service both to the local culture and the local church."[14]

Third, outsiders can contribute to local theologizing by helping locals see the conceptual gap between the outsider's theological tradition and the needs of the local context, and the corresponding need to fill that gap with meaningful local theology. As Bevans claims, "By his or her own honesty in presenting his or her theological position, the nonparticipant can stimulate people from the culture or situation to do their own theological thinking."[15] He explains,

> One way a nonparticipant can help in the construction of a local contextual theology is simply to do theology in a way that makes the most sense to him or her as a particular cultural subject. Inevitably, if this is done, one's students or congregation or readers will be struck by the difference from the way they think—some things will seem irrelevant, others challenging, still others will perhaps be found to be offensive. If participants in a particular context could take the further step of asking why a particular idea or theological approach is irrelevant or challenging or offensive, they are well on their way to actually doing theology as subjects in that context. . . . As they are confronted with what they are not, they might more easily discover who they are and how they might express their faith as who they are.[16]

In other words, the foreignness of the outsider's theological heritage can serve to stimulate local theologizing that is more indigenous in nature.

---

12. Bevans, *Models of Contextual Theology*, 20.

13. For example, Bevans, *Models of Contextual Theology*, 20, asserts, "Foreign students and visitors to the United States can highlight, more than native-born U.S. Americans, the negative features of U.S. individualism and its success ethic. A European or U.S. American missionary can remind family-centered cultures such as the Philippines that families can sometimes demand too much of an individual and that Christian values of justice and honesty might have a greater claim than blind family loyalty."

14. Bevans, *Models of Contextual Theology*, 20.

15. Bevans, *Models of Contextual Theology*, 20.

16. Bevans, *Models of Contextual Theology*, 21.

Dyrness provides other reasons for the legitimacy of Western outsider involvement in local theologizing in other parts of the world. First, he maintains that the Western theological tradition raises "perennial questions that theologians have attempted to answer through the ages."[17] In other words, not all of what preoccupies Western theological discourse is irrelevant to other contexts. Dyrness maintains,

> The practice of missionary teaching . . . reflects specific traditions of Western theology that respond to universal human needs and longings and specific core themes of Scripture. These specifics may well be challenged, but if they are given up, *some formulation will have to be developed* that will respond to the specific questions of human life: How do we live as a family? How is political and economic life to be ordered fairly and justly? And if these questions are to be answered, it is foolish to ignore the responses that God's people have developed throughout the centuries.[18]

The Western tradition has sought to answer meaningful questions that people ask across cultures. As such, Western theological agents can still make a valuable contribution to local theologizing.

Second, Dyrness appeals to the emerging discourse on Theological Interpretation of Scripture.[19] Advocates of this hermeneutical approach argue that "theological frameworks can enable interpretation rather than impede it. . . . Rather than interpreting Scripture simply in terms of its original cultural and historical setting, scholars are pointing out that truly formative readings are embedded in communal convictions about God and the work of the Spirit."[20] Such communal hermeneutics provide a path forward for the missionary outsider to contribute to local theologizing in other contexts. Dyrness continues,

> Since all readings of Scripture employ theological assumptions about God and how we learn of his purposes, we should welcome the opportunity to explore and learn from theological options from other places and times. Since we all belong to a common body of Christ, we should welcome the opportunity to read Scripture with these other believers. This engaged and

---

17. Dyrness, "Doing Theology," 34.
18. Dyrness, "Doing Theology," 35.
19. See chapter 4 for an overview of TIS and its bearing on the notion of hermeneutical community.
20. Dyrness, "Doing Theology," 37.

faithful reading of Scripture seems more attractive to non-Western Christians than the barren historical-critical method. It is a reading that both encourages spiritual formation and seeks to harvest the exegetical riches of the contemporary church and the church through the centuries.[21]

Traditioned theology—even that emanating from the West—can thus enrich theological reflection in other contexts. As such, the "Westernness" of many missionary outsiders has the potential to aid local theologizing rather than undermine it.

In addition to these arguments, the general notion that theology is a communal task warrants outsider involvement in the process of local theologizing.[22] In the broader hermeneutical community, outsiders and locals alike are theological members of one another. Therefore, each has a role to play. As Charles R. Taber argues, local theologizing should develop in "dialogue within the community of believers" and in "dialogue with the Church in the broadest sense."[23] Yet in this broad theological community, it remains important for outsiders to refrain from dictating the convictions of locals. M. M. Thomas thus claims, "Isolation is impossible, and undesirable even if it were possible. But ecumenism should not be confused with foreign imposition."[24] That is, rather than subtly continuing colonial practices of theological control, Western outsiders should enter into a genuine theological dialogue with local believers.[25]

21. Dyrness, "Doing Theology," 37.

22. Simon Chan, *Grassroots Asian Theology: Thinking the Faith from the Ground Up* (Downers Grove, IL: InterVarsity, 2014), 17, notes, "Doing theology is essentially an ecclesial endeavor requiring cooperation between the people of God and the theologian."

23. Charles R. Taber, "The Limits of Indigenization in Theology," in *Readings in Dynamic Indigeneity*, ed. Charles H. Kraft and Tom N. Wisley (Pasadena, CA: William Carey Library, 1979), 395.

24. M. M. Thomas, "Foreword," in *An Introduction to Indian Christian Theology*, by Robin H. S. Boyd (New Delhi: ISPCK, 1991), vi; Taber, "Limits of Indigenization," 396, suggests that the goal is "being able to learn both from the insights and the errors of others without falling into bondage to any."

25. William A. Dyrness and Oscar García-Johnson, *Theology Without Borders: An Introduction to Global Conversations* (Grand Rapids: Baker Academic, 2015), 127–28, assert, "For the dialogue among different communities to be constructive in global contexts, the interlocutors should speak in a decolonial language, with a glocal-constructive intent, and an attitude of respectful listening and learning." Bevans, *Models of Contextual Theology*, 21, adds, "But when a person does this, he or she must approach the host culture with both humility and honesty. He or she must have humility because he or she will always be on the margins of the society in which he or she has chosen to work; he or she can never be a real part of it or a direct contributor to it. And he or she

Moreover, the New Testament establishes a precedent for an ongoing outsider role in local theological development. The apostle Paul—himself an outsider to many of the regions among which he ministered—maintained a holy "anxiety for all the churches" (2 Cor 11:28) and taught and labored among them in order to "present everyone mature in Christ" (Col 1:28). This maturity meant, for him, that the word of Christ would dwell in local believers such that they might be able to encourage and exhort one another from the Scriptures (Col 3:16). Paul then passed this work on to other missionary co-laborers of his. He encouraged Timothy, "Devote yourself to the public reading of Scripture, to exhortation, to teaching" (1 Tim 4:13). To Titus he commanded, "But as for you, teach what accords with sound doctrine" (Titus 2:1). The picture which emerges here from the ministries of Paul and his co-laborers is one in which outside missionaries, rather than abandon newly planted local churches, labor diligently among them so that Christ might be formed in their members (Gal 4:19).

Thus, in hermeneutical community, there remains a role for outsiders in local theological development, and local theology benefits from the inclusion of both locals and outsiders. As Robert J. Schreiter argues, "The professional theologian can provide essential links to the larger Christian tradition. Outsiders bring important experience, but by themselves can come to exercise hegemony over the community. A rootedness in the community is essential for a local theology, but does not in itself guarantee insight. All of this underlines how much the theology emerging in local contexts is a communal enterprise."[26] Locals can provide contextual insight in light of their familiarity with the local culture, outsiders can often bring the wider Christian tradition to bear on the process, and all can search the Scriptures together to discern and express its meaning. In such a communal enterprise, multiple agents—each reflecting a different point of view—contribute to the development of local theologies.

---

must have honesty because only through honest sharing of himself or herself can he or she hope to contribute anything at all to people's understanding of their faith in terms of their cultural and social context. A genuine contextual theology, in other words, can indeed grow out of genuine dialogue between the participants in a particular culture and the stranger, the guest, the other."

26. Robert J. Schreiter, *Constructing Local Theologies* (Maryknoll, NY: Orbis, 1985), 20.

METAPHORS FOR THE OUTSIDER

Over recent decades, missiologists and theologians have captured aspects of the outsider's role using several different metaphors. These include the outsider as midwife, broker, and mediator. Each of these metaphors aligns well with a hermeneutical community approach to local theological development.

Outsider as Midwife

Leonardo Mercado, a theologian from the Philippines, was one of the first to explain the role of a theological specialist as that of a *midwife*. He sought to explain the relationship between the professional theologian and the common people in the development of local theologies. According to Mercado, the theologian's role "can be compared to that of a midwife, to borrow Socrates' expression. The midwife dose [sic] not give birth but only assists in the delivery. The theologian does not make his own theology. His assistance will be of various forms."[27] Although Mercado did not frame this metaphor in reference to outsiders and locals, his central insight remains applicable since missionary outsiders often serve as de facto professional theologians in various contexts.

Bevans has reappropriated this metaphor in recent scholarship as a way of understanding how someone who does not share the local people's rootedness in culture might nevertheless take part in developing contextual theology. He claims, "The role of the trained theologian, therefore, is not that of an expert who tells people the best way to express their faith. Rather her or his role is that of reflector and thematizer, the one who is able to provide the biblical and traditional background that will enable the people to develop their own theology. Her or his role is very much like a midwife—assisting at a birth with lots of experience and expertise, but not really directly involved in the birthing itself."[28] Thus the outsider, as a theological midwife, can aid the development of local theologies by bringing wider theological expertise to the table and assisting locals in using that expertise as they give birth to new expressions of theology.[29] In this way, the outsider does not dominate the process,

---

27. Leonardo N. Mercado, *Elements of Filipino Theology* (Tacloban City, Philippines: Divine Word University Publications, 1975), 13.

28. Mercado, *Elements of Filipino Theology*, 13.

29. H. D. Beeby, "Thoughts on Indigenizing Theology," *South East Asia J. Theol.*

but nevertheless plays an important role in helping to ensure a healthy theological "delivery."

Outsider as Broker

Another way of conceiving an outsider's involvement in local theologizing is to understand him or her as a *broker*. Krikor Haleblian may have been the first to suggest this metaphor. He maintains, "The believing community in each culture must take ultimate responsibility for contextualizing the gospel, but there is a place and a need for professionals who can act as 'brokers' in this difficult and ongoing task."[30] A broker is an intermediary agent, someone who can make exchanges between different parties. While Haleblian has professional theologians in view, the notion applies equally to missionaries, who often—in light of their own theological education—function as on-the-ground theologians among the people they serve.

Harvie M. Conn picked up this metaphor and envisioned it as a middle way between the theological imposition evident in colonial era missions and the potential withdrawal of outsiders from the work of theological development in the post-colonial era.[31] Given his belief that theology is a communal endeavor, there remains, for Conn, a role for the outsider in the task of developing local theologies. Similar to Haleblian, he claims, "The voice of the cultural outsider/missionary, acting as an idea 'broker,' can under the best of circumstances help to provide 'continual cross-fertilization and *mutual* correction.'"[32] The missionary outsider serves as a broker who, in some ways, stands in the gap between the local church and the church universal. As such, the outsider can play an important role in local theologizing by offering insight that might illuminate cultural blind spots and potential ways in which local theology might be erring toward syncretism. Moreover, without such a voice, local theology becomes more prone to provincialism.

Yet Conn is quick to hedge his claim. First, he insists that the brokerage benefit runs both ways. Not only does a local theology benefit

---

14.2 (1973) 38, also employs the midwife metaphor in discussing indigenous theology.

30. Krikor Haleblian, "The Problem of Contextualization," *Missiology Int. Rev.* 11.1 (1983) 99.

31. Conn, *Eternal Word*, 205.

32. Conn, *Eternal Word*, 205, emphasis original.

from the exchange of ideas through the outsider-broker, but the theology and church of the outsider gain as well. Conn declares, "It is not only the Western churches that can function as theological 'brokers' in stimulating new understanding of the Scriptures. Let the Third World churches help the West in its light from the temptation of theological parochialism.... Every church must learn to be both learner and teacher in theologizing."[33] Second, he recognizes potential ill effects of outsider involvement. As outsiders serve as hermeneutical community members in local theological development, they must not hold too fast to foreign theological methods and thus subvert the possibility of doing local theology in a truly local way. Conn explains, "Patterns of theological response constructed and then taught to a young church by missionary 'outsiders' can, with the best of intentions, create covert paradigms of theologizing. And these can continue in subtle ways, to form and control indigenous responsiveness to indigenous cultures long after the missionary and the missionary's creed have overtly stepped aside."[34] Withstanding these important caveats, Conn's notion of the outsider as broker falls squarely within the hermeneutical community emphasis. The outsider neither imposes his or her own theology nor withdraws completely from the task.

Outsider as Mediator

Yet another metaphor for the outsider's role in local theologizing is that of a *mediator*. This understanding of the missionary role stems from the ways contemporary global and local realities have converged to create an increasingly interconnected world.[35] In such a world, the old pattern of missionary movement, in which the West sends laborers to the rest of

---

33. Conn, *Eternal Word*, 252.
34. Conn, *Eternal Word*, 249.
35. Paul G. Hiebert, "The Missionary as Mediator of Global Theologizing," in *Globalizing Theology: Belief and Practice in an Era of World Christianity*, ed. Craig Ott and Harold A. Netland (Grand Rapids: Baker Academic, 2006), 288–89, notes, "In recent years, scholars have turned their attention to the emergence of world systems, but studies show that most people still live in local and regional settings, even though they may venture from home from time to time. Out of these discussions have emerged theories of a 'glocal' world in which different kinds of globalization interact in complex ways at global, regional, and local levels.... The glocalization of the world and the church has profound implications for missions in the twenty-first century, implications we have only begun to explore under the topics of truth, dialogue, religious pluralism, relativism, contextualization, ecumenism, partnership, and local and global theologies."

the world, has transformed into polycentric missionary activity.[36] Paul G. Hiebert explains, "In the past, missionaries went from the 'Christian' West to the uttermost parts of the world. Today, there are large churches and mission movements in many non-Western countries, and the West is now also a mission field."[37] Churches in the West are still actively sending missionaries, yet the flow of sending is hardly one way. In this new situation, the West no longer retains hegemonic control over the worldwide Christian movement.

An emerging understanding of missionary work in this polycentric world context features Western missionaries serving as mediators. Hiebert contends that in this new context today, "[A] growing number of missionaries are 'inbetweeners,' standing between different worlds, seeking to build bridges of understanding, mediating relationships, and negotiating partnerships in ministry."[38] Missionaries are mediators in several ways. They mediate between the gospel and the world, between Christianity and other religions, between church networks in different parts of the world, between theology and social sciences, and between the academic study of missions and its actual practice.[39]

Western missionaries also serve as mediators in the task of local theologizing. Churches all over the world are rightly developing and formulating their own theological convictions. As this happens, new questions are emerging regarding the relationship between different local theologies, as well as the relationship between such theologies and the notion that the gospel is universal truth for all peoples.[40] Missionaries are well-positioned to help navigate such issues. As Hiebert maintains, "Missionaries and transnational church leaders from around the world are called on to be mediators in doing global theologizing. They must help theologians from different cultures understand one another deeply and become more self-aware of their own cultural perspectives."[41] Thus

---

36. Two scholars who have recently explored such polycentrism in mission are Allen L. Yeh, *Polycentric Missiology: 21st-Century Mission from Everyone to Everywhere* (Downers Grove, IL: IVP Academic, 2016); Samuel Escobar, *The New Global Mission: The Gospel from Everywhere to Everyone* (Downers Grove, IL: IVP Academic, 2003).

37. Hiebert, "Missionary as Mediator," 297.

38. Hiebert, "Missionary as Mediator," 297.

39. Hiebert, "Missionary as Mediator," 297–99.

40. Hiebert, "Missionary as Mediator," 305–6.

41. Hiebert, "Missionary as Mediator," 307.

missionaries can serve as mediators within the broader, worldwide hermeneutical community.

The role of a mediator involves at least two components. First, it involves encouraging local Christian communities to self-theologize rather than rely on Western theological convictions. Hiebert and Eloise Hiebert Meneses contend, "We must . . . encourage young converts to study the Bible for themselves and formulate their own theological understandings of it, flawed as these are by their cultural biases. Then together with them we must form a hermeneutical community in which we listen and share our insights, correcting one another's biases and seeking together to understand and follow the Scripture more fully."[42]

Second, mediation in local theologizing involves acting as a resource person and catalyst.[43] Such a role is important when considering the aforementioned reality that context can often blind people to certain aspects of Scripture. Thus Hiebert, Tite Tiénou, and R. Daniel Shaw argue, "For this reason, missionaries and church leaders from outside play important roles in helping local churches to do theology, not by dictating the answers, but by acting as catalysts helping the people to understand Scripture better and to gently remind them of their cultural biases."[44] In some situations, missionaries can also provide vital links to the historic Christian theological tradition and thus help agents of local theology negotiate their convictions within a much broader hermeneutical community. Missionaries as mediators thus neither impose theology on others nor remove themselves from the process. Rather, they encourage local communities to theologize from their own context, and they provide resources and insight for the task.

ROLE OF THE OUTSIDER

Beyond endorsing helpful metaphors for the outsider's place in local theological development, a hermeneutical community approach recasts the particularities of the outsider's role in that process.[45] In order to

---

42. Paul G. Hiebert and Eloise Hiebert Meneses, *Incarnational Ministry: Planting Churches in Band, Tribal, Peasant, and Urban Societies* (Grand Rapids: Baker, 1995), 368–69.

43. Hiebert and Meneses, *Incarnational Ministry*, 164.

44. Paul G. Hiebert et al., *Understanding Folk Religion: A Christian Response to Popular Beliefs and Practices* (Grand Rapids: Baker, 1999), 385.

45. Lois Fuller, "The Missionary's Role in Developing Indigenous Christian

better situate the outsider's role in local theological development, this proposal will draw from the work of Brian A. DeVries, who provides an overview of different stages of contextualization.[46] Specifically, he outlines six such stages on a scale from "X-1" to "X-6": incarnational, missional, ecclesial, reformational, reflectional, and global contextualization.[47] According to him, the work of cross-cultural missions begins with incarnational contextualization (X-1) and then moves onward from there as the local church forms, grows, and presses on to maturity.

Important for the purpose of this chapter are the stages of missional contextualization (X-2) and ecclesial contextualization (X-3). According to DeVries, missional contextualization "involves the communication of the gospel message (the Word) by the missionary (sent one) to a person

---

Theology," *Evang. Missions Q.* 33.4 (1997) 404–9, has broached this very topic. She claims, "Although good beginnings have been made at indigenous Christian theology in many cultures, much still needs to be done. Missionaries want to encourage local believers to digest and apply Scripture to their own cultures and societies. A missionary is an outsider, however, who struggles to understand the local world view and thought patterns well enough to communicate convincing theology for a local situation" (407–8). Further, "Local believers are the best people to formulate indigenous Christian theology. But many of them have never attempted it because those who brought them the gospel did not encourage them to do so. The missionary role is to model this task, however inadequately, and to encourage others to do it" (409). In sum, Fuller contends that the missionary's role is to challenge and encourage locals to theologize, while also modeling the process. While these aims are good and helpful, they remain rather vague. This chapter seeks to delineate more clearly what should constitute the role of outsiders in local theological development.

46. Brian A. DeVries, "The Contexts of Contextualization: Different Methods for Different Ministry Situations," *Evang. Missions Q.* 55.4 (2019) 11–14.

47. DeVries, "Contexts of Contextualization," 11–14. Incarnational contextualization (X-1) is the endeavor of a missionary to contextualize his or her person—including one's "lifestyle, language, thinking, and even values and emotions" (11). Missional contextualization (X-2) is the process of an outsider communicating the gospel to local respondents "in such a way that is understandable and without any unintended distractions or misapplications" (12). Ecclesial contextualization (X-3) is the endeavor of a local church expressing the Christian message with a goal "to improve the accuracy of the local understanding and application of biblical truth (theology), to answer to local questions that challenge biblical thinking (apologetics), and to confront the sin of local traditions (prophetic preaching)" (12). Reformational contextualization (X-4) is the work of a local church embodying the Christian message before the public and transforming local culture through its witness (12). Reflectional contextualization (X-5) "describes the changes that take place in the missionary's own worldview" (12). At this stage, the missionary reorients him- or herself according to knowledge gained in the process of living and ministering cross-culturally. Global contextualization (X-6) takes place when churches from different contexts engage in conversation with one another in order to learn from each other and mutually grow in faith and understanding (13).

Hermeneutical Community

(receiver) in the local sociocultural context (receiving culture)."[48] At this stage, the agent of contextualization is the outsider, who seeks to "accurately communicate the gospel, within a different language and sociocultural context, in such a way that is understandable and without any unintended distractions or misapplications."[49] At the next stage—ecclesial contextualization—the agent becomes local churches and Christians who express their theological convictions as they relate to their own culture and context.[50]

DeVries and Hiebert both perceive the movement from missional contextualization to ecclesial contextualization as something that happens over generations. According to DeVries, ecclesial contextualization is done "often by second or third generation believers."[51] Similarly, Hiebert sees self-theologizing—which is characteristic of DeVries's ecclesial contextualization[52]—as a reality that develops slowly over time. He claims, "The development of a theology for a new cultural context does not take place overnight. As we have seen, the attention of a young church is focused on its growth and its immediate response to old beliefs and practices. The deeper problems of contextualization and of keeping the churches true to the Christian faith in the new setting often arise only with second- and third-generation leaders in the church."[53] If such theology simply develops organically over time, then one might recognize a rather limited role for outsiders in that development process.

However, in the hermeneutical community approach to local theological development advocated here, the outsider assumes an intentional role in fostering self-theology among local believers, thus moving them toward the kind of ecclesial contextualization that DeVries envisions. As Hiebert recognizes, local churches need to mature in theological conviction and expression: "In time . . . it is important for a church to wrestle with the question of contextualizing the gospel in its own cultural setting. Every church must make theology its own concern, for it must face the challenges to faith raised by its culture. And when this happens, the

---

48. DeVries, "Contexts of Contextualization," 11.
49. DeVries, "Contexts of Contextualization," 12.
50. DeVries, "Contexts of Contextualization," 12.
51. DeVries, "Contexts of Contextualization," 12.
52. DeVries, "Contexts of Contextualization," 12.
53. Paul G. Hiebert, *Anthropological Insights for Missionaries* (Grand Rapids: Baker, 1985), 213.

results will be more profound and enduring."[54] Therefore, considering the value and importance of self-theologizing, outsiders within a hermeneutical community approach seek to intentionally foster such local theologizing rather than waiting decades for it to develop.[55]

This section delineates five core components of the outsider's role in this process. These include teaching Scripture, modeling sound hermeneutics, cultivating theological agency, challenging blind spots, and broadening perspectives.[56] Although this proposal is broad and inexhaustive, it nevertheless provides a framework by which outsiders can more intentionally move local believers and churches toward ecclesial contextualization. In utilizing this framework, outsiders can thus help local churches become self-theologizing, which DeVries describes as "the confessing and teaching of biblical truth (Word) by indigenous people within the local church (receiver) in the language and worldview of the local context (receiving culture)."[57]

Additionally, a degree of progression exists among these components. That is, with a local church at an X-2 level—in which locals have not yet begun to self-theologize—the outsider's role will center mostly on teaching Scripture while modeling sound hermeneutics. As local believers grow in their understanding of Scripture and interpretation, the outsider then begins to cultivate theological agency more actively by creating space in which locals can study, interpret, apply, and express Scriptural truth in relation to their context. Then as locals grow in this work of theologizing, the outsider begins to challenge potential blind spots and broaden local theological perspectives.

In this movement from missional contextualization to ecclesial contextualization, the outsider can play a prominent role—a precedent that might appear to undermine the pursuit of self-theologizing and local theological agency. However, one should not conflate this prominence

---

54. Hiebert, *Anthropological Insights*, 214.

55. Stephen B. Bevans, "Singing the Lord's Song in a Foreign Land: The Foreigner as Theology Teacher," *South East Asia J. Theol.* 17.2 (1976) 50, claims, "While the foreign theologian cannot actually do theology indigenous to the culture in which he works, he can, I believe, play an active and even unique role in forming his students into indigenous theologians."

56. This chapter will explore the notion of cultivating theological agency in greater depth than the other components, partly because it is not discussed enough in the realm of theological development, and because it is perhaps the most crucial component of the outsider's work in shepherding local churches toward self-theologizing.

57. DeVries, "Contexts of Contextualization," 12.

with the kind of centrality and control evident in colonial patterns of theological development. For one, the outsider is prominent in this movement toward ecclesial contextualization more by default of his or her position as initial evangelist. That is, because he or she has already assumed a leading role in the missional contextualization phase, which features the outsider leading locals to faith and discipling them, he or she will serve as an important proponent in guiding the local church toward ecclesial contextualization. The practice of self-theologizing does not develop by the outsider breaking fellowship with the local church; it develops as the outsider shepherds the church in that direction. Thus, in cases where the outsider has helped plant new churches in foreign contexts, his or her prominent role in the early development of the church makes sense.

Another way that the prominence of outsiders in this proposal differs from the centrality of outsiders in colonial approaches to theological development is that this proposal features outsiders becoming less assertive over time. Through the progression of components of the outsider's role (i.e., teaching scripture, modeling sound hermeneutics, cultivating theological agency, challenging blind spots, and broadening perspectives), the outsider begins to cede his or her voice to locals, who ultimately assume the primary role in local theologizing. That is, in the move from missional to ecclesial contextualization, outsiders give increasingly more space to locals in the task of expressing theological conviction. The outsider's role thus shifts from being primary to being auxiliary.

Finally, a vital mark which guards the outsider's role from devolving into a means of colonial control over theology is the adoption of a learner's mentality. That is, outsiders here must recognize that they have as much to learn from local believers as those believers do from them. The apostle Paul sought not just to give but also to receive. He declared to the church in Rome his hope "that we may be mutually encouraged by each other's faith, both yours and mine" (Rom 1:12). It is likewise of paramount importance that missionary outsiders enter new contexts not just as teachers, but as learners who can gain much from the wisdom and insight of local members of the body of Christ. Outsiders from the West should thus welcome a theological reciprocity in which Majority World Christians likewise teach, challenge, and broaden the perspectives of their Western brethren. This kind of reciprocity balances the prominent role that outsiders might play in local theological development.

OUTSIDER ROLE IN LOCAL THEOLOGICAL DEVELOPMENT

With these caveats in place, the following core components form a role for the outsider that circumvents the extremes of colonial and post-colonial approaches to local theological development. Not only does each component individually seek to mitigate foreign theological control, but the progression of these components also leads to a phase of contextualization (i.e., ecclesial contextualization) in which local believers serve as the primary agents of local theologizing.[58] Accordingly, the outsider maintains a role in local theological development (contra post-colonial withdrawal), yet ultimately entrusts the task of theology to local believers (contra colonial imposition).

Teaching Scripture

The first component of the outsider's role—particularly in contexts where the church has not reached the ecclesial contextualization phase[59]—is teaching Scripture. The impetus for this core practice is two-fold. First, for evangelicals, the Bible serves as the normative authority and foundation for all theology—a commitment which derives, in part, from the Protestant Reformation's emphasis on *sola scriptura*.[60] Evangelicals have continued to champion that emphasis on the Bible for the life and theology of the church. David K. Clark explains, "Evangelical theology's affirmation of the Scripture Principle—the Reformation cry, *sola scriptura*—involves a dual commitment to the innate authority of the Bible and to an explicit, functional submission to that authority.... The painstaking task of biblical exegesis and of theological reflection—interpreting all of life in light of the Bible—begin with this understanding."[61] Eminent

---

58. The following sections seek to demonstrate how these components limit foreign control in the process of theological development. See also DeVries, "Contexts of Contextualization," 12.

59. According to DeVries, "Contexts of Contextualization," 12, churches at the ecclesial contextualization phase assume for themselves the responsibility to teach Scripture.

60. David K. Clark, *To Know and Love God: Method for Theology* (Wheaton, IL: Crossway, 2010), 59, posits, "For evangelicals, the Reformation heritage is especially important. The Reformers believed that theology and practice in the Catholic Church had become human-centered. Part of their reasserting the theocentric nature of theology was the Scripture Principle. While the medieval church affirmed the authority of Scripture, the Reformers insisted on the *sole* and *ultimate* authority of the Bible. The Scripture Principle, the commitment to *sola scriptura*, is an essential and defining feature of evangelical theology" (emphasis original).

61. Clark, *To Know and Love God*, 65.

evangelical theologian Carl F. H. Henry adds, "The Bible is the reservoir and conduit of divine truth, the authoritative written record and exposition of God's nature and will."[62] Henry's view of biblical authority typifies evangelical conviction concerning the Scriptures.[63]

Majority World evangelical theologians have likewise committed themselves to biblical authority in the task of theology.[64] For example, Indian theologian Sunand Sumithra, former director of the Theological Commission of the World Evangelical Alliance, asserts, "Evangelical theology is primarily the interpreting of the Bible in context. The Bible is, thus, the primary source, ultimate authority, and foundation for theology."[65] Theologian Tokunboh Adeyemo, former general secretary of the Association of Evangelicals in Africa, similarly contends, "God's eternal and unchanging message is both relevant and true to our ever-changing situations. It cannot be over-emphasized that as God is absolute, so is His message. This God's self-disclosure of Himself—the Scriptures—forms our primary source for theology."[66] In other words, any attempt to express local evangelical theology must begin with the biblical text.

Moreover, a second impetus for outsiders focusing on teaching Scripture is the need to mitigate the premature influence of Western theological systems. That is, outsiders should endeavor to teach the Bible rather than accumulated bodies of Western theological thought. According to Wilbert R. Shenk, what is needed is "an approach to theology which is a dynamic process of confronting the community of faith

---

62. Carl F. H. Henry, *God, Revelation and Authority*, vol. 4: *God Who Speaks and Shows* (Waco, TX: Word, 1979), 7.

63. Clark, *To Know and Love God*, 61, explains, "Henry's view of theological authority is typical of evangelicalism today. He defended the view that the Bible is the capstone of revelation. It alone is the unique, written revelation of God, a permanent, meaningful, and authoritative self-expression by God of his nature and will."

64. In a joint statement, "The Seoul Declaration: Toward an Evangelical Theology for the Third World," *Int. Bull. Mission Res.* 7.2 (1983) 64, Majority World evangelicals declared, "We have concertedly committed ourselves to building our theology on the inspired and infallible Word of God, under the authority of our Lord Jesus Christ, through the illumination of the Holy Spirit. No other sources stand alongside. Despite our varying approaches to doing theology, we wholeheartedly and unanimously subscribe to the primacy of the Scriptures."

65. Sunand Sumithra, "Towards Evangelical Theology in Hindu Cultures," in *Biblical Theology in Asia*, ed. Ken Gnanakan (Bangalore, India: Theological Book Trust, 1995), 143.

66. Tokunboh Adeyemo, "Towards an Evangelical African Theology," *Evang. Rev. Theol.* 7.1 (1983) 147.

with the full range of meaning of the biblical faith without resort to theological systems which become self-regulating. If a church is robbed of this experience in the first generation, by virtue of needing to accept a second-hand theological system from an alien people and culture it may be very difficult to change course later on."[67] In other words, local believers benefit from an encounter with Scripture before any encounter with established bodies of theological discourse. By not relying on such theological systems, locals gain an opportunity to fuse their horizons of understanding with the horizon of the biblical text, thus minimizing premature influences from without.[68]

This emphasis on teaching Scripture thus allows locals to engage the biblical text *directly* rather than having to go through the lens of Western theology. As Indonesian theologian Albert Widjaja claims, "Indigenous theology is not a theology which merely adjusts western theology into the though-form [sic] of the indigenous culture. Nor is it a ramification and elaboration of certain fundamental aspects of western theology to meet the presupposition of the native culture."[69] Rather, indigenous—i.e., local—theology must stem from direct exploration of the biblical text. According to Widjaja, "Scripture is the basic source from which theological knowledge comes. It is also the sole authority by which theology should be judged. Therefore, the Scripture has to be explored afresh.... In doing so, we may have a deeper understanding of God's message as we ponder directly upon all the original material of the Bible."[70]

Thus, because the Bible is the normative authority for all theological reflection, outsiders should focus on teaching the Bible rather than existing Western theologies so that locals have an opportunity to engage

---

67. Wilbert R. Shenk, "Theology and the Missionary Task," *Missiology* 1.3 (1973) 307.

68. D. A. Carson, "Reflections on Contextualization: A Critical Appraisal of Daniel Von Allmen's 'Birth of Theology,'" *East Afr. J. Evang. Theol.* 3.1 (1984) 48–49, explains, "One problem . . . is that the missionary may unwittingly intrude a lot of his own cultural baggage into the gospel he is preaching. . . . A second problem is that the new convert may have unwittingly picked up some of this unnecessary baggage from the missionary. But it is precisely in fostering the fusion of the convert's horizon of understanding with that of the biblical text, which both missionary and convert agree is the basis of authority for their shared faith, that there is a possibility of the convert's divesting himself of these unwise and sometimes unwitting accretions, a possibility of developing a genuinely contextualized theology."

69. Albert Widjaja, "Beggarly Theology: A Search for a Perspective Toward Indigenous Theology," *South East Asia J. Theol.* 14.2 (1973) 41.

70. Widjaja, "Beggarly Theology," 42.

directly with the biblical text.[71] Granted, outsiders cannot teach Scripture from a presuppositionless, unbiased, and neutral point of view.[72] However, an emphasis on Scripture over existing bodies of Western theology can help minimize *premature* foreign theological influence and maximize local engagement with Scripture. The teaching ministry of the outsider should help facilitate such engagement.

However, such an approach—in which the outsider shifts his or her focus away from existing theology and toward expounding Scripture afresh—might produce trepidation among those eager to guard "the faith that was once for all delivered to the saints" (Jude 3). Dean S. Gilliland explains, "It stands to reason that one who is proclaiming the gospel in another culture wants to hand over the experience, the full truth, without error, which has become his or her own."[73] In other words, missionary outsiders often desire—understandably—to guard theological orthodoxy among local churches, and one way of doing that is to insist on locals adhering to already established theological systems.

Yet one must be careful at this point to distinguish between the Bible and theology. Hiebert notes, "As evangelicals we hold to the truthfulness of the Bible. We also have strong theological convictions."[74] Yet in considering how these realities relate, Hiebert contends that one must be careful not to conflate the two.[75] Others concur. For example, Indian theologian Ken R. Gnanakan claims, "*Theology* and the Bible are not synonymous. Theology depends upon the Bible, but the Bible does not depend upon theology."[76] Taber adds, "We confuse the closing of the

---

71. Chris Marantika, "Towards an Evangelical Theology in an Islamic Culture," in *Biblical Theology in Asia*, ed. Ken Gnanakan (Bangalore, India: Theological Book Trust, 1995), 181, asserts, "Asian theologians . . . should begin to search the Scriptures, master God's revealed truth, and express it through the vehicle of their oriental thinking. . . . The Word of God, therefore, should become the centre and the sole source for doing an Asian evangelical theology." Simon Herrmann, "Research Serving Theology: A Model for the Era of World Christianity," *Missiology* 49.2 (2021) 166, rightly contends, "The standard is God's Word, not the theology of someone else."

72. Carson, "Reflections on Contextualization," 45, notes that it is impossible for one to teach from a *tabula rasa* and that existing theological convictions always color the content of teaching.

73. Dean S. Gilliland, "Contextual Theology as Incarnational Mission," in *The Word Among Us: Contextualizing Theology for Mission Today*, ed. Dean S. Gilliland (Dallas: Word, 1989), 14.

74. Hiebert, *Anthropological Insights*, 197–98.

75. Hiebert, *Anthropological Insights*, 198.

76. Ken R. Gnanakan, "Biblical Foundations: A South Asian Study," *Evang. Rev. Theol.* 7.1 (1983) 113, emphasis original.

canon and the closing of our theologizing, and end up with theological idols. Especially in the context of an emerging truly international Body, with many voices contributing to the enrichment of all, it would be folly for any segment of the Church, whether in or out of the west, to conclude that it had completed its task and that all that remained was to cross the t's and dot the i's. Rather, we must forever be reforming our theology."[77] That is, theology is provisional while biblical revelation is permanent. Such a differentiation allows evangelicals to acknowledge a plurality of theologies without compromising the final authority of Scripture.

Moreover, such trepidation (toward tabling existing theology) remains unnecessary in light of the ongoing role that historical theology plays in local theological development. That is, a focus on exploring Scripture afresh does not entail a rejection of past theological insight. As Rodrigo D. Tano, theologian from the Philippines, explains, "This does not mean the setting aside of a long tradition of useful theological activity in the west. It means rather that the Christian communities in the Third World can come to the text directly with their questions, needs and aspirations, and allow the text to speak to them."[78] Existing theologies maintain a place in local theological development, yet not at the expense of the primacy of Scripture.[79]

In sum, as the outsider focuses on teaching directly from Scripture, locals not only gain a foundation in scriptural truth but also an opportunity to root their convictions directly in the biblical text. According to Gilliland, the precedent of outsiders controlling local theological conviction by not allowing locals to explore Scripture anew reflects "that very spirit of domination and control which so subtly, so permanently keeps new Christians from discovering the Word of Truth in Jesus Christ for themselves in their own life and world."[80] The goal, rather, should be to help local Christians "be able to process, reflect upon, and organize

---

77. Taber, "Limits of Indigenization," 396–97.

78. Rodrigo D. Tano, "Toward an Evangelical Asian Theology," *Evang. Rev. Theol.* 7.1 (1983) 156.

79. Carson, "Reflections on Contextualization," 51, adds, "[A] truly contextualized theology is, in my view, one in which believers from a particular culture seek to formulate a comprehensive theology in the language and categories of their own culture, but based on the whole Bible itself. . . . But this does not entail the abandonment of all contact with other theologies, which is impossible, but only that the line of direct control must be from Scripture."

80. Gilliland, "Contextual Theology as Incarnational Mission," 14.

biblical truth so that the Book and the truth *become their own*."[81] That is, by focusing on teaching Scripture, outsiders can help locals take ownership of their theological convictions rather than outsource them to existing theologies from other contexts. Thus, the teaching of Scripture—the foundation for all theological reflection—serves an important role in local theological development.

Modeling Sound Hermeneutics

A second core component of the outsider's role is modeling sound hermeneutics. While majoring on the text of Scripture is important, such an emphasis can yet falter if sound hermeneutical practice does not accompany it. "Sound" here refers to a hermeneutic that recognizes Scripture as authoritative, seeks to ascertain authorial intent in understanding meaning, and also focuses on the content of the biblical text as the basis for theological development. Regarding the need for modeling hermeneutics, theologian Doug Heidebrecht claims, "The challenge for leaders is both to model good interpretive practice and to facilitate the community's involvement in the process of a close reading of biblical texts."[82] Bevans similarly contends that in cross-cultural situations, the foreign "theology teacher does not present answers in class, but models."[83] Although Bevans perhaps overstates his case, the point here is that outsiders should model sound interpretive practices as they teach Scripture to locals.

A major impetus for such modeling is the ever-present danger of misinterpreting Scripture according to worldviews that may not align with biblical truth. Ruth Julian elucidates this danger in local theological development:

> Unfortunately, without training, a dialogical approach between Scripture and worldview does not always happen. Instead, many lay-Christians use a linear approach to Bible study through which their worldview colors what is read but there is no return

---

81. Gilliland, "Contextual Theology as Incarnational Mission," 15, emphasis original.

82. Doug Heidebrecht, "Community Hermeneutics in Practice: Following the Interpretive Path Together," *Direction* 49.2 (2020) 131. Heidebrecht's focus here is on leaders within the Mennonite Brethren denomination leading their congregations in corporate study of the Scriptures. However, his assertion applies just as well to missionary outsiders seeking to promote local theological development.

83. Bevans, "Singing the Lord's Song," 56.

challenge. The Bible is not given the opportunity to speak back into the reader's life and point out the areas in that life which need to be changed. When this happens, the worldview that Christians bring to Scripture dictates the interpretation instead of Scripture guiding the interpretation.[84]

In other words, without acquiring a model for how to properly interpret the Bible, local believers remain susceptible to practicing a kind of eisegesis in which their contextual preunderstandings remain the operative, determinative factor in theological development rather than biblical exegesis.[85] Granted, this susceptibility does not just characterize local believers in Majority World contexts; it also characterizes those in the North Atlantic world who remain prone, for example, to reading modern, individualistic concepts into the text of Scripture.[86] The danger of thus misreading Scripture underscores the need for reading together in hermeneutical community.

Further, in modeling hermeneutics for local believers, outsiders should adopt a simple pattern for interpretation. The term "simple" here refers to models that entail a minimal number of steps to arrive at a baseline understanding of a given passage's meaning. Simplicity in hermeneutical practice helps mitigate a subtle form of theological control by outsiders that develops through an insistence that locals adopt elaborate hermeneutical methodologies.[87] Historical-critical tools, for example, can detach interpreters from their context while rooting the interpretive task in Enlightenment presuppositions.[88] By insisting that locals employ such

---

84. Ruth Julian, "Ground Level Contextualization," in *Local Theology for the Global Church: Principles for an Evangelical Approach to Contextualization*, ed. Matthew Cook et al. (Pasadena, CA: William Carey Library, 2010), 72–73.

85. As an example of this danger, Shenk, "Theology and the Missionary Task," 301, cites a study of Congolese churches by Efraim Anderson in 1968. Shenk summarizes, "While there is good evidence that the churches studied had come to have a solid appreciation for the Bible, and made use of it in the life of the church, there were significant problems in learning how to interpret the Bible vis-à-vis Congolese culture. More than once the Congolese read into a Bible passage, or concept, or word, a pagan-cultural notion, seeking validation of the cultural practice from the Bible."

86. E. Randolph Richards and Brandon J. O'Brien, *Misreading Scripture with Western Eyes: Removing Cultural Blinders to Better Understand the Bible* (Downers Grove, IL: InterVarsity, 2012), 192–210.

87. Conn, *Eternal Word*, 249.

88. Fernando F. Segovia, "Racial and Ethnic Minorities in Biblical Studies," in *Ethnicity and the Bible*, ed. Mark G. Brett, Biblical Interpretation Series 19 (New York: Brill, 1996), 478–79, explains that some scholars and theologians from the Majority World have "received their training almost exclusively in the academic institutions of

methods from the outset, outsiders inculcate Western theological sentiment among locals.[89] Conversely, by modeling simple hermeneutical practices—that do not require Western academic indoctrination—outsiders can help mitigate such foreign control in local theological development.

Beyond minimizing outsider control, a simple hermeneutical pattern also makes it easier for locals to interpret Scripture in their context.

---

the West, where historical criticism—the first paradigm—still reigned supreme by and large and where they were duly introduced to the fundamentals of the method at the hands of Western male scholars in their role as Doktorvätern or 'doctoral fathers,' master researchers and teachers as well as founders or links in all-important, patriarchal pedigree lines. As such, these outsiders were very much subject to the powerful centripetal and homogenizing forces of this training, with its emphasis on the classic ideals of the Enlightenment: all knowledge as science; the scientific method as applicable to all areas of inquiry; nature or facts as neutral and knowable; research as a search for truth involving value-free observation and recovery of the facts; the researcher as a giant of reason who surveys the facts with disinterested eyes. A further though much more implicit dimension of this process of academic socialization, quite in keeping as well with the cult of modernity emerging from the Enlightenment, should be noted as well: the profound conviction that such training not only represented progress over against traditional interpretations of the Bible (the triumph of light over darkness and reason over tradition) but also the superiority of the West over against all other cultures (the hermeneutics of over/against and the white man's burden). In other words, historical criticism was not only perceived and promoted as the sole and proper way to read and interpret the texts of antiquity but also as the ultimate sign of progress in the discipline, the offer of the West to the rest of the world and the means by which the backward and uncivilized could become modern and civilized." Beyond historical criticism, the Western academic setting for theology has also served to disjoin biblical studies and the particularities of the interpreter's identity. Nicholas Wolterstorff, "The Travail of Theology in the Modern Academy," in *The Future of Theology: Essays in Honor of Jürgen Moltmann*, ed. Miroslav Volf et al. (Grand Rapids: Eerdmans, 1996), 38, explains, "The discipline under which the modern university places its members, by virtue of its judgments as to acceptable and preferable scholarship, has indisputably promoted the flourishing of the natural and social sciences. It has, by contrast, inhibited the flourishing of a theology that exhibits the stamp of Christian conviction and answers to felt needs of the church. . . . Perhaps the deepest component in that understanding of university-appropriate learning which came to dominate the modern university is that such learning is to be a generically human enterprise. To put the point pictorially: Before entering the university halls of learning we are to strip off all our particularities—particularities of gender, race, nationality, religion, social class, age—and enter purely as normal adult human beings. If I have failed to strip off some particularity, and my fellows in the hall of learning notice this, they are to call it to my attention and order me back into the entry, there to remove the particularity which, unintentionally or not, I kept on."

89. For a helpful exploration of theological method in relation to Majority World Christianity, see Kevin J. Vanhoozer, "One Rule to Rule Them All? Theological Method in an Era of World Christianity," in *Globalizing Theology: Belief and Practice in an Era of World Christianity*, ed. Craig Ott and Harold A. Netland (Grand Rapids: Baker Academic, 2006), 85–126.

As Larry W. Caldwell has shown, in areas where the church is still young and developing, local theology students often find it difficult to implement the sophisticated Western hermeneutical methods they learn in class.[90] Therefore he urges, "It is imperative that we theological educators in Asia equip Asians to be able to discover and apply the truths of the Bible to their daily lives without having to rely upon either the interpretational dogma of Protestant scholars and/or upon a scholarly priesthood trained to interpret the Bible for them."[91] This imperative necessitates a simple hermeneutical pattern that locals can easily learn, implement, and reproduce.

Finally, while a simple hermeneutical model might not be nuanced enough to capture the fullness of meaning in some biblical texts, its simplicity nevertheless opens the door for locals to further nuance and develop the model in the future. As Bevans claims, "Whatever model is offered, the model remains a *model*: relative and not absolute. The model provides a framework which the student should criticize, and on which the student can build."[92] In other words, the particular model which the outsider promotes among local believers should be simple enough that those local believers can build upon it as they mature in the faith, thus developing more robust hermeneutical methods and abilities along the way.

Cultivating Theological Agency

A third—and perhaps most critical[93]—component of the outsider's role in a hermeneutical community approach to local theological development is the cultivation of theological agency. That is, part of the outsider's role is to equip local believers to become agents of their own theological convictions rather than mere recipients of theology from others. As

---

90. Larry W. Caldwell, "Towards the New Discipline of Ethnohermeneutics: Questioning the Relevancy of Western Hermeneutical Methods in the Asian Context," *J. Asian Mission* 1.1 (1999) 27–28, contends, "The Asian world—a billion of whom live in oral cultures or who are only functionally literate—may not be prepared socially or economically for the use of western hermeneutical methods, especially those based upon historical criticism. We must, therefore, re-evaluate the appropriateness of transporting oftentimes expensive and elitist hermeneutical methods into such cultures."

91. Caldwell, "Towards the New Discipline," 40.

92. Bevans, "Singing the Lord's Song," 56, emphasis original.

93. This component is potentially the most critical one because apart from it, outsiders can easily remain in positions of control over local theological conviction even while exemplifying the other components which this chapter delineates.

foregoing chapters have demonstrated, the colonial pattern of theological imposition undermined such local theological agency.[94] It rendered locals as objects rather than subjects of theology.[95] In a hermeneutical community approach, the outsider instead operates as a "catalyst" who, in Bevans's words, seeks "to get his students thinking on their own, and so to theologize as indigenous subjects."[96]

In other words, the aim of the outsider is not necessarily to teach theology, but to teach the "doing" of theology—to cultivate in local believers the ability to bring the Scriptures to bear on the realities they face in context. Conn observes that the way schools often teach theology (as abstract theory) has resulted in "a growing incapacity to do theology: our concentration is on theology, not theologizing. Students learn the cumulative cognitive results of the doing of theology."[97] In a similar vein, Bevans argues, "Teaching theology is a process far from the mere imparting of knowledge. It is rather the imparting of an attitude: the spirit of inquiry. Every theology teacher—indigenous or foreign—teaches theology inasmuch as he teaches his students *how* to theologize. . . . He teaches them not so much to know *theology*, but to be *theologians*."[98]

Further, if it is the responsibility of each generation to search the Scriptures and apply it their context, then outsiders must focus on cultivating such theological agency among newer generations of believers. D. A. Carson asserts, "Every generation in every culture (especially in those cultures that are undergoing rapid transition) must get involved in its own Bible study, and learn to express biblical truth in and apply it

---

94. Conn, *Eternal Word*, 247, summarizes, "Long under the covert domination of Western theological colonialism, the non-Western church accepts the psychodynamics of colonialism's division of the world into 'settlers' and 'natives.' 'The natives,' long accustomed to withdrawing 'theology from the 'educational bank' (the language of Paulo Freire), come to believe the self-image imposed by the missionary 'settlers.' They become spectators without a theology of their own, robbed of any free relationship with the Word and the world. They accept the identity created for them by missionary language. They are 'younger church,' passively dependent on the 'mother church.'"

95. H. S. Wilson, "A Tryst with Theology: Self Theologizing as a Perennial Discipleship Mandate," *Theol. Cult.* 10.1 (2013) 147, asserts, "Many Christian communities that came into existence as a result of mission from outside have often ended up being recipients of theologies formulated in a different context or done for them by people outside their community. In that process the subjectivity of the community is compromised."

96. Bevans, "Singing the Lord's Song," 61.

97. Conn, *Eternal Word*, 299.

98. Bevans, "Singing the Lord's Song," 55, emphasis original.

to its own context."[99] Accordingly, outsiders laboring in local theological development must not be content to impart pre-packaged theologies from other generations. Outsiders rather should intentionally equip local believers to become agents of theological conviction and expression.[100] As Heidebrecht claims, "The joy of discovering the Bible's meaning should not just be a second-hand experience."[101]

Opposition to Cultivating Agency

In response to the notion that locals should learn how to self-theologize, one might raise an understandable critique—that locals need not duplicate theology which others have already expressed and settled. For example, Francis Jr. S. Samdao posits, "Because of the creeds, Christians need not reinvent the trinitarian or Christological wheel."[102] Similarly, Jim Harries notes, "Not recognizing the *potential* value in Western theology . . . could be condemning the majority world to the need for reinventing the wheel."[103] Granted, neither Samdao nor Harries is against local theological agency and expression.[104] Moreover, the concern for not reinventing theological wheels can derive from a noble desire to remain in conversation with historical theology.[105] Yet the concern can also betray a sentiment common to the colonial approach to local theology—i.e.,

---

99. Carson, "Reflections on Contextualization," 50; see also Conn, *Eternal Word*, 233.

100. Charles W. Forman, ed., *Christianity in the Non-Western World* (Englewood Cliffs, NJ: Prentice-Hall, 1967), 128, asserts that "the essence of indigenization" is local believers "thinking for themselves."

101. Heidebrecht, "Community Hermeneutics in Practice," 131.

102. Francis Jr. S. Samdao, "On the Idea of Contextualization: Cultural Sensitivity and Catholic Sensibility," *Evang. Rev. Theol.* 46.1 (2022) 58.

103. Jim Harries, "Enabling the Majority World to Benefit from 'Superior' Western Theology," *Curr. Theol. Mission* 44.2 (2017) 18, emphasis original.

104. For example, Jim Harries, "Western Theology in Africa," *Int. Rev. Mission* 106.2 (2017) 258–60, argues against Westerners and Western thought dominating the task of theology in Africa. Further, Samdao, "On the Idea of Contextualization," at no point diminishes the need for theological contextualization by locals. Rather, he rightly advocates for such contextualization to acknowledge and remain "within the bounds of the catholicity of the church," thereby guarding against "independent ethnic theologies" (61).

105. For example, similar to Samdao and Harries, Vanhoozer, "One Rule to Rule Them All?," 119, reasons, "There is no need for each Christian community to reinvent the theological wheel. To affirm the catholic principle, then, is to affirm the importance of reading Scripture guided by the ancient-contemporary rule of faith."

Hermeneutical Community

the belief that local believers need not develop theology in reference to a given subject if such a theology already exists, especially if there remains wide support for such theology.[106]

Yet—in keeping with the above metaphor—while locals may not need to *reinvent* theological wheels, there remains great value in the work of *reconstructing* such wheels from the raw material of Scripture. As previously mentioned, such a process—when rooted in the biblical text—helps local believers take ownership of their theological convictions, because those convictions do not then derive from foreign theology but from the Scriptures themselves. According to Schreiter, "The concern for local theology is not only about the distinctiveness that may arise, but also about the engagement of a larger number of Christians in the enterprise of theological reflection. Such engagement contributes much to what makes a theology local, even if the results look similar to what is happening elsewhere."[107]

In other words, the point of developing local theology is not necessarily about reinventing something or creating something new; the point is to incorporate locals in a theological process, even if that process yields theology that resembles theology expressed in other contexts. For instance, while believers in any given context can profit from learning about Chalcedonian theology regarding the nature of the person of Jesus Christ, local believers still benefit from investigating the Scriptures directly as they seek to understand and express their Christological convictions. Further, as DeVries claims, "Because the foundation and authority of the truth remains the same and because the same Spirit guides the process [of theological development], the result, if faithfully performed, should yield a complementary expression in culturally acceptable terms of the same Bible truth."[108] Thus the aim for local theology is not reinvention; the aim is restating and explaining the relevance of biblical truth for the local context.

Another critique of outsiders intentionally promoting local theologizing comes from Daniel von Allmen in an essay entitled "The Birth of

---

106. Chapter 2 has highlighted this colonial theological sentiment.

107. Schreiter, *Constructing Local Theologies*, 37–38.

108. Brian A. DeVries, "Toward a Global Theology: Theological Method and Contextualization," *Verbum Eccles.* 37.1 (2016) 9, notes that the process of theological development will often yield similar results in different places. He asserts, "Because the foundation and authority of the truth remains the same and because the same Spirit guides the process, the result, if faithfully performed, should yield a complementary expression in culturally acceptable terms of the same Bible truth."

Theology: Contextualization as the Dynamic Element in the Formation of New Testament Theology."[109] In this article, von Allmen argues that it is paternalistic for missionary outsiders to insist on locals developing their own theologies. He contends, "In urging Africans to 'finally get down to making an African theology,' do foreigners not treat them like children who have to be shown what to do, stop them from following their own natural rhythm, and force them to rush through a process of 'indigenization' which, if it is to be a healthy one, must allow them to be first off all themselves, freely and unhampered, not led by the nose?"[110] According to von Allmen, outsiders should not insist on locals "doing theology," but rather should allow locals to develop theology on their own and in their own time.[111]

Von Allmen here is concerned to show how theology develops out of worship. He contends, "What the first Christians precisely did not begin by doing was to express their faith in the form of a systematically worked out theology."[112] Rather, "They responded to the preaching by worship; they sang the work that God had done for them, in hymns. That was the way in which the first Christians gradually discovered the implications of their faith in Jesus Christ."[113] Von Allmen thus remains leery of outsiders pushing locals to develop indigenous theology, in part, because that would appear to short-circuit what he believes to be the natural development of theology—a process in which indigenous response to the gospel in worship precedes indigenous response in theological reflection. Yet even after a local community has become a worshiping church, it can still remain beholden to Western theology.[114] The endeavor of an outsider to cultivate local theological agency in such cases is, therefore, not necessarily at odds with von Allmen's emphasis on the priority of indigenous worship.[115]

---

109. Daniel von Allmen, "Birth of Theology: Contextualization as the Dynamic Element in the Formation of New Testament Theology," *Int. Rev. Mission* 64.253 (1975) 37–52.

110. von Allmen, "Birth of Theology," 49.

111. von Allmen, "Birth of Theology," 51–52.

112. von Allmen, "Birth of Theology," 41.

113. von Allmen, "Birth of Theology," 41–42.

114. The case studies of chapter 2—particularly those from Africa and Asia—highlight this possibility.

115. von Allmen, "Birth of Theology," 51, appears to recognize this point. He claims, "We should look upon theological education as the communication of working techniques and building materials. Once this technical training has been given,

Another aspect of von Allmen's rejection of outsider initiative in local theological development is the historical response of some African churches to missionaries who suddenly pivoted toward a promotion of theological indigenization after a long precedent of suppressing such indigenization.[116] Regarding this response, Patrick A. Kalilombe of Malawi explains,

> One can hardly blame the local people for questioning the sincerity and good intentions of people who, as a group, have shown for years a consistent contempt for and misunderstanding of this same local culture. Why all of a sudden this strange about-turn? Why this rush to pre-empt a movement that should normally be initiated and conducted by the local people, in their own way, and at their own pace? ... What people are objecting to is not so much the changes in themselves. What puts people off is that such adaptations should again be imposed from outside just as they have always been.[117]

With this background in view, one can further understand von Allmen's hesitancy to recognize a role for outsiders in cultivating local theological agency.

Von Allmen, however, does not account for how Western theology has dominated Majority World theological education—a status quo that requires initiative to change. Over the course of the twentieth century, patterns of Western Protestant theological education spread throughout the world.[118] As a result of this diffusion, Western theological sensibilities came to dominate theological education in the Majority World.[119] Even

---

we should encourage African theologies, not to transcribe the received theology in African sermons or treatises of African theology, but rather to preach the Gospel itself in terms that are intelligible to their brethren, and in a way that is suited to their own temperament." Although the overall thrust of von Allmen's essay serves as an argument against outsiders cultivating local theological agency, it appears to leave the door open for outsiders to do just that—though von Allmen would certainly insist that such "encouragement" follow an indigenous response of worship.

116. von Allmen, "Birth of Theology," 48–49.

117. Patrick A. Kalilombe, "Self-Reliance of the African Church: A Catholic Perspective," in *African Theology en Route: Papers from the Pan African Conference of Third World Theologians, December 17–23, 1977, Accra, Ghana*, ed. Kofi Appiah-Kubi and Sergio Torres (Maryknoll, NY: Orbis, 1979), 38–39.

118. For an overview of this diffusion, see J. Snodgrass, "To Teach Others Also: An Apostolic Approach to Theological Education in Pioneer Missions" (PhD diss., Southeastern Baptist Theological Seminary, 2017), 79–134.

119. Scholars who have highlighted the Western character of theological education in the Majority World include Tite Tiénou, "Indigenous African Christian Theologies:

though this situation has begun to shift toward more contextualized approaches in recent decades, Western sensibilities still remain operative in various spheres of theological education in the Majority World, in part due to a reliance on textbooks and funding from the West.[120] Given this situation, for an outsider not to take initiative in promoting local theologizing is to perpetuate a pattern of foreign theological control over local theological conviction.

Further, von Allmen does not account for how a hunger for Western theological schooling among Majority World students often works against the prospect of developing local theologies. For example, Dyrness, who has extensive experience in Majority World theological education, highlights this challenge in the Philippines: "I remember advocating to my students that more theology needed to be done in Tagalog (the Philippine national language), that they needed to begin doing their own vernacular theological reflection. I still remember my shock when they responded that since most of the books they wanted to read were in English, they should learn theology from Western teachers who were educated in Western universities, and they should read and write their theology in English."[121] Such a hunger for Western theological education is evident among others as well.[122] This reality impedes the kind of

---

The Uphill Road," *Int. Bull. Mission. Res.* 14.2 (1990) 76; Jonathan T'ien-en Chao, "Development of National Faculty for Asian Theological Education," in *Voice of the Church in Asia: Report of Proceedings, Asia Theological Association Consultation (Hong Kong, December 27, 1973—January 4, 1974)*, ed. Bong Rin Ro (Singapore: Asia Theological Association, 1975), 91–98; Gabriel Oludele Adeloye, "Decolonizing Biblical Interpretation and Its Effect on the Church in Africa," *Pract. Theol. Baptist Coll. Theol. Lagos* 9 (2016) 199–200; Wilbert R. Shenk, "The Changing Role of the Missionary: From Civilization to Contextualization," in *Missions, Evangelism, and Church Growth*, ed. C. Norman Kraus (Scottdale, PA: Herald, 1980), 39–40.

120. Regarding the reality and influence of Western theological texts, Charles Nyamiti, "An African Theology Dependent on Western Counterparts?," *AFER* 17.3 (1975) 144, notes that the ongoing use of "Western textbooks as basis for our theological and spiritual formation" in Africa serves to "westernize the theological feeling and orientation of our students and lay people." Regarding the reality and influence of foreign funding in Majority World theological education, see Harries, "Enabling the Majority World," 16–17.

121. Dyrness, "Doing Theology," 31.

122. In a qualitative research study that included thirty-two Chinese and Korean graduate students enrolled at theological institutions in the United States, James Sung-Hwan Park, "West Is Best? Why Chinese and Korean Students Pursue Graduate Theological Study in the United States" (PhD diss., Trinity Evangelical Divinity School, 2017), 263, "identified three main perceptions and motivations of students who pursue graduate theological study in US seminaries. First, perceptions of quality. Interviewees

natural, unobstructed development of local theology that von Allmen anticipates among Majority World churches. Thus, far from being an act of paternalism—as von Allmen claims—the work of cultivating local theological agency by outsiders helps to break down these vestiges of theological paternalism.

Need for Cultivating Agency

In addition to counteracting the theological paternalism highlighted above, the work of cultivating theological agency is necessary for other reasons as well. First, growth in theological agency aids the maturation of local churches. According to Gnanakan and Sumithra, "The Church in Asia today will only be able to stand against opposing forces both from inside and outside, only as it manifests maturity in theology and theologization."[123] Hwa Yung adds, "It could be argued that one reason which has held back non-Western churches from moving on to real maturity is that they have been weighed down by an alien western theology that does not fully address their questions and issues contextually. Clearly, an essential part of the leadership development task is to train leaders to think contextually both in theology and ministry."[124] In other words, the act of searching the Scriptures to develop and express theological convictions helps Majority World Christians and churches grow in the faith.[125]

---

see American higher education as the global center of scholarship and knowledge production and find the quality of education offered by US seminaries superior to that of Asian seminaries. These perceptions of quality relate to motivations of studying in the global center of academic excellence and expertise. Second, perceptions of prestige. Interviewees see American schools as more prestigious than Asian schools, and consequently believe that degrees from American seminaries hold superior value compared to degrees from Asian seminaries. These perceptions of prestige are linked to motivations of enhancing status and career prospects. Third, perceptions of opportunity. Interviewees see America as a bigger and broader world and believe that experiencing America opens doors to ministering on a global scale. These perceptions are linked to motivations of becoming global citizens and leaders with a platform for global ministry."

123. Ken Gnanakan and Sunand Sumithra, "Theology, Theologization and the Theologian," in *Biblical Theology in Asia*, ed. Ken Gnanakan (Bangalore, India: Theological Book Trust, 1995), 39.

124. Hwa Yung, "Some Challenges for Leadership Development for Mission in East Asia," *Transformation* 21.4 (2004) 235.

125. Hiebert, *Anthropological Insights*, 208, contends, "To grow, spiritually young churches must search the Scriptures themselves, and if—for fear that they will leave

Second, local theological agency helps guard against theological syncretism. According to Adeyemo, "The theological deficiency of churches in Africa has led to the rise of many sects, heresies, cults and numerous other false movements all over the continent."[126] Similarly, Tiénou claims that this deficiency "can lead to monstrous heresies because of its lack of grappling with issues."[127] When a church's theology says little regarding the pressures local believers experience in non-Christian societies, the church remains susceptible to syncretizing elements of Christianity and pagan belief. However, theological agency can buttress the church in the face of this challenge. As Tiénou declares, "The Bible, at the present a closed book for many, when properly understood is the sure way of rectifying the present mistakes! Theology, having as its aim the maturing of all God's children, is not a luxury for us. It is a necessity!"[128] As local believers begin exploring the biblical text, rooting their convictions therein, and bringing those convictions to bear on the challenges they face in context, they will be much more equipped to stand firm against theological heresy.

Third, local believers need to grow in theological agency because ultimately they will be the ones most able to bring Scripture to bear on local cultural issues. Outsiders, by default, lack the kind of intimate knowledge of local cultures that comes with growing up in a given locale. According to Lois Fuller, "A missionary is an outsider . . . who struggles to understand the local world view and thought patterns well enough to communicate convincingly theology for a local situation."[129] Locals do not typically face this struggle. Carson rightly notes, "In time, the new hearer, now a convert, learns to fuse the horizon of his understanding with that of the biblical text and because he likely knows his own culture better then [sic] the missionary ever will, he has the potential, all things being equal, to become a far clearer and more effective witness and theologian in his own culture than the missionary does."[130] That is, local believers carry rich insight into the local culture and therefore have the potential

---

the truth—we do not allow them to do so, we condemn them to spiritual infancy and early death." Thus, "we need to teach all Christians to study and interpret the Bible for themselves and to apply its message to their lives" (216).

126. Tokunboh Adeyemo, "Contemporary Issues in Africa and the Future of Evangelicals," *Evang. Rev. Theol.* 2.1 (1978) 7.

127. Tite Tiénou, "The Church and Its Theology," *Evang. Rev. Theol.* 7.2 (1983) 246.

128. Tiénou, "Church and Its Theology," 246.

129. Fuller, "Missionary's Role in Developing," 408.

130. Carson, "Reflections on Contextualization," 48.

to point out more clearly the ways the Bible addresses and critiques local customs and sensibilities. Therefore, the cultivation of local theological agency remains an important component of the outsider's role in local theological development.[131]

Manner of Cultivating Agency

A key component of cultivating theological agency is granting local believers space to root their convictions in Scripture and give voice to those convictions as they relate to the issues they face. In other words, outsiders should establish some kind of forum in which locals can, and are expected to, participate in theological reflection. According to Shenk, "The missionary group initially provides the nucleus for developing the 'theological community' but as soon as there are Christians from the local community they must be brought in as participants and thus begin the process of developing a theology indigenous to that church in its culture."[132] In developing such a theological—i.e., hermeneutical—community, the outsider moves from teaching through *monologue* to teaching through *facilitation*. That is, the outsider's role is to facilitate among local believers a study of the biblical text and the application of the text to the local context. In doing so, the outsider yields his or her voice to allow locals—under the guidance of the Holy Spirit—to assume a more prominent role in the expression of theological conviction.

One way of creating such space for local theologizing is through Hiebert's process of "critical contextualization."[133] This process outlines four steps by which missionaries and local believers might address and evaluate local customs in light of biblical truth. First, "the local church leaders and the missionary lead the local congregation in uncritically gathering and analyzing the traditional beliefs and customs associated with some question at hand."[134] Second, "the pastor or missionary leads the church in a study of the Scriptures related to the question at hand. . . . Here the pastor or missionary plays a major role, for this is the area of his

---

131. Fuller, "Missionary's Role in Developing," 407–8, asserts, "Missionaries want to encourage local believers to digest and apply Scripture to their own cultures and societies."

132. Shenk, "Theology and the Missionary Task," 308.

133. Paul G. Hiebert, "Critical Contextualization," *Int. Bull. Mission. Res.* 11.3 (1987) 104–12.

134. Hiebert, "Critical Contextualization," 109.

or her expertise."[135] Third, the local believers "corporately... evaluate their own past customs in the light of their new biblical understanding, and ... make decisions regarding their response to their new-found truths."[136] Finally, the pastor or missionary helps the local congregation implement those decisions into contextual practices that reflect biblical truth.[137]

In Hiebert's process, however, the outsider still assumes a prominent role in interpreting Scripture for local believers.[138] Mark J. Hatcher rightly points out, "Hiebert's model permits an active role for the whole community in steps one, three, and four. Why not shift the leaders' role from presenting the truths expressed by biblical texts to facilitating the whole community's dialog with the texts and each other in pursuit of what God is communicating to them through the text?"[139] Hiebert grants that it is important for "the congregation [to] be actively involved in the study and interpretation of Scripture so that they will grow in their own abilities to discern truth."[140] Yet, the outsider still operates as a dominant voice in the reading and interpretation of Scripture, since, according to Hiebert, "this is where the pastor or missionary . . . has the most to offer in an understanding of biblical truth and in making it known in other cultures."[141]

For Hiebert, the major role that local believers play is not necessarily in the study and interpretation of Scripture but in the application of Scripture to local issues. He contends, "To involve the people in evaluating their own culture in the light of new truth draws upon their strength. They know their old culture better than the missionary, and are in a better position to critique it, once they have biblical instruction. Moreover, to involve them is to help them to grow spiritually by teaching them discernment and by helping them to learn to apply scriptural teaching to

---

135. Hiebert, "Critical Contextualization," 109.

136. Hiebert, "Critical Contextualization," 110.

137. Hiebert, "Critical Contextualization," 110.

138. Herrmann, "Research Serving Theology," 171, observes, "Even in models like Hiebert's critical contextualization model, in which local Christians are heavily involved and have the last say on the evaluation of cultural practices, the missionary is seen as the expert in interpreting Scripture."

139. Mark J. Hatcher, "Biblical Interpretation and the Shaping of Religious Worlds: A Study of Bible Study for Critical Contextualization" (PhD diss., Asbury Theological Seminary, 2004), 209.

140. Hiebert, *Anthropological Insights*, 187.

141. Hiebert, "Critical Contextualization," 110.

their own lives."[142] Here locals participate in a process of applying the biblical truth they learn from the outsider to the issues they face in context. Yet, as Hatcher contends, "Hiebert's model will more effectively achieve its goals if it made Bible interpretation to be a communal project."[143]

Although this process does not involve locals to the fullest extent in the process of hermeneutics and theological method, it serves as a step forward in the direction of cultivating theological agency among locals. It creates space in which local believers can interact with Scripture and apply it to their contexts without the outsider dictating decisions. Further, if an outsider were to involve locals more intentionally in step two—the study and interpretation of Scripture—then this process would serve even more to cultivate local agency in theological reflection.

Such a modified version of Hiebert's critical contextualization is but one way to begin cultivating theological agency among local believers. Whether by this manner or another, the important point of emphasis for outsiders is to provide an opportunity for local believers to study Scripture and express their biblical convictions as they relate to either central doctrines (e.g., Christology, ecclesiology, etc.) or pressing issues they face in context (e.g., polygamy, ancestor worship, etc.). As Simon Herrmann claims, "When Christians who take their faith seriously come together to reflect on their life in light of God's Word and then try to reach conclusions about how this reflection pertains to their life, they develop their theology for this area of life."[144] As they do so, local believers and churches will grow in maturity, stand more strongly against false teaching, and become less reliant upon the convictions of outsiders to guide their spiritual lives.

Challenging Blind Spots

A fourth core component of the outsider's role in local theological development is challenging cultural and theological blind spots among local believers. Such blinds spots are inevitable for all who come to the Scriptures seeking to discern and apply its truth because they do so from a limited point of view. As Taber claims, "[A] hermeneutic worked out exclusively within one civilization and history will have its strong points

---

142. Hiebert, "Critical Contextualization," 110.
143. Hatcher, "Biblical Interpretation," 209.
144. Herrmann, "Research Serving Theology," 166–67.

and its clear insights, but it will also have its inevitable weaknesses, errors and blind spots."[145] Similarly, Carson adds, "Precisely because each culture approaches the Scriptures with its own set of prejudices and blinkers [sic], it will be able to see, and (initially at least) be prevented from seeing, certain things that another culture might respond to (or fail to respond to) in quite a different way."[146]

Part of the value of including outsiders in local theological development is the corrective function they can play by pointing out such blind spots and illuminating overlooked or misunderstood aspects of Scripture in theological reflection. Conn avers, "Often, one pattern of studying the Scripture can block out other possible patterns. As a result, our cultural worldviews, our paradigms both help us and hinder us. . . . Theologizing becomes like studying a diamond. Using more than one perspective, looking at more than one facet of the diamond, helps us see the whole all the better. What is missed by one, another may see. What is seen incorrectly by one, another may correct."[147] That is, cultural outsiders can help shepherd local believers toward orthodoxy at points where they risk misunderstanding or misappropriating biblical texts.[148]

---

145. Charles R. Taber, "Missiology and the Bible," *Missiology* 11.2 (1983) 240.

146. Carson, "Reflections on Contextualization," 50.

147. Conn, *Eternal Word*, 337. Conn draws from Vern Poythress's notion of perspectivalism. For a deeper exploration of Poythress's thought as it relates to world Christianity, see Anna Daub, "Vern Poythress's Perspectivalism in a Global Context: A Symphony of Contextual Theologies Seeking Harmony" (PhD diss., Southeastern Baptist Theological Seminary, 2021).

148. Richards and O'Brien, *Misreading Scripture with Western Eyes*, 12, rightly point out that "the most powerful cultural values are those that go without being said. . . . [O]ften we are not even aware of what goes without being said in our own culture. This is why misunderstanding and misinterpretation happen." Outsiders, however, can sometimes be more aware of local cultural tenets which local believers might overlook. For example, Western missionaries in India might discern more readily how Hinduism's works-based notion of salvation can skew one's understanding of the salvation that Jesus offers. That is, after years of seeking salvation by works through devotion to particular gods, Hindu-background believers might be tempted to displace their former gods with Jesus but yet retain the same manner of gaining salvation (i.e., good works). In such a case, those missionaries who are well acquainted with *sola fide* and the recovery of grace-based salvation in the Reformation might be able to shepherd local believers toward a more orthodox understanding of soteriology. Conversely, Christians of the Majority World can help the Western church discern how certain Western values may not align with Scripture. Richards and O'Brien (192–210) point to the supremacy of the self in the West as one such value to which Westerners are most blind and demonstrate how that value has led Westerners to misinterpret certain passages of Scripture. In conclusion, they ask, "So how do we avoid misreading Scripture with Western eyes? How do we remove our cultural blinders? . . . If we want to know

The additional fact that locals might also serve to correct an outsider's theological understanding underscores the broader value of a hermeneutical community approach to theological development. As an example of such mutual correction, Carson posits, "The African, for instance, might expose the unbiblical individualism of his European counterpart, and show how much of the biblical language of the church is 'family' language—points on which the European may have been insensitive. On the other hand, the European may challenge the African to ask if his understanding of family solidarity may not have been carried too far—perhaps by introducing elements of ancestor worship into his theology, even though such worship has no sanction in Scripture."[149] Outsiders thus maintain an important role in local theologizing, and part of that role is to serve, when necessary, as a corrective agent—challenging theological blind spots and illuminating areas of Scripture that locals might misunderstand or unintentionally disregard.

Broadening Perspectives

A fifth core component of the outsider's role in local theological development is broadening local perspectives by introducing past and present theology from other contexts. Again, every person who approaches Scripture to discern and understand its message does so from a particular vantage point—one that is inevitably limited. One can, to an extent, transcend this limitation by interacting with theologies from outside of one's immediate historical context. By explicating biblical truth from different vantage points, such theologies serve as valuable checks and balances in the process of local theologizing.[150] In some cases, they can help redirect local theology when it begins to stray from historic Christian orthodoxy. As Simon Chan notes, "For a local theology to be authentically Christian, it must have substantial continuity with the larger Christian tradition."[151]

---

when we're reading ourselves into the Bible, rather than allowing the Bible to speak in its own terms, we need to commit ourselves to reading *together*. The worldwide church needs to learn to study Scripture together as a global community. Paying attention to our brothers and sisters abroad can open the echo chamber and allow new voices in" (216, emphasis original).

149. Carson, "Reflections on Contextualization," 53.
150. Schreiter, *Constructing Local Theologies*, 34.
151. Chan, *Grassroots Asian Theology*, 11.

Thus, the task of local theologizing must ultimately enter into a conversation with historical theology and theologies from other locales.[152]

Majority World theologians typically welcome such conversation with past and present theologies.[153] For example, ma Djongwé Daïdanso of Chad states, "We would not therefore cut ourselves radically from the theological legacy of the past and we would not ignore or neglect the theological attainments assembled and established by biblical Christianity for centuries."[154] Further, Kwame Bediako declares, "There can be no doubt that the Western theological heritage belongs to the whole Church, and that Third World churches must learn to make it their own, for they stand in continuity with, and in the company of, the people of God of all ages and nations."[155] In other words, historical theology and theologies from other contexts should continue to have a voice in local theological development.

To that end, outsiders serve as valuable theological mediators for locals by introducing theological thought from outside the immediate local context—theology that may not be readily available to local believers, particularly to those in areas where access to theological resources remains limited. As Schreiter maintains, "The expatriate can also be the bearer of the lived experience of other communities, experience that can challenge and enrich a local community. Without the presence of outside experience, a local church runs the risk of turning in on itself, becoming self-satisfied with its own achievements."[156] A missionary, for example, might introduce the Nicene Creed to local believers and encourage them

---

152. Vanhoozer, "One Rule to Rule Them All?," 122, contends, "No one interpretive community can mine all the treasures of the Word of God by itself. If biblical interpretation is indeed the soul of theology, then theologians had better attend to the global conversation."

153. For example, see Adeyemo, "Towards an Evangelical African Theology," 149; Emilio Antonio Núñez C., "Towards an Evangelical Latin American Theology," *Evang. Rev. Theol.* 7.1 (1983) 124; Hwa Yung, *Mangoes or Bananas? The Quest for an Authentic Asian Christian Theology*, 2nd ed. (Maryknoll, NY: Orbis, 2014), 190; Paul Siu, "Theologizing Locally," in *Local Theology for the Global Church: Principles for an Evangelical Approach to Contextualization*, ed. Matthew Cook et al. (Pasadena, CA: William Carey Library, 2010), 161; Sumithra, "Towards Evangelical Theology in Hindu Cultures," 151.

154. ma Djongwé Daïdanso, "An African Critique of African Theology," *Evang. Rev. Theol.* 7.1 (1983) 64.

155. Kwame Bediako, "The Willowbank Consultation Jan 1978: A Personal Reflection," *Themelios* 5.2 (1980) 31.

156. Schreiter, *Constructing Local Theologies*, 19. See also Benno van den Toren, "Growing Disciples in the Rainforest: A Contextualized Confession for Pygmy Christians," *Evang. Rev. Theol.* 33.4 (2009) 309–10.

to consider how it might challenge and shape their soteriological convictions. Such an introduction can potentially undermine local theological agency if it occurs too early in the process of theological development; however, it can help sharpen local conviction later in that process. By thus introducing other theologies past and present, outsiders broaden local perspectives and provide valuable checks and balances for locals as they seek to clarify and express their theological convictions in light of the issues that confront them.

Summary

These five core components constitute a framework for understanding the outsider's role within a hermeneutical community approach to local theological development. As outsiders teach Scripture, model sound hermeneutics, cultivate theological agency, challenge blind spots, and broaden perspectives, they not only aid the development of local theology but also steer clear of the pitfalls of colonial and post-colonial approaches to theological development. That is, this five-part role incorporates the voice of outsiders (contra post-colonial withdrawal) while at the same time mitigating their control over local theological conviction (contra colonial imposition). In sum, this approach recasts the outsider's role in local theological development; the outsider neither *imposes* theology nor *withdraws* from its development, but rather *facilitates* theological development by locals.[157]

EXAMPLES FOR THE OUTSIDER

As Rynkiewich has noted, precedents for this kind of outsider role are just beginning to emerge.[158] This section will explore several examples in which missionaries have embraced aforementioned components of

---

157. Heidebrecht, "Community Hermeneutics in Practice," 131, contends, "When leaders teach inductively and facilitate a process of active learning, the community is able to move toward a shared interpretation, which lays a foundation for the community's full participation in discerning the application of Scripture to their own lives."

158. Rynkiewich, "Mission, Hermeneutics, and the Local Church," 57. That such precedents are only recently emerging likely testifies to how presuppositions concerning the universality and normativity of Western theology have remained entrenched in the minds of Western missionaries and church leaders.

the outsider's role in local theological development.[159] In none of these precedents does the outsider embrace each of the five components delineated above. However, each precedent serves—to some degree—as an approximation of the outsider's role within a hermeneutical community approach to local theological development.

Doing Theology in Zaire—John Gration

One example of local theological development in which the outsider exemplified a component of the role outlined above comes from the work of John Gration in Zaire—currently the Democratic Republic of the Congo. Gration (1926–2012) taught missions at Wheaton College for two decades. Prior to that, he served as a theological educator in Zaire from 1953 to 1964.[160] After participating in Lausanne's Willowbank Consultation on the Gospel and Culture in 1978, however, he began to sense that he had adopted an inadequate approach to his educational ministry in Zaire. He confessed, "While no expatriate can ever ultimately contextualize the gospel for a group of believers, it became my growing conviction that I could have facilitated the process far more than I did."[161]

Having recognized his tendency toward colonial control over local theological conviction, Gration sought to pave a new path that would allow local believers to participate in the task of theologizing. Regarding the control that he previously exerted over local theological development, he explained, "I had delivered many prepackaged boxes of biblical 'truth' to my Zairian students. Although the content was biblical, it did not speak to many issues, crucial to the Zairian Church, of which I was only dimly aware. Furthermore, the delivery system fostered a mentality of theological dependency that matched the colonial context."[162] To reverse this trend, Gration sought to organize a forum in which the group of Zairian churches among whom he ministered might "begin to develop

---

159. In addition to the three examples explored here, one finds a similar example in the work of Gerald O. West, *Contextual Bible Study* (Pietermaritzburg: Cluster, 1993); The Ujamaa Centre for Community Development and Research, "Doing Contextual Bible Study: A Resource Manual," 2015, https://www.anglicancommunion.org/media/253823/6-Ujamaa-Manual-doing-contextual-Bible-study-a-resoruce-manual.pdf. See also van den Toren, "Growing Disciples in the Rainforest," 306–15.

160. John Gration, "Willowbank to Zaire: The Doing of Theology," *Missiology* 12.3 (1984) 297.

161. Gration, "Willowbank to Zaire," 297.

162. Gration, "Willowbank to Zaire," 297.

its own African theology, a theology that would be both biblical and culturally relevant and authentic."[163]

Process: Overview of Seminars

Gration began this work of cultivating theological agency by setting up two seminars in Zaire—one for local Swahili-speaking believers and one for local French-speaking believers.[164] These seminars lasted several days and included local pastors as well as local seminary professors and church administrators.[165] In leading these seminars, Gration sought not to dictate theological answers, but rather to establish a process by which local believers might study and apply Scripture to the local context. He explained, "While I was concerned about the ultimate product of the seminars, I was equally or more so concerned about the process. I was convinced that the desired product could never be attained without the proper process."[166]

At the start of these seminars, Gration introduced the first question that would occupy participants: "What is the gospel?"[167] Gration noted that as participants gave answers to the question, "these were all faithfully recorded by me on sheets of newsprint, but not without probing questions as to the meaning of the words being used. I assumed the position of one who was not antagonistic to the gospel, but who was totally ignorant of its special, technical vocabulary."[168] This discussion led to an excitement among participants as they began to probe previously unseen depths of the gospel's meaning.[169] Toward the end of the discussion, a participant in one seminar requested Gration to summarize the gospel, which he declined to do. He reasoned, "I graciously refused to come to closure at this point. I wanted to maintain the state of minor disequilibrium that I had created at the outset in order to enhance the continued learning process."[170]

---

163. Gration, "Willowbank to Zaire," 298.
164. Gration, "Willowbank to Zaire," 298–99.
165. Gration, "Willowbank to Zaire," 298–99.
166. Gration, "Willowbank to Zaire," 298.
167. Gration, "Willowbank to Zaire," 299.
168. Gration, "Willowbank to Zaire," 299.
169. Gration, "Willowbank to Zaire," 299.
170. Gration, "Willowbank to Zaire," 300.

After each group had considered and reflected on this question regarding the gospel, Gration introduced a second question: "What is (African) culture?"[171] After considering a general definition of culture, "customs and institutions, differing from tribe to tribe among those present, were more easily comprehended."[172] Participants also considered the "concepts of worldview and values."[173] After the group discussed these topics, Gration shared the definition of culture outlined by the participants at the Willowbank Consultation.[174]

Third, Gration raised the question of the relationship between the gospel and African culture. This question launched participants into the heart of the seminar.[175] Gration noted, "We broke into small buzz groups to discuss how and where the gospel had touched, and in some cases transformed, African culture. An ancillary question asked why the gospel had so widely attracted Africans."[176] Answers to these questions varied between the two seminars. According to Gration, "The French seminar was in general more reluctant to be as positive or absolute in its affirmations. This group was generally more analytical and seemed more perceptive in seeing both sides of an issue. Thus while both groups saw the deep hostility of tribalism as something the gospel has greatly ameliorated, the French seminar participants were far more emphatic in their concern for the strong lingering evidences of it even in the life of the church."[177] Answers from the Swahili-speaking seminar reflected "early gospel preaching in their midst as well as the meeting of specific felt needs within the African milieu by the gospel message."[178]

Finally, Gration posed to each seminar a question concerning the local church's unfinished theological task: "Where has the gospel not touched or adequately transformed African culture?"[179] As seminar participants discussed this question, Gration recorded answers on large sheets of paper for everyone to see, then "items with a common denominator were

---

171. Gration, "Willowbank to Zaire," 300.
172. Gration, "Willowbank to Zaire," 300.
173. Gration, "Willowbank to Zaire," 300.
174. Gration, "Willowbank to Zaire," 300.
175. Gration, "Willowbank to Zaire," 300.
176. Gration, "Willowbank to Zaire," 300.
177. Gration, "Willowbank to Zaire," 300.
178. Gration, "Willowbank to Zaire," 300–301.
179. Gration, "Willowbank to Zaire," 301.

Hermeneutical Community

grouped together."[180] After the group pooled and collated answers to this question, they chose three particular answers/topics to explore further during the rest of the seminar time: "the dynamic interaction between text and context, the text of Scripture and the context of African culture."[181] Gration noted that he took no part in choosing the topics, but remained silent and allowed local participants to make the decision.[182]

To explore the chosen topics related to this fourth question, the seminars divided into smaller groups, which then each considered one of the three issues. Gration explained the process which occupied the small groups:

> Each of the three groups chose one of the topics with which they would grapple in the light of Scripture. They were given some preliminary and basic instructions relative to the process to be followed. Having defined and clarified the problem to be addressed, they were then to go to the Scriptures and seek out as much relevant biblical data on this subject as they could, using the limited tools of concordances and Bible indexes that were at their disposal. From what the Bible says on the subject, derived by sound exegesis and hermeneutics, they were to find biblical illustrations, draw principles and formulate propositions relative to these topics.[183]

The seminar participants thus individually studied Scripture as it related to their assigned topic and discussed their insights within the small group to which they belonged. Afterward, each small group reported their findings back to the entire seminar body.[184] Gration then noted, "In both the Swahili and French seminars there was evidence of a serious dialogue with Scripture. Because of time restrictions the dialogue was limited, but the 'conversation' had begun. Scripture assumed a new relevancy as it not only provided answers to questions that were being asked but itself raised new questions."[185]

As an outcome of this process, the three small groups in the French seminar compiled working papers that consolidated and expressed

---

180. Gration, "Willowbank to Zaire," 302.
181. Gration, "Willowbank to Zaire," 303.
182. Gration, "Willowbank to Zaire," 302.
183. Gration, "Willowbank to Zaire," 303.
184. Gration, "Willowbank to Zaire," 303.
185. Gration, "Willowbank to Zaire," 303.

their theological reflections on the topics at hand.[186] A representative from each of those groups recorded their statements on newsprint for the entire group to see, which, according to Gration, "elicited some very stimulating discussions."[187] Further, Gration highlighted the import of this process as it played out: "Again and again, it was obvious that the Africans were breaking new ground in their thinking. The barriers between African culture and biblical truth were gradually being broken down."[188]

Component: Cultivating Theological Agency

In this brief process, Gration did not assume the full role outlined above, which is understandable considering the short time available to him and the seminar participants. At the time of the seminars, Gration no longer lived in Zaire; he led the seminars as a visitor with limited time to invest in local theologizing. Further, considering his long precedent of dominating local theological development among these churches in Zaire, Gration sought to minimize his influence on the process. He noted that during his decade there as a resident theological educator, the lecture format had composed 97 percent of his teaching ministry.[189] In order to begin reversing this precedent, Gration refrained from vocalizing his opinions or the insight of foreign theology during his limited time with local believers in these seminars. Thus, he did not embody aforementioned components of the outsider's role like teaching Scripture, modeling sound hermeneutics, challenging blind spots, and broadening perspectives.

However, in these seminars, Gration exemplified a crucial component of the outsider's role in a hermeneutical community approach to local theological development—cultivating theological agency. Through these seminars, he created a forum in which local believers could study Scripture in light of contextual issues and begin voicing their theological convictions arising from their study. Rather than give answers to the questions at hand, Gration imparted a process by which local believers could arrive at answers on their own. He noted that, as a result, "there was never any question as to ownership."[190] That is, the local participants began to

---

186. Gration, "Willowbank to Zaire," 304.
187. Gration, "Willowbank to Zaire," 304.
188. Gration, "Willowbank to Zaire," 304.
189. Gration, "Willowbank to Zaire," 304.
190. Gration, "Willowbank to Zaire," 299.

take ownership of their theological convictions rather than relying on what Gration—an outsider—had to say. He explained, "Their work was incomplete, to be sure. At this point, however, I was far more interested in process than in product. I had faithfully delivered the 'product' across 15 years of teaching, often to realize later that some of the boxes had remained unopened or at best their content only partially used. In this new situation, Africans would pose their own questions, discover their own answers and fill their own boxes. In a word, they would be theologizing."[191]

Gration hoped that this pattern of cultivating local agency could help reverse the precedent of foreign theological imposition.[192] He noted, "Although I recognized that a genuine African ethnotheology could only be produced by Africans themselves, yet I felt that as an expatriate I could have a significant role in the process—as much by what I *didn't* do this time around as by what I did."[193] In Gration's view, outsiders, rather than withdraw from the work of local theological development, can play an important role in such development by serving as a "facilitator and/or catalyst."[194] He asserted, "Missionaries can have a significant role in the contextualization process. We have molded the forms, established the patterns and created the sometimes inappropriate models that now exist in the very warp and woof of many third world churches. Now older, veteran missionaries can (and maybe should) assume a pivotal role in helping to initiate a new process of contextualization that can reverse or at least redirect much of what has been established in years gone by."[195] In sum, Gration's process serves as a helpful example of how outsiders can cultivate theological agency among local believers. One might further strengthen Gration's process by expanding it to include cross-cultural critique and a consideration of theologies from other eras and contexts, but it nevertheless serves as an effective means of facilitating self-theologizing.

---

191. Gration, "Willowbank to Zaire," 303.

192. Gration, "Willowbank to Zaire," 298, explains, "Because I am convinced that the process I employed is needed in other parts of the world and is virtually reproducible anywhere, I wish to share the pattern followed in each seminar, make some observations on what took place, and finally indicate what I feel should be the next steps."

193. Gration, "Willowbank to Zaire," 298, emphasis original.

194. Gration, "Willowbank to Zaire," 306.

195. Gration, "Willowbank to Zaire," 305.

Contextualizing Christianity in Ghana—W. Jay Moon

Another example of an outsider adopting a hermeneutical community approach to local theological development comes from the work of W. Jay Moon in West Africa. Moon is currently a professor of evangelism and church planting at Asbury Theological Seminary. Prior to this post, Moon served for thirteen years as a missionary in Ghana. During that time, he employed a modified version of Hiebert's critical contextualization process to help local believers explore indigenous proverbs and their potential use in contextualizing the communication of Christianity.[196] This process featured a hermeneutical community that included both Moon and local Christians. Such an approach was important for Moon, who believes, "Contextualization is best done in a hermeneutical community. . . . Both the etic and emic perspectives provide valuable insight for contextualization."[197]

An impetus for Moon's approach was the lack of contextualization among churches in Africa. He notes, "While the church in Africa is growing at a tremendous rate, the Scripture has not reached deeply into the worldview of the culture. . . . Contextualization then, is an urgent need since Christianity has yet to deal adequately with everyday concerns, let alone issues of life and death. Missionaries and national church leaders are searching up and down the river for tools and insights that will facilitate an engagement of the Scripture and culture. So far, there has largely been disappointment."[198] Moon developed his hermeneutical community approach as a means of filling this gap and guarding the church against "split-level Christianity,"[199] in which local believers

---

196. W. Jay Moon, "Using Proverbs to Contextualize Christianity in the Builsa Culture of Ghana, West Africa" (PhD diss., Asbury Theological Seminary, 2005).

197. Moon, "Using Proverbs to Contextualize," 223. Here Moon draws from the seminal work of linguist Kenneth L. Pike, who developed the "etic" and "emic" concepts. Pike, *Language in Relation to a Unified Theory of the Structure of Human Behavior*, 2nd rev. ed. (Paris: Mouton & Co., 1967), 37, explains, "The etic viewpoint studies behavior as from outside of a particular system, and as an essential initial approach to an alien system. The emic viewpoint results from studying behavior as from inside the system. (I coined the words etic and emic from the words phonetic and phonemic, following the conventional linguistic usage of these latter terms. The short terms are used in an analogous manner, but for more general purposes.)"

198. Moon, "Using Proverbs to Contextualize," 1-2.

199. Moon, "Using Proverbs to Contextualize," 4. On "split-level Christianity," see Jaime Bulatao, "Split-Level Christianity," *Philipp. Sociol. Rev.* 13.2 (1965) 119–21; Paul G. Hiebert et al., "Responding to Split-Level Christianity and Folk Religion," *Int. J. Front. Missions* 16.4 (1999) 173–82; Hiebert et al., *Understanding Folk Religion*, 10–21.

adhere to Christian conviction on the surface but maintain worldviews which the gospel has yet to fully penetrate.

Process: Modified Critical Contextualization

The process which Moon employed and advocates involves six components. First, a "catalyst" summons a group of believers to act as a "hermeneutical community" as it explores local proverbs and how they might relate to Christianity.[200] Because Moon believes that local proverbs in that context "serve as open windows into the worldview of the culture,"[201] he views them as means of facilitating engagement between Scripture and context, and thus useful "for evangelism, discipleship, and contextualization."[202] According to Moon, the community which engages such local proverbs should involve both locals and outsiders if possible.[203] The work of the catalyst at this early stage is "to gather people and consider how to work out the logistics of transportation, food, and lodging, when needed."[204]

Second, the gathered group exegetes and analyzes indigenous proverbs. Moon elaborates, "Participants should be prepared to discuss a proverb with the group. They should state the proverb and then explain its meaning/origin in the culture. They should explain the context that this proverb is often used, as well as explain its meaning with other oral literature when needed (e.g., a story or song may be needed to explain the proverb more fully). The other participants should also contribute to this exegesis."[205] This step corresponds with Hiebert's first step in the process of critical contextualization—"exegesis of the culture."[206] According to Moon, "The aim is to dig down to the roots of the proverb to see the cultural values that this proverb reveals."[207]

Third, the group seeks to identify passages of Scripture that address themes from the indigenous proverb(s). Moon claims, "Scripture should

---

200. Moon, "Using Proverbs to Contextualize," 240.
201. Moon, "Using Proverbs to Contextualize," 3.
202. Moon, "Using Proverbs to Contextualize," 240.
203. Moon, "Using Proverbs to Contextualize," 240.
204. Moon, "Using Proverbs to Contextualize," 241.
205. Moon, "Using Proverbs to Contextualize," 241.
206. Hiebert, "Critical Contextualization," 109.
207. Moon, "Using Proverbs to Contextualize," 241.

be identified that speaks to the deeper roots identified above."[208] He recognizes that not all such themes will align with biblical truth. Thus, the searching of Scripture plays an important role in the process. Moon explains that the study of Scripture "helps participants to identify which roots the Scripture will affirm, modify, or reject. The aim is to encourage critical reflection so that participants do not fall into the typical responses of rejecting everything or accepting everything."[209]

Fourth, the hermeneutical community then considers how its investigation of Scripture might impact the local church, its teaching, and its life in the culture.[210] Some questions to consider at this stage include:

a. Does this analysis affect other traditional practices or beliefs?
b. Does this provide helpful information into wider issues like witchcraft, funeral practices, ancestors, sacrifices, marriage relationships, polygamy, or other "thorny issues"?
c. Does this fill in some missing information concerning some particular problems that we are struggling to resolve biblically in our culture?
d. Does this shed light on some passages that we have a hard time understanding or obeying?[211]

Fifth, the group then pursues consensus concerning practical ministry suggestions in light of their exploration of the indigenous proverb(s) and Scripture. Moon explains, "This is where the pieces are pulled together and the group seeks to make application for their own lives and ministry."[212] Questions to consider at this point include:

a. How can the results of this analysis be used in teaching, evangelism, counseling, and discipling?
b. What is the best way to remember and communicate this? This will be helpful for transforming not only our own lives but also the life of the church.

---

208. Moon, "Using Proverbs to Contextualize," 241.
209. Moon, "Using Proverbs to Contextualize," 241.
210. Moon, "Using Proverbs to Contextualize," 242.
211. Moon, "Using Proverbs to Contextualize," 242.
212. Moon, "Using Proverbs to Contextualize," 242.

c. What occasions would this be useful for (e.g., weddings, funerals, baby dedications, baptism, communion, church discipline, etc.)?

d. In addition to the proverb, what other oral literature, object lessons, metaphors, pictures (e.g., GR picture books), etc. would be helpful in communicating this truth?[213]

Sixth, a participant from the group records what transpired in this hermeneutical community process. Moon notes, "By recording the discussion, others can review and use it later when other issues arise. It becomes a part of church history that may help others to deal with similar issues."[214] Further, according to Moon, it is best to use the local language to document the process and its results. He contends, "This maintains the integrity of the thinking processes and conceptual categories used," and also "encourages creative indigenous expressions to truly emerge in the contextualization process."[215]

Finally, according to Moon, the group—having become familiar with this process—can then begin to explore more difficult proverbs and other cultural issues. He asserts, "This will stretch the participants to understand and apply the process more fully."[216] Moreover, this hermeneutical community endeavor can take place among various groups and locales. Moon explains, "Adaptations can be made for dealing with youth, the elderly, and various officials. In addition, various venues can be used, such as the local church, theological schools, regional training centers . . . etc."[217]

Moon maintains that this process is widely applicable and that one can utilize it to examine cultural topics beyond indigenous proverbs.[218] He asserts, "While analyzing proverbs provides a process to use for contextualization, the bigger fish to catch is the engagement of Scripture with cultural issues."[219] That is, beyond investigating local proverbs, one can employ this process to discern how Scripture bears upon issues that confront the church in context and how the church should respond to such issues. This process thus resembles Hiebert's process of critical

---

213. Moon, "Using Proverbs to Contextualize," 242–43.
214. Moon, "Using Proverbs to Contextualize," 243.
215. Moon, "Using Proverbs to Contextualize," 243.
216. Moon, "Using Proverbs to Contextualize," 243.
217. Moon, "Using Proverbs to Contextualize," 243.
218. Moon, "Using Proverbs to Contextualize," 261–63.
219. Moon, "Using Proverbs to Contextualize," 254.

contextualization.[220] However, unlike Hiebert's process, Moon's method here includes local believers in the work of studying and interpreting Scripture.

Component: Cultivating Theological Agency

Moon's modified process of critical contextualization serves as an example of cultivating theological agency among local believers. The outsider here serves as a "catalyst" who helps to "initiate and sustain the contextualization process."[221] As such, the outsider does not dominate the process, but rather contributes in ways that are helpful yet limited. Moon explains, "[Catalysts] are instrumental in drawing together the stakeholders, going outside the group for wider perspectives, and patiently guiding the group to informed consensus instead of reacting with the knee-jerk responses of total acceptance or total rejection."[222] By serving as a catalyst rather than a catechist, the outsider provides space for locals to directly engage the biblical text rather than receive theological answers from the outsider. In the process, locals gain an opportunity to grow in their ability to read, interpret, apply, and express scriptural truth, thereby becoming agents of their own theological convictions.

As with Gration's process, Moon's process here focuses mainly on facilitating an engagement between the gospel and the local culture—in this case through the window of indigenous proverbs. Moon does not offer it as a comprehensive approach to local theological development. Thus, if one wanted to facilitate more comprehensive development, he or she would need to augment this approach with methods for teaching Scripture, modeling sound hermeneutics, challenging blind spots, and broadening perspectives. Nevertheless, Moon's method serves as a helpful means of cultivating theological agency among local churches.

Confessing the Faith in North India—N. Shank and K. Shank

A third example of how outsiders contribute to local theological development in a hermeneutical community approach comes from the work of N. Shank and K. Shank in North India. The two have served

220. Hiebert, "Critical Contextualization," 109–10.
221. Moon, "Using Proverbs to Contextualize," 224.
222. Moon, "Using Proverbs to Contextualize," 224.

as missionary practitioners for over two decades, laboring to plant churches among unreached people groups. During this time, they have developed a training model that attempts to lead local church leaders toward contextual theologizing. Their training manual—*Confessing the Faith Within Church Planting Movements: A Guide for Training Church Planting Networks Toward Contextual Theology* (henceforth *Confessing the Faith*)—outlines a method by which missionary outsiders can take an active role in facilitating local theological development. They explain, "The goal for this effort is a developed confession of faith owned and useful to a church planting network capable of guiding and protecting churches through the challenges of culture without and false teaching within (Acts 20:29–31, Titus 1:9)."[223]

Process: Overview of Training

A suggested prerequisite for this training is a course surveying the Old and New Testaments that establishes for trainees a foundation in biblical theology (with a focus on the metanarrative of Scripture) and hermeneutics. Shank and Shank suggest such a course because participants need to be able to engage passages of Scripture and discern their meaning.[224] They claim, "Without this skill among participants the trainer will find [the Confessing the Faith] manual less effective," since it requires participants to study Scripture inductively on their own.[225]

For such a course, Shank and Shank utilize a training entitled *Foundations for Emerging Leaders: A Guide for Long Term Discipleship in New Churches*[226] (henceforth *Foundations*). This training consists of a series of modules in which new church leaders—most of whom have had no formal theological education—can grow in their ability to lead and shepherd churches.[227] C. Hawkins and J. Houk, who developed the *Foun-*

---

223. N. Shank and K. Shank, *Confessing the Faith Within Church Planting Movements: A Guide for Training Church Planting Networks Toward Contextual Theology*, 2011, https://www.imb.org/wp-content/uploads/2022/04/57-Seconds-S1E14-Confessing-the-Faith.pdf, 1.

224. Shank and Shank, *Confessing the Faith*, 1.

225. Shank and Shank, *Confessing the Faith*, 1.

226. C. Hawkins and J. Houk, *Foundations for Emerging Leaders: A Guide for Long Term Discipleship in New Churches* (unpublished manual, 2013).

227. Hawkins and Houk, *Foundations for Emerging Leaders*, 10, note, "*Foundations* is more than a set of training materials, but it seeks to integrate what our new leaders already know with what they still need to learn. In this way, *Foundations* is a process for

dations training, explain, "*Foundations* is a series of six courses designed to teach a basic overview of the Bible and a simple hermeneutic in a way emerging church leaders can understand, employ, and teach to others. In Bible school terms, *Foundations* teaches Old Testament and New Testament Survey, Beginning Hermeneutics, and a Preaching Practicum."[228] They state further, "*Foundations* ensures emerging leaders are equipped to rightly handle the Word of Truth. We hold the ability to teach and guard against false teaching as a central objective for those completing the *Foundations* course."[229] Trainers thus employ the *Foundations* process to impart an understanding of Scripture (i.e., select passages from creation to consummation) and model for participants a simple hermeneutic they can use in studying, interpreting, and teaching Scripture.[230]

With a foundation in Scripture and hermeneutics in tow, emerging leaders then participate in *Confessing the Faith*, a series of workshops in which "emerging leader(s) can be led through a process of expressing his or their faith."[231] Each workshop in this training broaches an important Christian doctrine (e.g., soteriology, ecclesiology, etc.). For each, the objective is four-fold:

1. A systematic survey of the Bible's teaching on the doctrine.
2. The creation and/or introduction of frequently asked questions within the cultural context of the church planting leaders.
3. Progress toward consensus answers to these questions as a group.
4. The creation of a "statement of faith" related to the doctrine among the participants.[232]

In leading these workshops, the missionary serves to facilitate participant study and interpretation of Scripture, as well as the expression of their emerging theological convictions.

---

providing tools as new leaders and churches become self-feeding."

228. Hawkins and Houk, *Foundations for Emerging Leaders*, 10.

229. Hawkins and Houk, *Foundations for Emerging Leaders*, 4–5. Further, they assert, "As churches are released to function, the Pauline emphasis on identifiable local leadership includes the ability to protect and lead the flock in truth. *Foundations* provides multiple intense workshops for the development of sound hermeneutics as a foundational aspect of local leadership" (5).

230. Hawkins and Houk, *Foundations for Emerging Leaders*, 4–5, 8–14.

231. Shank and Shank, *Confessing the Faith*, 2.

232. Shank and Shank, *Confessing the Faith*, 2.

Hermeneutical Community

This process involves five steps on the part of the facilitator. First, it involves soliciting and listing questions related to the doctrine at hand and relevant to the local culture and context.[233] According to the *Confessing the Faith* manual, "Asking participants to create the questions ensures the audience drives the discussion based on ministry realities rather than assumed direction."[234] Then, after writing out the participants' questions, the facilitator leads the group to select and prioritize several questions that will occupy them throughout the rest of the training.[235] Shank and Shank note, "Priority can be set based on false or incomplete teaching, barriers within worldview or local religions or divisive topics creating unrest among churches."[236]

Second, after the group prioritizes questions pertaining to the particular doctrine, the facilitator grants participants time to individually study relevant passages of Scripture to discern what the Bible says regarding that doctrine.[237] For this study, the facilitator gives an initial list of various passages, drawn from the "Baptist Faith and Message 2000" (BF&M),[238] as a starting point.[239] Shank and Shank utilize the BF&M because, as Baptists, they believe it presents "foundational doctrines essential to the faith and teaching of churches" and that it provides a foundation for sound ecclesiological practice.[240] Yet the facilitator typically encourages the group to seek out other scriptural passages that might also inform a sound understanding of the doctrine in focus.

Third, the facilitator leads participants to pursue answers to the prioritized questions through discussion in small groups, a process which lasts several hours.[241] Once the groups have written out answers along with the biblical references for those answers, the facilitator moves

---

233. Shank and Shank, *Confessing the Faith*, 2.
234. Shank and Shank, *Confessing the Faith*, 7.
235. Shank and Shank, *Confessing the Faith*, 2.
236. Shank and Shank, *Confessing the Faith*, 7.
237. Shank and Shank, *Confessing the Faith*, 2.
238. Southern Baptist Convention, "Baptist Faith and Message 2000," https://bfm.sbc.net/bfm2000/.
239. Shank and Shank, *Confessing the Faith*, 2, 8.
240. N. Shank, email to the author, January 4, 2023. Additionally, Shank states, "As a Baptist I do not see the BF&M (or any confession) as authoritative. It has no authority of its own, but I appreciate and see value in churches choosing to associate and cooperate with other like-minded churches. I see a confession as a tool making such association and cooperation possible over time."
241. Shank and Shank, *Confessing the Faith*, 3.

toward step four—writing answers from the small groups on a board or chart paper and facilitating large group discussion in response.[242] In steps three and four, the goal for the workshop leader is not to lecture, but to "facilitate as much discussion as possible."[243] The facilitator should "seek consensus but . . . not force agreement on any one question."[244]

Finally, after the group has moved toward consensus, the facilitator leads participants to create a statement of faith regarding the specific doctrine under consideration. According to the *Confessing the Faith* manual, "Using the questions and answers created in steps 1–4 (recorded on the chart papers) the participants should be encouraged to write as comprehensive a statement as possible. The statement will be written in paragraph form with the verses listed at the bottom of the provided chart paper."[245] Though the facilitator is to encourage comprehensiveness when possible, the manual states, "The process of creating a statement relevant to cultural issues and perhaps misunderstandings or false teaching within the local group should be prioritized over a comprehensive statement."[246]

In sum, this five-fold process of *Confessing the Faith* aims to deepen doctrinal understanding among emerging churches and church leaders and to buttress them against false teaching from within and cultural challenges from without. Shank and Shank assert, "We consider the ability to refute those teaching false doctrine to be the role of local emerging leaders (Titus 1:9). Our goal is for this workshop to provide an intentional response in such cases and perhaps create a tool across multiple churches for the fellowship of sound doctrine."[247] Moreover, through such workshops, the outsider serves as a facilitator who neither withdraws from local theological development nor dominates the process. Rather, the outsider joins with and empowers local believers to act as a local hermeneutical community.

---

242. Shank and Shank, *Confessing the Faith*, 3, 9.
243. Shank and Shank, *Confessing the Faith*, 8.
244. Shank and Shank, *Confessing the Faith*, 8.
245. Shank and Shank, *Confessing the Faith*, 3.
246. Shank and Shank, *Confessing the Faith*, 9. For an example of such a confession, see appendix.
247. Shank and Shank, *Confessing the Faith*, 10.

Components: Teaching Scripture, Modeling Sound Hermeneutics, Cultivating Theological Agency, Challenging Blind Spots

In this process of *Confessing the Faith*, the outsider embodies several components of the role outlined above. First, the outsider endeavors to teach Scripture through a prerequisite course like *Foundations*. In this course, the outsider leads locals toward a more robust understanding of the Bible. Hawkins and Houk explain, "*Foundations* provides an overview of the Bible. Each *Foundations* workshop begins with and builds upon an overview of Old and New Testament survey. In a pattern of 'spiral learning' trainees are led through constant review of the meta-narrative of scripture to ensure a right understanding of context, biblical history and theme development across scripture."[248] Thus, the focus here for the outsider is on teaching Scripture itself rather than existing theologies.[249]

Second, through the *Foundations* training, the outsider models a sound hermeneutic for locals to learn and implement. The hermeneutical tool which *Foundations* promotes is sound in that it not only recognizes Scripture as authoritative, but it also focuses on the content of the biblical text as the basis for theological development. That is, it aims at exegesis while seeking to mitigate eisegesis. It revolves around four simple questions regarding any given passage: "What do we learn about God? What do we learn about Man? Is there a sin to avoid? Is there an example or command to follow?"[250] By answering these questions, a student of Scripture can gain a baseline understanding of what a passage says. Hawkins and Houk elaborate, "By beginning with what the Bible says, many exegetical fallacies can be avoided. A healthy mature teacher should never begin with a thought from his head or an action that he desires the church to do. Instead, the healthy mature teacher should be in God's Word regularly listening for the Holy Spirit to tell him what to teach. This leads the pastor far down the road to Biblically based messages."[251] During the early stages of *Foundations*, the outsider leads the group in asking and answering these four questions as they study

---

248. Hawkins and Houk, *Foundations for Emerging Leaders*, 5.

249. Hawkins and Houk, *Foundations for Emerging Leaders*, 14, yet note, "The *Foundations* courses are not trainings in the traditional sense but are designed as workshops. As groups of pastors gather together, they receive some instruction from a teacher. At the same time, a large amount of time is devoted to learning and preparing messages together in small groups."

250. Hawkins and Houk, *Foundations for Emerging Leaders*, 12.

251. Hawkins and Houk, *Foundations for Emerging Leaders*, 12.

Scripture together, thus setting an example for the group to follow as they later study passages on their own and in small groups.[252]

Third, in the process of *Confessing the Faith*, the outsider cultivates theological agency among locals. That is, rather than impose foreign doctrinal formulations, the outsider leads locals toward reading, interpreting, applying, and expressing Scriptural truth in order for them to develop theology in their own words and language. Throughout the process, the outsider assumes the role of facilitator, allowing local believers to directly engage the biblical text and fostering discussion among the group as they together seek to understand and articulate the truth of Scripture.[253] The missionary thus serves as a kind of theological midwife, helping locals give birth to theology—a theology which belongs not to the midwife, but to those laboring to express biblical truth for their own context.[254] In this process, local believers thus begin to take ownership of their theological convictions rather than rely on missionary outsiders to tell them what to believe regarding doctrinal and contextual issues.

Finally, the outsider also serves to challenge blind spots in this process of *Confessing the Faith*. The manual includes excerpts, under each doctrine, from the BF&M.[255] However, Shank and Shank list such excerpts in their training manual not to demand conformity to them but to help the outsider discern if there are "obvious omissions" in the theological statements which the participants have developed.[256] They acknowledge that "each cultural setting will determine the need for various topics to be included. The process of creating a statement relevant to cultural issues and perhaps misunderstandings or false teaching within the local group should be prioritized over a comprehensive statement" on a particular doctrine.[257] Thus, such excerpts from a Western confession of faith serve not as a control over local theological conviction and expression, but as one means of checks and balances to help ensure that local theology remains within the bounds of orthodoxy.

---

252. Hawkins and Houk, *Foundations for Emerging Leaders*, 15.

253. Shank and Shank, *Confessing the Faith*, 9.

254. The "midwife" metaphor—rather than the "broker" or "mediator" metaphors described earlier—better describes the outsider's role here, since it implies the *creation* of something new, which in this case, is a new theological confession.

255. Southern Baptist Convention, "Baptist Faith and Message 2000."

256. Shank and Shank, *Confessing the Faith*, 9.

257. Shank and Shank, *Confessing the Faith*, 9.

Shank and Shank's model thus spans from early leadership development (through teaching Scripture and modeling sound hermeneutics) to formal theologizing (through cultivating theological agency and challenging blind spots). One might further strengthen this process of *Confessing the Faith* by following it with a consideration of historical theology and theologies from other locales. Such consideration—i.e., broadening of perspective—could help emerging churches more fully root themselves in the historic Christian tradition and broaden their fellowship in sound doctrine. Yet Shank and Shank's model nevertheless serves as an innovative way forward in the process of sound theological development among local churches.

CONCLUSION

In a hermeneutical community approach to local theological development, the outsider neither dominates the process nor withdraws from it. Rather, he or she serves as one voice among others seeking to understand and articulate the faith "once for all delivered to the saints" (Jude 3). The outsider assumes an active role in guiding churches toward what DeVries calls "ecclesial contextualization"—a stage of growth in which local churches become agents of their own theological convictions.[258] This role includes teaching Scripture, modeling sound hermeneutics, cultivating theological agency, challenging blind spots, and broadening perspectives. These components align with the Willowbank Report's evangelical vision for theological development, which denounces both theological imperialism and theological provincialism.[259]

---

258. DeVries, "Contexts of Contextualization," 12.

259. Lausanne Theology and Education Group, "The Willowbank Report," in *Down to Earth: Studies in Christianity and Culture*, ed. Robert T. Coote and John R. W. Stott (Grand Rapids: Eerdmans, 1980), 334.

6

A Way Forward for Missionary Outsiders

THIS BOOK HAS ARGUED that a hermeneutical community approach to local theological development delineates a constructive role for outsiders that avoids the colonial extreme of theological imposition and the post-colonial extreme of theological withdrawal. During much of the colonial era, missionary outsiders assumed that Western theology was universally normative and therefore imposed such theology on the churches they planted throughout the Majority World. In the post-colonial era, many have rejected that assumption and practice and have advocated for the development of local theology that might address cultural and contextual challenges which local churches face.

The untenable nature of colonial theological imposition and the ambiguity toward outsiders in post-colonial reactions to such imposition have rendered the outsider's role in local theological development unclear. To address this lack of clarity, this book appeals to the concept of hermeneutical community. A hermeneutical community approach to local theological development delineates a role for outsiders in which the outsider remains present in the process (contra extreme post-colonial sentiment), yet in a way that fosters self-theologizing rather than inhibit it (contra colonial patterns of theological imposition).

SUMMARY

Chapter 1 of this book introduced the importance of local theologizing and the historical precedent of Western theological imposition in the Majority World—which undermines such local theologizing. It then highlighted responses to this precedent and described how those responses have rendered the outsider's role in local theological development unclear. With this context in place, the chapter introduced the thesis of this work and sought to show its significance for missiological reflection and practice.

Chapter 2 provided a descriptive analysis of theological imposition in three different historical cases which demonstrate the precedent of theological imposition. First, it analyzed the theological control that late sixteenth-century Jesuit missionaries exerted over the native church in Peru. In doing so, it focused heavily on the ministry of José de Acosta. Then, the chapter considered how theological imposition factored into the ministry of the Church Missionary Society in Uganda around the turn of the twentieth century. Finally, it examined how Western missionary leaders controlled theological discussions within the Protestant union movement in South India during the first half of the twentieth century.

With each case, the chapter demonstrated how theological imposition factored into the ministry of outsiders. Having analyzed each case, the chapter synthesized the findings to identify commonalities in the practice and presuppositions of the aforementioned missionary groups. In each case, outsiders betrayed an assumption of Western theological normativity and universality and also remained in positions of control over local theological conviction.

Chapter 3 then explored post-colonial reactions to Western theological imposition. It assessed reactions in both ecumenical and evangelical circles. In examining ecumenical reactions, the chapter focused on the body of literature that developed among theologians of the Ecumenical Association of Third World Theologians (EATWOT). Central to this literature are the papers that Majority World theologians presented at major EATWOT conferences. The chapter revealed significant misgivings among such theologians who were eager, for various reasons, to counteract the colonial pattern of Western theological imposition.[1]

---

1. For example, chapter 3 explained how EATWOT has critiqued the theological method of much of Western theology. Rather than rooting theology in the text of

A WAY FORWARD FOR MISSIONARY OUTSIDERS

In its analysis of evangelical responses to colonial theological imposition, this chapter focused heavily on the literature associated with three major evangelical associations—the Latin American Theological Fraternity, the Association of Evangelicals of Africa, and the Asia Theological Association. Similar to the treatment of EATWOT discourses, this study of evangelical literature revealed misgivings among Majority World evangelical theologians concerning the precedent of foreign theological imposition.[2] Chapter 3 then synthesized and evaluated Majority World critiques of theological imposition and then demonstrated how such critiques have rendered the outsider's role in local theological development unclear.

Chapter 4 then critically assessed the notion of "hermeneutical community." It presented a descriptive analysis of how the concept developed in six different bodies of hermeneutical thought—Anabaptist hermeneutics, philosophical hermeneutics, theological hermeneutics, postliberal hermeneutics, Pentecostal hermeneutics, and ecumenical hermeneutics. The chapter then assessed the merits of hermeneutical community from a biblical perspective, demonstrating how various biblical passages lend credence to the practice of hermeneutical community. In particular, it showed from Acts 15:1–35 how theological authority (i.e., the right to theologize) did not rest solely with the mother church in Jerusalem, but instead remained diffused among multiple churches and their members. Further, the chapter showed from 1 Cor 14:16–23, 1 Pet 3:15, Rom 15:14, and 1 Pet 2:9 how theological agency (i.e., the responsibility to theologize) resides with all members of the church. Finally, chapter 4 demonstrated the relevance and function of hermeneutical community for contemporary local theological development.

Finally, having established the notion of hermeneutical community and its relevance, this book, in chapter 5, applied that notion to the outsider's role in local theological development. This chapter illustrated how the concept provides warrant for outsider involvement, offered metaphors for understanding the outsider's role, and demonstrated

---

Scripture—a common approach in the West—EATWOT members grant primacy to history and praxis in the development of theology, believing that both history and praxis can serve as conduits of divine revelation.

2. While Majority World evangelicals typically reject the theological method which EATWOT espouses, they nevertheless critique other aspects of Western theology. As chapter 3 has shown, for example, these evangelicals critique both the dualism they perceive in Western theology and the irrelevance of such theology in the face of contextual issues in the Majority World.

how a hermeneutical community approach recasts the role that outsiders should play in local theological development. It delineated five core components to that role, which—while not necessarily exhaustive—are essential for outsiders. These include (1) teaching Scripture, (2) modeling sound hermeneutical method, (3) cultivating theological agency, (4) challenging blind spots, and (5) broadening perspectives. Finally, this chapter highlighted and briefly evaluated three contemporary examples of how missionary outsiders have adopted roles commensurate with a hermeneutical community approach to local theological development.

IMPLICATIONS

One implication of this study is that outsiders should remain involved in the work of local theological development. As this book has sought to show, there is great value in incorporating multiple perspectives—both outside and local—in the work of searching Scripture, discerning its meaning, and applying it to contextual challenges facing the church. The perspectives of outsiders can serve as checks and balances in that process and as a means of broadening local perspectives. No faction of the church has cornered the market on doctrinal truth; all "see in a mirror dimly" (1 Cor 13:12). Therefore, it behooves those involved in local theological development to pool insight through the incorporation of multiple voices—outsiders included.

Another implication is that cross-cultural missionaries, in their work of establishing local churches, should actively promote and foster what Brian A. DeVries calls "ecclesial contextualization."[3] That is, they should not render or leave local believers and churches as passive recipients of theological conviction. Rather, missionaries should intentionally cultivate theological agency among locals so that they, on their own, might be able to address contextual challenges with biblical truth. Such self-theologizing is vital for churches if they are to survive the pressures of their surrounding culture. Thus, missionary outsiders, rather than assume that local theology will develop organically over time, should facilitate self-theologizing early in the life of local churches.

This research also carries implications for contemporary patterns of theological education. For example, the practice of "parachute"

---

3. Brian A. DeVries, "The Contexts of Contextualization: Different Methods for Different Ministry Situations," *Evang. Missions Q.* 55.4 (2019) 12.

theological education appears to subtly perpetuate Western theological imposition in the Majority World.[4] Parachute theological education is the pattern of outsiders dropping in on a location for a short period of time to teach theology to local believers. Such an approach, however, often fails to account for local cultural issues and the culturally shaped learning styles of locals.[5] These oversights can lead outsiders to impart foreign, irrelevant, and hard-to-understand theologies to locals.[6] Moreover, such parachute theological education often treats local believers as mere recipients of instruction who depend on others (i.e., outsiders) to teach them sound doctrine. Rarely does this approach engender an ability to self-theologize; locals remain objects of instruction rather than agents of theological conviction.

While parachute theological education may be better than an absence of theological education, its effectiveness in promoting lasting, relevant theological development remains questionable. To improve on such an approach, organizations, churches, and seminaries that send short-term teachers overseas might do well to (1) equip those outgoing educators to better understand the cultures and people to whom they are going to teach, (2) have outgoing educators focus on imparting to locals a *process* for theologizing more than imparting doctrines of theology, and (3) augment the short time which outsiders spend among local believers with longer periods of instruction through other means (e.g., online seminars, partnerships with resident missionaries or nationals,

---

4. The notion of "parachute" theological education here draws from the work of John Cheong, "Polycentrism in Majority World Theologizing: An Engagement with Power and Essentialism," in *Majority World Theologies: Theologizing from Africa, Asia, Latin America, and the Ends of the Earth*, ed. Allen L. Yeh and Tite Tiénou, Evangelical Missiological Society Series 26 (Pasadena, CA: William Carey Library, 2018), 35, who asserts, "When one- or two-day seminar speakers are often parachuted into the region from the minority world (often with theological or teaching content that is culturally insensitive), majority world Christians must ask whether they help in developing theology or teachers that addresses local challenges. Do they tackle ancestor veneration (a major barrier to the gospel in Asia), food offered to idols, or Christlike living in extended family context?"

5. James E. Plueddemann, *Teaching Across Cultures: Contextualizing Education for Global Mission* (Downers Grove, IL: IVP Academic, 2018), 30, contends, "Effective teaching demands that the teacher be as well versed in the learner's culture as in the subject matter. *To be a teacher of students, one must first be a student of students.* The key problem for many crosscultural teachers is assuming that their subject matter expertise can be transmitted to their students without taking into account the context and cultural values of the learner. These teachers need a paradigm shift" (emphasis original).

6. Cheong, "Polycentrism in Majority World Theologizing," 35.

etc.). Such measures could help overcome underlying weaknesses in the parachute theological education model.

Similarly, this research implicates approaches to theological development which focus mostly on the transfer of theological content from outsiders to locals, whether in the context of short-term theological training or residential seminaries. As John Cheong explains, "Minority world theologians who visit the majority world typically bring a pre-set syllabus to majority world contexts with little input from the nationals. Doing so often ignores their insights into local needs and resources, and it also risks Westernizing their curriculum, valorizing Western theological resources as essential and universal while marginalizing local capacity."[7] The same can be true for Western faculty teaching in Majority World seminaries.

In either context, Western educational efforts that focus on transferring theological content to other parts of the world almost invariably impose Western theology on local recipients. This pattern encourages locals to imbibe Western theological tenets, despite the fact that such tenets often fail to make sense of the challenges that confront local Christians.[8] Organizations that focus on theological development in the Majority World could address this problem by focusing less on imparting theological content—through set curricula, theological books, etc.—and more on imparting a sound theological process which local believers can utilize to bring scriptural truth to bear on contextual issues.

Another implication of this research is how it might shape pedagogical practices of faculty in theological institutions. That is, if local theological agency is valuable for believers and churches across the world, then how might theology professors teach their students and, at the same time, help them become agents of their own convictions? This task might be particularly difficult for faculty responsible for teaching systematic theology.[9] One way to cultivate theological agency among students in such a scenario could be for the foreign instructor to begin the semester by equipping students to explore, understand, and interpret the passages of Scripture associated with central theological doctrines. Then, over the course of the semester, the instructor could lead students through a

---

7. Cheong, "Polycentrism in Majority World Theologizing," 30.

8. For a helpful exploration of this reality, see Paul G. Hiebert, "The Flaw of the Excluded Middle," *Missiology Int. Rev.* 10.1 (1982) 35–47.

9. That is, because systematic theology typically presents theological knowledge as a fixed set of tenets ready for the student to assimilate rather than develop.

process of correlating passages, systematizing them under various headings, and expressing their truth accordingly. By the end of the semester, students would not only have a gained a wealth of systematic theological knowledge; they would have also grown in their own capacity to theologize, since—rather than listen passively to lectures—they would have participated in the exploration and explication of doctrinal truth.

This study also carries implications for Western churches, which—like local churches in the Majority World—stand to benefit from incorporating outsiders in their process of theological development. Just as Western outsiders can aid the development of local theology in the Majority World, so too can Majority World Christians aid the ongoing work of local theologizing in the West. Such aid could occur, for example, by Western seminaries inviting more Majority World theologians to teach in those institutions or by local churches inviting nearby pastors of diaspora congregations into theological conversations on important local issues. In fact, it is quite possible that voices from the Majority World can help Western churches better navigate Western cultural issues like growing individualism and rising secularism. Andrew Walls even posits, "Shared reading of the Scriptures and shared theological reflection will be to the benefit of all, but the oxygen-starved Christianity of the West will have most to gain."[10]

Additionally, this research presents implications for how Western churches and church leaders equip and disciple new believers. One reason that Western missionaries have historically not entrusted the task of theologizing to local believers might be that Western church leaders have often reserved for themselves the right and responsibility to teach theology to members of their churches. In such cases, church leaders serve as the theological authorities while members remain passive recipients of theological instruction. Many missionaries thus have no precedent to follow when it comes to cultivating theological agency within local churches among whom they minister. Yet, if one of the responsibilities of pastors is to "equip the saints for the work of ministry" (Eph 4:12), and if the word of Christ is "to dwell [in members of the church] richly, teaching and admonishing one another in all wisdom," (Col 3:16), then it might behoove even Western church leaders to pursue theological development along similar lines to the proposal offered in chapter 5 of this book. In doing so, they can begin to cultivate theological agency among

---

10. Andrew F. Walls, *The Cross-Cultural Process in Christian History: Studies in the Transmission and Appropriation of Faith* (Maryknoll, NY: Orbis, 2002), 47.

believers whom they disciple and thus equip them to stand firm in the faith.

FURTHER RESEARCH

In the wake of this study, several areas of research warrant further investigation. This book delimits its focus to the outsider's role in a local church's transition from "missional contextualization"[11] (in which the outsider remains the agent of theological conviction) to "ecclesial contextualization"[12] (in which local believers and churches become agents of theological conviction and expression). Beyond this realm, it remains to be seen how a hermeneutical community approach to local theological development might work itself out in the context of higher theological education. Specifically, how might a Western instructor in a Majority World theological institution embrace hermeneutical community for teaching his or her students? In what ways could the instructor teach theology yet do so without dictating the convictions of students? The previous section offered a preliminary suggestion, but further research in this area could help seminaries better shape their curricula and pedagogical practices to cultivate self-theologizing.

Another suggestion for further research is empirical study which mines the effects, challenges, and benefits of hermeneutical community in local theological development. Such studies could yield helpful information for practitioners seeking to effectively facilitate self-theologizing. For example, one might explore if, and how, the creation and use of indigenous statements of faith have strengthened networks of local pastors and churches against false teaching. Another study might assess whether those statements of faith have served to unite or divide congregations in specific church networks which hold to such indigenous confessions. Additionally, an empirical study which examines the intersection of foreign financial support and self-theologizing could help missionary practitioners discern if and how foreign subsidies undermine local theological agency.[13]

---

11. DeVries, "Contexts of Contextualization," 11–12.

12. DeVries, "Contexts of Contextualization," 12.

13. Cheong, "Polycentrism in Majority World Theologizing," 35, posits, "A major hurdle is the lack of freedom for nationals to self-theologize when working with such parachurch ministries. This is difficult because minority world leaders of such ministries often have relationships with majority world Christians that involve material and/

Further, an assessment of current practices in local theological development across various mission organizations could help stakeholders discern if and how such practices fall into the errors of foreign theological imposition or foreign theological withdrawal. As the previous section noted, contemporary patterns of parachute theological education and theological content transfer within the Majority World appear to perpetuate Western theological imposition. Conversely, missionaries who emphasize numerical church growth through broad evangelism while neglecting the work of discipleship and leadership development within local churches appear to fall into the danger of theological withdrawal. Studies which explore such organizational practices could help strengthen or, perhaps, correct patterns of theological development.

Finally, a deeper exegetical study of the biblical text in relation to the ideas of *theological authority* and *theological agency* could help further ground this book's hermeneutical community proposal. Chapter 4 explored Acts 15:1–35 and its bearing on theological authority, then explored 1 Cor 14:26–33, 1 Pet 3:15, Rom 15:14, and 1 Pet 2:9 to discern how they undergird the notion of theological agency. In order to explore these two concepts in more depth, one might study how pneumatological convictions (e.g., the indwelling of the Spirit cited in John 16:13–15) might similarly serve as a foundation for theological authority and agency among all believers and churches.

CONCLUSION

Over a century ago, Roland Allen highlighted the precedent and inadequacy of imposing Western theology on churches abroad.[14] He elaborated,

> In so acting we have adopted a false method of education. Slavery is not the best training for liberty. It is only by exercise that powers grow. To do things for people does not train them to do them for themselves. We are learning more and more in things educational that the first duty of the teacher is not to solve all difficulties for the pupil, and to present him with the ready-made answer, but to awaken a spirit, to teach it to realize its own powers, by setting before it difficulties, and showing it how

---

or financial support that the latter fear losing."

14. Roland Allen, *Missionary Methods: St. Paul's or Ours* (London: Robert Scott, 1912), 187–99.

> to approach and overcome them. The work of the missionary is education in this sense: it is the use of means to reveal to his converts a spiritual power which they actually possess and of which they are dimly conscious. As the converts exercise that power, as they yield themselves to the indwelling Spirit, they discover the greatness of the power and the grace of the Spirit, and in so doing they reveal it to their teacher.... The work of the missionary cannot be done by imposing things from without. The one result which he desires is the growth and manifestation of a Spirit from within.[15]

In other words, Allen recognized the importance of missionaries allowing theological conviction to develop locally rather than importing it wholesale from the outside.

Many before and after Allen have likewise promoted the ideal of local believers and churches growing in their ability to theologically instruct one another,[16] but none is more famous than the apostle Paul himself. As chapter 4 demonstrated, he praised the Roman church for being "full of goodness, filled with all knowledge and able to instruct one another" (Rom 15:14).[17] Paul was evidently confident enough in the Roman church that he saw no need for further foundation-laying work among them, and he instead sought to quickly pass on from Rome to continue his ministry in regions beyond (Rom 15:20, 24).[18] Part of Paul's

---

15. Allen, *Missionary Methods*, 193.

16. As chapter 3 noted, those who promoted such local theologizing include Charles Cuthbert Hall, *The Universal Elements of the Christian Religion: An Attempt to Interpret Contemporary Religious Conditions* (New York: Fleming H. Revell, 1905), 42–46, 51–53, 154–56; Arthur J. Brown, *Rising Churches in Non-Christian Lands* (New York: Missionary Education Movement of the United States and Canada, 1915), 188–90; Kenneth Scott Latourette, *Missions Tomorrow* (New York: Harper and Brothers, 1936), 211–12; G. C. Oosthuizen, *Theological Discussions and Confessional Developments in the Churches of Asia and Africa* (Franeker, Netherlands: T. Wever, 1958); J. H. Bavinck, *An Introduction to the Science of Missions*, trans. David Hugh Freeman (Grand Rapids: Baker, 1960), 203–4; Michael Hollis, *Paternalism and the Church: A Study of South Indian Church History* (New York: Oxford University Press, 1962), 15, 35–36; John V. Taylor, *The Primal Vision: Christian Presence amid African Religion* (Philadelphia: Fortress, 1963), 21–24; Wilbert R. Shenk, "Theology and the Missionary Task," *Missiology* 1.3 (1973) 295–96; Paul G. Hiebert, *Anthropological Insights for Missionaries* (Grand Rapids: Baker, 1985), 193–224.

17. Thomas R. Schreiner, *Romans*, 2nd ed., BECNT (Grand Rapids: Baker Academic, 2018), 739, explains that this declaration is not mere flattery on Paul's part. Rather, Paul here recognizes the church's growth in spiritual maturity.

18. Paul would later spend significant time in Rome during his imprisonment (Acts 27–28). This reality, however, does not compromise his reasoning in Rom 15 concerning

confidence resided in the fact that the believers in Rome were "able to instruct one another" (Rom 15:14). That is, those within the church at Rome had become agents of their own theological convictions, able to reason from Scripture and bring it to bear on the challenges they faced.

As missionary outsiders plant and establish local churches today, they too must guide those believers toward such growth in goodness, knowledge, and the ability to instruct one another. By adopting a hermeneutical community approach to theological development, outsiders can do just that. Moreover in doing so, outsiders can help local churches achieve perhaps the most elusive mark of ecclesial indigeneity—the ability and practice of self-theologizing.

---

his missionary plans vis-à-vis the state of the church at Rome.

Appendix

Indigenous Statement of Faith on Soteriology

THE FOLLOWING STATEMENT OF faith developed out of a network of churches in North India. Leaders among the network assembled to consider the doctrine of salvation from a biblical perspective. At the end of their gathering—having gone through the *Confessing the Faith* process—they jointly declared:

> Salvation is received not through religious works, but through the grace of God alone. To be saved one must repent of sins, confess Jesus as the Lord by mouth, and believe in him by heart, because God made him alone to be the Savior. Jesus Christ sacrificed himself on the cross by paying the penalty for sin and reconciled the world to God. Jesus alone is the source of eternal life, and salvation is found in him and none other. Those who believe in him receive eternal life, become a new creation, know the true God, and become God's children. They then walk by the Holy Spirit, are filled by the fruit of the Spirit, and receive spiritual gifts. In this way, those who are saved will not lose their salvation, because God is the one to give eternal life which cannot be destroyed. They are secured and sanctified and remain pure until the second coming of the Lord Jesus. No one can separate them from the love of God because the Holy Spirit has sealed them. However, a believer is required to obey God's commands, do good works, keep the fear of the Lord, and work out his/her salvation.

INDIGENOUS STATEMENT OF FAITH ON SOTERIOLOGY

Gen 3:15; Matt 1:21; 4:17; 16:21–26; Luke 1:68–69; 2:28–32; John 1:12, 29; 3; 5:24; 14:21; 15:1–16; 17:3; Acts 2:21, 38–39; 4:12; 15:11; 16:30–31; 17:30–31; 20:32; Rom 1:8–18; 3:23–25; 5:8–10; 6:1–23; 8:29–39; 10:9–10, 13; 1 Cor 1:30; 15:10; 2 Cor 5:17–20; Gal 3:13; 5:22–25; Eph 1:14–14; 4:30; 1–7; 2:9–22; 2:10; 4:12; Phil 2:12; Col 1:9–22; 1 Thess 5:23–24; 2 Tim 1:12; Titus 2:11–14; Heb 5:8–9; 9:24; Jas 2:14–26; 1 Pet 2:1–23; 1 John 1:2–23, 28–29; 3:9; 4:7[1]

---

[1]. This statement is a translation from its Hindi and Nepali iterations. Its authors listed at the bottom those verses that informed their confession on soteriology.

Bibliography

Abesamis, Carlos H. "Doing Theological Reflection in a Philippine Context." In *The Emergent Gospel: Theology from the Underside of History: Papers from the Ecumenical Dialogue of Third World Theologians, Dar es Salaam, August 5-12, 1976*, edited by Sergio Torres and Virginia Fabella, 112-23. Maryknoll, NY: Orbis, 1978.
———. "Faith and Life Reflections from the Grassroots in the Philippines." In *Asia's Struggle for Full Humanity: Towards a Relevant Theology: Papers from the Asian Theological Conference, January 7-20, 1979, Wennappuwa, Sri Lanka*, edited by Virginia Fabella, 123-39. Maryknoll, NY: Orbis, 1980.
Abraham, K. C., ed. "African Report." In *Third World Theologies: Commonalities and Divergences: Papers and Reflections from the Second General Assembly of the Ecumenical Association of Third World Theologians, December 1986, Oaxtepec, Mexico*, 28-56. Eugene, OR: Wipf & Stock, 2004.
———, ed. "Asian Report." In *Third World Theologies: Commonalities and Divergences: Papers and Reflections from the Second General Assembly of the Ecumenical Association of Third World Theologians, December 1986, Oaxtepec, Mexico*, 3-27. Eugene, OR: Wipf & Stock, 2004.
———, ed. "Commonalities, Divergences, and Cross-Fertilization Among Third World Theologies: A Document Based on the Seventh International Conference of the Ecumenical Association of Third World Theologians, Oaxtepec, Mexico, December 7-14, 1986." In *Third World Theologies: Commonalities and Divergences: Papers and Reflections from the Second General Assembly of the Ecumenical Association of Third World Theologians, December 1986, Oaxtepec, Mexico*, 195-213. Eugene, OR: Wipf & Stock, 2004.
———, ed. "Latin American Report." In *Third World Theologies: Commonalities and Divergences: Papers and Reflections from the Second General Assembly of the Ecumenical Association of Third World Theologians, December 1986, Oaxtepec, Mexico*, 57-80. Eugene, OR: Wipf & Stock, 2004.
Acosta, José de. *De Procuranda Indorum Salute—Jose De Acosta S.J. 1540-1600: An English Introduction and Translation*. Translated by G. Stewart McIntosh. 2020. Kindle.
———. *Natural and Moral History of the Indies*. Edited by Jane E. Mangan. Translated by Frances M. López-Morillas. Chronicles of the New World Order. Durham, NC: Duke University Press, 2002.
Adam, A. K. M., et al., eds. *Reading Scripture with the Church: Toward a Hermeneutic for Theological Interpretation*. Grand Rapids: Baker Academic, 2006.

BIBLIOGRAPHY

Adeloye, Gabriel Oludele. "Decolonizing Biblical Interpretation and Its Effect on the Church in Africa." *Practical Theology (Baptist College of Theology, Lagos)* 9 (2016) 198–208.

Adeyemo, Tokunboh. "The African Church and Selfhood." *Evangelical Review of Theology* 5.2 (1981) 36–45.

———. "Contemporary Issues in Africa and the Future of Evangelicals." *Evangelical Review of Theology* 2.1 (1978) 3–11.

———. "Towards an Evangelical African Theology." *Evangelical Review of Theology* 7.1 (1983) 147–54.

African Report Group. "In Search of an African Theology." In *Irruption of the Third World: Challenge to Theology: Papers from the Fifth International Conference of the Ecumenical Association of Third World Theologians, August 17–29, 1981, New Delhi, India*, edited by Virginia Fabella and Sergio Torres, 56–60. Maryknoll, NY: Orbis, 1983.

Ahn, Jae Woong. "The Christian Conference of Asia and the Ecumenical Movement." *Church and Society* 92.1 (2001) 7–12.

"All Africa Conference of Churches and the Lusaka Assembly." *African Ecclesial Review* 16.2 (1974) 329–34.

Allen, Roland. *Missionary Methods: St. Paul's or Ours*. London: Robert Scott, 1912.

Allison, Gregg R. "Theological Interpretation of Scripture: An Introduction and Preliminary Evaluation." *Southern Baptist Journal of Theology* 14.2 (2010) 28–37.

Amalorpavadass, D. S. "The Indian Universe of a New Theology." In *The Emergent Gospel: Theology from the Underside of History: Papers from the Ecumenical Dialogue of Third World Theologians, Dar es Salaam, August 5–12, 1976*, edited by Sergio Torres and Virginia Fabella, 137–56. Maryknoll, NY: Orbis, 1978.

Amaya, Ismael E. "A Latin American Critique of Western Theology." *Evangelical Review of Theology* 7.1 (1983) 13–27.

Amirtham, Samuel, and John S. Pobee, eds. "Introduction." In *Theology by the People: Reflections on Doing Theology in Community*, edited by Samuel Amirtham and John S. Pobee, 1–26. Geneva: World Council of Churches, 1986.

———, eds. *Theology by the People: Reflections on Doing Theology in Community*. Geneva: World Council of Churches, 1986.

Anderson, Gerald H. "A Moratorium on Missionaries?" *Christian Century* 91.2 (1974) 43–45.

Anderson, Rufus. *Foreign Missions: Their Relations and Claims*. New York: Charles Scribner, 1869.

Anizor, Uche, and Hank Voss. *Representing Christ: A Vision for the Priesthood of All Believers*. Downers Grove, IL: IVP Academic, 2016.

Ankrah, Kodwo E. "Church and Politics in Africa." In *African Theology en Route: Papers from the Pan African Conference of Third World Theologians, December 17–23, 1977, Accra, Ghana*, edited by Kofi Appiah-Kubi and Sergio Torres, 155–61. Maryknoll, NY: Orbis, 1979.

Appiah-Kubi, Kofi. "Preface." In *African Theology en Route: Papers from the Pan African Conference of Third World Theologians, December 17–23, 1977, Accra, Ghana*, edited by Kofi Appiah-Kubi and Sergio Torres, viii–x. Maryknoll, NY: Orbis, 1979.

Appiah-Kubi, Kofi, and Sergio Torres, eds. "Final Communiqué." In *African Theology en Route: Papers from the Pan African Conference of Third World Theologians, December 17–23, 1977, Accra, Ghana*, 189–95. Maryknoll, NY: Orbis, 1979.

BIBLIOGRAPHY

Archer, Kenneth J. *A Pentecostal Hermeneutic: Spirit, Scripture and Community.* Cleveland, TN: CPT, 2005.

———. "Pentecostal Hermeneutics: Retrospect and Prospect." *Journal of Pentecostal Theology* 8 (1996) 63–81.

———. "Pentecostal Hermeneutics and the Society for Pentecostal Studies: Reading and Hearing in One Spirit and One Accord." *Pneuma* 37.3 (2015) 317–39.

———. "Spirited Conversation About Hermeneutics: A Pentecostal Hermeneut's Response to Craig Keener's Spirit Hermeneutics." *Pneuma* 39 (2017) 179–97.

Archer, Melissa L. "'I Was in the Spirit on the Lord's Day': A Pentecostal Engagement with Worship in the Apocalypse." PhD diss., Bangor University, 2013.

Armas Medina, Fernando de. *Cristianizacion Del Peru (1532–1600).* Sevilla: Escuela de Estudios Hispano-Americanos de Sevilla, 1953.

Arrastía, Cecilio. "La Iglesia como Comunidad Hermenéutica." *Apuntes* 1.1 (1981) 7–13.

Asian Report Group. "Toward a Relevant Theology in Asia." In *Irruption of the Third World: Challenge to Theology: Papers from the Fifth International Conference of the Ecumenical Association of Third World Theologians, August 17–29, 1981, New Delhi, India*, edited by Virginia Fabella and Sergio Torres, 61–76. Maryknoll, NY: Orbis, 1983.

Athyal, Saphir F. "A History of the Asia Theological Association." In *Voice of the Church in Asia: Report of Proceedings, Asia Theological Association Consultation (Hong Kong, December 27, 1973–January 4, 1974)*, edited by Bong Rin Ro, 1–6. Singapore: Asia Theological Association, 1975.

———. "Toward an Asian Christian Theology." In *What Asian Christians Are Thinking: A Theological Source Book*, edited by Douglas J. Elwood, 68–84. Quezon City, Philippines: New Day, 1978.

Atkinson, William. "Worth a Second Look? Pentecostal Hermeneutics." *Evangel* 21.2 (2003) 49–54.

Autry, Arden C. "Dimensions of Hermeneutics in Pentecostal Focus." *Journal of Pentecostal Theology* 1.3 (1993) 29–50.

Balasuriya, Tissa. "Divergences: An Asian Perspective." In *Third World Theologies: Commonalities and Divergences: Papers and Reflections from the Second General Assembly of the Ecumenical Association of Third World Theologians, December 1986, Oaxtepec, Mexico*, edited by K. C. Abraham, 113–19. Eugene, OR: Wipf & Stock, 2004.

———. "A Third World Perspective." In *Doing Theology in a Divided World: Papers from the Sixth International Conference of the Ecumenical Association of Third World Theologians, January 5–13, 1983, Geneva, Switzerland*, edited by Virginia Fabella and Sergio Torres, 197–205. Maryknoll, NY: Orbis, 1985.

———. "Towards the Liberation of Theology in Asia." In *Asia's Struggle for Full Humanity: Towards a Relevant Theology: Papers from the Asian Theological Conference, January 7–20, 1979, Wennappuwa, Sri Lanka*, edited by Virginia Fabella, 16–27. Maryknoll, NY: Orbis, 1980.

Banninga, John J. "Union in South India." *Christian Century* 64.15 (1947) 459–61.

Barefoot, C. S. "Local Ownership of the Theological Task." *Great Commission Baptist Journal of Missions* 2.2 (2023) 1–16.

Barnes, Monica. "Catechisms and Confessionarios: Distorting Mirrors of Andean Societies." In *Andean Cosmologies Through Time: Persistence and Emergence*, edited by Robert V. H. Dover et al., 67-94. Bloomington: Indiana University Press, 1992.

Barrett, C. K. *A Commentary on the First Epistle to the Corinthians*. New York: Harper & Row, 1968.

Barth, Karl. *God in Action: Theological Addresses*. Translated by E. G. Homrighausen and Karl J. Ernst. New York: Round Table, 1936.

———. "No Boring Theology!" *South East Asia Journal of Theology* 11.1 (1969) 3-5.

Bauckham, Richard. "James and the Jerusalem Church." In *The Book of Acts in Its Palestinian Setting*, edited by Richard Bauckham, 415-80. Grand Rapids: Eerdmans, 1995.

Bauer, Walter, and William F. Arndt. *A Greek-English Lexicon of the New Testament and Other Early Christian Literature*. Edited by Frederick W. Danker. 3rd ed. Chicago: University of Chicago Press, 2000.

Bautista, Lorenzo, et al. "The Asian Way of Thinking in Theology." In *Biblical Theology in Asia*, edited by Ken Gnanakan, 123-37. Bangalore, India: Theological Book Trust, 1995.

Bavinck, J. H. *An Introduction to the Science of Missions*. Translated by David Hugh Freeman. Grand Rapids: Baker, 1960.

Bebbington, David W. *Evangelicalism in Modern Britain: A History from the 1730s to the 1980s*. London: Routledge, 1989.

Bediako, Kwame. "The Willowbank Consultation Jan 1978: A Personal Reflection." *Themelios* 5.2 (1980) 25-32.

Beeby, H. D. "Thoughts on Indigenizing Theology." *South East Asia Journal of Theology* 14.2 (1973) 34-38.

Bell, G. K. A., ed. "The General Assembly of the South India United Church. Resolutions of Acceptance. September 1946." In *Documents on Christian Unity: Third Series 1930-48*, 228-29. New York: Oxford University Press, 1948.

———, ed. "The General Council of the Church of India, Burma, and Ceylon. Resolution of Acceptance. January 1945." In *Documents on Christian Unity: Third Series 1930-48*, 228. New York: Oxford University Press, 1948.

———, ed. "The South India Provincial Synod of the Methodist Church. Resolution of Acceptance. January and July 1943." In *Documents on Christian Unity: Third Series 1930-48*, 224. New York: Oxford University Press, 1948.

———, ed. "Statement Drawn Up by Thirty-Three Ministers of the Anglican and South India United Churches at Tranquebar, May 1 and 2, 1919." In *Documents on Christian Unity: A Selection from the First and Second Series 1920-30*, 122-25. New York: Oxford University Press, 1955.

Bevans, Stephen B. *An Introduction to Theology in Global Perspective*. Maryknoll, NY: Orbis, 2009.

———. *Models of Contextual Theology*. Rev. and exp. ed. Maryknoll, NY: Orbis, 2002.

———. "Singing the Lord's Song in a Foreign Land: The Foreigner as Theology Teacher." *South East Asia Journal of Theology* 17.2 (1976) 49-62.

Billings, J. Todd. *The Word of God for the People of God: An Entryway to the Theological Interpretation of Scripture*. Grand Rapids: Eerdmans, 2010.

Black, Max. "The Gap Between 'Is' and 'Should.'" *Philosophical Review* 73.2 (1964) 165-81.

Boesak, Allan. "Coming In out of the Wilderness." In *The Emergent Gospel: Theology from the Underside of History: Papers from the Ecumenical Dialogue of Third*

BIBLIOGRAPHY

World Theologians, Dar es Salaam, August 5–12, 1976, edited by Sergio Torres and Virginia Fabella, 76–95. Maryknoll, NY: Orbis, 1978.

———. "Liberation Theology in South Africa." In *African Theology en Route: Papers from the Pan African Conference of Third World Theologians, December 17–23, 1977, Accra, Ghana*, edited by Kofi Appiah-Kubi and Sergio Torres, 169–75. Maryknoll, NY: Orbis, 1979.

Boff, Leonardo. "Theological Characteristics of a Grassroots Church." In *The Challenge of Basic Christian Communities: Papers from the International Ecumenical Congress of Theology, February 20–March 2, 1980, São Paulo, Brazil*, edited by Sergio Torres and John Eagleson, 124–44. Maryknoll, NY: Orbis, 1981.

Bosch, David J. *Transforming Mission: Paradigm Shifts in Theology of Mission*. Maryknoll, NY: Orbis, 1991.

Boucher, David. "Invoking a World of Ideas: Theory and Interpretation in the Justification of Colonialism." *Theoria* 63.2 (2016) 6–24.

Breman, Christina M. *The Association of Evangelicals in Africa: Its History, Organization, Members, Projects, External Relations, and Message*. Zoetermeer, Netherlands: Boekencentrum, 1996.

———. "A Bird's Eye View of A.E.A.: The Association of Evangelicals in Africa." *Africa Journal of Evangelical Theology* 17.1 (1998) 3–12.

Brock, Charles. *Indigenous Church Planting: A Practical Journey*. Neosho, MO: Church Growth International, 1994.

Brown, Arthur J. *Rising Churches in Non-Christian Lands*. New York: Missionary Education Movement of the United States and Canada, 1915.

Bruce, F. F. *The Book of the Acts*. Rev. ed. NICNT. Grand Rapids: Eerdmans, 1988.

———. "The Church of Jerusalem in the Acts of the Apostles." *Bulletin of the John Rylands University Library of Manchester* 67.2 (1985) 641–61.

Bulatao, Jaime. "Split-Level Christianity." *Philippine Sociological Review* 13.2 (1965) 119–21.

Burgaleta, Claudio M. *José de Acosta, S.J. (1540–1600): His Life and Thought*. Chicago: Loyola University Press, 1999.

Buthelezi, Manas. "Toward Indigenous Theology in South Africa." In *African Theology en Route: Papers from the Pan African Conference of Third World Theologians, December 17–23, 1977, Accra, Ghana*, edited by Kofi Appiah-Kubi and Sergio Torres, 56–75. Maryknoll, NY: Orbis, 1979.

Calderón, Jorge Alverez. "Peruvian Reality and Theological Challenges." In *Irruption of the Third World: Challenge to Theology: Papers from the Fifth International Conference of the Ecumenical Association of Third World Theologians, August 17–29, 1981, New Delhi, India*, edited by Virginia Fabella and Sergio Torres, 42–49. Maryknoll, NY: Orbis, 1983.

Caldwell, Larry W. "Towards the New Discipline of Ethnohermeneutics: Questioning the Relevancy of Western Hermeneutical Methods in the Asian Context." *Journal of Asian Mission* 1.1 (1999) 21–43.

Callahan, James. "The Bible Says: Evangelical and Postliberal Biblicism." *Theology Today* 53.4 (1997) 449–63.

Campbell, Charles L. *Preaching Jesus: New Directions for Homiletics in Hans Frei's Postliberal Theology*. Eugene, OR: Wipf & Stock, 2006.

Carr, Burgess. "Internationalizing the Mission." *IDOC/International Documentation* 63 (1974) 72–74.

BIBLIOGRAPHY

Carson, D. A. "Hermeneutics: A Brief Assessment of Some Recent Trends." *Themelios* 5.2 (1980) 12–20.

———. "Reflections on Contextualization: A Critical Appraisal of Daniel Von Allmen's 'Birth of Theology.'" *East Africa Journal of Evangelical Theology* 3.1 (1984) 16–59.

Cartledge, Mark J. "Text-Community-Spirit: The Challenges Posed by Pentecostal Theological Method to Evangelical Theology." In *Spirit and Scripture: Exploring a Pneumatic Hermeneutic*, edited by Kevin L. Spawn and Archie T. Wright, 130–42. New York: T&T Clark International, 2012.

Cartwright, Michael G. "The Practice and Performance of Scripture: Grounding Christian Ethics in a Communal Hermeneutic." *Annual of the Society of Christian Ethics* 8 (1988) 31–53.

Carvajal, Orlando P. "The Context of Theology." In *The Emergent Gospel: Theology from the Underside of History: Papers from the Ecumenical Dialogue of Third World Theologians, Dar es Salaam, August 5–12, 1976*, edited by Sergio Torres and Virginia Fabella, 193–226. Maryknoll, NY: Orbis, 1978.

Casada, James A. "James A. Grant and the Introduction of Christianity in Uganda." *Journal of Church and State* 25.3 (1983) 507–22.

Cervantes, Fernando. "'The Defender of the Indians': Bartolomé de Las Casas in Context." *The Way* 38.3 (1998) 271–81.

Chakkarai, V. "The South India Rapprochement." In *Rethinking Christianity in India*, edited by G. V. Job et al., 277–83. Madras, India: A. N. Sudarisanam, 1939.

Chan, Simon. *Grassroots Asian Theology: Thinking the Faith from the Ground Up*. Downers Grove, IL: InterVarsity, 2014.

Chandran, J. Russell. "Development of Christian Theology in India: A Critical Survey." In *The Emergent Gospel: Theology from the Underside of History: Papers from the Ecumenical Dialogue of Third World Theologians, Dar es Salaam, August 5–12, 1976*, edited by Sergio Torres and Virginia Fabella, 157–72. Maryknoll, NY: Orbis, 1978.

———. "A Methodological Approach to Third World Theology." In *Irruption of the Third World: Challenge to Theology: Papers from the Fifth International Conference of the Ecumenical Association of Third World Theologians, August 17–29, 1981, New Delhi, India*, edited by Virginia Fabella and Sergio Torres, 79–86. Maryknoll, NY: Orbis, 1983.

Chao, Jonathan T'ien-en. "Development of National Faculty for Asian Theological Education." In *Voice of the Church in Asia: Report of Proceedings, Asia Theological Association Consultation (Hong Kong, December 27, 1973–January 4, 1974)*, edited by Bong Rin Ro, 91–100. Singapore: Asia Theological Association, 1975.

———. "Some Ideas on the Direction of Chinese Theological Development." *Occasional Bulletin* 20.6 (1969) 1–14.

Chenchiah, P. "Church Union: A Study of Underlying Ideas." In *Rethinking Christianity in India*, edited by G. V. Job et al., 209–28. Madras, India: A. N. Sudarisanam, 1939.

Cheong, John. "Polycentrism in Majority World Theologizing: An Engagement with Power and Essentialism." In *Majority World Theologies: Theologizing from Africa, Asia, Latin America, and the Ends of the Earth*, edited by Allen L. Yeh and Tite Tiénou, 24–40. Evangelical Missiological Society Series 26. Pasadena, CA: William Carey Library, 2018.

BIBLIOGRAPHY

Cheung, Alex T. M. "A Narrative Analysis of Acts 14:27–15:35: Literary Shaping in Luke's Account of the Jerusalem Council." *Westminster Theological Journal* 55.1 (1993) 137–54.

Chikane, Frank. "Spirituality of the Third World: Conversion and Commitment." In *Spirituality of the Third World: A Cry for Life: Papers and Reflections from the Third General Assembly of the Ecumenical Association of Third World Theologians, January, 1992, Nairobi, Kenya*, edited by K. C. Abraham and Bernadette Mbuy-Beya, 173–81. Eugene, OR: Wipf & Stock, 2005.

Chow, Wilson W. "Biblical Foundations: An East Asian Study." *Evangelical Review of Theology* 7.1 (1983) 102–12.

Christian Conference of Asia. "The Confessing Church in Asia and Its Theological Task." In *What Asian Christians Are Thinking: A Theological Source Book*, edited by Douglas J. Elwood, 41–46. Quezon City, Philippines: New Day, 1978.

———. "Confessing the Faith in Asia Today." In *What Asian Christians Are Thinking: A Theological Source Book*, edited by Douglas J. Elwood, 7–15. Quezon City, Philippines: New Day, 1978.

Chul-Ha, Han. "An Asian Critique of Western Theology." *Evangelical Review of Theology* 7.1 (1983) 34–47.

The Church in the Mission Field: Report of Commission II. Edinburgh: Oliphant, Anderson and Ferrier, 1910.

Church of South India. *The Constitution of the Church of South India with Amendments up to 31st December 1951.* Madras: The Christian Literature Society for India, 1952.

"Churches Renewed in Mission: Report of Section III of the Bangkok Conference." *International Review of Mission* 62.246 (1973) 216–23.

Churchill, Winston S. *My African Journey.* Toronto: William Briggs, 1909.

Clark, David K. *To Know and Love God: Method for Theology.* Wheaton, IL: Crossway, 2010.

Coe, Shoki. "In Search of Renewal in Theological Education." *Theological Education* 9.4 (1973) 233–43.

Conder, Tim, and Daniel Rhodes. *Free for All: Rediscovering the Bible in Community.* Grand Rapids: Baker, 2009.

Conn, Harvie M. "Contextualization: Where Do We Begin?" In *Evangelicals and Liberation*, edited by Carl E. Armerding, 90–119. Grand Rapids: Baker, 1977.

———. *Eternal Word and Changing Worlds: Theology, Anthropology, and Mission in Trialogue.* Grand Rapids: Zondervan, 1984.

Cook, Matthew. "Contextual but Still Objective?" In *Local Theology for the Global Church: Principles for an Evangelical Approach to Contextualization*, edited by Matthew Cook et al., 75–89. Pasadena, CA: William Carey Library, 2010.

Cook, Matthew, et al., eds. *Local Theology for the Global Church: Principles for an Evangelical Approach to Contextualization.* Pasadena, CA: William Carey Library, 2010.

Couch, Beatriz Melano. "New Visions of the Church in Latin America: A Protestant View." In *The Emergent Gospel: Theology from the Underside of History: Papers from the Ecumenical Dialogue of Third World Theologians, Dar es Salaam, August 5–12, 1976*, edited by Sergio Torres and Virginia Fabella, 193–226. Maryknoll, NY: Orbis, 1978.

Court, Deborah. "Ethnography and Case Study: A Comparative Analysis." *Academic Exchange Quarterly* (2003). https://www.thefreelibrary.com/Ethnography+and+case+study%3a+a+comparative+analysis.-a0111848865.

Cranfield, C. E. B. *A Critical and Exegetical Commentary on the Epistle to the Romans.* 2 vols. ICC. Edinburgh: T&T Clark, 1979–80.

Croatto, J. Severino. "Biblical Hermeneutics in the Theologies of Liberation." In *Irruption of the Third World: Challenge to Theology: Papers from the Fifth International Conference of the Ecumenical Association of Third World Theologians, August 17-29, 1981, New Delhi, India*, edited by Virginia Fabella and Sergio Torres, 140–68. Maryknoll, NY: Orbis, 1983.

Cunningham, Richard B. "Theologizing in a Global Context: Changing Contours." *Review and Expositor* 94.3 (1997) 351–62.

Cushner, Nicholas P. *Why Have You Come Here? The Jesuits and the First Evangelization of Native America.* New York: Oxford University Press, 2006.

Daïdanso, ma Djongwé. "An African Critique of African Theology." *Evangelical Review of Theology* 7.1 (1983) 63–72.

Danker, Frederick W. "Reciprocity in the Ancient World and in Acts 15:23–29." In *Political Issues in Luke-Acts*, edited by Richard J. Cassidy and Philip J. Scharper, 49–58. Maryknoll, NY: Orbis, 1983.

Darch, John H. *Missionary Imperialists? Missionaries, Government and the Growth of the British Empire in the Tropics, 1860–1885.* Studies in Christian History and Thought. Colorado Springs: Paternoster, 2009.

Daub, Anna. "Vern Poythress's Perspectivalism in a Global Context: A Symphony of Contextual Theologies Seeking Harmony." PhD diss., Southeastern Baptist Theological Seminary, 2021.

Davids, Peter H. *The First Epistle of Peter.* Grand Rapids: Eerdmans, 1990.

de Carvalho, Emílio J. M. "Hope for the Future." In *Irruption of the Third World: Challenge to Theology: Papers from the Fifth International Conference of the Ecumenical Association of Third World Theologians, August 17-29, 1981, New Delhi, India*, edited by Virginia Fabella and Sergio Torres, 276–77. Maryknoll, NY: Orbis, 1983.

———. "Opening Statement." In *Doing Theology in a Divided World: Papers from the Sixth International Conference of the Ecumenical Association of Third World Theologians, January 5–13, 1983, Geneva, Switzerland*, edited by Virginia Fabella and Sergio Torres, 5–8. Maryknoll, NY: Orbis, 1985.

DeHart, Paul J. *The Trial of the Witnesses: The Rise and Decline of Postliberal Theology.* Malden, MA: Blackwell, 2006.

de la Rosa, Alexandre Coello. "La Doctrina de Juli a Debate (1575–1585)." *Revista de Estudios Extremeños* 63.2 (2007) 951–89.

Delavignette, Robert. *Christianity and Colonialism.* Translated by J. R. Foster. New York: Hawthorn, 1964.

Dennis, James S. *Christian Missions and Social Progress: A Sociological Study of Foreign Missions.* 3 vols. New York: Fleming H. Revell, 1897–1906.

de Souza, Luis A. Gómez. "Structures and Mechanisms of Domination in Capitalism." In *The Challenge of Basic Christian Communities: Papers from the International Ecumenical Congress of Theology, February 20–March 2, 1980, São Paulo, Brazil*, edited by Sergio Torres and John Eagleson, 161–88. Maryknoll, NY: Orbis, 1981.

BIBLIOGRAPHY

Devadutt, V. E. "What Is an Indigenous Theology?" In *Readings in Dynamic Indigeneity*, edited by Charles H. Kraft and Tom N. Wisley, 313–24. Pasadena, CA: William Carey Library, 1979.

Devasahayam, D. M. "The South India Church Union Movement." In *Rethinking Christianity in India*, edited by G. V. Job et al., 229–75. Madras, India: A. N. Sudarisanam, 1939.

de Villiers, Pieter G. R. "Communal Discernment in the Early Church." *Acta Theologica* 17 (2013) 132–55.

DeVries, Brian A. "The Contexts of Contextualization: Different Methods for Different Ministry Situations." *Evangelical Missions Quarterly* 55.4 (2019) 11–14.

———. "Toward a Global Theology: Theological Method and Contextualization." *Verbum et Ecclesia* 37.1 (2016) 1–12.

Dickson, Kwesi A. "The African Theological Task." In *The Emergent Gospel: Theology from the Underside of History: Papers from the Ecumenical Dialogue of Third World Theologians, Dar es Salaam, August 5–12, 1976*, edited by Sergio Torres and Virginia Fabella, 46–49. Maryknoll, NY: Orbis, 1978.

Doctrina Christiana y Catecismo para Instrucción de los Indios. Lima, 1584.

Dorrien, Gary J. "A Third Way in Theology? The Origins of Postliberalism." *Christian Century* 118.20 (2001) 16–21.

Dostal, Robert J. "Gadamer: The Man and His Work." In *The Cambridge Companion to Gadamer*, edited by Robert J. Dostal, 13–35. Cambridge, UK: Cambridge University Press, 2002.

Driver, John. *Community and Commitment*. Scottdale, PA: Herald, 1976.

Dube, Musa W. *Postcolonial Feminist Interpretation of the Bible*. St. Louis, MO: Chalice, 2000.

———. "The Subaltern Can Speak: Reading the Mmutle (Hare) Way." *Journal of Africana Religions* 4.1 (2016) 54–75.

Dube, Musa W., and R. S. Wafula, eds. *Postcoloniality, Translation, and the Bible in Africa*. Eugene, OR: Pickwick, 2017.

Dunn, James D. G. *The Acts of the Apostles*. Valley Forge, PA: Trinity Press International, 1996.

du Plessis, Johannes. *The Evangelisation of Pagan Africa: A History of Christian Missions to the Pagan Tribes of Central Africa*. Cape Town: J.C. Juta, 1929.

Durston, Alan. *Pastoral Quechua: The History of Christian Translation in Colonial Peru, 1550–1650*. Notre Dame, IN: University of Notre Dame Press, 2007.

Dussel, Enrique D. "The Political and Ecclesial Context of Liberation Theology in Latin America." In *The Emergent Gospel: Theology from the Underside of History: Papers from the Ecumenical Dialogue of Third World Theologians, Dar es Salaam, August 5–12, 1976*, edited by Sergio Torres and Virginia Fabella, 175–92. Maryknoll, NY: Orbis, 1978.

Dyrness, William A. "Doing Theology out of a Western Heritage: Gains and Losses." In *Theology Without Borders: An Introduction to Global Conversations*, by William A. Dyrness and Oscar García-Johnson, 23–41. Grand Rapids: Baker Academic, 2015.

———. *Invitation to Cross-Cultural Theology: Case Studies in Vernacular Theologies*. Grand Rapids: Zondervan, 1992.

———. *Learning About Theology from the Third World*. Grand Rapids: Zondervan, 1990.

Dyrness, William A., and Oscar García-Johnson. *Theology Without Borders: An Introduction to Global Conversations*. Grand Rapids: Baker Academic, 2015.

EATWOT. "Communiqué: Ecumenical Dialogue of Third World Theologians, Dar es Salaam, August 12, 1976." In *The Emergent Gospel: Theology from the Underside of History: Papers from the Ecumenical Dialogue of Third World Theologians, Dar es Salaam, August 5–12, 1976*, edited by Sergio Torres and Virginia Fabella, 272–74. Maryknoll, NY: Orbis, 1978.

———. "The Final Statement." In *Asia's Struggle for Full Humanity: Towards a Relevant Theology: Papers from the Asian Theological Conference, January 7–20, 1979, Wennappuwa, Sri Lanka*, edited by Virginia Fabella, 152–60. Maryknoll, NY: Orbis, 1980.

———. "Final Statement: Ecumenical Dialogue of Third World Theologians, Dar es Salaam, August 12, 1976." In *The Emergent Gospel: Theology from the Underside of History: Papers from the Ecumenical Dialogue of Third World Theologians, Dar es Salaam, August 5–12, 1976*, edited by Sergio Torres and Virginia Fabella, 259–71. Maryknoll, NY: Orbis, 1978.

———. "The Irruption of the Third World: Challenge to Theology: Final Statement of the Fifth EATWOT Conference, New Delhi, August 17–29, 1981." In *Irruption of the Third World: Challenge to Theology: Papers from the Fifth International Conference of the Ecumenical Association of Third World Theologians, August 17–29, 1981, New Delhi, India*, edited by Virginia Fabella and Sergio Torres, 191–206. Maryknoll, NY: Orbis, 1983.

Ellington, Scott A. "Pentecostalism and the Authority of Scripture." In *Pentecostal Hermeneutics: A Reader*, edited by Lee Roy Martin, 149–70. Leiden: Brill, 2013.

Ens, Adolf. "Theology of the Hermeneutical Community in Anabaptist-Mennonite Thought." In *The Church as Theological Community: Essays in Honour of David Schroeder*, edited by Harry Huebner, 69–80. Winnipeg: CMBC Publications, 1990.

Ervin, Howard M. "Hermeneutics: A Pentecostal Option." *Pneuma* 3.1 (1981) 11–25.

Escobar, Samuel. *The New Global Mission: The Gospel from Everywhere to Everyone*. Downers Grove, IL: IVP Academic, 2003.

Estep, William R. *The Anabaptist Story*. Nashville: Broadman, 1963.

Fabella, Virginia. "An Introduction." In *Asia's Struggle for Full Humanity: Towards a Relevant Theology: Papers from the Asian Theological Conference, January 7–20, 1979, Wennappuwa, Sri Lanka*, edited by Virginia Fabella, 3–15. Maryknoll, NY: Orbis, 1980.

Fee, Gordon D. *The First Epistle to the Corinthians*. Rev. ed. Grand Rapids: Eerdmans, 2014.

Ferro, Marc. *Colonization: A Global History*. Translated by K. D. Prithipaul. Quebec: World Heritage, 1997.

Fish, Stanley. *Is There a Text in This Class? The Authority of Interpretive Communities*. Cambridge, MA: Harvard University Press, 2000.

Fleming, Bruce C. E. *Contextualization of Theology: An Evangelical Assessment*. Pasadena, CA: William Carey Library, 1980.

Flemming, Dean E. *Contextualization in the New Testament: Patterns for Theology and Mission*. Downers Grove, IL: IVP Academic, 2005.

Forman, Charles W., ed. *Christianity in the Non-Western World*. Englewood Cliffs, NJ: Prentice-Hall, 1967.

BIBLIOGRAPHY

Fowl, Stephen E. *Engaging Scripture: A Model for Theological Interpretation*. Malden, MA: Blackwell, 1998.

——. *Theological Interpretation of Scripture*. Cascade Companions. Eugene, OR: Cascade, 2009.

Fowl, Stephen E., and L. Gregory Jones. *Reading in Communion: Scripture and Ethics in Christian Life*. Eugene, OR: Wipf & Stock, 1998.

Frei, Hans W. *The Eclipse of Biblical Narrative: A Study in Eighteenth and Nineteenth Century Hermeneutics*. New Haven, CT: Yale University Press, 1974.

——. "The 'Literal Reading' of Biblical Narrative in the Christian Tradition: Does It Stretch or Will It Break?" In *Theology and Narrative: Selected Essays*, by Hans W. Frei, 117–52. Edited by George Hunsinger and William C. Placher. New York: Oxford University Press, 1993.

——. "Theology and the Interpretation of Narrative: Some Hermeneutical Considerations." In *Theology and Narrative: Selected Essays*, by Hans W. Frei, 94–116. Edited by George Hunsinger and William C. Placher. New York: Oxford University Press, 1993.

——. *Types of Christian Theology*. Edited by George Hunsinger and William C. Placher. New Haven, CT: Yale University Press, 1992.

Frykenberg, Robert Eric. *Christianity in India: From Beginnings to the Present*. New York: Oxford University Press, 2010.

Fuller, Lois. "The Missionary's Role in Developing Indigenous Christian Theology." *Evangelical Missions Quarterly* 33.4 (1997) 404–9.

Gadamer, Hans-Georg. *Truth and Method*. 2nd rev. ed. New York: Continuum, 2004.

García-Johnson, Oscar. "Transoccidentalism and the Making of Global Theology." In *Theology Without Borders: An Introduction to Global Conversations*, by William A. Dyrness and Oscar García-Johnson, 1–22. Grand Rapids: Baker Academic, 2015.

Gardner, Paul. *1 Corinthians*. ZECNT. Grand Rapids: Zondervan, 2018.

Garland, David E. *1 Corinthians*. BECNT. Grand Rapids: Baker Academic, 2003.

Gatu, John. "Missionary, Go Home." *IDOC/International Documentation* 63 (1974) 70–72.

George, K. M. *Church of South India: Life in Union (1947–1997)*. Delhi: ISPCK, 1999.

Gilliland, Dean S. "Contextual Theology as Incarnational Mission." In *The Word Among Us: Contextualizing Theology for Mission Today*, edited by Dean S. Gilliland, 9–31. Dallas: Word, 1989.

——, ed. *The Word Among Us: Contextualizing Theology for Mission Today*. Dallas: Word, 1989.

Gilmartin, Mary. "Colonialism/Imperialism." In *Key Concepts in Political Geography*, edited by Carolyn Gallaher et al., 115–23. London: Sage, 2009.

Gish, Arthur G. *Living in Christian Community*. Scottdale, PA: Herald, 1979.

Gnanakan, Ken R. "Biblical Foundations: A South Asian Study." *Evangelical Review of Theology* 7.1 (1983) 113–22.

Gnanakan, Ken, and Sunand Sumithra. "Theology, Theologization and the Theologian." In *Biblical Theology in Asia*, edited by Ken Gnanakan, 39–46. Bangalore, India: Theological Book Trust, 1995.

Goba, Bonganjalo. "A Black South African Perspective." In *Doing Theology in a Divided World: Papers from the Sixth International Conference of the Ecumenical Association of Third World Theologians, January 5–13, 1983, Geneva, Switzerland*, edited by Virginia Fabella and Sergio Torres, 53–58. Maryknoll, NY: Orbis, 1985.

BIBLIOGRAPHY

———. "Emerging Theological Perspectives in South Africa." In *Irruption of the Third World: Challenge to Theology: Papers from the Fifth International Conference of the Ecumenical Association of Third World Theologians, August 17-29, 1981, New Delhi, India*, edited by Virginia Fabella and Sergio Torres, 19-29. Maryknoll, NY: Orbis, 1983.

González, Antonio. "Anabaptist Hermeneutics and Theological Education." *Mennonite Quarterly Review* 84.2 (2010) 207-28.

González, Justo L. *Mañana: Christian Theology from a Hispanic Perspective*. Nashville: Abingdon, 1990.

Gonzalez, Ricardo. "El Juli Jesuítico: ¿Modelo Misional o Proyección Historiográfica?" *IHS Antiguos Jesuitas En Iberoamérica* 2.1 (2014) 85-100.

Graham, Carol. "The Inauguration of the Church of South India." *International Review of Mission* 37.1 (1948) 49-53.

Gration, John. "Willowbank to Zaire: The Doing of Theology." *Missiology* 12.3 (1984) 297-309.

Green, Chris E. W. "Foretasting the Kingdom: Toward a Pentecostal Theology of the Lord's Supper." PhD diss., Bangor University, 2012.

Green, Gene L. "The Challenge of Global Hermeneutics." In *Global Theology in Evangelical Perspective: Exploring the Contextual Nature of Theology and Mission*, edited by Jeffrey P. Greenman and Gene L. Green, 50-64. Downers Grove, IL: IVP Academic, 2012.

Green, Gene L., et al., eds. *Majority World Theology: Christian Doctrine in Global Context*. Downers Grove, IL: IVP Academic, 2020.

Green, Joel B. *Practicing Theological Interpretation: Engaging Biblical Texts for Faith and Formation*. Grand Rapids: Baker Academic, 2011.

Greenman, Jeffrey P. "Learning and Teaching Global Theologies." In *Global Theology in Evangelical Perspective: Exploring the Contextual Nature of Theology and Mission*, edited by Jeffrey P. Greenman and Gene L. Green, 237-52. Downers Grove, IL: IVP Academic, 2012.

Greenman, Jeffrey P., and Gene L. Green, eds. *Global Theology in Evangelical Perspective: Exploring the Contextual Nature of Theology and Mission*. Downers Grove, IL: IVP Academic, 2012.

Griffiths, Tudor. "Bishop A. R. Tucker of Uganda and the Implementation of an Evangelical Tradition of Mission." PhD diss., University of Leeds, 1998.

Grigorenko, Donald. "Reconceiving Theology: Influencing Factors to the Formation of Theology." *International Journal of Frontier Missiology* 35.2 (2018) 63-68.

Grondin, Jean. *The Philosophy of Gadamer*. Translated by Kathryn Plant. Montreal: McGill-Queen's University Press, 2003.

Grudem, Wayne A. *The Gift of Prophecy in 1 Corinthians*. Washington, DC: University Press of America, 1982.

Gutiérrez, Gustavo. "The Irruption of the Poor in Latin America and the Christian Communities of the Common People." In *The Challenge of Basic Christian Communities: Papers from the International Ecumenical Congress of Theology, February 20-March 2, 1980, São Paulo, Brazil*, edited by Sergio Torres and John Eagleson, 107-23. Maryknoll, NY: Orbis, 1981.

———. "Reflections from a Latin American Perspective: Finding Our Way to Talk About God." In *Irruption of the Third World: Challenge to Theology: Papers from the Fifth International Conference of the Ecumenical Association of Third World*

Theologians, August 17–29, 1981, New Delhi, India, edited by Virginia Fabella and Sergio Torres, 222–34. Maryknoll, NY: Orbis, 1983.

———. "Two Theological Perspectives: Liberation Theology and Progressivist Theology." In *The Emergent Gospel: Theology from the Underside of History: Papers from the Ecumenical Dialogue of Third World Theologians, Dar es Salaam, August 5–12, 1976*, edited by Sergio Torres and Virginia Fabella, 227–55. Maryknoll, NY: Orbis, 1978.

Haenchen, Ernst. *The Acts of the Apostles: A Commentary*. Philadelphia: Westminster, 1971.

Haleblian, Krikor. "The Problem of Contextualization." *Missiology: An International Review* 11.1 (1983) 95–111.

Hall, Charles Cuthbert. *The Universal Elements of the Christian Religion: An Attempt to Interpret Contemporary Religious Conditions*. New York: Fleming H. Revell, 1905.

Hansen, Holger Bernt. "Church and State in Early Colonial Uganda." *African Affairs* 85.338 (1986) 55–74.

———. "European Ideas, Colonial Attitudes and African Realities: The Introduction of a Church Constitution in Uganda 1898–1909." *International Journal of African Historical Studies* 13.2 (1980) 240–80.

Harder, Lydia. "Discipleship Reexamined: Women in the Hermeneutical Community." In *The Church as Theological Community: Essays in Honour of David Schroeder*, edited by Harry Huebner, 199–220. Winnipeg: CMBC Publications, 1990.

———. "A Hermeneutics of Discipleship: Toward a Mennonite/Feminist Approach to Biblical Authority." ThD diss., Toronto School of Theology, 1993.

Harries, Jim. "Enabling the Majority World to Benefit from 'Superior' Western Theology." *Currents in Theology and Mission* 44.2 (2017) 16–19.

———. "Western Theology in Africa." *International Review of Mission* 106.2 (2017) 241–60.

Harris, Brian. "Beyond Bebbington: The Quest for Evangelical Identity in a Postmodern Era." *Churchman* 122.3 (2008) 201–19.

Hastings, Adrian. "From Mission to Church in Buganda." *Zeitschrift Für Missionswissenschaft Und Religionswissenschaft* 53.3 (1969) 206–28.

Hatcher, Mark J. "Biblical Interpretation and the Shaping of Religious Worlds: A Study of Bible Study for Critical Contextualization." PhD diss., Asbury Theological Seminary, 2004.

Hauerwas, Stanley. *Unleashing the Scripture: Freeing the Bible from Captivity to America*. Nashville: Abingdon, 1993.

Hawkins, C., and J. Houk. *Foundations for Emerging Leaders: A Guide for Long Term Discipleship in New Churches*. Unpublished manual, 2013. PDF file.

Hector, Kevin W. "Postliberal Hermeneutics: Narrative, Community, and the Meaning of Scripture." *Expository Times* 122.3 (2010) 105–16.

Heidebrecht, Doug. "Community Hermeneutics in Practice: Following the Interpretive Path Together." *Direction* 49.2 (2020) 123–40.

Henry, Carl F. H. *God, Revelation and Authority*. Vol. 4, *God Who Speaks and Shows*. Waco, TX: Word, 1979.

———. "Narrative Theology: An Evangelical Appraisal." *Trinity Journal* 8.1 (1987) 3–19.

Herrmann, Simon. "Research Serving Theology: A Model for the Era of World Christianity." *Missiology* 49.2 (2021) 163–75.

BIBLIOGRAPHY

Hey, Sam. "Changing Roles of Pentecostal Hermeneutics." *Evangelical Review of Theology* 25.3 (2001) 210–18.

Hiebert, Paul G. *Anthropological Insights for Missionaries*. Grand Rapids: Baker, 1985.

———. *Anthropological Reflections on Missiological Issues*. Grand Rapids: Baker, 1994.

———. "Beyond Anti-Colonialism to Globalism." *Missiology: An International Review* 19.3 (1991) 263–81.

———. "Critical Contextualization." *International Bulletin of Missionary Research* 11.3 (1987) 104–12.

———. "The Flaw of the Excluded Middle." *Missiology: An International Review* 10.1 (1982) 35–47.

———. "The Missionary as Mediator of Global Theologizing." In *Globalizing Theology: Belief and Practice in an Era of World Christianity*, edited by Craig Ott and Harold A. Netland, 288–308. Grand Rapids: Baker Academic, 2006.

Hiebert, Paul G., and Eloise Hiebert Meneses. *Incarnational Ministry: Planting Churches in Band, Tribal, Peasant, and Urban Societies*. Grand Rapids: Baker, 1995.

Hiebert, Paul G., et al. "Responding to Split-Level Christianity and Folk Religion." *International Journal of Frontier Missions* 16.4 (1999) 173–82.

———. *Understanding Folk Religion: A Christian Response to Popular Beliefs and Practices*. Grand Rapids: Baker, 1999.

Hodkinson, Phil, and Heather Hodkinson. "The Strengths and Limitations of Case Study Research." Paper presented at the Learning and Skills Development Agency conference, "Making an Impact on Policy and Practice." Cambridge, December 5–7, 2001.

Hollis, Michael. *Paternalism and the Church: A Study of South Indian Church History*. New York: Oxford University Press, 1962.

———. *The Significance of South India*. Richmond, VA: John Knox, 1966.

Hosne, Ana Carolina. *The Jesuit Missions to China and Peru, 1570–1610: Expectations and Appraisals of Expansionism*. New York: Routledge, 2013.

Houston, Sam. "Narrative and Ideology: The Promises and Pitfalls of Postliberal Theology." *Religion and Theology* 23 (2016) 161–87.

Hume, David. *Treatise of Morals: And Selections from the Treatise of the Passions*. Edited by James H. Hyslop. Boston, 1893.

Hunsinger, George. "Postliberal Theology." In *The Cambridge Companion to Postmodern Theology*, edited by Kevin J. Vanhoozer, 42–57. Edinburgh: Cambridge University Press, 2003.

Hutchison, William R. *Errand to the World: American Protestant Thought and Foreign Missions*. Chicago: University of Chicago Press, 1993.

International Council on Biblical Inerrancy. "Chicago Statement on Biblical Inerrancy." *Journal of the Evangelical Theological Society* 21.4 (1978) 289–96.

Jenkins, Philip. *The New Faces of Christianity: Believing the Bible in the Global South*. New York: Oxford University Press, 2006.

———. *The Next Christendom: The Coming of Global Christianity*. 3rd ed. New York: Oxford University Press, 2011.

Jennings, Willie James. *The Christian Imagination: Theology and the Origins of Race*. New Haven, CT: Yale University Press, 2010.

Jenson, Robert W. "Hermeneutics and the Life of the Church." In *Reclaiming the Bible for the Church*, edited by Carl E. Braaten and Robert W. Jenson, 89–105. Eugene, OR: Wipf & Stock, 2016.

Job, G. V. "The Christian Movement in India." In *Rethinking Christianity in India*, edited by G. V. Job et al., 3–45. Madras, India: A. N. Sudarisanam, 1939.

Job, G. V., et al., eds. *Rethinking Christianity in India*. Madras, India: A. N. Sudarisanam, 1939.

Jobes, Karen H. *1 Peter*. BECNT. Grand Rapids: Baker Academic, 2005.

Johns, Jackie David, and Cheryl Bridges Johns. "Yielding to the Spirit: A Pentecostal Approach to Group Bible Study." *Journal of Pentecostal Theology* 1 (1992) 109–34.

Johnson, Luke Timothy. *The Acts of the Apostles*. SP 5. Collegeville, MN: Liturgical, 1992.

———. *Scripture and Discernment: Decision-Making in the Church*. Nashville: Abingdon, 1996.

Joseph, M. P. *Theologies of the Non-Person: The Formative Years of EATWOT*. New York: Palgrave MacMillan, 2015.

Julian, Ruth. "Ground Level Contextualization." In *Local Theology for the Global Church: Principles for an Evangelical Approach to Contextualization*, edited by Matthew Cook et al., 57–73. Pasadena, CA: William Carey Library, 2010.

Just, Arthur A., Jr. "The Apostolic Councils of Galatians and Acts: How First-Century Christians Walked Together." *Concordia Theological Quarterly* 74.3-4 (2010) 261–88.

Kalilombe, Patrick A. "Self-Reliance of the African Church: A Catholic Perspective." In *African Theology en Route: Papers from the Pan African Conference of Third World Theologians, December 17–23, 1977, Accra, Ghana*, edited by Kofi Appiah-Kubi and Sergio Torres, 36–58. Maryknoll, NY: Orbis, 1979.

Kappen, Sebastian. "Orientations for an Asian Theology." In *Asia's Struggle for Full Humanity: Towards a Relevant Theology: Papers from the Asian Theological Conference, January 7–20, 1979, Wennappuwa, Sri Lanka*, edited by Virginia Fabella, 108–22. Maryknoll, NY: Orbis, 1980.

Kato, Byang H. "Another Look at Moratorium." *Christianity Today* 20.7 (1976) 41–42.

———. *Theological Pitfalls in Africa*. Kisumu, Kenya: Evangel, 1975.

Katoppo, Henriette. "Asian Theology: An Asian Woman's Perspective." In *Asia's Struggle for Full Humanity: Towards a Relevant Theology: Papers from the Asian Theological Conference, January 7–20, 1979, Wennappuwa, Sri Lanka*, edited by Virginia Fabella, 140–51. Maryknoll, NY: Orbis, 1980.

Keener, Craig S. *Acts: An Exegetical Commentary*. 4 vols. Grand Rapids: Baker Academic, 2012–15.

———. "The Spirit and Biblical Interpretation: Spirit Hermeneutics." *Asian Journal of Pentecostal Studies* 23.2 (2020) 123–46.

Kelly, J. N. D. *A Commentary on the Epistles of Peter and of Jude*. New York: Harper & Row, 1969.

Ki-Hong, Kim. "Key Theological Issues in Asia: Influence of Modern Western Theology in the Asian Church." In *Biblical Theology in Asia*, edited by Ken Gnanakan, 91–99. Bangalore, India: Theological Book Trust, 1995.

Kipling, Rudyard. "The White Man's Burden." In *The Five Nations*, 79–81. London: Methuen and Co., 1903.

Kirk, J. Andrew. *Theology and the Third World Church*. Downers Grove, IL: InterVarsity, 1983.

Kitagawa, Joseph M. *The Christian Tradition: Beyond Its European Captivity*. Philadelphia: Trinity Press International, 1992.

Klassen, William. "The Voice of the People in the Biblical Story of Faithfulness." In *The Church as Theological Community: Essays in Honour of David Schroeder*, edited by Harry Huebner, 140–67. Winnipeg: CMBC Publications, 1990.

Kohn, Hans. "Reflections on Colonialism." In *The Idea of Colonialism*, edited by Robert Strausz-Hupé and Harry W. Hazard, 2–16. New York: Frederick A. Praeger, 1958.

Kruse, Colin G. *Paul's Letter to the Romans*. PNTC. Grand Rapids: Eerdmans, 2012.

Kwan, Simon. "Theological Indigenisation as Anti-Colonialist Resistance: A Chinese Conception of the Christian God as a Case Study." *Studies in World Christianity* 15.1 (2009) 22–50.

Kwok, Pui-lan. "Discovering the Bible in the Non-Biblical World." In *Voices from the Margin: Interpreting the Bible in the Third World*, edited by R. S. Sugirtharajah, 289–305. Maryknoll, NY: Orbis, 1995.

———. *Discovering the Bible in the Non-Biblical World*. Eugene, OR: Wipf & Stock, 2003.

———. *Introducing Asian Feminist Theology*. Sheffield: Sheffield Academic, 2000.

———. *Postcolonial Imagination and Feminist Theology*. Louisville, KY: Westminster John Knox, 2005.

———. "Teaching Theology from a Global Perspective." In *Teaching Global Theologies: Power and Praxis*, edited by Pui-lan Kwok et al., 11–27. Waco, TX: Baylor University Press, 2015.

Kwok, Pui-lan, et al., eds. *Teaching Global Theologies: Power and Praxis*. Waco, TX: Baylor University Press, 2015.

Land, Steven J. "A Passion for the Kingdom—Revisioning Pentecostal Spirituality." *Journal of Pentecostal Theology* 1 (1992) 19–46.

Latourette, Kenneth Scott. *Missions Tomorrow*. New York: Harper and Brothers, 1936.

Lausanne Theology and Education Group. "The Willowbank Report." In *Down to Earth: Studies in Christianity and Culture*, edited by Robert T. Coote and John R. W. Stott, 308–42. Grand Rapids: Eerdmans, 1980.

Lee, Peter K. H. "Between the Old and the New." In *The Emergent Gospel: Theology from the Underside of History: Papers from the Ecumenical Dialogue of Third World Theologians, Dar es Salaam, August 5–12, 1976*, edited by Sergio Torres and Virginia Fabella, 124–36. Maryknoll, NY: Orbis, 1978.

Lindbeck, George A. *The Nature of Doctrine: Religion and Theology in a Postliberal Age*. Louisville, KY: Westminster John Knox, 1984.

———. "Scripture, Consensus, and Community." In *Biblical Interpretation in Crisis: The Ratzinger Conference on Bible and Church*, edited by Richard John Neuhaus, 74–101. Grand Rapids: Eerdmans, 1989.

Lints, Richard. *The Fabric of Theology: A Prolegomenon to Evangelical Theology*. Grand Rapids: Eerdmans, 1993.

MacCormack, Sabine. *Religion in the Andes: Vision and Imagination in Early Colonial Peru*. Princeton, NJ: Princeton University Press, 1993.

Mananzan, Mary John. "Response from the Philippines." In *Spirituality of the Third World: A Cry for Life: Papers and Reflections from the Third General Assembly of the Ecumenical Association of Third World Theologians, January, 1992, Nairobi, Kenya*, edited by K. C. Abraham and Bernadette Mbuy-Beya, 182–87. Eugene, OR: Wipf & Stock, 2005.

Mande, Wilson Muyinda. "An Ethics for Leadership Power and the Anglican Church in Buganda." PhD diss., University of Aberdeen, 1996.

Manshardt, Clifford. "Church Union in South India." *Journal of Religion* 9.4 (1929) 607–13.

———. "Movements Toward Church Union in South India." *Journal of Religion* 6.6 (1926) 617–24.

———. "The Movement Toward Church Union in South India." *Journal of Religion* 9.1 (1929) 109–15.

Marantika, Chris. "Towards an Evangelical Theology in an Islamic Culture." In *Biblical Theology in Asia*, edited by Ken Gnanakan, 181–99. Bangalore, India: Theological Book Trust, 1995.

Marshall, I. Howard. *1 Peter*. IVPNTC. Downers Grove, IL: InterVarsity, 1991.

Martin, Lee Roy. "Introduction to Pentecostal Hermeneutics." In *Pentecostal Hermeneutics: A Reader*, edited by Lee Roy Martin, 1–9. Leiden: Brill, 2013.

Matson, A. T. "The Instructions Issued in 1876 and 1878 to the Pioneer CMS Parties to Karagwe and Uganda: Part I." *Journal of Religion in Africa* 12.3 (1981) 192–237.

———. "The Instructions Issued in 1876 and 1878 to the Pioneer CMS Parties to Karagwe and Uganda: Part II." *Journal of Religion in Africa* 13.1 (1982) 25–46.

Mattia, Joan Plubell. "Walking the Rift: Alfred Robert Tucker in East Africa Idealism and Imperialism 1890–1911." PhD diss., University of Birmingham, 2007.

Mbiti, John S. "The Biblical Basis for Present Trends in African Theology." In *African Theology en Route: Papers from the Pan African Conference of Third World Theologians, December 17–23, 1977, Accra, Ghana*, edited by Kofi Appiah-Kubi and Sergio Torres, 83–94. Maryknoll, NY: Orbis, 1979.

———. "Theological Impotence and the Universality of the Church." In *Third World Theologies*, edited by Gerald H. Anderson and Thomas F. Stransky, 6–18. Mission Trends 3. New York: Paulist, 1976.

Mbuy-Beya, Bernadette. "African Spirituality: A Cry for Life." In *Spirituality of the Third World: A Cry for Life: Papers and Reflections from the Third General Assembly of the Ecumenical Association of Third World Theologians, January, 1992, Nairobi, Kenya*, edited by K. C. Abraham and Bernadette Mbuy-Beya, 64–76. Eugene, OR: Wipf & Stock, 2005.

McCaughey, Mary. *The Church as Hermeneutical Community and the Place of Embodied Faith in Joseph Ratzinger and Lewis S. Mudge*. Religions and Discourse 58. Oxford: Peter Lang, 2015.

McClendon, James Wm., Jr. *Systematic Theology*. Vol. 2, *Doctrine*. Nashville: Abingdon, 1994.

McKim, Donald K., ed. *"fides quaerens intellectum."* In *Westminster Dictionary of Theological Terms*, 104. Louisville, KY: Westminster John Knox, 1996.

McNally, Robert Edwin. "The Council of Trent, the Spiritual Exercises and the Catholic Reform." *Church History* 34.1 (1965) 36–49.

Mercado, Leonardo N. *Elements of Filipino Theology*. Tacloban City, Philippines: Divine Word University Publications, 1975.

Mesters, Carlos. "The Use of the Bible in Christian Communities of the Common People." In *The Challenge of Basic Christian Communities: Papers from the International Ecumenical Congress of Theology, February 20–March 2, 1980, São Paulo, Brazil*, edited by Sergio Torres and John Eagleson, 197–210. Maryknoll, NY: Orbis, 1981.

Michaels, J. Ramsey. *1 Peter*. WBC 49. Grand Rapids: Zondervan, 1988.

Mignolo, Walter. "Epistemic Disobedience and the Decolonial Option: A Manifesto." *Transmodernity* 1.2 (2011) 44–66.

Míguez-Bonino, José. "Commonalities: A Latin American Perspective." In *Third World Theologies: Commonalities and Divergences: Papers and Reflections from the Second General Assembly of the Ecumenical Association of Third World Theologians, December 1986, Oaxtepec, Mexico*, edited by K. C. Abraham, 105–10. Eugene, OR: Wipf & Stock, 2004.

———. "The Present Crisis in Mission." *IDOC/International Documentation* 63 (1974) 74–78.

Mischke, Werner. *The Global Gospel: Achieving Missional Impact in Our Multicultural World*. Scottsdale, AZ: Mission ONE, 2015.

Mofokeng, Takatso. "Response from South Africa." In *Spirituality of the Third World: A Cry for Life: Papers and Reflections from the Third General Assembly of the Ecumenical Association of Third World Theologians, January, 1992, Nairobi, Kenya*, edited by K. C. Abraham and Bernadette Mbuy-Beya, 136–38. Eugene, OR: Wipf & Stock, 2005.

Moon, W. Jay. "Using Proverbs to Contextualize Christianity in the Builsa Culture of Ghana, West Africa." PhD diss., Asbury Theological Seminary, 2005.

Moore, Rick D. "Canon and Charisma in the Book of Deuteronomy." *Journal of Pentecostal Theology* 1 (1992) 75–92.

Moore, Stephen D., and Fernando F. Segovia, eds. *Postcolonial Biblical Criticism: Interdisciplinary Intersections*. The Bible and Postcolonialism. New York: T&T Clark International, 2007.

Morimoto, Anri. "Asian Theology in the Ablative Case." *Studies in World Christianity* 17.3 (2011) 201–15.

———. "Contextualised and Cumulative: Tradition, Orthodoxy and Identity from the Perspective of Asian Theology." *Studies in World Christianity* 15.1 (2009) 65–80.

Moses, David G. "The Spiritual Significance of Church Union in South India." *Christianity and Crisis* 7.21 (1947) 2–4.

Mounce, Robert H. *Romans*. NAC 27. Nashville: B&H, 1995.

Muñoz, Ronaldo. "Ecclesiology in Latin America." In *The Challenge of Basic Christian Communities: Papers from the International Ecumenical Congress of Theology, February 20–March 2, 1980, São Paulo, Brazil*, edited by Sergio Torres and John Eagleson, 150–60. Maryknoll, NY: Orbis, 1981.

Murray, Stuart. *Biblical Interpretation in the Anabaptist Tradition*. Studies in the Believers Church Tradition 3. Kitchener, Ontario: Pandora, 2000.

———. *Post-Christendom: Church and Mission in a Strange New World*. 2nd ed. Eugene, OR: Cascade, 2018.

Mushete, Ngindu. "The History of Theology in Africa: From Polemics to Critical Irenics." In *African Theology en Route: Papers from the Pan African Conference of Third World Theologians, December 17–23, 1977, Accra, Ghana*, edited by Kofi Appiah-Kubi and Sergio Torres, 23–35. Maryknoll, NY: Orbis, 1979.

Mveng, Engelbert. "A Cultural Perspective." In *Doing Theology in a Divided World: Papers from the Sixth International Conference of the Ecumenical Association of Third World Theologians, January 5–13, 1983, Geneva, Switzerland*, edited by Virginia Fabella and Sergio Torres, 72–75. Maryknoll, NY: Orbis, 1985.

———. "Third World Theology—What Theology? What Third World? Evaluation by an African Delegate." In *Irruption of the Third World: Challenge to Theology:*

Papers from the Fifth International Conference of the Ecumenical Association of Third World Theologians, August 17-29, 1981, New Delhi, India, edited by Virginia Fabella and Sergio Torres, 217-21. Maryknoll, NY: Orbis, 1983.

Nacpil, Emerito. "Mission but not Missionaries." *International Review of Mission* 60.239 (1971) 356-62.

Neill, Stephen. *Colonialism and Christian Missions.* New York: McGraw-Hill, 1966.

———. "Co-Operation and Unity." *International Review of Mission* 44.176 (1955) 439-46.

———. *A History of Christian Missions.* 2nd ed. New York: Penguin, 1990.

———. *A History of Christianity in India 1707-1858.* New York: Cambridge University Press, 1985.

Nel, Marius. "Attempting to Define a Pentecostal Hermeneutics." *Scriptura* 114 (2015) 1-21.

Nelson, F. Burton. "The Church of South India: A Report." *Covenant Quarterly* 22.3 (1964) 31-39.

Nicholls, Bruce J. "From Colosse to India: Some Reflections on the Life of the Church in Cultural Contexts." In *Integral Mission: The Way Forward: Essays in Honour of Dr. Saphir Athyal*, edited by C. V. Mathew, 393-408. Tiruvalla, India: Christava Sahitya Samithi, 2006.

Nikolajsen, Jeppe Bach. "The Formative Power of Scripture: The Church as a Hermeneutical Community." *European Journal of Theology* 27.2 (2018) 130-38.

Núñez C., Emilio Antonio. "The Problem of Curriculum." In *New Alternatives in Theological Education*, edited by C. René Padilla, 73-87. Oxford: Regnum, 1988.

———. "Towards an Evangelical Latin American Theology." *Evangelical Review of Theology* 7.1 (1983) 123-31.

Nyamiti, Charles. "An African Theology Dependent on Western Counterparts?" *African Ecclesial Review* 17.3 (1975) 141-47.

———. "Approaches to African Theology." In *The Emergent Gospel: Theology from the Underside of History: Papers from the Ecumenical Dialogue of Third World Theologians, Dar es Salaam, August 5-12, 1976*, edited by Sergio Torres and Virginia Fabella, 31-45. Maryknoll, NY: Orbis, 1978.

Oduyoye, Mercy Amba. "Commonalities: An African Perspective." In *Third World Theologies: Commonalities and Divergences: Papers and Reflections from the Second General Assembly of the Ecumenical Association of Third World Theologians, December 1986, Oaxtepec, Mexico*, edited by K. C. Abraham, 100-104. Eugene, OR: Wipf & Stock, 2004.

———. "The Value of African Religious Beliefs and Practices for Christian Theology." In *African Theology en Route: Papers from the Pan African Conference of Third World Theologians, December 17-23, 1977, Accra, Ghana*, edited by Kofi Appiah-Kubi and Sergio Torres, 109-16. Maryknoll, NY: Orbis, 1979.

———. "Who Does Theology? Reflections on the Subject of Theology." In *Doing Theology in a Divided World: Papers from the Sixth International Conference of the Ecumenical Association of Third World Theologians, January 5-13, 1983, Geneva, Switzerland*, edited by Virginia Fabella and Sergio Torres, 143-49. Maryknoll, NY: Orbis, 1985.

O'Malley, John W. *The First Jesuits.* Cambridge, MA: Harvard University Press, 1993.

———. *The Jesuits: A History from Ignatius to the Present.* New York: Rowman & Littlefield, 2014.

BIBLIOGRAPHY

Oosthuizen, G. C. *Theological Battleground in Asia and Africa: The Issues Facing the Churches and the Efforts to Overcome Western Divisions.* New York: Humanities, 1972.

———. *Theological Discussions and Confessional Developments in the Churches of Asia and Africa.* Franeker, Netherlands: T. Wever, 1958.

Osborne, Grant R. *The Hermeneutical Spiral: A Comprehensive Introduction to Biblical Interpretation.* Rev. and exp. ed. Downers Grove, IL: IVP Academic, 1991.

———. *Romans.* IVPNTC. Downers Grove, IL: IVP Academic, 2004.

Otieno, Luckio O. "Theological Developments in the All Africa Conference of Churches—1958–1978." MA thesis, University of Nairobi, 1983.

Ott, Craig. "Conclusion: Globalizing Theology." In *Globalizing Theology: Belief and Practice in an Era of World Christianity*, edited by Craig Ott and Harold A. Netland, 309–36. Grand Rapids: Baker Academic, 2006.

Ott, Craig, and Harold A. Netland, eds. *Globalizing Theology: Belief and Practice in an Era of World Christianity.* Grand Rapids: Baker Academic, 2006.

Packer, J. I. "Infallible Scripture and the Role of Hermeneutics." In *Scripture and Truth*, edited by D. A. Carson and John D. Woodbridge, 325–58. Grand Rapids: Baker, 1992.

Padilla, C. René. "Biblical Foundations: A Latin American Study." *Evangelical Review of Theology* 7.1 (1983) 79–88.

———. "The Contextualization of the Gospel." In *Readings in Dynamic Indigeneity*, edited by Charles H. Kraft and Tom N. Wisley, 286–312. Pasadena, CA: William Carey Library, 1979.

———. "Evangelical Theology in Latin American Contexts." In *The Cambridge Companion to Evangelical Theology*, edited by Timothy Larsen and Daniel J. Treier, 259–73. New York: Cambridge University Press, 2007.

———. "The Interpreted Word: Reflections on Contextual Hermeneutics." *Themelios* 7.1 (1981) 18–23.

———, ed. *New Alternatives in Theological Education.* Oxford: Regnum, 1988.

Padilla, Washington. "Non-Formal Theological Education." In *New Alternatives in Theological Education*, edited by C. René Padilla, 97–139. Oxford: Regnum, 1988.

Padilla DeBorst, Ruth. "Who Sets the Table for Whom? Latin American Congresses on Evangelization (CLADE) 1969–2012: A Revision with Eyes Toward a New Celebration." *Journal of Latin American Theology* 5.2 (2010) 107–24.

Palmer, Richard E. *Hermeneutics: Interpretive Theory in Schleiermacher, Dilthey, Heidegger, and Gadamer.* Evanston, IL: Northwestern University Press, 1969.

Park, James Sung-Hwan. "West Is Best? Why Chinese and Korean Students Pursue Graduate Theological Study in the United States." PhD diss., Trinity Evangelical Divinity School, 2017.

Parratt, John. "Introduction." In *An Introduction to Third World Theologies*, edited by John Parratt, 1–15. New York: Cambridge University Press, 2004.

Penyak, Lee M., and Walter J. Petry, eds. "The Requerimiento." In *Religion in Latin America: A Documentary History*, 25–27. Maryknoll, NY: Orbis, 2006.

Peterson, David G. *The Acts of the Apostles.* PNTC. Grand Rapids: Eerdmans, 2009.

Petrina, Stephen. "Methods of Analysis: Historical Case Study." 2020. https://blogs.ubc.ca/researchmethods/files/2020/11/Historical-Case.pdf.

Pieris, Aloysius. *An Asian Theology of Liberation.* Maryknoll, NY: Orbis, 1988.

———. "The Place of Non-Christian Religions and Cultures in the Evolution of Third World Theology." In *Irruption of the Third World: Challenge to Theology: Papers from the Fifth International Conference of the Ecumenical Association of Third World Theologians, August 17–29, 1981, New Delhi, India*, edited by Virginia Fabella and Sergio Torres, 113–39. Maryknoll, NY: Orbis, 1983.

———. "Towards an Asian Theology of Liberation: Some Religio-Cultural Guidelines." In *Asia's Struggle for Full Humanity: Towards a Relevant Theology: Papers from the Asian Theological Conference, January 7–20, 1979, Wennappuwa, Sri Lanka*, edited by Virginia Fabella, 75–95. Maryknoll, NY: Orbis, 1980.

Pike, Kenneth L. *Language in Relation to a Unified Theory of the Structure of Human Behavior*. 2nd rev. ed. Paris: Mouton & Co., 1967.

Placher, William C. "Paul Ricoeur and Postliberal Theology: A Conflict of Interpretations?" *Modern Theology* 4.1 (1987) 35–52.

Plueddemann, James E. *Teaching Across Cultures: Contextualizing Education for Global Mission*. Downers Grove, IL: IVP Academic, 2018.

Polhill, John B. *Acts*. NAC 26. Nashville: Broadman, 1992.

Porter, Andrew. "Introduction." In *The Imperial Horizons of British Protestant Missions, 1880–1914*, edited by Andrew Porter, 1–13. Studies in the History of Christian Missions. Grand Rapids: Eerdmans, 2003.

Porter, Stanley E., and Jason C. Robinson. *Hermeneutics: An Introduction to Interpretive Theory*. Grand Rapids: Eerdmans, 2011. Kindle.

Potter, F. M. "Churches Unite in South India." *Christian Century* 64.43 (1947) 1263–65.

Rayan, Samuel. "Reconceiving Theology in the Asian Context." In *Doing Theology in a Divided World: Papers from the Sixth International Conference of the Ecumenical Association of Third World Theologians, January 5–13, 1983, Geneva, Switzerland*, edited by Virginia Fabella and Sergio Torres, 124–42. Maryknoll, NY: Orbis, 1985.

———. "Reflections on a Live-In Experience: Slumdwellers." In *Asia's Struggle for Full Humanity: Towards a Relevant Theology: Papers from the Asian Theological Conference, January 7–20, 1979, Wennappuwa, Sri Lanka*, edited by Virginia Fabella, 50–56. Maryknoll, NY: Orbis, 1980.

———. "Theological Priorities in India Today." In *Irruption of the Third World: Challenge to Theology: Papers from the Fifth International Conference of the Ecumenical Association of Third World Theologians, August 17–29, 1981, New Delhi, India*, edited by Virginia Fabella and Sergio Torres, 30–41. Maryknoll, NY: Orbis, 1983.

Reese, Robert. "John Gatu and the Moratorium on Missionaries." *Missiology* 42.3 (2014) 245–56.

Reinhard, Wolfgang. *A Short History of Colonialism*. New York: Manchester University Press, 2011.

"Report of the Seventeenth Session of the Joint Committee on Church Union in South India." Madras, 1941. Yale Divinity School archives.

"Report of the Thirteenth Session of the Joint Committee on Church Union." Madras, 1935. Yale Divinity School archives.

Richard, Pablo. "A Theology of Life: Rebuilding Hope from the Perspective of the South." In *Spirituality of the Third World: A Cry for Life: Papers and Reflections from the Third General Assembly of the Ecumenical Association of Third World Theologians, January, 1992, Nairobi, Kenya*, edited by K. C. Abraham and Bernadette Mbuy-Beya, 92–108. Eugene, OR: Wipf & Stock, 2005.

Richards, E. Randolph, and Brandon J. O'Brien. *Misreading Scripture with Western Eyes: Removing Cultural Blinders to Better Understand the Bible*. Downers Grove, IL: InterVarsity, 2012.

Ro, Bong Rin. "Contextualization: Asian Theology." In *What Asian Christians Are Thinking: A Theological Source Book*, edited by Douglas J. Elwood, 47–58. Quezon City, Philippines: New Day, 1978.

———. "Theological Trends in Asia." *Themelios* 13.2 (1988) 55–57.

———. *Train Asians in Asia: A New Mission Strategy*. Asian Perspective 35. Taichung, Taiwan: Asia Theological Association, 1987.

Rogers, Andrew P. *Congregational Hermeneutics: How Do We Read?* New York: Routledge, 2016.

Root, Michael. "What Is Postliberal Theology? Was There a Yale School? Why Care?" *Pro Ecclesia* 27.4 (2018) 399–411.

Rynkiewich, Michael A. "Mission, Hermeneutics, and the Local Church." *Journal of Theological Interpretation* 1.1 (2007) 47–60.

Treier, Michael A. "Mission, Hermeneutics, and the Local Church." *Journal of Theological Interpretation* 1.1 (2007) 47–60.

Said, Edward W. *Culture and Imperialism*. New York: Knopf, 1993.

"Salvation and Social Justice: Report of Section II of the Bangkok Conference." *International Review of Mission* 62.246 (1973) 198–201.

Samdao, Francis Jr. S. "On the Idea of Contextualization: Cultural Sensitivity and Catholic Sensibility." *Evangelical Review of Theology* 46.1 (2022) 51–61.

Sanneh, Lamin. *Encountering the West: Christianity and the Global Cultural Process: The African Dimension*. Maryknoll, NY: Orbis, 1993.

———. *Translating the Message: The Missionary Impact on Culture*. American Society of Missiology Series 13. Maryknoll, NY: Orbis, 1989.

Saracco, J. Norberto. "Search for New Models of Theological Education." In *New Alternatives in Theological Education*, edited by C. René Padilla, 25–35. Oxford: Regnum, 1988.

Savage, Peter F. "The 'Doing of Theology' in a Latin American Context." *Theological Students Fellowship Bulletin* 5.4 (1982) 2–8.

Schnabel, Eckhard J. *Acts*. ZECNT. Grand Rapids: Zondervan, 2012.

Schreiner, Thomas R. *1, 2 Peter, Jude*. NAC 37. Nashville: Broadman & Holman, 2003.

———. *1 Corinthians: An Introduction and Commentary*. TNTC. Downers Grove, IL: IVP Academic, 2018.

———. *Romans*. 2nd ed. BECNT. Grand Rapids: Baker Academic, 2018.

Schreiter, Robert J. *Constructing Local Theologies*. Maryknoll, NY: Orbis, 1985.

———. *The New Catholicity: Theology Between the Global and the Local*. Maryknoll, NY: Orbis, 1997.

Schwaller, John Frederick. *The History of the Catholic Church in Latin America: From Conquest to Revolution and Beyond*. New York: New York University Press, 2011.

Segovia, Fernando F. *Decolonizing Biblical Studies: A View from the Margins*. Maryknoll, NY: Orbis, 2000.

———. "Racial and Ethnic Minorities in Biblical Studies." In *Ethnicity and the Bible*, edited by Mark G. Brett, 469–92. Biblical Interpretation Series 19. New York: Brill, 1996.

Segovia, Fernando F., and Mary Ann Tolbert, eds. *Reading from This Place*. Vol. 1, *Social Location and Biblical Interpretation in the United States*. Minneapolis: Fortress, 1995.

———, eds. *Reading from This Place*. Vol. 2, *Social Location and Biblical Interpretation in Global Perspective*. Minneapolis: Fortress, 2000.

———, eds. *Teaching the Bible: The Discourses and Politics of Biblical Pedagogy*. Minneapolis: Fortress, 2011.

Segundo, Juan Luis. *The Liberation of Dogma: Faith, Revelation, and Dogmatic Teaching Authority*. Eugene, OR: Wipf & Stock, 2004.

———. *The Liberation of Theology*. Translated by John Drury. Maryknoll, NY: Orbis, 1976.

"The Seoul Declaration: Toward an Evangelical Theology for the Third World." *International Bulletin of Missionary Research* 7.2 (1983) 64–65.

Sepúlveda, Juan Ginés de. *Tratado Sobre las Justas Causas de la Guerra Contra los Indios*. Bilingual edition, Latin-Spanish. Mexico: Fondo de Cultura Económica, 1979.

Setiloane, Gabriel M. "Where Are We in African Theology?" In *African Theology en Route: Papers from the Pan African Conference of Third World Theologians, December 17–23, 1977, Accra, Ghana*, edited by Kofi Appiah-Kubi and Sergio Torres, 59–65. Maryknoll, NY: Orbis, 1979.

Shank, N., and K. Shank. *Confessing the Faith Within Church Planting Movements: A Guide for Training Church Planting Networks Toward Contextual Theology*. 2011. https://www.imb.org/wp-content/uploads/2022/04/57-Seconds-S1E14-Confessing-the-Faith.pdf.

Shenk, Wilbert R. *Changing Frontiers of Mission*. Maryknoll, NY: Orbis, 1999.

———. "The Changing Role of the Missionary: From Civilization to Contextualization." In *Missions, Evangelism, and Church Growth*, edited by C. Norman Kraus, 33–58. Scottdale, PA: Herald, 1980.

———. "Theology and the Missionary Task." *Missiology* 1.3 (1973) 295–310.

Shepherd, Arthur. *Tucker of Uganda: Artist and Apostle, 1849–1914*. London: Student Christian Movement, 1929.

Shepherd, Gregory J. *José de Acosta's "De Procuranda Indorum Salute": A Call for Evangelical Reforms in Colonial Peru*. New York: Peter Lang, 2014.

Siebert, Bradley G. "Tested in the Faith Community: The Congregational Hermeneutics of the Mennonites." Paper presented at the 48th Annual Meeting of the Conference on College Composition and Communication. Phoenix, AZ, March 12–15, 1997.

Simbo, Billy K. "An African Critique of Western Theology." *Evangelical Review of Theology* 7.1 (1983) 28–33.

Sinn, Simone. "Hermeneutics and Ecclesiology." In *The Routledge Companion to the Christian Church*, edited by Gerard Mannion and Lewis S. Mudge, 576–93. New York: Routledge, 2008.

Siu, Paul. "Theologizing Locally." In *Local Theology for the Global Church: Principles for an Evangelical Approach to Contextualization*, edited by Matthew Cook et al., 143–64. Pasadena, CA: William Carey Library, 2010.

Smith, W. Alan. "Intersubjectivity and Community: Some Implications from Gadamer's Philosophy for Religious Education." *Religious Education* 88.3 (1993) 378–93.

Snodgrass, J. "To Teach Others Also: An Apostolic Approach to Theological Education in Pioneer Missions." PhD diss., Southeastern Baptist Theological Seminary, 2017.

Sobrino, Jon. "The Witness of the Church in Latin America." In *The Challenge of Basic Christian Communities: Papers from the International Ecumenical Congress of Theology, February 20–March 2, 1980, São Paulo, Brazil*, edited by Sergio Torres and John Eagleson, 161–88. Maryknoll, NY: Orbis, 1981.

Song, Choan-Seng. "From Israel to Asia: A Theological Leap." In *Third World Theologies*, edited by Gerald H. Anderson and Thomas F. Stransky, 211–22. Mission Trends 3. New York: Paulist, 1976.

———. "Let Us Do Theology with Asian Resources." *East Asia Journal of Theology* 3.2 (1985) 202–8.

———. "Theological Transpositions." *Theologies and Cultures* 7.2 (2010) 10–28.

———. *Third-Eye Theology: Theology in Formation in Asian Settings*. Cambridge, UK: Lutterworth, 1980.

Southern Baptist Convention. "Baptist Faith and Message 2000." https://bfm.sbc.net/bfm2000/.

Stanley, Brian. "Afterword." In *The Church Mission Society and World Christianity, 1799–1999*, edited by Kevin Ward and Brian Stanley, 344–52. Grand Rapids: Eerdmans, 2000.

———. "East African Revival: African Initiative Within a European Tradition." *Churchman* 92.1 (1978) 6–22.

Steuernagel, Valdir. "The Relevance and Effects of European Academic Theology on Theological Education in the Third World." *Evangelical Review of Theology* 27.3 (2003) 203–12.

Stock, Eugene. *The History of the Church Missionary Society: Its Environment, Its Men and Its Work*. 4 vols. London: Church Missionary Society, 1899–1916.

Story, Lyle. "Luke's Instructive Dynamics for Resolving Conflicts: The Jerusalem Council." *Journal of Biblical and Pneumatological Research* 3 (2011) 99–118.

Stott, John R. W. "Foreword." In *Down to Earth: Studies in Christianity and Culture*, edited by Robert T. Coote and John R. W. Stott, vii–x. Grand Rapids: Eerdmans, 1980.

Strauss, Steve. "Creeds, Confessions, and Global Theologizing: A Case Study in Comparative Christologies." In *Globalizing Theology: Belief and Practice in an Era of World Christianity*, edited by Craig Ott and Harold A. Netland, 140–56. Grand Rapids: Baker Academic, 2006.

———. "The Role of Context in Shaping Theology." In *Contextualization and Syncretism: Navigating Cultural Currents*, edited by Gailyn Van Rheenen, 99–128. Evangelical Missiological Society Series 13. Pasadena, CA: William Carey Library, 2006.

Strong, David K., and Cynthia A. Strong. "The Globalizing Hermeneutic of the Jerusalem Council." In *Globalizing Theology: Belief and Practice in an Era of World Christianity*, edited by Craig Ott and Harold A. Netland, 127–39. Grand Rapids: Baker Academic, 2006.

Sugirtharajah, R. S. *Asian Biblical Hermeneutics and Postcolonialism: Contesting the Interpretations*. Maryknoll, NY: Orbis, 1998.

———. *The Bible and Asia: From the Pre-Christian Era to the Postcolonial Age*. Cambridge, MA: Harvard University Press, 2013.

———. "Inter-Faith Hermeneutics: An Example and Some Implications." In *Voices from the Margin: Interpreting the Bible in the Third World*, edited by R. S. Sugirtharajah, 306–18. Maryknoll, NY: Orbis, 1995.

———. *Postcolonial Criticism and Biblical Interpretation.* New York: Oxford University Press, 2009.
———. *Postcolonial Reconfigurations: An Alternative Way of Reading the Bible and Doing Theology.* St. Louis, MO: Chalice, 2003.
———, ed. *Vernacular Hermeneutics.* Sheffield: Sheffield Academic, 1999.
———, ed. *Voices from the Margin: Interpreting the Bible in the Third World.* Maryknoll, NY: Orbis, 1995.
Sumithra, Sunand. "Towards Evangelical Theology in Hindu Cultures." In *Biblical Theology in Asia*, edited by Ken Gnanakan, 141–64. Bangalore, India: Theological Book Trust, 1995.
Sundkler, Bengt. *Church of South India: The Movement Towards Union, 1900–1947.* London: Lutterworth, 1954.
———. "Towards a Christian Theology in Africa." In *Readings in Dynamic Indigeneity*, edited by Charles H. Kraft and Tom N. Wisley, 493–515. Pasadena, CA: William Carey Library, 1979.
Sundkler, Bengt, and Christopher Steed. *A History of the Church in Africa.* New York: Cambridge University Press, 2000.
Taber, Charles R. "The Limits of Indigenization in Theology." In *Readings in Dynamic Indigeneity*, edited by Charles H. Kraft and Tom N. Wisley, 372–99. Pasadena, CA: William Carey Library, 1979.
———. "Missiology and the Bible." *Missiology* 11.2 (1983) 229–45.
Tamez, Elsa. "Women's Rereading of the Bible." In *Voices from the Margin: Interpreting the Bible in the Third World*, edited by R. S. Sugirtharajah, 48–57. Maryknoll, NY: Orbis, 1995.
Tano, Rodrigo D. "Toward an Evangelical Asian Theology." *Evangelical Review of Theology* 7.1 (1983) 155–71.
Taylor, Charles. "Gadamer on the Human Sciences." In *The Cambridge Companion to Gadamer*, edited by Robert J. Dostal, 126–42. Cambridge, UK: Cambridge University Press, 2002.
Taylor, John V. *The Growth of the Church in Buganda.* London: SCM, 1958.
———. *The Primal Vision: Christian Presence amid African Religion.* Philadelphia: Fortress, 1963.
———. *Processes of Growth in an African Church.* International Missionary Council Research Pamphlets 6. London: SCM, 1958.
Taylor, Mark. *1 Corinthians.* NAC 28. Nashville: Broadman & Holman, 2014.
Tennent, Timothy C. *Theology in the Context of World Christianity: How the Global Church Is Influencing the Way We Think About and Discuss Theology.* Grand Rapids: Zondervan, 2007.
Theological Education Fund. "A Working Policy for the Implementation of the Third Mandate of the Theological Education Fund." In *Contextualization of Theology: An Evangelical Assessment*, by Bruce C. E. Fleming, 83–87. Pasadena, CA: William Carey Library, 1980.
Thetele, Constance Baratang. "Women in South Africa: The WAAIC." In *African Theology en Route: Papers from the Pan African Conference of Third World Theologians, December 17–23, 1977, Accra, Ghana*, edited by Kofi Appiah-Kubi and Sergio Torres, 150–54. Maryknoll, NY: Orbis, 1979.
Thiselton, Anthony C. *The First Epistle to the Corinthians: A Commentary on the Greek Text.* Grand Rapids: Eerdmans, 2000.

Thomas, John Christopher. "Reading the Bible from Within Our Traditions: A Pentecostal Hermeneutic as Test Case." In *Between Two Horizons: Spanning New Testament Studies and Systematic Theology*, edited by Joel B. Green and Max Turner, 108–22. Grand Rapids: Eerdmans, 2000.

———. "'What the Spirit Is Saying to the Church': The Testimony of a Pentecostal in New Testament Studies." In *Spirit and Scripture: Exploring a Pneumatic Hermeneutic*, edited by Kevin L. Spawn and Archie T. Wright, 115–29. New York: T&T Clark International, 2012.

———. "Women, Pentecostalism, and the Bible: An Experiment in Pentecostal Hermeneutics." In *Pentecostal Hermeneutics: A Reader*, edited by Lee Roy Martin, 81–94. Leiden: Brill, 2013.

Thomas, M. M. "Foreword." In *An Introduction to Indian Christian Theology*, by Robin H. S. Boyd, v–vi. New Delhi: ISPCK, 1991.

Thompson, Mark D. "The Origin of the Thirty-Nine Articles." *Churchman* 125.1 (2011) 37–50.

Thompson, Richard P. "Scripture, Christian Canon, and Community: Rethinking Theological Interpretation Canonically." *Journal of Theological Interpretation* 4.2 (2010) 253–72.

Tiénou, Tite. "The Church and Its Theology." *Evangelical Review of Theology* 7.2 (1983) 243–46.

———. "Evangelical Theology in African Contexts." In *The Cambridge Companion to Evangelical Theology*, edited by Timothy Larsen and Daniel J. Treier, 213–24. Cambridge, UK: Cambridge University Press, 2007.

———. "Forming Indigenous Theologies." In *Toward the Twenty-First Century in Christian Mission*, edited by James M. Phillips and Robert T. Coote, 245–52. Grand Rapids: Eerdmans, 1993.

———. "Indigenous African Christian Theologies: The Uphill Road." *International Bulletin of Missionary Research* 14.2 (1990) 73–77.

———. "Indigenous Theologizing: From the Margins to the Center." *Journal of NAIITS* 6 (2008) 109–24.

———. *The Theological Task of the Church in Africa*. 2nd rev. and exp. ed. Theological Perspectives in Africa 1. Achimota, Ghana: Africa Christian, 1990.

Torres, Sergio. "Introduction." In *The Emergent Gospel: Theology from the Underside of History: Papers from the Ecumenical Dialogue of Third World Theologians, Dar es Salaam, August 5–12, 1976*, edited by Sergio Torres and Virginia Fabella, vii–xxiii. Maryknoll, NY: Orbis, 1978.

———. "The Irruption of the Third World: A Challenge to Theology." In *Irruption of the Third World: Challenge to Theology: Papers from the Fifth International Conference of the Ecumenical Association of Third World Theologians, August 17–29, 1981, New Delhi, India*, edited by Virginia Fabella and Sergio Torres, 3–15. Maryknoll, NY: Orbis, 1983.

———. "Opening Address." In *The Emergent Gospel: Theology from the Underside of History: Papers from the Ecumenical Dialogue of Third World Theologians, Dar es Salaam, August 5–12, 1976*, edited by Sergio Torres and Virginia Fabella, 1–6. Maryknoll, NY: Orbis, 1978.

Torres, Sergio, and John Eagleson, eds. *The Challenge of Basic Christian Communities: Papers from the International Ecumenical Congress of Theology, February 20–March 2, 1980, São Paulo, Brazil*. Maryknoll, NY: Orbis, 1981.

———, eds. "Final Document: International Ecumenical Congress of Theology, February 20–March 2, 1980, São Paulo, Brazil." In *The Challenge of Basic Christian Communities: Papers from the International Ecumenical Congress of Theology, February 20–March 2, 1980, São Paulo, Brazil*, edited by Sergio Torres and John Eagleson, 161–88. Maryknoll, NY: Orbis, 1981.

Treier, Daniel J. *Introducing Theological Interpretation of Scripture: Recovering a Christian Practice*. Grand Rapids: Baker Academic, 2008.

———. "What Is Theological Interpretation? An Ecclesiological Reduction." *International Journal of Systematic Theology* 12.2 (2010) 144–61.

A Treasure in Earthen Vessels: An Instrument for an Ecumenical Reflection on Hermeneutics. Faith and Order Paper 182. Geneva: World Council of Churches, 1998.

Tucker, Alfred R. *Eighteen Years in Uganda and East Africa*. 2 vols. London: Edward Arnold, 1908.

Tutu, Desmond. "The Theology of Liberation in Africa." In *African Theology en Route: Papers from the Pan African Conference of Third World Theologians, December 17–23, 1977, Accra, Ghana*, edited by Kofi Appiah-Kubi and Sergio Torres, 162–68. Maryknoll, NY: Orbis, 1979.

The Ujamaa Centre for Community Development and Research. "Doing Contextual Bible Study: A Resource Manual." 2015. https://www.anglicancommunion.org/media/253823/6-Ujamaa-Manual-doing-contextual-Bible-study-a-resoruce-manual.pdf.

van den Toren, Benno. "Can We See the Naked Theological Truth?" In *Local Theology for the Global Church: Principles for an Evangelical Approach to Contextualization*, edited by Matthew Cook et al., 91–108. Pasadena, CA: William Carey Library, 2010.

———. "Growing Disciples in the Rainforest: A Contextualized Confession for Pygmy Christians." *Evangelical Review of Theology* 33.4 (2009) 306–15.

Van Engen, Charles E. "The Glocal Church: Locality and Catholicity in a Globalizing World." In *Globalizing Theology: Belief and Practice in an Era of World Christianity*, edited by Craig Ott and Harold A. Netland, 157–79. Grand Rapids: Baker Academic, 2006.

Vanhoozer, Kevin J., ed. *Dictionary for Theological Interpretation of the Bible*. Grand Rapids: Baker, 2005.

———. *Is There a Meaning in This Text? The Bible, the Reader, and the Morality of Literary Knowledge*. Grand Rapids: Zondervan, 2009.

———. "One Rule to Rule Them All? Theological Method in an Era of World Christianity." In *Globalizing Theology: Belief and Practice in an Era of World Christianity*, edited by Craig Ott and Harold A. Netland, 85–126. Grand Rapids: Baker Academic, 2006.

Vanhoozer, Kevin J., et al., eds. *Theological Interpretation of the Old Testament: A Book-by-Book Survey*. Grand Rapids: Baker Academic, 2008.

Vanhoozer, Kevin J., et al., eds. *Theological Interpretation of the New Testament: A Book-by-Book Survey*. Grand Rapids: Baker Academic, 2008.

Vargas Ugarte, Rubén, ed. *Concilios Limenses (1551–1772)*. Vol. 1. Lima: Tipografia Peruana, 1951.

Venn, Henry. "The Native Pastorate and Organization of Native Churches. First Paper, Issued 1851. Minute upon the Employment and Ordination of Native Teachers."

In *Memoir of Henry Venn, B.D.: Prependary of St. Paul's, and Honorary Secretary of the Church Missionary Society*, by William Knight, 412–14. London, 1882.

———. "The Native Pastorate and Organization of Native Churches. Second Paper, Issued July, 1861." In *Memoir of Henry Venn, B.D.: Prependary of St. Paul's, and Honorary Secretary of the Church Missionary Society*, by William Knight, 414–20. London, 1882.

von Allmen, Daniel. "Birth of Theology: Contextualization as the Dynamic Element in the Formation of New Testament Theology." *International Review of Mission* 64.253 (1975) 37–52.

Voss, Hank. *The Priesthood of All Believers and the Missio Dei: A Canonical, Catholic, and Contextual Perspective*. Eugene, OR: Pickwick, 2016.

Waddell, Robby. "Hearing What the Spirit Says to the Churches: Profile of a Pentecostal Reader of the Apocalypse." In *Pentecostal Hermeneutics: A Reader*, edited by Lee Roy Martin, 171–203. Leiden: Brill, 2013.

Wagenaar, Hinne. "'Stop Harassing the Gentiles': The Importance of Acts 15 for African Theology." *Journal of African Christian Thought* 6.1 (2003) 44–54.

Walker, R. H. "The Native Church of Uganda." *Church Missionary Review* 64.2 (1913) 431–38.

Walls, Andrew F. *The Cross-Cultural Process in Christian History: Studies in the Transmission and Appropriation of Faith*. Maryknoll, NY: Orbis, 2002.

———. "Globalization and the Study of Christian History." In *Globalizing Theology: Belief and Practice in an Era of World Christianity*, edited by Craig Ott and Harold A. Netland, 70–82. Grand Rapids: Baker Academic, 2006.

Ward, Kevin. "A History of Christianity in Uganda." In *From Mission to Church: A Handbook of Christianity in East Africa*, edited by Zablon Nthamburi, 81–112. Nairobi: Uzima, 1991.

———. "Introduction." In *The Church Mission Society and World Christianity, 1799–1999*, edited by Kevin Ward and Brian Stanley, 1–12. Grand Rapids: Eerdmans, 2000.

Ward, Marcus. *The Pilgrim Church: An Account of the First Five Years in the Life of the Church of South India*. London: Epworth, 1953.

Warnke, Georgia. *Gadamer: Hermeneutics, Tradition and Reason*. Oxford: Polity, 1987.

West, Gerald O. *Contextual Bible Study*. Pietermaritzburg: Cluster, 1993.

Westphal, Merold. *Whose Community? Which Interpretation? Philosophical Hermeneutics for the Church*. Grand Rapids: Baker Academic, 2009.

White, Peter. "Decolonising Western Missionaries' Mission Theology and Practice in Ghanaian Church History: A Pentecostal Approach." *Die Skriflig* 51.1 (2017) 1–7.

Wiarda, Timothy. "The Jerusalem Council and the Theological Task." *Journal of the Evangelical Theological Society* 46.2 (2003) 233–48.

Wickremesinghe, Lakshman. "Christianity in the Context of Other Faiths." In *Asia's Struggle for Full Humanity: Towards a Relevant Theology: Papers from the Asian Theological Conference, January 7–20, 1979, Wennappuwa, Sri Lanka*, edited by Virginia Fabella, 28–36. Maryknoll, NY: Orbis, 1980.

Widjaja, Albert. "Beggarly Theology: A Search for a Perspective Toward Indigenous Theology." *South East Asia Journal of Theology* 14.2 (1973) 39–45.

Williams, C. Peter. "The Church Missionary Society and the Indigenous Church in the Second Half of the Nineteenth Century: The Defense and Destruction of the

BIBLIOGRAPHY

———. "Venn Ideals." In *Converting Colonialism: Visions and Realities in Mission History, 1706–1914*, edited by Dana L. Robert, 86–111. Grand Rapids: Eerdmans, 2008.

———. "'Not Transplanting': Henry Venn's Strategic Vision." In *The Church Mission Society and World Christianity, 1799–1999*, edited by Kevin Ward and Brian Stanley, 147–72. Grand Rapids: Eerdmans, 2000.

Wilson, H. S. "A Tryst with Theology: Self Theologizing as a Perennial Discipleship Mandate." *Theologies and Cultures* 10.1 (2013) 132–56.

Witherington, Ben, III. *The Acts of the Apostles: A Socio-Rhetorical Commentary*. Grand Rapids: Eerdmans, 1998.

Wolterstorff, Nicholas. "The Travail of Theology in the Modern Academy." In *The Future of Theology: Essays in Honor of Jürgen Moltmann*, edited by Miroslav Volf et al., 35–46. Grand Rapids: Eerdmans, 1996.

Wood, Charles M. *The Formation of Christian Understanding: Theological Hermeneutics*. Valley Forge, PA: Trinity Press International, 1993.

Wrogemann, Henning. *Intercultural Hermeneutics*. Vol. 1 of *Intercultural Theology*. Translated by Karl E. Böhmer. Downers Grove, IL: IVP Academic, 2016.

Yalden-Thomson, D. C. "Hume's View of 'Is-Ought.'" *Philosophy* 53.203 (1978) 89–93.

Yap, Kim Hao. *From Prapat to Colombo: History of the Christian Conference of Asia, 1957–1995*. Hong Kong: Christian Conference of Asia, 1995.

Yeh, Allen L. *Polycentric Missiology: 21st-Century Mission from Everyone to Everywhere*. Downers Grove, IL: IVP Academic, 2016.

Yeh, Allen L., and Tite Tiénou, eds. *Majority World Theologies: Theologizing from Africa, Asia, Latin America, and the Ends of the Earth*. Evangelical Missiological Society Series 26. Pasadena, CA: William Carey Library, 2018.

Yoder, John Howard. "The Hermeneutics of the Anabaptists." *Mennonite Quarterly Review* 41.4 (1967) 291–308.

———. "The Hermeneutics of Peoplehood: A Protestant Perspective on Practical Moral Reasoning." *Journal of Religious Ethics* 10.1 (1982) 40–67.

Yong, Amos. *Spirit-Word-Community: Theological Hermeneutics in Trinitarian Perspective*. Eugene, OR: Wipf & Stock, 2002.

Yung, Hwa. "The Integrity of Mission in the Light of the Gospel: Some Reflections from Asian Christianity." *Svensk Missionstidskrift* 93.3 (2005) 325–46.

———. "Some Challenges for Leadership Development for Mission in East Asia." *Transformation* 21.4 (2004) 234–37.

———. *Mangoes or Bananas? The Quest for an Authentic Asian Christian Theology*. 2nd ed. Maryknoll, NY: Orbis, 2014.

www.ingramcontent.com/pod-product-compliance
Lightning Source LLC
Chambersburg PA
CBHW052144300426
44115CB00011B/1508